Principles of
Digital Audio and Video

For a complete listing of the *Artech House Audiovisual Library,*
turn to the back of this book.

Principles of
Digital Audio and Video

Arch C. Luther

Artech House, Inc.
Boston • London

Library of Congress Cataloging-in-Publication Data
Luther, Arch C.
    Principles of digital audio and video / Arch C. Luther.
      p.   cm.
    Includes bibliographical references and index.
    ISBN 0-89006-892-5 (alk. paper)
    1.Digital television.   2. Sound—Recording and reproducing—Digital
techniques   3. Digital video.   I. Title.
    TK6680.5.L88   1997
    621.388—dc21   97-12550
                                                  CIP

British Library Cataloguing in Publication Data
Luther, Arch C.
    Principles of digital audio and video
    1. Digital video 2. Sound – Recording and reproducing – Digital techniques
    3. Multimedia systems 4. Digital communications
    I. Title
    621.3'82
    ISBN 0-89006-892-5

Cover design by Jennifer Makower

© 1997 ARTECH HOUSE, INC.
685 Canton Street
Norwood, MA 02062

International Standard Book Number: 0-89006-892-5
Library of Congress Catalog Card Number: 97-12550
10 9 8 7 6 5 4 3 2 1

Principles of
Digital Audio and Video

Arch C. Luther

Artech House, Inc.
Boston • London

Library of Congress Cataloging-in-Publication Data
Luther, Arch C.
    Principles of digital audio and video / Arch C. Luther.
        p.   cm.
    Includes bibliographical references and index.
    ISBN 0-89006-892-5 (alk. paper)
    1.Digital television.   2. Sound—Recording and reproducing—Digital
techniques   3. Digital video.   I.   Title.
    TK6680.5.L88   1997
    621.388—dc21   97-12550
                                                          CIP

British Library Cataloguing in Publication Data
Luther, Arch C.
    Principles of digital audio and video
    1. Digital video 2. Sound – Recording and reproducing – Digital techniques
    3. Multimedia systems 4. Digital communications
    I. Title
    621.3'82
    ISBN 0-89006-892-5

Cover design by Jennifer Makower

© 1997 ARTECH HOUSE, INC.
685 Canton Street
Norwood, MA 02062

International Standard Book Number: 0-89006-892-5
Library of Congress Catalog Card Number: 97-12550
10 9 8 7 6 5 4 3 2 1

Contents

Preface

Audio and video systems throughout the world are facing the transition to digital technology. New A/V services based on digital technology are emerging. This is creating a need for a comprehensive tutorial on digital technology with a focus on audio and video applications. That is the objective of this book.

This book is intended for engineers or engineering students. I assume the reader has a background in electrical engineering or computer science. Since engineers today are generally multilingual and I do not necessarily mean they know several spoken or written languages—but that they understand the languages of mathematics, engineering drawing, computer software, or any of the other ways that engineers express themselves. However, recognizing that individual engineers are fluent in different engineering languages, I have tried to express concepts in more than one way. For example, if you are not comfortable with mathematical notation, you will usually find the concepts also explained in text or diagrams.

The focus of this book is on fundamental concepts, philosophies, and applications of digital audio and video. This level of coverage is suitable for readers who are designing systems rather than components. It will help the reader learn how to evaluate and select system approaches and components. Good engineering is a matter of taking into account all the issues surrounding a problem before coming to conclusions. To the extent possible, I have tried to raise all the issues about digital audio and video technology that should be considered in system decisions.

Existing analog technology is often a basis for its digital equivalent, so some of the analog technology has to be presented by way of background, but that is limited as much as possible to give most of the book to digital technology.

Description of specific hardware or software is avoided except for examples. As hardware and software change so rapidly, this book would be obsolete in a few months if its presentation depended heavily on such details.

The first chapter begins with digital technology as if the reader does not know much about it, but it does this in a broad way to bring out the meaning of its application to audio and video systems. Chapters 2 and 3 cover the fundamentals of audio and video, including psychophysical aspects. Since the end result of these systems is that humans are listening to and watching the output, it is important to understand the characteristics of human hearing and vision.

Audio and video applications always result in some sort of system. This may range from the system contained in your stereo rack to a worldwide system of signal sources, communication, distribution, and receiving instruments. Chapter 4 discusses this range and the considerations that apply in different systems. The important subject of analog-digital conversion is covered in depth by Chapter 5. Chapter 6 covers video cameras, and Chapters 7 and 8 cover digital transmission and digital processing, respectively.

Most digital A/V systems depend on data compression, and that is the subject of Chapter 9. Then, Chapter 10 covers video displays, and digital recording and storage are covered by Chapter 11. Chapter 12 covers A/V postproduction (mixing, editing, etc.), and chapter 13 is about digital multimedia, which is the integration of audio and video with computers. Finally, Chapter 14 discusses philosophically where all this digital technology may take us in the future.

The end result is that the reader should have an overview of all aspects of digital audio and video technology and be able to participate with it as a user, developer, or decision-maker.

Acknowledgments

Many people other than the author have contributed their comments, information, and reviews to this book. I would especially like to acknowledge the support of Luigi Gallo, Jukka Hamalainen, Tom Leacock, Johann Safar, John Smiley, Larry Thorpe, and Mark Walsh.

Chapter 1

Digital Concepts

1.1 HISTORY

Electronic reproduction of sound and pictures has existed for more than 50 years. Some historical background is useful to understand how the technology grew to where it is today.

1.1.1 Electronic Sound and Pictures

Electronic reproduction of sound was developed in the form of the telephone in the late nineteenth century. In the early twentieth century, the electronic phonograph and the radio enlarged the applications for electronic sound so that nearly every home in the civilized world today contains one or more of these instruments.

In the immediate post-World War II period, electronic motion pictures emerged as television. Soon every home was enjoying electronic pictures and sound and the world changed forever. Television systems use analog technology for pictures and sound, which requires a real-time continuous communication between signal sources and receivers—the technologies available had to operate that way. However, these systems have become highly developed, cost reduced, widely distributed, and enjoyed by billions of people worldwide. In this book, the word "television" always means the analog systems now in use.

In a broad sense, it is difficult to argue that there is anything wrong with television systems; they are still providing satisfactory service fifty or more years since their development. However, another kind of sound-and-picture reproduction technology has appeared that offers massive advantages in cost, performance, and features. Totally new services are becoming possible. Welcome to digital audio and video, which is the subject of this book.

1.1.2 Digital Technology

The roots of digital technology also go back to the nineteenth and early twentieth centuries, but the objective was quite different—electronic computation. Electronic digital technology was difficult with the components of those days and, as a result, many early electronic computers used analog technology. Analog computers were workable for applications that did not require a high degree of numerical precision, but they were not usable for the high-precision computing tasks that are so vital to today's business, financial, industrial, and military worlds. That was the market for which electronic digital computers were developed.

By the post-World War II period, digital computers were available, but they were expensive, massive, difficult to operate, unreliable, and applicable only to tasks that could not be completed any other way and for users who could afford great expense. This all changed in the 1960s with the development of solid-state integrated circuits. Computing costs dropped by orders of magnitude, computing speed and reliability increased by similar factors, and mass proliferation of digital computers began.

The application of digital computer technology to the reproduction of sound and pictures was investigated early on, but the numbers and costs exceeded what practical applications could stand by several orders of magnitude. As a result, early computers did not support realistic sound and pictures.

1.1.3 Integrated Circuit Technology

An important aspect of integrated circuit (IC) that was recognized early in its development is that the theoretical potential of the technology was enormous compared with the capabilities of early devices. Gordon Moore, who later was one of the founders of Intel Corporation, saw this and predicted in 1965 that the number of devices on a single chip would double approximately every 18 months. Since the cost of a chip was not expected to grow very much, this prediction, now known as *Moore's Law*, said that the performance-cost capability of devices would grow at nearly the same rate as the number of devices per chip. For 30 years, this prediction has been true! The result is that present IC chips regularly contain millions of devices—a growth of over six orders of magnitude since the first ICs were built. Figure 1.1 shows the curve of Moore's Law. The industry expects that this progression will continue for the foreseeable future.

IC technology adapts better to digital circuits than to analog circuits, although both are available. Ignoring the cost of conversion between analog and digital signals, for equivalent functionality, digital ICs are less expensive than analog ICs. However, conversion is expensive, so digital applications at first were pursued only in two situations: (1) where the task could not be done at all in analog systems, so the costs are justifiable on that basis (an example is frame storage of video) and (2) when enough digital functionality is included that the digital savings pay for the conversion cost (an example is nonlinear editing.) This latter class of digital applications is driving the entire system to becoming digital, in which

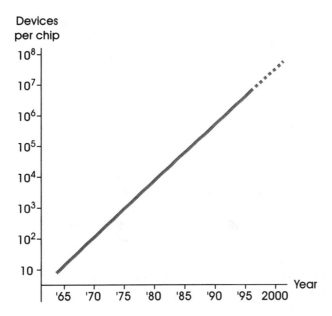

Figure 1.1 *Moore's Law.*

case conversion occurs only once at each end of the system. The cost situation is only one of the reasons in favor of digital. Others are listed in Section 1.2.2.2.

1.2 ANALOG AND DIGITAL

The above discussion has mentioned analog and digital systems. This section defines and compares them.

1.2.1 Analog Systems

Natural phenomena are generally viewed as continuously varying functions of time, space, or other independent variables. Above the atomic level, physical objects and media behave smoothly without steps or granularity. Of course, a limiting noise level is always present, which sets the smallest gradations that are meaningful. The flow of water in a river, the heat of a fire, the illumination falling on a scene and its resultant reflected intensity—all are continuous functions. This is called *analog.*

In electronic representation of analog quantities, the relevant physical quantity is converted directly to an electronic voltage as a function of time. Devices for this purpose are called *transducers.* The subsequent electronic processing operates on the analog voltage to accomplish the purpose of the system. At the end of the system, the analog voltage may be converted back to the appropriate physical quantity (light intensity, sound pressure, etc.) for presentation to the user. Analog electronic systems like this are easy to understand and are simple; however, they have important theoretical limitations that must be considered for a successful design.

1.2.1.1 Analog Limitations

The following analog limitations are inherent in all system to some degree or other.

- Noise and interference—the presence of a limiting noise level in analog systems has already been mentioned. A certain amount of random noise is unavoidable in all electronic circuits because of thermal agitation of electrons. In addition, other spurious signals may be present because of electromagnetic interference (EMI). Since an analog signal itself is a completely continuous function, the noise and interference looks like part of the signal and cannot be entirely eliminated. Furthermore, as circuits are added to an analog system, more noise sources come into play and the noise content of the signal increases.

- Distortion—An analog signal depends on a proportional relationship between the physical quantity and its corresponding electrical voltage. Analog circuits tend to introduce nonlinearities that upset the exact proportionality. As with noise, distortion cannot be detected unless one already knows what the signal is. In testing for distortion, the system is presented with a known signal and the output is compared with the input. The difference is distortion (also noise generated by the system.) However, when the system is in actual use, the original signal cannot be obtained at the same time for such a comparison. Distortion accumulates in extended systems in the same way as noise.

- Instability—small variation in signal levels occur in all circuits as a result of temperature dependency and other factors. In an analog system, these are indistinguishable from the signals themselves and result in drift of signal parameters with time.

1.2.2 Digital Systems

In a digital system, information is conveyed by a series of *digits*, or *symbols* that have a specified, discrete number of possible values. For example, in the familiar Arabic numeral system, each symbol has ten possible values (0, 1, 2, 3, 4, 5, 6, 7, 8, 9). Numbers larger than 9 require more than one symbol for representation. The number of possible values per symbol is called the *base* and systems are possible using any base from 2 up.

To represent analog quantities in a digital system, an *analog-to-digital conversion* (ADC) process must be used to produce a series of digital symbols. By carefully choosing the parameters of this process, analog signals can be represented to any desired degree of precision. Normally, the precision is chosen so that signal variations are reproduced down to the limiting noise level of the analog signal source, but not below it. ADC is the subject of Chapter 5. Because displays and loudspeakers are analog devices, a reverse conversion, *digital-to-analog conversion* (DAC), is necessary to present digital audio and video signals to users.

Digital symbols can be reproduced precisely without error when the variations introduced by circuits or transmission are less than the reciprocal of the base. For example, in a base-10 system, variations of a symbol value up to approximately 10 percent of full amplitude can be eliminated by the process of *quantization*, where the symbol is forced to take the digital value that it is closest to. Because the noise immunity is highest for the lowest base value, most digital systems use base-2, called *binary*. This is so widespread that the words *digital* and *binary* are often thought of as equivalent, which they are not. Most computer, digital audio, and digital video systems are binary, although systems of other bases may be used for special tasks such as transmission or recording. Binary systems have a special name for their symbols: *bits*, which comes from binary digits.

There are application for other bases (such as base-10); some of the important base systems are:

Base	Name	Values
2	binary	0, 1
3	ternary	0, 1, 2
4	quaternary	0, 1, 2, 3
8	octal	$0-7$
10	decimal	$0-9$
12	duodecimal	$0-11$
16	hexadecimal	$0-15$

The base-16 (*hexadecimal*, also called *hex*) is important in computers because it is a convenient way to express binary values. To express 16 values, the hexadecimal system uses the numbers 0 to 9 for the first 10 values and then the letters A to F for the values 10 to 15. An 8-bit byte can be expressed as two hexadecimal digits, a 16-bit word is four digits, and so forth. For example, the binary value 1111 1111 is FF in hex. To avoid confusion with regular decimal numbers (i.e., when the hex value contains only the numerals), hex numbers are always prefixed or postfixed as follows: 0xF3 or F3H.

1.2.2.1 Digital Limitations

Because of the conversion from analog to digital (and back again), and because the digital symbols must be individually processed, digital systems are more difficult to understand and they are conceptually very complex. However, today the complexity problem is largely hidden inside of integrated circuits that have been developed for common digital tasks, including the conversions.

1.2.2.2 Digital Advantages

The many real and potential advantages of digital systems are discussed in the following list. The discussion emphasizes the features that apply to digital audio and video systems as well as digital systems in general.

1. **Precise representation**—The precision of representing analog quantities is established at the point of conversion from analog to digital. Based on the parameters chosen for sampling rate (see Section 1.4.2.1) and symbols (usually bits) per sample, the analog-equivalent performance of the digital system is determined. If desired, subsequent digital processing and transmission can be designed so that perfect reproduction is maintained throughout systems of any size. Such systems having perfect reproduction are said to be *transparent*. However, some digital processes for audio and video are deliberately nontransparent; the best example is video and audio data compression, where the digital signals are modified to reduce the amount of data without causing observable aural or visual impairments. Compression is the subject of Chapter 9.

2. **Storage**—Many processes are facilitated by the ability to store significant amounts of data. For example, analog video can be enhanced by storing multiple lines of video in real time and comparing the data from line to line to generate correction signals. This is very expensive to do with analog technology, but it is so easy and inexpensive to do with digital devices that one of the first applications of digital video was to accomplish just this task.

   Once the ability exists to store a frame or more of video, many processes are practical that were simply impossible with analog technology. For example, there is no longer any need for a video display to operate at the same standards as the incoming video; different resolutions or different numbers of lines can be used. Thus, a new flexibility is available in setting video standards. This has been exploited in the new *high-definition television* (HDTV) standards; HDTV receivers can accept and display signals generated at several different scanning standards. Another product made possible by digital frame storage technology is the *frame synchronizer* (see Section 4.6.1) that is widely used in broadcasting to synchronize multiple video sources.

   Recording is another form of storage. With audio and video, recording means that a signal stream is stored as it comes in over a period of time and then can be played back at normal rates at a later time. Excellent analog video and audio recording equipment is available, but digital recording (which is also available) offers advantages in higher signal performance, reliability, and, in the case of digital disk recording, nearly instantaneous random-access playback.

3. **Complex processes**—In analog processing, a separate circuit is usually required for each step of a complex process. Digital systems can be built that way, too, but there is another option where a single processor is *programmed* to perform the

entire complex process. This is the concept of the *central processing unit* (CPU) of most digital computers (see Section 1.6).

By means of the program, called the *software*, a CPU can accomplish almost any computing task. The only limitation to this is speed—as a process becomes more complex, it will be slower. In the case of audio, modern CPUs are fast enough to do thousands of operations on each element of a digital audio stream as it passes in real time. However, that is not the case for video, where the stream may move 1,000 times faster than audio. Special video processing chips have been designed to solve that problem. As the progression shown by Moore's Law continues to make faster CPUs, the need for special video processors will reduce.

4. **Error-free transmission**—Signal transmission channels are generally analog and are subject to the problems of noise and distortion mentioned in Section 1.2.1.1. This is true whether the signal being transmitted is in analog or digital format, but digital formats can be made immune to the noise and distortion, whereas the errors accumulate in extended analog systems until they obliterate the signal. Designers of analog systems must make their signal transmission modules sufficiently noiseless and distortion free that the accumulation can be tolerated. This is expensive.

If the total noise and distortion in a channel for digital transmission is less than the reciprocal of the symbol base, the system theoretically can be error free. However, the statistics of random noise are such that there is always a small probability that very large noise levels can momentarily occur and, to achieve practical error performance, additional steps are usually employed. Most digital transmission systems are designed to deliver error levels less than one error in a billion symbols (error rate = 10^{-9}); sometimes far less.

Such small error rates are achieved by adding extra information to the data stream at the transmitting end of the system. The receiving end of the transmission path then uses this extra data for detecting and correcting errors. This is called *error protection*. Some of the many ways to do it are described in Chapter 7.

5. **Low cost**—The ultimate attraction to digital systems is that they are often cheaper than equivalent analog systems, if the latter are even possible. This is because of the remarkable reduction of the cost of ICs due to Moore's Law and the massive market created for them in the computer industry. There is reason to believe this will continue, and future digital system components will be still lower in cost. As this happens, more and more digital applications will become practical.

The result of these advantages is that digital electronic systems are replacing analog systems as fast as they can be developed and deployed.

1.3 BINARY NUMBER SYSTEMS

A single binary symbol (bit) has only two values: 0 and 1. By itself, one bit is useful only as a switch—on or off. However, by using groups of bits together, numbers of any size can be represented. This is called *encoding*. A common grouping is to consider eight bits as a group—this is a *byte*. In the simplest interpretation, each bit in sequence represents a successively higher power of two. This is *pure binary* encoding and is illustrated in Figure 1.2. In this way, eight bits can represent values between 0 and 255, sixteen bits cover the range from 0 to 65,535, thirty-two bits go from 0 to 4,294,967,295, and so on. Notice that these ranges cover only positive *integral* numbers. Negative values or irrational numbers are not supported. Integer representation is useful for video signals, but not for audio because audio signals are *bipolar*, having both positive *and* negative values.

1.3.1 Encoding Negative Numbers

A bipolar signal can be encoded by placing the analog zero at the center of the pure binary range as shown in Figure 1.3. For example, with eight bits, zero is binary 1000 000. Positive values go upward from there (the most significant bit (MSB) remaining at 1) and negative values go down (MSB = 0.) The 8-bit range is from -128 to $+127$ or for n bits it is $-2^{(n-1)}$ to $2^{(n-1)} - 1$. This is called *offset binary* and it works, but it proves awkward in arithmetic

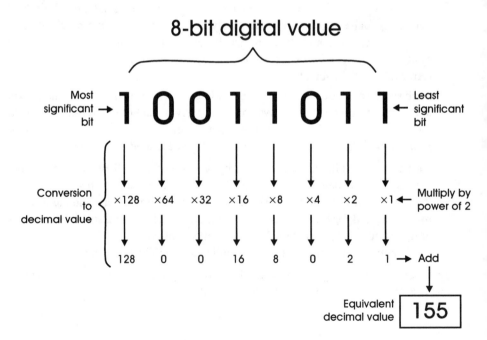

Figure 1.2 *Pure binary encoding for 8 bits.*

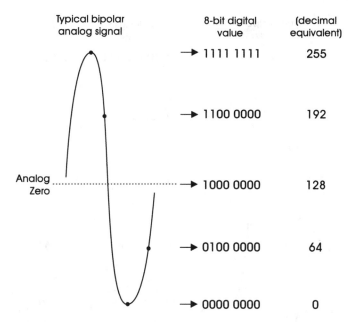

Figure 1.3 *Offset-binary encoding of a bipolar signal.*

because the analog zero value is not digital zero. This means that the offset value gets processed by arithmetic functions and causes a shift of the signal zero level.

A better encoding method for bipolar signals is called *two's-complement*, illustrated in Figure 1.4. In this method, encoded analog zero remains at binary zero so that it will not be affected by arithmetic processing. The MSB is zero for positive numbers and 1 for negative numbers. Two's-complement encoding is achieved by performing offset binary encoding and then simply inverting the MSB. It provides the same range as offset binary.

1.3.2 Encoding Irrational Numbers

Nonintegral values are expressed in decimal notation by the use of the decimal point. In computers, this is accomplished with *floating-point encoding*. In a specified word length, (32, 64, or sometimes 80 bits), bits are assigned for a mantissa and an exponent. The mantissa is a pure binary number with a separate sign bit and the exponent is a variant of offset binary signed representation. The encoded value is the mantissa with sign applied multiplied by 2 raised to the power of the exponent. This is illustrated in Figure 1.5. Most general-purpose CPUs include special hardware for floating-point calculations.

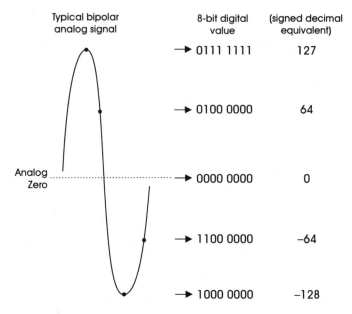

Typical bipolar analog signal	8-bit digital value	(signed decimal equivalent)
	0111 1111	127
	0100 0000	64
Analog Zero	0000 0000	0
	1100 0000	–64
	1000 0000	–128

Figure 1.4 Two's-complement encoding.

1.3.3 Encoding Text Characters

The storage, processing, and display of text characters is extremely important in computers. Special encoding schemes have been developed for text; the most important one is the *American Standard Code for Information Interchange* (ASCII) code that encodes English text characters in 7-bit or 8-bit values. Since the English alphabet has 26 characters, which grows to 52 characters with upper and lower cases, and additional punctuation characters are needed, it becomes reasonable to encode text in 7 bits (127 values plus zero.) The additional values are used for control codes, such as tabs, line feed and page feed, and so forth,

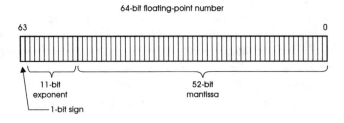

64-bit floating-point number

63 ... 0

11-bit exponent
52-bit mantissa
1-bit sign

Figure 1.5 Floating-point encoding for 64-bit values.

that provide for a minimal amount of text formatting. The ASCII numeric codes are usually encoded digitally as pure binary in bytes (8 bits). The eighth bit offers the opportunity for 128 more characters. Many systems define the additional characters to support other languages.

The structure of the ASCII code provides many features that simplify the binary coding of text. For just one example, switching from upper-case to lower-case is simply the setting of bit 5, because the codes for each letter differ by a value of 32.

For languages such as Chinese and Japanese that have many more than 255 characters, a double-byte (16-bit) code is also available.

1.3.4 Binary Arithmetic

In any system that deals with numbers, it is necessary to perform arithmetic functions (addition, subtraction, multiplication, etc.) and this is true of binary systems. Binary arithmetic is very similar to the familiar decimal arithmetic; some examples are shown in Figure 1.6.

Figure 1.6(a) shows the properties of 1-bit addition. This kind of diagram is known as a *truth table*—it displays (in the rectangle) the results of addition from all possible combinations of the two 1-bit values x and y. Notice that this is exactly the same as the addition of decimal values 0 and 1 except that the table entry for $1 + 1$ shows a value of 0 instead of 2

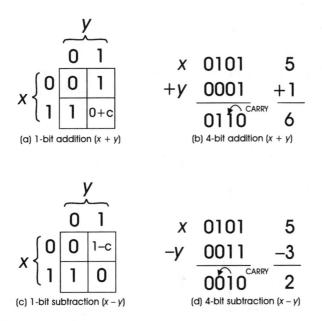

(a) 1-bit addition $(x + y)$

(b) 4-bit addition $(x + y)$

(c) 1-bit subtraction $(x - y)$

(d) 4-bit subtraction $(x - y)$

Figure 1.6 *Binary arithmetic.*

and the 'c' indicates that a *carry* occurs. Of course a single bit cannot have a value of 2, so the result of binary addition of 1 and 1 is zero and a carry command to add 1 to the next higher significant bit. This is shown in the example of Figure 1.6(b), where 4-bit values are added.

The examples of Figure 1.6(c) and Figure 1.6(d) are for binary subtraction. Subtraction of 1 from 0 results in a carry that subtracts 1 from the next higher bit.

Binary multiplication is often performed by adding the multiplicand to itself repeatedly as specified by the multiplier, although more sophisticated (and faster) algorithms are also available (see Section 8.3.1). Binary division is accomplished by the same technique as long division for decimals.

Arithmetic works the same for either pure binary or two's-complement encoding. However, other encodings (such as floating-point) require their own specific arithmetic processes. These may be supported either with special hardware or (in a computer) emulated by software. The latter approach is much slower than hardware approaches but it costs almost nothing.

1.3.4 Binary Logic

Logical elements are the building blocks of digital circuits. Figure 1.7 shows truth tables for the four fundamental elements, OR, AND, NOT, and XOR. The following list expresses the functions in words:

OR is 1 when either x or y is 1 or when both are 1.

AND is 1 only when both x and y are 1.

NOT is the negation of x, or its inversion.

XOR (exclusive-OR) is 1 when either x or y is 1, but not when both are 1.

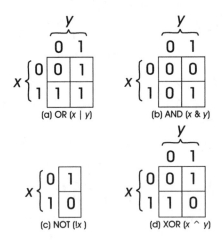

Figure 1.7 Logical functions.

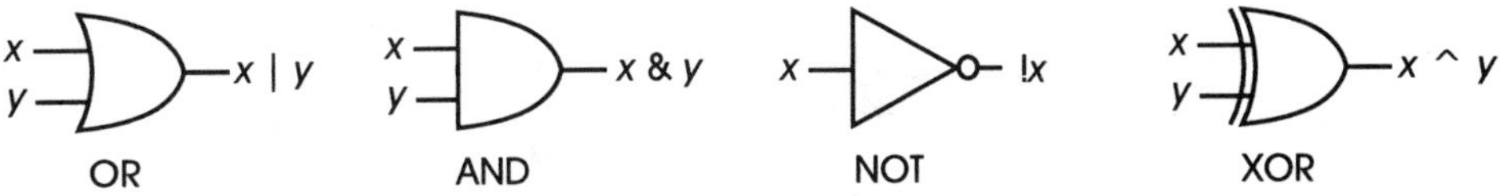

Figure 1.8 *Symbols for logic diagrams.*

Logical operations can also be expressed mathematically. The mathematics of logic was developed by the nineteenth century English mathematician, George Boole, and his system is known as *Boolean algebra*. These techniques are widely used to describe and work with the complex logic operations that are contained in most digital ICs.

Another way of viewing logic is with diagrams. This is probably the most widely used method of describing logic. The building blocks of logic diagrams are shown in Figure 1.8. Each logical block is implemented in an IC as a circuit that involves one or more transistors. Signals in a digital IC are expressed as being either high (1) or low (0), where low is usually zero voltage and high is approximately the power supply voltage. Sometimes this is reversed, a situation that is called *active low* operation. The logic circuits for active low are not the same as those for active high, so a specific system must operate in only one way.

The basic logic circuits operate instantaneously—as soon as valid inputs are presented to a circuit, the output becomes valid as quickly as the frequency response of the circuit will allow. This determines the speed of the logic—usually in the nanosecond range (10^{-9} seconds.)

Logic is also an important part of software. The notation used in C-language software is shown in the captions of Figure 1.7.

1.3.5 Flip-Flops

The *flip-flop* is a single-bit memory circuit that has many uses in digital systems. Figure 1.9 shows the basic idea of the flip-flop. The figure shows a block diagram, truth table, and a time diagram for an operation of latching an analog signal. The fundamental circuit element is a one-bit memory circuit. The flip-flop circuit receives the signal on its D (data) input and a rising transition on the C (clock) line determines when the cicruit will sample the D input and store its value. The output is the stored value, which remains valid until the flip-flop is either cleared or latched on another input. Thus the output of a flip-flop can be read without concern for critical timing.

1.4 DIGITAL SYSTEMS

The preceding discussion has mentioned some of the components of digital audio and video systems. Figure 1.10 shows how they relate to each other in an actual system that can receive analog audio and video and deliver it to one or more end users. The components are

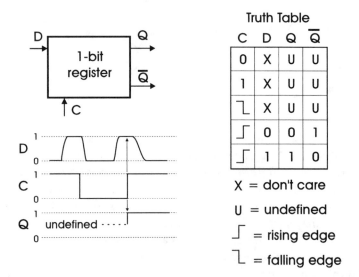

Figure 1.9 *Operation of a flip-flop circuit.*

introduced below and covered further in subsequent chapters. The chapter references are also indicated in Figure 1.10.

1.4.1 Analog Signal Sources

Except for computer-generated artificial sources such as music synthesis, animation, and simulation, all audio and video originate in nature and must be captured by microphones and video cameras. These units inherently deliver analog signals because all transducers for audio or video are analog. Video cameras sometimes contain ADC circuits in the same box. This is especially true in the case of "digital video cameras," which include analog sensors but deliver digital outputs. Because of the advantages of digital signal processing, some analog cameras will convert to digital signals for their internal processing and convert back to analog for output to an analog system. Cameras are the subject of Chapter 6.

Certain tasks of a complete system are often performed by analog equipment. For example, if an analog camcorder is used to capture video, the signal is recorded on analog videotape. When this tape is played into the digital system, the source (so far as the digital system can tell) is a videotape player. Of course, such signals will already contain any degradation introduced by the analog videotape, which cannot be removed by the subsequent digital system. As all-digital equipment becomes more widely used, this kind of problem will slowly disappear.

Audio signal sources are covered more fully in Chapter 3 and video sources are covered in Chapters 2 and 6.

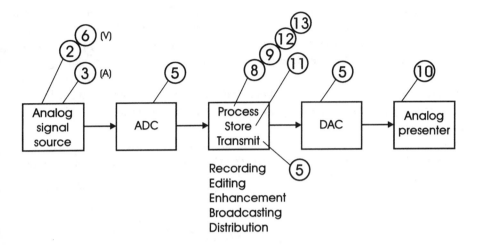

Figure 1.10 *A digital audio or video system. Numbers in circles are chapter references.*

1.4.2 Analog-to-Digital Conversion

A true analog signal is continuous in both time and amplitude. Audio signals are always like this, but video signals are a little different. The *charge-coupled device* (CCD) used for sensing in most video cameras is made up of discrete sensing areas that give the signals from these devices a discreteness in time although they are still continuous in amplitude. This may or may not be the same discreteness required by the digital system. The introductory discussion here is continued in depth in Chapter 5.

1.4.2.1 Sampling

To convert an analog signal to digital (to *digitize* it), it is made into a stream of digital words, which implies that both the time and amplitude are made discrete. The time problem is tackled first, by *sampling* the signal[*], which is a process of reading the amplitude at equally spaced intervals in time. The time spacing determines the *sampling rate* or *sampling frequency*, which, in turn, determines the response of the digital system to rapid changes in the analog voltage. Samples are analog values that are associated with specific points along the input analog waveform. In the case of video, an individual sample is referred to as a *pixel*, which is a contraction (and respelling) of <u>pic</u>ture <u>el</u>ements. For audio, individual samples are just called *samples*.

---

[*] Sampling does not have to be the first operation; it is also possible to quantize first and sample second.

The numbers for sampling are covered thoroughly in Chapter 5. It is sufficient here to say that the sampling frequency must be high enough that the digital stream will respond to the highest frequencies present in the analog signal. According to the *Nyquist criterion*, this means that the sampling frequency must be at least twice the highest analog signal frequency. This is to avoid a phenomenon called *aliasing*, which is the generation of spurious components at the difference between the signal and sampling frequencies. When the sampling frequency is higher than the Nyquist criterion, those difference frequencies will fall outside the signal passband.

For example, to sample an NTSC video signal that has a bandwidth (highest frequency) of 4.2 MHz, the sampling frequency must exceed 8.4 MHz. In practice, sampling frequencies are usually chosen higher than that.

1.4.2.2 Quantization

The second step of digitization is *quantization*, which is the process of forcing the analog samples to take the nearest digital value. The most important parameter of quantization is *bits per sample* (bps), which determines how many quantization levels are used. That number is 2^{bps}; for example, 8 bits gives 256 levels, 12 bits gives 4,096 levels, and so forth. Depending on the encoding, quantization levels are equally spaced (linear) or nonlinear. Most quantization is linear, but nonlinear quantization is sometimes used with audio systems, especially to optimize performance with small bps (12 or less.)

1.4.2.3 Encoding

Although quantization determines the bps, the encoding determines the meaning of those bits. Encoding must be standardized so that subsequent equipment knows exactly how to interpret the samples. It may be as simple as linear, pure binary encoding, or it may be more complex, such as is the case for color video, where encoding of three color parameters must be accounted for in each sample (see Section 2.6.2).

Encoding may also be changed in subsequent processes in order to facilitate a specific task, such as transmission. At the end of the special task, the encoding is put back to standard. This reencoding-deencoding process may or may not be transparent.

1.4.2.4 ADC Hardware

Most ADC hardware combines the processes of sampling, quantization, and encoding in a single device. The sampling frequency is determined by a separate *clock generator* device, and it is usually precisely standardized or synchronized to the incoming signal (in the case of video.) The bps value is determined inside the ADC device and cannot be changed externally, except by simply ignoring one or more of the least-significant bits, which is workable but is a waste of the hardware capability.

1.4.2.5 Data Rate

ADC creates a digital bit stream at a rate determined by the sampling frequency and the bps. The data rate, R, in bits/sec is

$$R = f_s \times bps \tag{1.1}$$

where:

f_s is the sampling frequency in Hertz.

So, for the example above of sampling NTSC video at 8.4 MHz and using 8 bps, the data rate is $8.4 \times 10^6 \times 8 = 67.200,000$ bits/sec. These calculations often generate large numbers, so it is convenient to speak of *kilobits* (Kb = 1,000 bits) or *megabits* (Mb = 1,000,000).

Unfortunately, computer memory and storage systems use a different definition of *kilo-* and *mega-*. There, these words are defined based on powers of 2. For example, the nearest power of 2 to 1,000,000 is 2^{20} or 1,048,576—this is also called a *megabit*. Table 1.1 shows the definitions based on powers of 2 as they are used for computer memory and storage (but not for data rates.)

A further "simplification" is, instead of counting individual bits, to count *bytes* (8 bits). This is convenient because computer memory and storage capacity is specified in bytes. The number of bits is simply divided by 8 to get bytes, so the data rate example above becomes 8,400,000 bytes/sec or 8.4 MB/sec. Note that in the abbreviation, capital B is for bytes and lower case b refers to bits.

Practical systems have standardized digitization parameters. Table 1.2 shows numbers for several different audio and video standards. The considerations for choosing sampling parameters are covered in Chapter 5.

Table 1.1

Large Numbers Used for Sizing of Digital Memory or Storage

Name	Abbreviation*	Size	
		Power	Value
kilobit	kb	2^{10}	1,024
megabit	Mb	2^{20}	1,048,576
gigabit	Gb	2^{30}	1,073,741,824
terabit	Tb	2^{40}	1,099,511,627,776

* For bytes, abbreviation is kB, MB, etc.

Table 1.2

Audio and Video Sampling Standards

Name	f_s	bps	Data rate (bytes/sec)
Audio			
CD-DA stereo	44.1 kHz	16	176,400
WAV mono	11.05 kHz	8	11,050
WAV stereo	22.1	16	88,400
Video *			
CCIR 601 4:4:4	13.5 MHz	24	40.50×10^6
SMPTE 274M HDTV	74.25 MHz	24	222.75×10^6

* Video data rates do not account for data dropped
during blanking intervals.

1.5 DIGITAL SYSTEM ENVIRONMENTS

Digital systems require a certain amount of overhead hardware to provide for system control and clocking. The logic circuits that make up a digital system respond to the signals that are present at their inputs but there has to be organization and control to determine when signals will come in and when they will change from one state to the next. There is usually an established system timing determined by one or more *clock* signals, which are simply sources of specific frequencies. For example, in an ADC circuit, there must be a clock that determines the sampling frequency. The same clock is used in later circuits to interpret the output data stream from the ADC.

Usually clock signals move within a system on separate lines from the data. In the case of a communication link that has only one channel, provision must be made for some way for the receiving end to reconstruct a clock from the communication signal itself. Many communication formats provide this by a structure that is said to be *self-clocking*.

1.5.1 Clocking and Latching

Although digital signals have only two significant states (low and high, 0 and 1, etc.) the circuits handling the signals are basically analog and pass through intermediate levels while transitioning from one state to the other. This is accommodated by specifying exact times when the signal level in a digital circuit can be expected to be valid. To ensure accuracy, signals should be read from one circuit to another only during these valid periods. The process for doing this is called *clocking* or *latching*. A flip-flop circuit (see Section 1.3.5) is used to capture the digital signal during its valid period by clocking the flip-flop during that time.

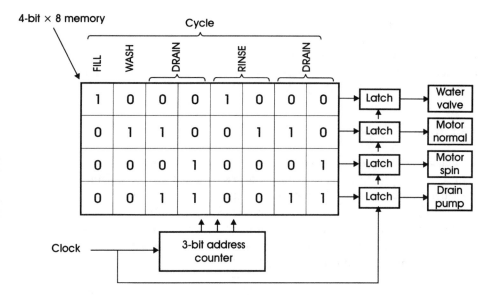

Figure 1.11 *Example of a state machine—clothes washer controller.*

1.5.2 State Machines

A binary logic system, no matter how complex, has a truth table that specifies a unique set of outputs for every combination of the inputs. This is insufficient to perform many processes and means must be provided for the successive application of many logic operations to perform a real task. The most flexible and capable environment for this purpose is the digital computer (described in Section 1.6) but in many cases a full computer would be overkill. A simpler organization is what is known as a *state machine*, shown in Figure 1.11. In this architecture, a memory array contains control signals that are used to configure a logic processor to perform the different functions required by the task at hand. A clock signal steps through the memory reading out one control signal after another in sequence to step the system through its processing steps. This is a similar concept to the mechanical controllers that used to control clothes washers to go through the modes of fill, wash, rinse, spin, and so forth. Of course, a modern clothes washer has an electronic state machine for this purpose.

The design shown in the figure has only one clock cycle per state, so the durations of the states are all the same. An easy modification can fix that—by adding several more bits to the state memory to specify the number of clock cycles that each state will take. For example, if four bits were added, 15 different durations would be available for each state.

It is also possible to model a state machine in software on a computer. This is sometimes useful as an overall architecture for a program; the state determines the "mode" that the program is in.

1.6 DIGITAL COMPUTERS

A computer is the preferred architecture for most digital processing tasks and computers are widely used for digital audio and video systems. Therefore, computer architectures are important to the readers of this book.

1.6.1 Basic Architecture

Computers can be built in many sizes or powers, but they all share the same architectural elements. There are three fundamental parts to a computer: (1) a digital memory that can store data and commands, (2) a processor unit that is capable of reading or writing the memory and performing different processes under control of the command information, and (3) some *input/output* equipment that interfaces the rest of the computer to the user (keyboard, mouse, displays, speakers, etc.) and to external *peripherals* such as hard disks, printers, communications equipment, and the like.

1.6.2 The CPU

The central element of a computer is its CPU, defined in Section 1.2.2.2 and diagrammed in Figure 1.12. The elements of a CPU are connected by means of a *bus*, which is a parallel

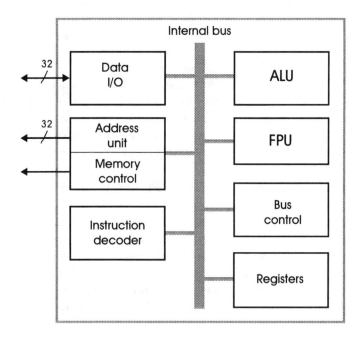

Figure 1.12 *Block diagram of a CPU.*

path for many lines of data. CPUs are classified by the number of data bus lines (8, 16, 32, 64, etc.) The numbers mean that the computer processes that number of bits in parallel. Today's personal computer CPUs are generally 32 bits. The CPU's bus extends outside the CPU for connection of external memory and peripherals. This is the purpose of the *data I/O* and *address unit* of the CPU.

There are three kinds of information that pass over the CPU's bus: data, addresses, and commands. The data are the information that the computer processes and are stored in external memory and the addresses are numbers that refer to locations for reading or writing in that memory.

The commands are called *instructions* and also have addresses in the memory. The total group of available instructions is called the *instruction set*. The larger the instruction set, the more powerful the computer, except that there is a special class of computer designed to use a small instruction set but execute them extremely rapidly—such computers are called *reduced instruction-set computers* (RISC). All other computers are *complex instruction-set computers* (CISC). The *instruction decoder* in the CPU reads the instructions and tells the rest of the CPU what action to perform.

The processing element of a CPU is its *arithmetic logic unit* (ALU). As the name implies, it does arithmetic and logic functions on the data. Most CPUs also have a *floating-point unit* (FPU), which provides hardware support to speed up operations with floating-point data formats. Data are brought from external memory into the CPU for processing and are placed back in external memory after processing. Because external memory accesses take time, a CPU has a small amount of internal memory in the form of *registers*.

1.6.3 Data Buses

A data bus is a structure of many parallel lines to which multiple processing units may be connected. All the processing units see the same data but all except for the intended unit will ignore it. This is accomplished by a series of control lines in the bus that all units watch for their own unique code to appear. When that happens, they respond immediately by latching the data from the bus into their internal circuits. By this means, all units are serviced in series. The *bus control* part of the CPU handles this.

The CPU bus extends outside the CPU for connection of other system units. It is called the *system bus* and must include not only data lines but address lines and control lines to support connection of other devices including memory. Figure 1.13 is a block diagram of a typical computer system.

Because all data moving around in a computer pass through the same bus, the bus can be a bottleneck when a lot of activity is going on. This can be alleviated by splitting some of the heaviest traffic off the system bus onto a *local bus*. Most modern computers have one or more local buses servicing the mass storage and the video display. The most common PC local bus is the *peripheral connect interface* (PCI) bus.

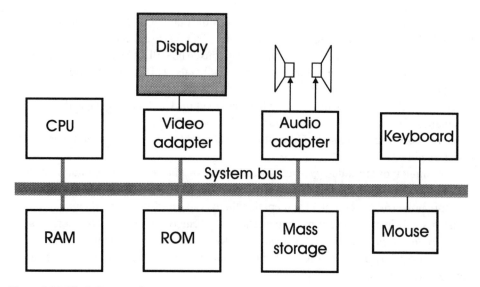

Figure 1.13 *Block diagram of a computer system.*

1.6.4 Memory

Next to the CPU, the memory is probably the most important part of a computer system. Although there is a small amount of memory in a CPU, a system needs much more than that to handle programs and data. This is the system's *main memory*, which is made of *random-access memory* (RAM) devices connected in an array that is as wide as the data bus (32 bits). It can be as large in the other dimension as the addressing system will support.

Addressing is provided by additional lines in the bus specifically for this purpose. Memory is accessed in a special cycle of operation where the CPU first places an address on the bus and tells the bus control to begin a memory cycle. The memory receives the address and places the data from that address onto the bus, following which the target unit for the memory access is given its control code and it reads the data from the bus. Depending on the system design, a memory cycle can occur in 100 ns or so.

For example, if 24 addressing lines are provided in the bus, the system can support memory up to 16,777,216 × 32 bits. This is 64 MB of memory, accessible in 4-byte groups. Because memory is a significant cost, many systems do not contain all the memory that their addressing system could handle.

1.6.5 Peripherals

Units on the bus other than the CPU and main memory are *peripherals*. They include permanent storage units such as hard disks, CD-ROM drives, floppy disks, or tape drives. These *mass storage* units are used to hold programs and data and, if the storage medium is removable, to exchange programs and data between systems. The basic measure of mass storage capacity is the megabyte, although many systems now have storage measured in gigabytes. Because mass storage units involve mechanical technology, the cost reduction over time has not been as dramatic as Moore's Law, but there have been steady reductions as the need for more storage has enlarged the market for these devices.

Other peripheral devices for a computer handling digital audio and video include *user interface* units such as keyboard, mouse, video display, and audio speakers. Video displays are the subject of Chapter 10; audio speakers and their digital interfaces are discussed in Chapter 3.

1.6.6 Software

A computer does not do anything unless it has *software*—the lists of instructions that tell the CPU to perform specific tasks. A package of software programs that makes the computer do a complete task, such as word processing or a database, is called an *application*. However, there are other kinds of software, operating in layers as shown in Figure 1.14.

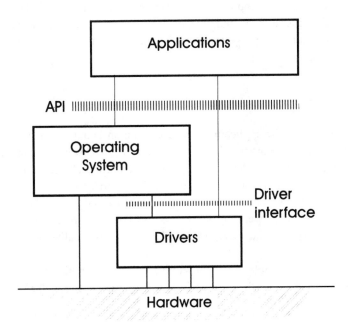

Figure 1.14 *Computer software hierarchy.*

1.6.6.1 Languages

Runnable (executable) software must be located in main memory so that it is accessible to the CPU. It must consist of instructions for the specific CPU of the system. Although it is possible to write programs directly in the instruction format, typical CPU instructions are very detailed and difficult to work with by programmers. It is usually necessary to have a different format for writing programs—a *higher level language* that relates more to the tasks that will make up programs than to the CPU instruction set. Typical languages are BASIC, Pascal, C, SmallTalk, and so forth.

Programs written in a higher level language must be converted to CPU instructions before they can be run. There are two ways to do that: compilation and interpretation. *Compilation* is performed by the programmer using a programming tool called a *compiler* that reads the high-level language code and creates an executable file that contains the CPU instructions for running the application. This executable file is all that is needed to run the application—the high-level language code is kept by the programmer and is not distributed to users.

The approach is different for *interpretation*. In that case, the higher level code is distributed to users and they have another program called an *interpreter* that can read the program code, convert it to CPU instructions, and run them in real time. Because of the extra step of interpretation while running the program, interpreted programs always run slower than the same program if compiled.

1.6.6.2 Operating Systems

Although is it possible to write applications that could run on a computer without support from any other software, there are many mundane tasks that are best handled in a standard way by software that remains resident in the computer at all times. That is the purpose of the *operating system* layer. Tasks such as interfacing the keyboard and mouse, controlling mass storage, and many other things are needed by all applications and can be provided by an operating system. Every operating system is designed to present an *application programming interface* (API) that is available to all applications to call upon the operating system services.

An API also makes it possible to run the same applications on different hardware as long as software is provided with the different hardware to bring out a standard API. This is done by providing another level of software called *drivers*.

1.6.6.3 Drivers

There can be a lot of complexity to writing the software that directly interfaces to a piece of hardware. Details such as port numbers, memory addresses, and hardware physical parameters should be hidden from most application programmers. This is the purpose of the *driver* layer—it brings specific hardware up to a level that the operating system can use. In this respect, an operating system has another programming interface that it uses to communicate with drivers. Hardware specifics are hidden at this level so that changes and updates to the hardware can be accommodated by updating the driver software while the operating system and its API remains unchanged. This way, the same applications continue to run as before.

1.7 DIGITAL TRANSMISSION

Transmission is the process of moving data from one location to another. It can be as simple as the transmission that occurs via the data bus within a single computer to worldwide transmission via satellite, telephone line, radio communication, or any other electronic medium.

The computer data bus is a *parallel* path, having many wires for data, addresses, clocks, and so forth. This is practical only for short distances, in which the cost and limited bandwidth of multiwire cables can be tolerated. For longer distances, it is necessary to transmit on a single channel by converting the data to a *serial* format. This is a tradeoff because the bandwidth of the single serial path must increase to n times the bandwidth of each wire in an n-wire parallel arrangement. However, the simplicity of a single transmission channel is appropriate for most long-distance communications.

All transmission media are analog channels, but binary digital signals are so tolerant of channel characteristics that they are easily handled. In fact, the capability of most communication channels is much greater than what binary transmission requires, and there is opportunity to increase the data capacity of the channel by using some form of *modulation*. Most modulation schemes increase the bits per symbol of the transmitted signal, so they are trading system signal-to-noise ratio for signal bandwidth. For example, if two bits are transmitted per symbol, the channel data rate is doubled compared with that of one bit per symbol. However, the channel signal-to-noise ratio must double for the same error performance. This is usually a reasonable tradeoff because most analog channels have noise performance much better than that needed for one-bit-per-symbol digital transmission.

Many methods are available for digital transmission over various channel types. These are the subject of Chapter 7.

Chapter 2

Video Fundamentals

2.1 NATURAL IMAGES

Television is a highly developed analog audio and video system. The fundamentals behind television are based on the properties of human vision, which also apply to digital video systems.

The purpose of an electronic image reproduction (video) system is to capture natural scenes and reproduce them at a distance in either space or time or both (see Figure 2.1). Natural scenes are what one sees as he or she looks around in the real world—they are created by light from the sun or artificial sources being reflected by the physical objects of the scene. This gives the objects their observable properties of color and brightness. The word "observable" is important—the reproduction of a scene should be in terms of what an observer sees or, more accurately, what one *thinks* one sees. This is a *psychophysical* criterion, which may be different from the physical quantities of brightness and color.

Unfortunately for easy characterization, natural scenes are seldom illuminated by a single light source of known properties. The illumination at any point in the scene is a summation of the light from identifiable sources plus light reflected from surrounding objects. This latter illumination has already been modified by the reflectance properties of the surrounding objects, resulting in an effective illumination whose brightness and color varies throughout the scene. To further complicate the situation, the human eye has learned to adapt to these local variations in illumination to the extent that one is generally not aware of them when observing the scene directly. The image reproduction system must accomplish the same result.

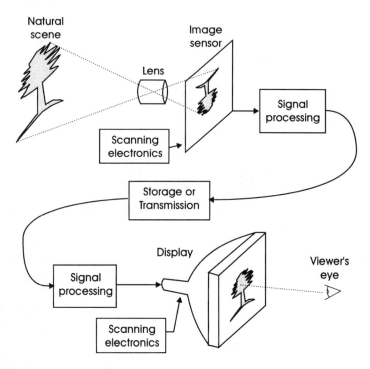

Figure 2.1 *Electronic image reproduction.*

2.2 HUMAN VISION

The eye is a remarkable device—it contains more than 100,000,000 (10^8) sensors with a brightness control system that allows clear vision over a brightness range of more than ten million to one. The two eyes together with the brain give the ability to recognize objects in three-dimensional space. Although most electronic reproduction systems do not come close to these properties, by designing them with the properties of the eye in mind, they are satisfactory for many purposes.

2.2.1 Resolution

The resolving power of an average eye with 20/20 vision and in the center of vision is approximately one minute of arc (1/60th of a degree or 1′.) This is called the *acuity* of the eye and the figure given applies for gray scale objects only; the acuity for colored objects is less (see Section 2.4.1). The acuity means, for example, that one can visually resolve objects spaced about 0.4 in when seen from a distance of 100 ft. Since the field of view of the eye is nearly 180 deg, one could theoretically resolve a total of 180 × 60 = 10,800 objects across the full field of view. However, the eye's resolution falls off away from the center of vision, so the total of objects resolved is actually much less.

An electronic imaging system that would resolve such large numbers of objects in a single picture is typically not practical, so electronic imaging systems are usually designed so that their display screen occupies less than the eye's total field of view. Therefore, most of the image is viewed by the part of the eye that has full resolution, and the full-resolution acuity should be used in electronic imaging calculations. The other feature of the eye that means full acuity should be used is the ability of the eye to move so as to bring the items of interest into the center of vision. A wide-angle display viewed closely faces the problem that viewers will choose to look directly at whatever part of the screen that interests them. At any particular time, this could be anywhere on the screen, so the entire screen must have high resolution.

As discussed in Section 1.4.2.1, digital systems describe images as a series of pixels. Display systems should be designed so that individual pixels are not visible because they can interfere with the appearance of the picture. This is usually achieved by having enough pixels in the image that a viewer at the design viewing distance or greater will not be able to resolve them. An important parameter for these considerations is the *viewing ratio*, which is defined as the ratio of the viewer's distance from the screen to the height of the picture:

$$VR = \frac{d}{PH} \tag{2.1}$$

where

VR = viewing ratio
d = viewer's distance from the screen in any units
PH = picture height in the same units as d

Using the above acuity figures, the maximum number of pixels visible at a particular viewing ratio is

$$\text{visible pixels} = \frac{3{,}440}{VR} \tag{2.2}$$

Notice that for a picture with a fixed number of pixels, there is a maximum size of the picture for a given distance before the pixels will become visible or, alternatively, there is a minimum viewing ratio that applies. Some examples of this are given in Table 2.1. These

Table 2.1

Minimum Viewing Ratios

System	Lines or pixels/PH	Viewing Ratio
NTSC television	483	7.2
HDTV	1080	3.2
Computer display	768	4.5*

* Computers typically operate much lower than this.

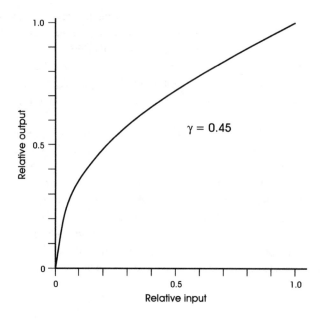

Figure 2.2 *Gamma correction curve for γ=0.45.*

considerations apply to either analog or digital video systems. In the case of analog video systems, one can use lines rather than pixels per picture height. Visibility of scan lines is even more disturbing than visibility of pixels.

2.2.2 Gray Scale Reproduction

Proper image reproduction requires that the light output at the final display be proportional to the light intensity reflected from the original scene at every point. This would ordinarily mean that the video signal be a linear function of the scene brightness. However, because the typical device (e.g., CRT) has a nonlinear intensity versus signal function, many system standards have included correction for that in the video signal because linearity correction is expensive to include in a display or television receiver.

Most video camera sensors do have a linear light response, so cameras usually include what is known as *gamma correction* to introduce the required nonlinear amplitude characteristic to the signal. Gamma refers to an exponential approximation to the transfer characteristic. For example, the gamma of a typical CRT is about 2.2. This means that a camera must introduce gamma correction with an exponent of 1/2.2 or 0.45. Such a characteristic is shown by the curve in Figure 2.2.

Unfortunately, many computer standards call for different gamma correction than does television, and it may sometimes be necessary to make corrections when converting between television signals and computer signals.

2.2.3 Refresh Rate and Flicker

One does not see rapid changes of illumination because of a visual property called *persistence of vision*, which means that the visual system responds slowly to rapid changes of illumination. However, if the illumination varies cyclically at a low frequency as when illuminated by a low-frequency electric lamp, the eye may perceive an annoying effect that we call *flicker*. The onset of flicker depends on the amount of illumination (flicker is easier to see at higher brightness levels) and is also easier to see in peripheral vision. This latter effect fortunately helps to make us more sensitive to rapidly moving (possibly dangerous) objects that will first appear in peripheral vision. Controlling flicker is important because prolonged exposure to flickering light can cause headaches or even serious psychological symptoms.

Electronic display devices have a reverse persistence effect—their light output decays after a short time. Therefore, electronic images must be refreshed periodically to maintain the effect of steady illumination. The refresh rate must be high enough to avoid flicker under the desired viewing conditions. Typical refresh rates are tabulated in Table 2.2. The low refresh rate in a motion picture theater is possible because the theater is darkened and the pictures are not too bright. The computer display is an opposite situation—the display is often in a brightly illuminated room, the screen must be bright, and the low viewing ratio means that parts of the screen appear in peripheral vision.

There is a certain amount of adaptation to flicker that takes place when the same kind of viewing occurs regularly. For example, the 50-Hz refresh rate used in some countries is deemed completely satisfactory to the natives, but one arriving from a 60-Hz refresh rate country may at first think the pictures flicker terribly. Over time, one becomes adapted to it.

Table 2.2

Display Refresh Rates

System	Refresh rate (Hz)	Environment	VR
NTSC television	60 (59.94)	Living room	7
PAL television	50	Living room	7
Computer display	72	Bright office	1–2
Motion picture theater	48	Dark room	5–10

2.2.4 Reproducing Motion

The illusion of motion is created in a video system by updating the screen contents at a rate high enough for the viewer to perceive continuous motion. In a television system, that is accomplished at the camera and display scanning rates.

In the simplest situation, a video camera creates a separate frame for each refresh cycle of the video display. This is the way conventional analog television operates—the frame rates of the camera and the display are identical; in fact they are *synchronized*. In this mode of operation, the signal generated by the camera goes continuously to the display, with no intervening storage or processing. When television standards were first set, storage and processing had not been invented, so the system was designed for the display to be re-freshed by continuously delivering new signals from the camera, even when the image was stationary.

Today, with digital video technology, storage and processing are inherent in the system and it is not necessary for the camera and display to have the same frame rates or even to be synchronized. The camera can be operated at a frame rate that is sufficient for reproducing motion and the display can operate at a higher frame rate that provides the desired flicker performance. It is even possible to stop repeated transmission of stationary images or parts of images that are stationary to reduce data transmission requirements (see Chapter 9).

As shown above, flicker reduction requires frame rates of 50 Hz or more and the display should scan at such a rate, but motion reproduction is usually satisfactory with frame rates of 30 Hz or even lower. Thus, camera scanning need only be fast enough to support motion reproduction. In digital systems, it is possible to meet both of these criteria.

When one watches an object that moves rapidly through a scene, it appears to move smoothly but it is blurred because of the persistence-of-vision effect mentioned above. However, if the eye *tracks* the moving object, the blurring of the object is reduced, but the background now becomes blurred. A reproduction system cannot handle both of these situations at the same time because the camera device that captures the electronic image has a similar persistence-of-vision effect. This is called *motion smearing* and it occurs be-cause the camera has a finite exposure time.

This has not been much of a problem with television systems operated at their designed viewing ratios because the picture was not really large enough for the viewer to track mov-ing objects anyway. Moving objects are usually tracked by the camera, and the viewer does not have to do tracking. However, with larger, higher resolution screens coming into use, enough of the viewer's field of view may be involved that he or she would like to track dif-ferent parts of the scene. Then, the camera should not track the objects and it should have a shorter exposure time so the moving objects are sharper.

2.3 SCANNING

A natural scene reflects light from all its points simultaneously, and the eye of an observer senses all those points in parallel with its 10^8 sensors. It is up to the brain to make sense of

(a) Scanning raster

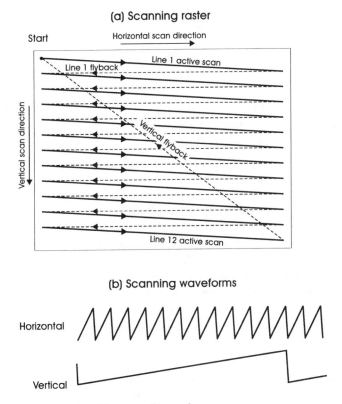

(b) Scanning waveforms

Figure 2.3 *Progressive scanning, (a) pattern, (b) waveforms.*

this fantastic stream of parallel data (which it does admirably). However, such a massively parallel architecture is not practical in electronics, so an electronic imaging system has a different problem—it must convert the parallel data into one, or at most a few, electronic signals that vary with time. The means to do that is *scanning*.

Scanning is just like the way one reads an English text document. Beginning at the upper left corner of the text, the reader's eye moves horizontally from left to right along the first line of text; at the end of that line, the eye snaps back to the left and moves down to the next line and resumes horizontal scanning. This process continues until the bottom of the page is reached.

Thus, scanning is the process of moving a sensing element (the eye in the previous paragraph) over all the points of an image (the page of text) in sequence until the entire scene (the page) has been covered. Of course, this could be done in many patterns, such as a radial scan as in a radar, a spiral motion, or even randomly. The developers of television chose a rectangular scanning pattern (called a *raster*) composed of separate horizontal and vertical motions. This has proved to be advantageous in that the entire scene is covered by an element that moves at a uniform speed, and its hardware implementation is very simple. This type of scanning is illustrated in Figure 2.3(a).

2.3.1 Electronic Scanning

To have a stable scanning pattern, the horizontal and vertical scanning frequencies must be synchronized in an exact integral relationship. To produce a pattern of N horizontal lines, the horizontal scanning frequency is highest and it must be in the ratio N to the vertical scanning frequency:

$$f_H = f_V \times N \tag{2.3}$$

The vertical scanning frequency is also the frame rate for the system. For example, if the frame rate is to be 60 Hz, then vertical scanning is also 60 Hz. For 525 scan lines, then the horizontal scan frequency is exactly $525 \times 60 = 31{,}500$ Hz.

In addition to this frequency relationship, scanning signals should be designed to produce *linear* scanning, which means that the scanning speed will be uniform over the entire image. This is important in both the camera and display to assure exact reproduction of the geometry of the scene on the display. Any nonlinearity of the scanning will cause geometric distortion of some part of the image. Although one could theoretically use an exact nonlinear scanning pattern, such patterns are difficult to maintain, and the nonuniform scanning speed causes other problems such as variation in resolution, sensitivity, and brightness. All video scanning standards use linear scanning.

2.3.2 Blanking Intervals

The position of the scanned element must move linearly with time in straight-line fashion. This applies while the scanning is moving from left to right across one line of the screen (the *active scan* time), but it is not necessary while the scan snaps back to the left for the next line. This period, the horizontal *flyback* interval, should be a short as possible. In early television, flyback time was limited by the circuits that scanned displays, and it was necessary to assign nearly 18% of the total time to horizontal flyback. That is wasteful because no visible information can be transmitted during that time. In fact, to make sure that nothing from that interval appears on the screen, the signal is *blanked out* by forcing it to a voltage that represented black on the screen. This has given rise to the more often used name for the flyback period: *horizontal blanking interval*. Linear scanning with an 18% blanking interval requires a *sawtooth* kind of waveform. This is shown in Figure 2.2(b).

Vertical scanning is also linear, but the television standards specify a shorter flyback period in recognition that early vertical scanning circuits could achieve a faster flyback. The *vertical blanking interval* (VBI) is 8% for television.

2.3.3 Signal Bandwidth and Horizontal Resolution

As in the reading of text where the eye recognizes one text character after another, scanning in a video camera effectively moves a sensing element across the scene, while generating a varying output voltage that is proportional to the intensity of the reflected light at each point the sensing element crosses. (There is no actual moving element in a video camera, but the result is the same as if there were. Camera sensors are described in Chapter 6.)

Recognizing that a physical sensing element has a finite size, the sensor averages all the light it sees within a small area called its *aperture*. This averaging causes a loss of fine detail or a falloff of high frequency response if we look at the electrical signal. The effect of the aperture, called the *aperture response*, is shown in Figure 2.4. The figure shows a round aperture, but an aperture can have any shape and also may have a nonuniform distribution of sensitivity within that shape. This makes the averaging process actually one of integration over the area of the aperture. The result, as the figure shows, is rounding of edges on all transitions and actual loss of amplitude when the pattern spacing becomes smaller than the aperture size.

It is apparent from the foregoing that the video frequencies generated by scanning depend on the fine detail in the scene and the speed of scanning. It is useful to view the fine detail in terms of how the system reproduces pattern of equally spaced black and white lines. Vertical-line patterns test the system's *horizontal resolution*, and horizontal-line patterns test the system's *vertical resolution*.

For horizontal resolution, the video frequency f_v generated by a pattern of uniformly spaced black and white vertical lines is given by (2.4):

$$f_V = \frac{1}{2} \frac{f_H \times N_P \times AR}{1 - HB} \tag{2.4}$$

where

$f_H =$ the horizontal-line scanning frequency

$N_P =$ the number of black and white lines in a distance equal to the picture height

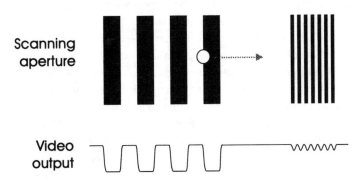

Figure 2.4 *Aperture response in scanning.*

$AR =$ the *aspect ratio*, the ratio of the width to the height of the screen (1.33 for NTSC television)

$HB =$ the fraction of time spent in horizontal blanking (0.18 for NTSC television)

Equation (2.4) counts the total number of black and white lines across the active width of the picture generated by a pattern of vertical lines that have the same spacing as N_p horizontal lines in a distance equal to the picture height. The factor ½ in (2.4) then accounts for the fact that one cycle of f_V is produced by one black and one white line, so the frequency is one-half the total lines counted multiplied by the horizontal-line frequency. The counting of total black and white lines in a distance equal to the picture height is a convention used in television for the specification of resolution or aperture response. Such numbers are specified in *TV lines* (TVL). Thus, specifying 300 TVL for a particular line pattern means that if the pattern were extended to cover a distance equal to the picture height, there would be 300 total black and white lines in the extended pattern.

2.3.4 Interlaced Scanning

The type of scanning described so far is called *progressive scanning* because all lines of each frame are scanned in sequence. Equation (2.4) showed that the maximum video frequency generated by scanning is directly proportional to the horizontal-scanning frequency, which, of course, is equal to the vertical-scanning frequency multiplied by the number of lines in the raster. Since the vertical-scanning frequency must be high enough to avoid flicker in the image, one can see that the video bandwidth needed is a direct function of how many lines are in the picture and what is the vertical frequency. However, video frequencies can be lowered without creating too great a flicker problem by using what is known as *interlaced scanning*.

This is achieved by scanning only part of the raster lines in each vertical scan. For example, one vertical scan can scan all the odd-numbered lines, and a second vertical scan can scan all the even-numbered lines. This is 2:1 interlacing, and it reduces video frequencies by 2:1 compared with progressive scanning at the same vertical frequency. Since the vertical frequency is unchanged, flicker is (almost) not a problem.

Interlaced scanning is accomplished by modifying the scanning numbers to have an odd number of total lines (e.g., 525 or 625) and making the horizontal-scanning frequency be one-half the product of the line number and the vertical-scanning frequency. This frequency relationship automatically results in the interlaced scanning pattern shown in Figure 2.5. As seen in the figure, the first vertical scan ends at the center of a line, so the second vertical scan starts in the center of a line, placing its lines exactly between the lines of the first scan. Since it takes two vertical scans to scan the complete raster, the frame frequency is half of the vertical scanning frequency. The two vertical scans that make up a frame are called *fields*; one has all the odd-numbered lines of the raster and the other has all the even-numbered lines.

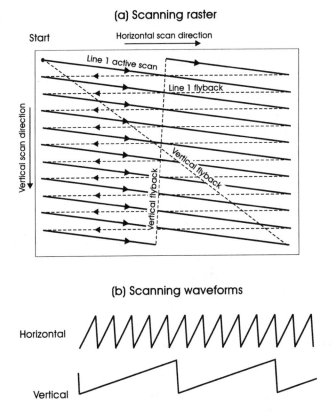

(a) Scanning raster

(b) Scanning waveforms

Figure 2.5 *Interlaced scanning, (a) pattern, (b) waveforms.*

2.3.4.1 Artifacts of Interlaced Scanning

Although interlaced scanning does reduce video frequencies by 2:1 and is widely used in television, it has two problems that are important today, especially in digital systems. These include a flicker problem known as *interline flicker* and a motion artifact called *gear-toothing*.

Interline flicker shows up in any image that does not have the same information on adjacent lines. Any pattern of sharp horizontal or near-horizontal lines will show flicker because the edge information appears in only one scan field, thus giving a refresh rate of one-half the vertical-scan frequency for that information. This problem shows most clearly on computer-generated text that typically has sharp edges. It is possible to filter the computer text to reduce the problem but that blurs the text enough that larger characters have to be used. For TV-screen display, computer text has to be limited to fewer than 40 characters across the screen, which is half or less the number of text characters that most noninterlaced computer screens can show. Although this limitation is not too bad for television viewing at large viewing distances, interlacing is completely unsatisfactory for most computer applications, and is not recommended for computer screens. It also is not desirable for HDTV screens at low viewing ratios.

The gear-toothing effect occurs when rapidly moving objects are scanned with interlacing. This effect is caused by the difference in the position of the moving object between the two vertical scans of an interlaced frame. Alternate lines show the object in different positions. The effect is somewhat masked by the normal motion blurring that occurs, but it becomes obvious if the camera is operated with short exposure time, or if the image is still-scanned for stop-motion effects.

2.3.5 Vertical Resolution

Unlike horizontal resolution, which is limited by the system bandwidth, vertical resolution is limited by the line-scanning pattern. Horizontal or near-horizontal patterns of fine detail are sampled by the scanning lines at a spatial frequency represented by the number of active scanning lines. Since the Nyquist criterion (see Section 1.4.2.1) points out that frequencies above one-half the sampling rate are not correctly sampled, one would think that the vertical resolution limit measured in TVL should be one-half the number of active lines. However, it subjectively appears to be somewhat higher than that because the aliasing distortion (see Section 5.2.1) does not completely mask the signal. Early television developers had a name for the ratio between the apparent limiting vertical resolution and the number of active lines—the *Kell factor*. This ranged from about 0.5 to 0.9 and usually was taken at 0.7.

The combination of interlaced scanning and vertical aliasing on horizontal edges causes artifacts in reproducing natural images that are seen as flickering on near-horizontal edges and flickering herringbone patterns in scene areas that have strong horizontally-oriented patterns such as a checkerboard coat.

The vertical sampling effect occurs in any system employing line scanning, so it exists in digital video systems as well as television. Its complete elimination requires that input frequencies above the Nyquist limit be filtered out ahead of the sampling process. That means the filtering must be done optically in the camera before the scanning process takes place in the image sensor. Some cameras have such filters (see Chapter 6).

2.3.6 Angular Resolution

The concept of resolution is generalized in *angular resolution*, which is resolution measured at any angle to the horizontal or vertical. This is observed and measured by studying system response to a test pattern called a *zone plate* (Figure 2.6). Here, the concentric circles require resolution capability in all directions.

Figure 2.6 *The zone plate pattern for measurement of angular resolution.*

2.4 COLOR REPRESENTATION

The discussion so far has applied primarily to monochrome (gray scale) images. Reproduction of color requires more.

2.4.1 Color Properties of Light

Natural light sources consist of a mixture of electromagnetic waves in the spectrum of visible wavelengths from 400 to 700 nm (10^{-9} meters). White light has an approximate uniform spectral distribution over that range, although there are many variations of "white" light. Colored lights have nonuniform distributions that enhance one or more regions of the spectrum. The process of reflection of white light from the surfaces of natural objects may be wavelength selective, which is what causes an object to have its characteristic color. Light waves at the wavelengths of the characteristic color are reflected; other wavelengths are more or less absorbed instead of being reflected.

The eye recognizes color by means of the three different kind of cone receptors in the retina. These respond differently to different colors and send three-dimensional signals to the brain, where color recognition occurs. Because of the recognition process, what one sees as color is a perception that may not be the same as the physical color. A color reproduction system looks at the physical color information (spectral distributions), but it must reproduce the perception of color that a viewer is going to expect.

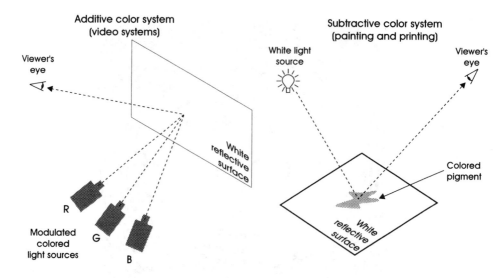

Figure 2.7 *Additive and subtractive color systems.*

Research into the behavior of color vision going back to Sir Isaac Newton in the 17th century has shown that the perception of any color can be represented by just three variables. This is consistent with the three types of color receptors in the eye and is known as the *trichromatic* theory of color. It is the basis for color photography, color printing, color painting, and color video systems.

2.4.2 Primary Colors

The trichromatic theory states that any color can be reproduced by a combination of three colors, known as *primary colors* (Figure 2.7). The primary color set used in color video systems is the *additive set:* red, green, and blue. (This is called *RGB*.) "Additive" means they reproduce colors by adding colored light sources. When equal amounts of the additive primaries are mixed, the resulting color is gray or white.

Another example of primary colors is the set used for color painting by artists and in color printing. These primaries, technically called magenta, cyan, and yellow, are known (incorrectly) by some people as "red," "blue," and yellow. They are the *subtractive* primaries, because they are used in the form of pigments to modify the light reflected from white paper by absorbing (subtracting) certain colors that would otherwise be reflected. If equal amounts of the subtractive colors are applied to a white surface, the resulting reflected color is gray or black. Note that a "white" surface reflects all colors equally.

The subtractive primaries are the *complements* of the additive primaries, which means that each subtractive primary is the sum of two additive primaries (Figure 2.8). As shown

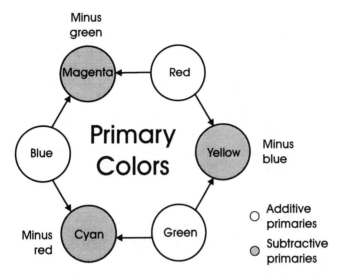

Figure 2.8 *Additive and subtractive primary colors. The arrows show how the subtractive primaries are the complements of the additive primaries.*

by the arrows in the figure, magenta is red and blue, cyan is green and blue, and yellow is red and green. The subtractive primaries are sometimes referred to by the name of the additive primary that they do *not* contain. For example, magenta is known as "minus green."

2.4.3 Component Color Video Systems

In a color video system, the cameras must deliver three color *components* to control the red, blue, and green light sources of the display. Professional video cameras do this by using three simultaneously scanned image sensors that have appropriate color filtering to achieve the desired spectral responses (see Section 6.3). The output of the sensors provides the signals to control the three guns of a color CRT for display. Lower cost cameras use only one sensor that has stripes or patches of color filters on it to capture the three colors from spatially adjacent areas on the sensing surface. Electronic processing of the signal from a single-sensor camera allows the RGB color components to be extracted. The details of both types of cameras are discussed in Chapter 6.

Handling color component signals on three parallel circuits is awkward when a large system having many video signal interconnections must be built. It becomes impossible when analog color signals have to be transmitted or broadcast over a single transmission channel. Therefore, there is a need for *composite* color systems that combine the three color components into a single signal.

Note that in a digital system where the RGB components are generated digitally, the combination of digital channels for each of the three components into a single channel is simply a parallal-to-serial conversion. However, creating a composite signal in an analog system is not such a simple task and generally involves performance compromises. Because of this, any system designed to be digital from scratch should not use analog composite signals at all. However, many systems are changing from analog to digital over time and digitizing the analog composite signals as described below is a useful expedient during the transition period.

Some of the techniques that make possible analog composite color systems are also useful in digital systems; the following discussion explains those. However, the discussion of actual composite systems is just an overview. The references [1,2] contain more complete descriptions of NTSC, PAL, and SECAM composite color systems.

2.4.4 Composite Color Systems

Another property of the eye is an important contributor to color video systems. As a result of the way the information from the eye is collected and processed in the brain, the eye has less acuity for colored objects than for gray scale objects. Therefore, a video system may have reduced resolution for colors and the pictures will not appear degraded to the eye. For a video system to exploit this property of the eye, the primary color signals generated by a camera must be restructured into separate color and monochrome the same way that the eye does. Since the trichromatic theory says that *any* three signals can represent color, it is possible to perform a linear matrix transformation of the R, G, and B component signals into a monochrome signal (called *luminance*) and two signals that represent color. The color signals are *color-difference* signals, meaning that they go to zero when there is no color. That is done by subtracting the luminance signal from the color components.

2.4.4.1 Luminance and Color-Difference Components

The luminance signal has a spectral response in accordance with the *luminosity curve* (Figure 2.9), which shows the relative brightness that the eye perceives for different spectral colors. The luminance signal Y is synthesized by combining the R, G, and B signals according to Eq. (2.5):

$$Y = 0.59G + 0.30R + 0.11B \tag{2.5}$$

Note that the weighting of the colors in the luminance equation is in accordance with the visual perception of brightness of the colors—green appears brightest, red is darker, and blue appears darkest.

Color difference signals are obtained by subtracting Y from the R and B signals to create an $R-Y$ signal and a $B-Y$ signal. These latter signals can be transmitted at about half-bandwidth because of the eye's poorer acuity for colors. Luminance and color-difference signals are widely used in both analog and digital video systems.

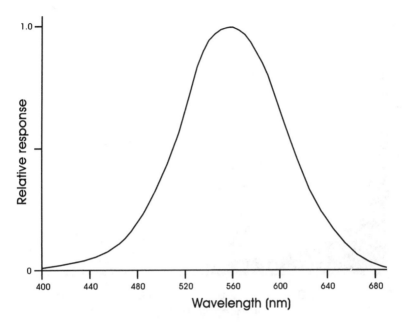

Figure 2.9 *The luminosity curve.*

2.4.4.2 Analog Frequency Interleaving

Another property of video signals makes possible the analog combination of luminance and color-difference components into a single channel. That is the recognition that the frequency components generated by a scanned video signal are mostly clustered around the harmonics of the horizontal-scanning frequency. Mathematically, this can be proven by performing Fourier analysis on typical video signals, but it also can be seen intuitively by observing that the most significant component of a video waveform is the horizontal blanking signal, which is simply a series of pulses at line-scanning frequency. Of course, the spectrum of such pulses would consist of the line-scanning frequency and its harmonics. This is illustrated in Figure 2.10.

The nature of this spectrum is that the signal energy is concentrated close to the harmonics of line frequency, which means that it is possible to interleave with the video another signal whose frequency components would fall mostly between the line harmonics. If that is done correctly, the interference between the two signals is minimized (but not zero.)

2.4.4.3 The NTSC Composite Color System

The first successful composite color system was the *National Television Systems Committee* (NTSC) system developed in the United States in the 1950s. It combines the three color component signals into a single composite signal that fits in the same 6-MHz

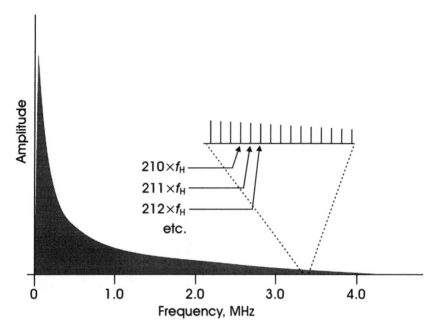

Figure 2.10 *Spectrum of monochrome video.*

channel bandwidth that was used for monochrome broadcasting. Further, the signal remains compatible with the monochrome standards so that existing monochrome receivers could view the color signals (in monochrome, of course.) The NTSC system is still in use today, more than 40 years after its development.

In NTSC or PAL color television, the interleaved signal is a modulated subcarrier that contains the color-difference information modulated on two quadrature suppressed carriers. The suppressed-carrier feature means that the carrier goes to zero for no signal, which occurs when or where there is no color in the picture. Thus, the color subcarrier signal vanishes in monochrome pictures or monochrome regions of color pictures. Because the color signals result from scanning at the same horizontal frequency as the luminance signal, the modulated color subcarrier signal has the same property that its sidebands are separated by the horizontal-scan frequency. Proper interleaving is achieved by correctly locating the subcarrier frequency to fall between the line-scan harmonics. This occurs automatically if the subcarrier frequency is an odd multiple of half the horizontal-scanning frequency. Figure 2.11 shows the spectrum of a properly interleaved color subcarrier.

The color subcarrier is placed near the top of the luminance bandwidth of the system, which takes into account another feature of video signals—that the high frequency components are typically small and that high frequency interference is less visible than lower frequencies. Both of these considerations reduce the visibility of crosstalk between the interleaved components.

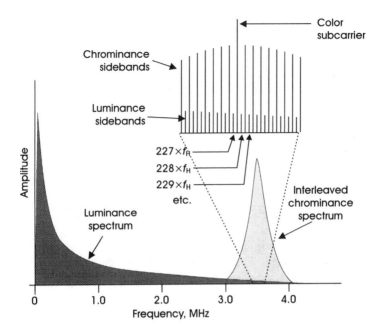

Figure 2.11 Spectrum of composite color video showing frequency interleaving.

A final feature contributes to the minimization of crosstalk between the components of the NTSC signal: the recognition that the eye's acuity for color varies with the color. By choosing the color components with this in mind, it is possible to reduce the bandwidth of one component even more than one-half. This requires changing from the $R - Y$ and $B - Y$ color differences to other signals that are called I and Q (for *inphase* and *quadrature*, which refers to the two modulation axes on the amplitude and phase modulated subcarrier of NTSC.) The matrix equations for these signals are

$$I = 0.6R - 0.28G - 0.32B \qquad (2.6)$$

$$Q = 0.21R - 0.51G + 0.30B \qquad (2.7)$$

In the NTSC standard, the I signal is transmitted with a bandwidth of 1.3 MHz, the Q signal has a bandwidth of 0.5 MHz, and the Y signal (with the color subcarrier interleaved) uses the full video bandwidth of 4.2 MHz. There are other considerations in choosing the exact numbers for the NTSC system, but they are beyond the scope necessary here. The actual numbers are given in Table 2.3.

The NTSC field frequency of 59.94 Hz is slightly different from the nominal 60 Hz for an important reason. To minimize possible cross-modulation interference between the 4.5-MHz sound carrier frequency and the color subcarrier, it is desirable that the line-scanning frequency be an integral submultiple of 4.5 MHz. (That makes the interleaved color subcarrier *not* an integral multiple, which is the desirable condition.) The closest frequency to

Table 2.3

System Parameters of NTSC, PAL, and SECAM Composite Color Systems

Item	NTSC	PAL	SECAM
Total lines	525	625	625
Interlace	2:1	2:1	2:1
Field rate (Hz)	59.94	50.0	50.0
f_H (Hz)	15,734.26	15,625	15,625
Luminance bandwidth (MHz)	4.2	5.0 or 5.5	6.0
f_{SC} (Hz)	3,579,545	4,433,619	4,250,000
			4,406,250
Chrominance bandwidth (MHz)	$I = 1.3$	$U = 1.3$	$D_R = 1.3$
	$Q = 0.5$	$V = 1.3$	$D_B = 1.3$

the monochrome standard's line frequency of 15,750 Hz is the 286th submultiple of 4.5 MHz, which is 15,734.26 Hz. Dividing that by 525 and multiplying by 2 (for the interlace) gives the field frequency of 59.94 Hz.

2.4.4.4 The PAL Composite Color System

The color television system for Europe was developed a few years after the NTSC system was in service, and thus, it benefited from the early experience with NTSC. The European system is called *Phase-Alternating Line* (PAL) and it takes account of the somewhat greater bandwidths available for broadcasting in Europe. As with NTSC, PAL offers compatibility with the previous monochrome broadcasting on the Continent.

Most European countries had a 625-line monochrome system with 50-Hz vertical scanning (the United Kingdom and France excepted, which had 405/50 and 819/50 systems, respectively.) With the greater available video bandwidth of 5.5 MHz, the PAL system can use a higher color subcarrier frequency and the same color-difference bandwidth in each channel. Since the color-difference bandwidths are the same, the PAL system used $B - Y$ and $R - Y$ components directly. These are given the names U and V. Their equations are

$$U = 0.493 \, (B - Y) \tag{2.8}$$

$$V = \pm 0.877 \, (R - Y) \tag{2.9}$$

However, the most important difference in PAL is what gives it its name: phase-alternating line, indicated by the $\pm$ sign in Eq. (2.9). This phase of the color subcarrier for the V component is alternated (reversed) from one line to the next. The effect of that is to largely cancel small errors in subcarrier phase that otherwise result in color-hue distortion. (This was a difficult problem with early NTSC equipment, although it has long since been alleviated by careful design of components and systems.)

The numbers for PAL are also in Table 2.3.

2.4.4.5 The SECAM Composite Color System

A different composite-color video system was developed in France. It is called *Sequential Couleur Avec Mémoire* (SECAM) and it uses two frequency-modulated subcarriers to carry the $B - Y$ and $R - Y$ color-difference components. This eliminates all system problems of maintaining color subcarrier amplitude and phase because these parameters are not important to FM. However, it has its own set of problems and is used only in France and countries associated with the former Soviet Union.

The parameters of SECAM are also in Table 2.3.

2.4.4.6 Problems with Composite Color

Although there are tens of thousands of TV stations broadcasting to hundreds of millions of receivers around the world, all using composite color, a perceptive video engineer can see that these systems still leave a lot to be desired. The result of color modulation and interleaving is not perfect; there are color edge effects, loss of monochrome resolution, the reduced color resolution is too much for reproducing computer-generated images, the interlaced scanning has artifacts, and the signals are not very tolerant of interferences or distortions produced by transmission or video recording. In general, television viewers are satisfied with the present systems, but them they don't have anything to compare them to. On the other hand, video engineers are not satisfied and they have been making continuous improvements as best they can within the standards.

In the final analysis, the existing television standards are the limiting item, and after 40 or more years, the world deserves a new system. That has been the goal of the people developing the new High-Definition TV (HDTV) standards. Using digital technology, the limitations of composite video can be eliminated and, by use of digital video compression, much higher resolution signals can be transmitted in the same 6-MHz channels now reserved for NTSC.

Of course, any system has limitations, but the HDTV standards represent more than an order of magnitude improvement in most system capabilities. This will make the difficulties of transition from analog to digital worth the trouble. In this digital world, there is no room for composite color.

2.5 ANALOG VIDEO SIGNALS

Video signals generated by scanning are processed in the camera and formatted according to the standard for which the camera is designed. In addition to specifying scanning frequencies, analog video standards specify the video waveform, which includes definition of the *synchronizing* information that is contained in the blanking intervals.

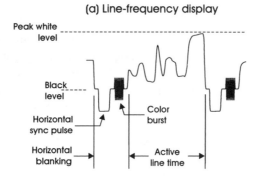

(a) Line-frequency display

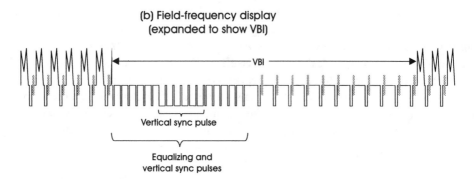

(b) Field-frequency display
(expanded to show VBI)

Figure 2.12 *NTSC video waveforms.*

2.5.1 Video Waveforms

Figure 2.12 shows the video waveforms for the NTSC television standard. The figure is not an exact replica of the standards; for that, consult reference [1].

Analog video waveforms are usually viewed with a waveform display or oscilloscope that is synchronized to the signal at either frame, field, or line rates. At any of these rates, the video information usually appears to be random and, of course, it will be changing if the picture is changing. However, the blanking and synchronizing parts of the video are stationary and repetitive, so they appear clearly.

Figure 2.12(a) is a line-rate display showing details of the horizontal blanking interval, which include the horizontal synchronizing pulse and the color synchronizing burst. The latter consists of a minimum of eight cycles at the color subcarrier frequency. Figure 2.12(b) shows details of the vertical blanking interval. A wide pulse is contained in this interval for vertical scan synchronization, but it is serrated with narrow pulses to continue horizontal synchronization during the wide pulse. Because the relationship between horizontal and vertical pulses shifts between odd and even fields due to the frequency ratio needed for interlacing, the serrations in the vertical sync and the surrounding equalizing pulses are at double-horizontal frequency. This makes the vertical pulse and its surroundings look the same on both odd and even fields.

Since most video systems consist of several units and video signals must be sent between units, video interconnection standards also exist to define cables, connectors, and voltage levels. This assures that units from different manufacturers can be connected into systems.

2.5.2 Analog Video Specifications

Since the input and output of a video system are analog even when the system is "all-digital," analog video measurements may still be used to evaluate a digital system. This section discusses the most important video parameters.

2.5.2.1 Video Frequency Response

A video channel must pass all the frequency components of the signal generated by scanning the scene. This ranges from dc (zero frequency) up to the highest frequency corresponding to the maximum horizontal resolution of the system. For a system that starts with a camera, frequency response is measured by placing one or more test charts in front of the camera and observing the system response with a picture monitor and a waveform monitor. Some test charts are designed to be all-purpose, and others are designed to show specific attributes of performance. Figure 2.13 shows two test charts for use in front of a camera. The high-frequency response of an electrooptical device such as a camera's imager is often referred to as the *modulation transfer function* (MTF) of the device (see Section 6.4.5).

The *multiburst* chart is designed to be viewed with a waveform monitor synchronized to horizontal scanning. The bursts of increasing frequency provide six points of response testing. The lowest frequency burst is 0.5 MHz, so this pattern tests the high-end response only.

The *pulse and bar* pattern is designed to test both high- and low-frequency response using a waveform monitor to display the system's transient response. The narrow pulse has a special *sine-squared* shape of a width such that its spectrum is entirely within the video system bandwidth (wider system bandwidths require shorter pulses.) Therefore, the pulse should be reproduced *exactly* by the system. Because this is a transient-response test, it tests both the amplitude and phase response of the system. Mid-frequencies are tested by examining the response on the flat-bar part of the waveform using horizontal synchronization of the waveform monitor. The pulse top should be flat, with no smearing or sagging. Low-frequency response is tested by examining the pattern with vertical sync of the waveform monitor. Again, the pulse top should be flat and level.

When a video signal input to the system is available, the system frequency response is tested by applying test signals from an electronic signal generator and observing the result

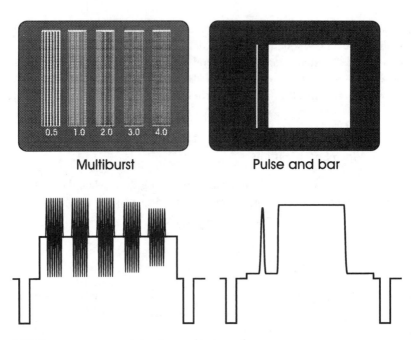

Figure 2.13 *Frequency response test pattern and test waveforms.*

with picture and waveform monitors. Some of the test charts and test signals correspond, but the all-purpose charts do not have corresponding simple waveforms. Of course, testing with video signals does not test the camera, but if that is not necessary, they are the best way to test a system.

The *wedge* test pattern (Figure 2.14) is usually presented as part of an all-purpose chart. It is observed on a picture monitor; the point on the wedge where the bars fade out is the limiting resolution of the system. Wedge tests are available for both horizontal and vertical resolution.

Figure 2.15 shows an all-purpose test chart designed by the author. It is not a chart to place before a camera but, rather, it is a digital file that can be displayed on a digital system. The block background is actually color blocks, but their outlines form a grating pattern (see Section 2.5.2.5). There are wedge patterns for both horizontal and vertical. However, the wedge patterns contain aliasing distortion. When displayed on a 1024 × 768 resolution digital display, the wedges should be reproduced exactly; if not, the display system is introducing distortion. The pattern also has gray scale blocks and a color bar pattern.

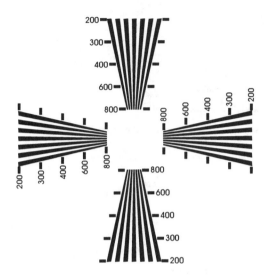

Figure 2.14 *Resolution wedge test patterns.*

Figure 2.15 *An all-purpose test pattern for digital displays.*

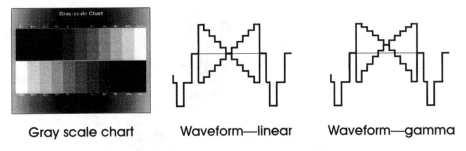

Gray scale chart   Waveform—linear   Waveform—gamma

Figure 2.16 *Gray scale test pattern showing linear waveform and with gamma.*

2.5.2.2 Gray Scale

Gray scale response is tested with a *stairstep* pattern or with a stairstep signal. These are shown in Figure 2.16. The pattern (or the signal) contains equal steps of gray scale, which should be reproduced linearly by the system. By having two patterns, one going up and the other going down, the midpoint response can be compared. With a truly linear system, the traces will cross over exactly at the 50% level. If the system under test contains gamma correction, then the stairsteps will cross at a different point, as shown in the third view of the figure.

2.5.2.3 Signal-to-Noise Ratio

Signal-to-noise ratio (SNR) is ordinarily measured by removing the signal and measuring residual noise. However, in an analog video system, there is no such thing as no signal—at least the sync and blanking signals must always be present. SNR measurement is thus done by supplying a *flat-field* signal, which is usually a 50%-brightness uniform gray. A *gated noise meter* must be used to measure the variation (which is the noise) of the gray field. Alternatively, the flat field may be observed on the waveform monitor and the thickness of the line representing the flat field is estimated. A rule of thumb is that the peak-to-peak thickness of the noise on the flat field is approximately six times the noise level. Thus the SNR would be

$$SNR = 6 \frac{black\text{-}to\text{-}white\text{-}signal\ level}{line\ thickness} \tag{2.10}$$

This method can be used to estimate the noise on each of the steps of a gray scale pattern to test system noise versus brightness.

The flat-field noise test is more difficult with a camera because the camera may introduce background variations (called *shading*) on the flat field, which can be confused with noise.

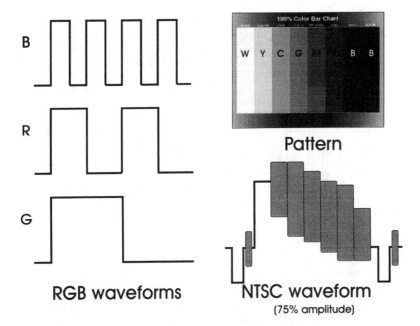

Figure 2.17 *RGB color-bar signals and pattern.*

2.5.2.4 Color Parameters

Color testing depends on whether the system is component or composite. In a component system, color performance is determined by proper matching of the signal levels. For a video signal test of this, an RGB color-bar pattern signal can be input to the system. A properly adjusted system will reproduce the RGB color-bar signals at its output. A color-bar pattern and its RGB waveforms are shown in Figure 2.17.

A composite system will produce waveforms that are specific to its format. For example, the NTSC waveform for a color-bar pattern is shown in the third block of Figure 2.17. The color-bar pattern in an NTSC or PAL system can also be viewed on a special display called a *vectorscope*, which shows a polar coordinate display of the subcarrier amplitude and phase.

2.5.2.5 Scan Linearity

With the almost total replacement of vacuum tube imagers with CCDs (see Chapter 6), scanning linearity is not the problem it used to be. That is because CCDs are built with a near-perfect pattern of pixels and the only thing else that can affect linearity electronically is the stability of clocking the CCD, which can also be nearly perfect. That leaves optical distortions as the only problem, and this is controlled in the design of the optics and can be

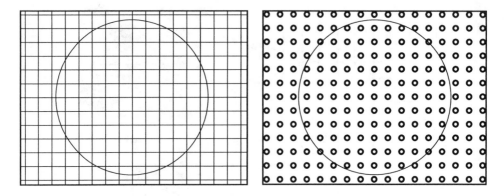

Figure 2.18 *Grating pattern and ball chart used for testing scan linearity.*

minimized. However, displays are still mostly CRTs, and they continue to have the problem of scan linearity.

Linearity measurement is usually done with two patterns, the ball chart and the grating, shown in Figure 2.18. The concept of measurement is that the ball chart is placed in front of a camera, and the resulting signal is mixed with an electronically generated grating pattern. The signals are aligned so the grating lines fall in the center of the circles. Because the circles are 4% outside diameter and 1% thickness (percent of scan height), if all grating lines fall within the center of the circles, linearity is better than ±1%. If some lines fall on the circles, linearity is within ±2% and if any lines are completely outside the circles, linearity is greater than 2%.

The above approach tests the camera linearity and not the display. To test a display, one of the patterns must be electronically generated and fed to the display, while the other pattern in the form of a transparent overlay is placed over the screen and aligned with the display. Then the same kind of observations can be made. Since there can be parallax errors because the screen overlay is a short distance from the actual phosphor of the display, care must be taken when doing this measurement.

2.6 DIGITAL VIDEO SYSTEMS

In digital video systems, the same kinds of standards are required. Some digital systems are defined in terms of direct sampling of analog composite waveforms—these are *composite digital* systems. Other systems operate directly with RGB signals and avoid the color processing of composite signals. They are called *component digital* systems. Analog composite processing involves compromises in signal quality which cannot be removed in the digitizing process, whereas component systems avoid those compromises from the beginning and thus have higher picture quality. The following discussion is an overview of digital video systems; detailed discussions are in other chapters.

2.6.1 Composite Digital Systems

In composite digital systems, the analog NTSC or PAL signal is generated as usual in analog equipment, and the A-D conversion is performed on that single signal. Because the color subcarrier is a high-energy component in these signals and it must be reproduced accurately in amplitude and phase, it is usual to use a sampling frequency that is synchronized to the color subcarrier. Most systems synchronize the sampling clock at 3× or 4× subcarrier, with 8 bits/sample. This gives the data rates shown in Table 2.4.

Some composite digital systems process the signals to change the encoding, remove blanking intervals, or make other modifications to better exploit the advantages of being digital.

2.6.2 Component Digital Systems

Component systems require digitizing of the three separate color components at nearly the same frequency required for digitizing the single composite signal, so there is inherently more data generated by digitizing components.

Early in the development of digital television, the *Consultative Committee for International Radio* (CCIR), now known as the *International Telecommunications Union* (ITU), an international standardizing body in telecommunications, undertook to set standards for component sampling of TV signals. To facilitate international exchange of digital signals, a single sampling frequency was proposed that was unrelated to any analog system's color subcarrier frequency. This was a reasonable choice since a truly component system does not contain a color subcarrier anywhere. The frequency is 13.5 Mhz; it's derivation is explained in Section 5.3.3.

The ITU standard, now known as ITU-R Recommendation BT.601, also provided for the use of color difference components as in NTSC or PAL that could be reduced in bandwidth and sampled at a submultiple of the basic sampling frequency. This is known as *color subsampling* and can occur at a division factor of 2:1 or 4:1 below the 13.5-MHz

Table 2.4

Sampling Parameters of Composite Digital Systems

Standard	Sampling	Bits/sample	Data rate (Mb/s)
NTSC	$3 f_{SC}$	8	85.9
NTSC	$4 f_{SC}$	8	114.5
PAL	$3 f_{SC}$	8	106.3
PAL	$4 f_{SC}$	8	141.8

basic frequency. Of course, subsampling involves the tradeoff of reducing the color band-widths and therefore violates the concept of component processing. In spite of that, at least the 2:1 subsampling is widely used. A simple designation for the ITU-601 systems has been defined:

4:4:4 Full-bandwidth sampling of R, G, B components

4:2:2 Full-bandwidth Y, 2:1 horizontally-subsampled R–Y, B–Y

4:1:1 Full-bandwidth Y, 4:1 horizontally-subsampled R–Y, B–Y

4:2:0 Full-bandwidth Y, 2:1 horizontally- and vertically-subsampled R–Y, B–Y

Note that the color difference components are R–Y and B–Y. For simplicity, this format is often referred to as YUV or YCrCb. Table 2.5 shows the data rates of these various sam-pling choices.

2.6.3 Digital Tape Recording Standards

Early development of digital television equipment focused in two main areas: video re-cording and video special effects. This is because these were the areas where the use of digital technology in an otherwise analog system made the most difference. The field of special effects (see Chapter 12) initially involved standalone digital hardware that inter-faced to the system with analog signals. Thus, there was no need to standardize the internal digital workings of the hardware. However, recorders had to be able to interchange tapes and standards were crucial. The discussion here is only about sampling parameters of the digital video recorder standards. For other details about digital recorders, see Chapter 11.

The Society of Motion Picture and Television Engineers (SMPTE) has taken the lead in developing recorder standards. Their first digital recorder standard, SMPTE D-1, is a com-ponent standard for recording YUV signals sampled in the ITU-601 4:2:2 format. A total data rate of 216 Mb/s is generated and recorded on ¾-inch tape stored in a cassette. Note that the actual recorded data rate is higher than the generated rate because of the error pro-tection and channel coding overhead.

The SMPTE D-2 standard uses the same physical tape cassette as the D-1 but is a com-posite format and a different formulation of tape is used. Sampling is at $4 \times f_{SC}$ for both NTSC and PAL. The total generated data rates are 115 and 142 Mb/s for NTSC and PAL.

Table 2.5

Sampling Parameters of Component Digital Systems Based on ITU-R Rec. BT.601

Standard	f_S (MHz)	Bits/sample	Data rate (Mb/s)
4:4:4	13.5	8	324
4:2:2	13.5/6.75	8	216
4:1:1	13.5/3.375	8	162

In the course of development of analog magnetic video recording for other markets, ½-inch tape systems came into use. They were smaller and cost less, so it was natural to develop high-performance digital systems based on the ½-inch tape decks. This led to the SMPTE D-3 (composite) and D-5 (component) standards. Again, both of these systems use the same tape cassette, holding ½-inch tape. The sampling parameters of these standards are the same as D-2 and D-1, respectively.

Another initiative of the worldwide standards community was the development of an HDTV production system whose output could be converted for distribution in any of the world's television standards (including HDTV, which was not yet standardized at the time.) This standard was originally defined as an analog standard and it has seen some use. A companion digital format was later defined, and this led to the SMPTE D-6 standard which handles a generated data rate of 1.2 Gb/s and uses the D-2 style of ¾-inch tape cassette. To achieve the much higher data rate, the tape runs faster and many more tape tracks are used (see Chapter 11).

Most recently, ¼-inch digital tape systems have been introduced in both the consumer, semiprofessional, and professional markets. These are digital systems from the ground up and there is no equivalent analog version. In most cases, the recorders are integrated with a camera in a camcorder format, so there is essentially no analog processing involved. The ¼-inch system is called *Digital Video Cassette* (DVC) and is available in both consumer and professional (DVCPRO) versions.

The DVC systems are distinguished from all the SMPTE D-series recorders by their use of digital data compression, which is not used in the D-series. Compression is a tradeoff in the eyes of video professionals because it is not transparent, meaning that there is some picture quality degradation due to the compression process. Although the systems are designed so that any degradation is not visible in one pass through the recording system, it will accumulate just like analog distortion when rerecording is done. Because of this problem, the DVCPRO standard calls for less aggressive compression than the consumer standard. The result is that DVCPRO has a shorter playing time but its multigeneration performance will be better. DVC operates at a data rate of 25 MB/s and DVCPRO uses 50 Mb/s.

2.6.4 Digital Disc Standards

The computer-based CD-ROM has been used for video recording by employing massive amounts of data compression. The tradeoff of picture quality is severe and is not acceptable for professional use. However, that is changing with the development of the *Digital Versatile Disc* (DVD) format based on optical recording technology that is similar to CD-ROM.

DVD increases the recording density from the 650 MB per side of CD-ROM to 4.7 GB per side. This, combined with a two-side, two-layer format, allows up to 17 GB to be recorded on a single 12-cm disc. Using the MPEG-2 compression technique (see Chapter 9), video performance that is the equivalent of NTSC or PAL studio performance can be obtained with playing times of one hour per side or layer. This corresponds to a data rate of 10 Mb/s. Like CD-ROM, DVD is a play-only technology or, at most, record-once. Therefore, it is useful for program distribution but does not replace magnetic tape formats for general-purpose record-play service. DVD is covered more fully in Chapter 11.

REFERENCES

1. Benson, K. B., and Whitaker, J. C., *Television Engineering Handbook*, New York, McGraw-Hill, 1992.

2. Inglis, A. F., and Luther, A. C., *Video Engineering*, New York, McGraw-Hill, 1996.

Chapter 3

Audio Fundamentals

3.1 NATURAL SOUND

Sounds are rapid pressure variations in the atmosphere (air) such as are produced by many natural processes. For example, wind rustling through trees, the crashing of ocean surf, the calls of birds—all are natural sounds. Similar pressure variations are produced by many man-made systems, sometimes deliberately and sometimes spuriously. An orchestra makes deliberate sound for the purpose of musical enjoyment while the sound produced by an aircraft taking off is generally viewed as spurious sound.

The human ear responds to atmospheric pressure variations when they are in the frequency range between about 30 Hz to about 15,000 Hz and the brain perceives them to be what we call sound. The magnitude or amplitude of the pressure variations creates the sensation of *loudness*.

Sounds move through the atmosphere according to the rules of wave propagation so that a sound can be heard at a distance from its source. Therefore, sound pressure variations are often called sound *waves*. Sound waves are analog—any value of instantaneous air pressure is possible.

Sound waves move through the air at a velocity v of 1131 ft/sec at room temperature and sea level. According to wave theory, the relationship between frequency f and wavelength λ is

$$\lambda = v/f \tag{3.1}$$

For example, the wavelength for a frequency of 440 Hz (A above middle C) is about 2.57 ft. Sound wavelengths are large, as evidenced by the dimensions of organ pipes, which have to be either $\frac{1}{4}$- or $\frac{1}{2}$-wavelength long.

Many other properties of sound waves are important in the design of audio components; this is the science of *acoustics*. Sound waves will reflect off hard (nonabsorbent) surfaces, producing the effects of *echo* and *reverberation*. Sound waves are *diffracted*—they will go through openings and around corners. They are also *refracted*—they will bend when encountering changes in velocity of propagation such as with regions of different air temperature or density. The important of these effects is a function of local conditions and wavelength; it is safe to say that mathematically modeling the propagation of sound in any real environment is complex indeed.

3.1.1 Ambiance

Natural sound involves more than source and listener because sound waves reflect off surrounding objects in the environment. The listener hears the reflected sounds as well as the sound coming directly from the source. These other sound components contribute to what is known as the *ambiance* of the sound, which is important to the full reproduction of the sound experience by an electronic system.

One of the major elements of sound ambiance is caused by reflections, which occur in closed spaces (such as a concert hall). Because of the finite speed of sound, sound waves bouncing around a room take longer to reach the listener than the direct sound and therefore appear as delayed sounds. The extreme case of this is the *echo*, where there is a single reflection that is delayed enough to be recognized as a repeat of the original sound. Echo becomes noticeable when the delay of the reflected sound is greater than about 50 ms, corresponding to a distance of 56 ft. Echo is most prominent with larger delays, such as those that occur in a canyon or other large natural space.

In a smaller space, there may be multiple reflections, none of which is delayed enough or distinct enough to be called an echo, but the sound continues to bounce around the room until it eventually dies out because of the partial absorption that occurs at each reflection—this is *reverberation*.

Reverberation contributes to the feeling of space and is important in sound reproduction. For example, if the reproduction does not pick up the reverberation (such as will occur if the pickup device is placed very close or even directly on the sound source), the sound will appear *dead*. This can be corrected by adding artificial reverberation, which is usually done by digital processing. Original recordings that will undergo subsequent editing are often taken under relatively dead conditions with the intention that artificial reverb will be added in editing. This gives the editor more control over the sound.

Reverberation is quantized in terms of the time for the reverberation to decay to 1/1000th of the original sound. For a hall designed primarily for speech presentation, a reverberation time of about 1 second is good. However, for presentation of music, a longer reverberation time is desirable, up to about 2 seconds. You have probably experienced the effect of too much reverberation on speech—it becomes unintelligible.

Sound measurements on components such as microphones or loudspeakers often need to be made in a completely benign environment to separate the characteristics of the component from the characteristics of the environment. A special room, called an *anechoic chamber*, is used for this purpose. Such a room absorbs all sound impinging on its

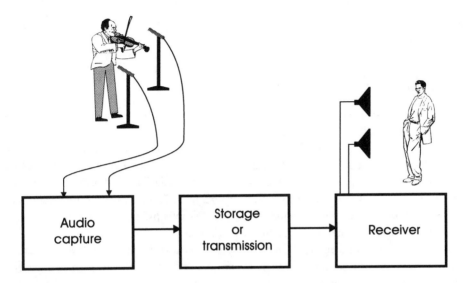

Figure 3.1 *Electronic sound reproduction system.*

perimeter so there are no reflections. It is the ultimate of "dead" space. When a person speaks in such a room, he or she can hardly hear his or her own voice, which becomes a very unsettling sensation.

3.2 ELECTRONIC REPRODUCTION OF SOUND

Electronic sound is called *audio*. A typical audio system is shown in Figure 3.1. Sound is picked up from the source by one or more microphones and the resulting audio signals are passed through the system until they reach the loudspeakers that convert the electrical signals back to sound waves.

The objective of electronic sound reproduction is to deliver sound waves at a distance of space and time that the hearer will perceive to be the same as if he or she were hearing the source directly. Other objectives can be to enhance natural sound so that the electronic sound actually sounds better than the original or to create new sounds that do not exist in nature at all.

3.3 HUMAN HEARING

Our ears are no less remarkable than our eyes. In combination with the brain, they can receive sound waves over a wide range of amplitudes and instantly recognize direction, frequency, source characteristics, and information content in the case of speech. It is important in the design of electronic audio system to understand the capabilities and limitations of this fantastic biological system. The study of the hearing process is known as *psychoacoustics*.

3.3.1 Loudness

The human response to the amplitude of sound waves is known as *loudness*. It ranges from the threshold of audibility at low sound levels to the threshold of pain for very loud sounds. This is a range of 10^{12} (1,000,000,000,000:1) or more in sound power level expressed in W/m^2. Because of the wide range, it is customary to express sound levels logarithmically, using decibels (dB). The reference level (0 dB) is usually taken as the threshold of hearing. 120 dB (e.g., the sound level 1,500 ft away from a large jet plane taking off) is approximately the threshold of pain—sound at this level is uncomfortably loud; at somewhat higher sound levels, actual hearing damage can occur.

At any one time, one cannot hear multiple sounds at different levels over this entire range because the loud sounds tend to mask the quieter sounds. However, since most useful sounds (speech or music) tend to have intermittent quiet periods and the ear will respond very rapidly to sound level changes, it is important for high-quality reproduction systems to have signal-to-noise ratios as much as 80 or 90 dB if noise is to be completely inaudible. On the other hand, if intelligibility is the only objective, the ear can understand speech at SNRs of 30 dB or even lower.

3.3.2 Frequency Response

The *frequency response* of human hearing is usually considered to cover the range from 30 to 15,000 Hz. However, it varies significantly among individuals and with loudness. Figure 3.2 shows curves of the sound level that creates the sensation of equal loudness at different frequencies and levels. These curves are based on psychophysical research first conducted by Fletcher and Munson. The lower curves show a deviation of more than 40 dB over the frequency range, with the maximum variation occurring at low frequencies. As the sound becomes louder, there is less variation in sensation with frequency; at 120 dB, all frequencies sound equally loud (i.e., very).

Depending on the purpose of the system, it is not always necessary to reproduce the full frequency range. For example, the telephone, which is designed for intelligible reproduction of speech, has a bandwidth of only 300 to 3,000 Hz. On the other hand, high-fidelity reproduction of music does require the full frequency band of 30 to 15,000 Hz. Many audio systems do even more than that, providing 20 to 20,000 Hz response.

3.3.3 Direction of Sound

Our ears and our brain make it possible for a listener to recognize the direction to a sound source. This is known as *binaural* capability. It is supported by *stereo* electronic systems

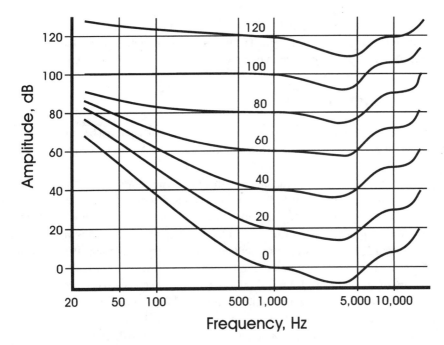

Figure 3.2 *Curves of the signal amplitude to maintain constant loudness versus frequency and 1,000-Hz loudness.*

that have two or more channels reproducing sound captured by separated pickups at the source. This provides a spatial distribution of sound that is extremely effective, especially for music. Systems of *surround sound* have been developed with five or more channels to reproduce sound all around the listener. Stereo is discussed further in Section 3.10.

3.4 AUDIO PICKUP

The principal device for converting sound waves to electrical signals (pickup) is the *microphone*, which comes in many forms. In general, a microphone contains a means for converting sound waves to mechanical motion in a magnetic or electric field or on an electromechanical transducer element such as a piezoelectric device. The conversion can be based on either the pressure variations in the sound wave or on the velocity of air particles in the wave. Pressure-sensitive microphones tend to be nondirectional, whereas velocity-sensitive microphones are basically bidirectional. Other patterns are obtained by combining the sensing techniques. Typically, microphone behavior is a complex combination of acoustic and electronic factors.

Capturing good sound depends critically on the choice of microphones, their placement, and the recording environment. The technique for handling microphones is known as *miking* and is an art very much in demand on the professional recording scene.

3.5 ANALOG AUDIO SIGNALS

Signals resulting from audio pickup are typically very small and must be amplified to suitable levels for processing or conversion to digital formats. As discussed in Section 3.3.1, electrical noise is an important consideration in this process.

Most natural sounds are a complex combination of sound waves of different frequencies and waveshapes. Therefore, the spectrum of a typical audio signal will be equivalently complex, containing one or more fundamental frequencies, their harmonics, and possibly crossmodulation products. Because most of the fundamental frequencies of sound waves are below about 5,000 Hz, the spectral content above that frequency consists of harmonics only. They are typically lower in amplitude than the fundamentals, which means the energy density of an audio spectrum will fall off at high frequencies. This is a characteristic that can be exploited in data compression or noise reduction systems.

Audio signals are bipolar, so they fluctuate above and below zero value. Since there can be a low-frequency cutoff in the frequency response, there is no dc component in an audio signal.

Unlike video signals that have an inherent structure based on the scanning process, analog audio signals are completely without structure. There is no place in an audio signal where signal values are predictable or where additional information might be inserted. Of course, once an audio signal has been digitized, structure can be built into the digital bit stream format. This is necessary for such purposes as clock recovery and error protection in digital audio systems.

3.5.1 Analog Signal Specifications

Analog audio technology is very mature, signal specifications are well understood, and effective methods of measurement are available and widely used. The following sections discuss the most important specifications, their measurement, and the significance of each specification in a digital environment [1].

One principle of analog spec-setting is important here. Because analog impairments inherently accumulate as system components are cascaded, products intended for use in large systems must have much tighter specifications than would be indicated by the actual needs of a listener. This is a fact of analog life, but it does not necessarily apply in an all-digital system. The principal impairments in a digital system occur at the ADC and DAC, and the rest of the system can be designed to introduce no further errors no matter how large the system becomes. Therefore, the only applications of analog-style specifications are on the ADC and DAC units of a digital system. The rest of the system can be evaluated only on the basis of digital error performance.

The previous paragraph is a little oversimplified because there are some digital processes that could affect the analog-equivalent system performance. One of these is *data compression*; if that exists in the system, its effect on system performance must be evaluated. Further, if the compression and decompression processes are performed repeatedly in the system, there is potential for the distortions to accumulate. This could happen if compression is used within one part of the system, such as a recorder, but the rest of the system is uncompressed digital. In that case, compression-decompression occurs every time the signal passes through a recorder.

3.5.1.1 Frequency Response

Provision for analog cascading has caused frequency response specifications such as 20 Hz to 20 kHz ±0.1 dB. While this certainly represents transparent performance for one pass, it is far tighter than a total system has to be. As mentioned above, most people cannot hear much outside the range of 30 to 15,000 Hz, and no one could detect a response variation of 0.1 dB. However, some CD players have specifications like this, which is simply a digital *tour de force*.

The analog-equivalent frequency response of a digital system will be determined first by the sampling frequency and second by the filtering used at the points of ADC and DAC. The remainder of a digital system will not affect the frequency response. Using the oversampling technique discussed in Section 3.6 and Chapter 5, the performance described above is, in fact, relatively easy to obtain in a digital audio system. Overkill, yes, but not much cost can be saved by lowering the performance, so users of digital systems have come to expect that kind of performance.

Analog frequency response is measured by applying a series of sinusoidal input signals at different frequencies to the unit under test and observing the amplitude of the output signals. This may be done manually with discrete frequencies or by automatic equipment that sweeps the frequency across the range and plots the output. Because of the low frequencies involved, frequency response measurements can take from a few seconds (automatic) to a few minutes (manual). The response is usually presented as a graph of amplitude vs. frequency, as shown in Figure 3.3.

Because of the wide frequency range, the frequency scale is logarithmic and the ordinate is given in dB relative to the response at some "center" frequency, usually 1,000 Hz. Most units will show a "flat" response over a center frequency range with a falloff at each end. In some cases, there may be resonances or other disturbances within the band. Frequency response is specified by giving a tolerance value within which the response must hold over the specified frequency range. The example in Figure 3.3 is flat within ±2.0 dB over the range from 20 to 20,000 Hz.

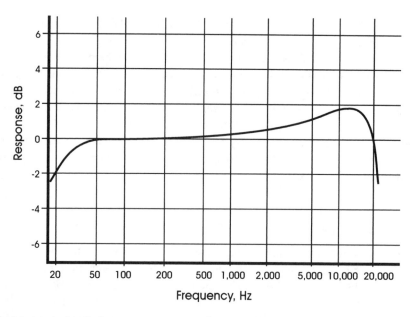

Figure 3.3 *A typical audio frequency response graph.*

3.5.1.2 Signal-to-Noise Ratio

All electronic systems have noise; it is just a matter of keeping it small enough compared with the desired signals for acceptable system performance. In an analog audio system, SNR is specified in dB relative to a "normal" signal level. For audio systems, both noise and signal are measured in *root-mean-square* (rms) values. The system is set up for normal signal level to be 0 dB, the signal is removed, and the resulting output (which is defined to be noise) is measured relative to 0 dB. It is a simple measurement with a single number result.

More information about noise can be obtained by examining the spectrum of the noise signal. This can be important to audio systems because the sensitivity of the ear to noise falls off at the ends of the frequency range, whereas a good measurement system will have uniform response over the frequency range. This can be accommodated by using a *weighting filter* in the noise measurement that accounts for the ear's frequency response (see Figure 3.2). Obviously, such a filter must be standardized for noise measurements by different people to be meaningfully compared. Several standards have been developed for this purpose, so when weighted noise measurements are made, the specific weighting technique must be specified. The most widely used weightings are the A-weighting and the CCIR weighting [2].

In a digital audio system, analog-equivalent SNR is unlikely to be affected by the digital parts of the system. It is a consideration only in the ADC and DAC processes. Measuring the digital parts of a system with no signal present is meaningless; the digital equivalent of analog SNR is usually considered to be the bit error rate.

3.5.1.3 Distortion

Nonlinearities of the transfer characteristic in an analog system cause distortion. In the frequency domain, distortion can be thought of as spurious frequency components that are created because of the presence of a signal. These components are harmonics of the signal, leading to the name *harmonic distortion*. Specifications are given in terms of total harmonic distortion (THD) and, when THD exceeds about 1%, distortion may become audible. Analog system components often specify much smaller values to allow for accumulation in large systems.

Analog distortion measurements are done by applying a pure tone (sinusoidal) signal to the system and at the measuring point filtering out the pure tone signal with a sharp notch filter. What remains after this filter is THD. However, it also contains the system's noise, which may limit measurement of small distortions in noisy systems. THD is specified as a percentage of the normal signal level, both determined by rms measurement.

Distortion may be a function of signal frequency and this can be significant in the design of a system, but most specifications ignore that problem and specify distortion for a signal frequency of 1,000 Hz. In a digital audio system, analog-equivalent distortion is only affected by the ADC and DAC parts of the system. Measurement of analog distortion on the digital parts of the system is meaningless.

3.5.1.4 Phase Shift

If the time delay through an analog system changes with signal frequency, the system will show *phase shift* errors. To a first approximation, the ear apparently does not hear such errors, and the importance of phase shift in audio equipment is somewhat controversial. However, it is measurable and is sometimes specified for high-quality system components. Note that this parameter is very important in video systems, where it is called *envelope delay distortion*.

Phase shift is measured by applying a sinusoidal signal at the input and comparing the phase of the output signal with the input. If the phase shift is an exactly linear function of the input frequency, it represents a constant delay and there is no distortion. However, if the phase versus frequency curve is not linear, there is a degree of distortion. Because of the question about how important this is in audio equipment, there are no standards for its specification or measurement.

For digital systems, phase shift is most likely to occur only in the ADC and DAC components. Most digital filters have no phase shift errors, although an IIR digital filter (see Section 8.3.2) can introduce phase errors. Because of this property, IIR filters are rarely used in audio systems.

3.5.1.5 Wow and Flutter

Analog audio signals passing through devices such as magnetic tape recorders or vinyl disk players can undergo frequency modulation due to nonuniformity of the mechanical motion of tape or disk. This is specified by the parameters of *wow and flutter* (W&F). It is measured by applying a test signal (usually 3.15 kHz) to the system and measuring the output through an FM discriminator tuned to the test frequency. W&F is specified as the total rms frequency modulation expressed as a percentage of the test frequency. A good system will have readings below 0.1 percent, which is not audible.

Several standards are available for this measurement; they vary with respect to the test frequency, type of metering used (rms, peak, quasi-peak, etc.), and the filtering in the measuring channel. Most measurements restrict W&F bandwidth to the range from 0.5 to 200 Hz, but there are also standards for measuring at much higher bandwidths to pick up FM due to scraping action in tape mechanisms.

In a digital system, W&F depends on the stability of the sampling clocks used in the ADC and DAC components. Since these are produced by electronic oscillators that can easily deliver very high stability, digital system W&F specifications are often as low as 0.001 percent.

3.6 AUDIO ANALOG-TO-DIGITAL CONVERSION

The parameters of audio ADC are sampling frequency and bits/sample. As discussed in Section 1.4.2 and in Chapter 5, the intended use of the system determines the desired bandwidth and SNR performance, which lead to the specification of sampling frequency and bits/sample. Digital audio systems range from the Compact Disc-Digital Audio high-fidelity system to the several systems designed for telephone-quality speech transmission. In between are the audio standards for personal computer usage where the considerations of data storage lead to lower sampling rates and the use of data compression. Table 3.1 shows some typical audio sampling standards.

Because analog audio signals are bipolar, all systems are based on two's complement encoding of the samples, although compressed systems may not transmit the samples

Table 3.1

Typical Audio Sampling Standards

Name	f_s	bps	Bandwidth (kHz)	Data rate (bytes/s)
CD-DA stereo	44.1 kHz	16	20	176,400
WAV mono (speech)	11.05 kHz	8	5	11,050
WAV stereo (music)	22.1	16	10	88,400
Telephone (μ-law)	8.0	8	3.5	64,000

directly in that format.

Most systems employ linear quantization except for the telephone systems that use μ-law nonlinear quantization (see Section 5.2.2.7). This optimizes the use of the small bits/sample choice in these system.

The use of an analog input filter ahead of ADC to eliminate input frequencies higher than one-half the sampling frequency is especially important in audio ADC because sampling such frequencies creates spurious frequency components at the difference between the audio frequency and the sampling frequency. These are called *aliasing* frequencies and the filter is called an *anti-aliasing* filter. Since such frequencies are not related to any frequency in the audio, they are easily heard. An analog filter for this purpose must have a sharp cutoff, and it is difficult to design and expensive to manufacture.

A technique that facilitates the filtering requirements is *oversampling*. In this method, the analog audio is sampled higher than the desired final sampling rate and little, if any, input filtering is used. After sampling, a digital filter is used to remove any aliasing components, which are clustered around the high sampling frequency and, because of the high sampling frequency, do not overlap the desired audio passband. The resulting digital samples are then reduced to the final output rate by *decimation* (removal of extra samples.) A variation of this technique uses a large oversampling factor (72) but digitizes at only one bit/sample. The output filtering removes aliasing and restores the desired output sampling rate and bits/sample. Oversampling techniques are described further in Section 5.3.1.

Note that the oversampling technique is applicable to audio signals, where signal bandwidth is low, but it is rare at video bandwidths because the necessary sampling frequencies become too high for practical circuits.

3.7 MUSIC

Periodic sounds at certain frequencies are very pleasing to the ear and when combined in appropriate ways they create the phenomenon known as music. Everyone learns the basic principles of music in grade school and most of us develop some degree of appreciation of it. Many even learn to play an instrument and thus do their part in creating music. Although it is outside the scope of this book to go into either the technical or the artistic aspects of music, there are several properties of music that are relevant to the design of electronic reproduction systems.

3.7.1 Pitch

Most music is made up of *notes*, which are short bursts of sound at a specific frequency. That frequency is the *pitch* of the note. Pitch may be expressed either as a frequency in Hertz or in musical notation based on a musical *scale*. Western music is based on an *equally tempered* scale that consists of notes spaced apart in the ratio of $2^{1/12}$ (1.05946). Most people can easily recognize a pitch difference of about one-quarter of this value and they will say a note is out of tune if it exceeds that amount of error compared with the basic scale. Some people can even recognize such an error when listening to a note by itself—this is known as *perfect pitch*.

The pitch of a note may be constant during a note or it may deliberately vary in certain ways. One deliberate variations is *vibrato*, which is about 1% FM of the pitch at a frequency between 0.5 and 20 Hz. In certain types of music, the musician may use *portamento*, which is the sweeping of pitch from one note to the next, or *pitch bending*, which can be almost any kind of pitch variation.

It is important to reproduce pitch with an absolute accuracy good enough to satisfy listeners who have perfect pitch and to reproduce the deliberate variations used by the musicians. The pitch must also have good enough short-term stability that flutter is not heard. Both of these requirements are on the *time base* of the reproduction system and they refer to time base *accuracy* and *stability*.

3.7.2 Timbre

A musical note consists of a fundamental frequency, certain of its harmonics, other related frequencies, and possible modulation of the amplitude and frequency of one or more of the components. The combination of all these creates the sensation that we call *timbre*. It is the property that distinguishes the sounds of different instruments when they are playing the same notes. It is difficult to put into words all the nuances of timbre but what is important here is that a sound reproduction system must reproduce enough of the frequency components and in the proper relationship to each other that timbre variations come through. This leads to the requirement for the widest bandwidth of sound reproduction. Music is usually recognizable when reproduced in a narrow bandwidth, say, 5,000 Hz, but it loses much of the distinguishing qualities of timbre. A full bandwidth of at least 15,000 Hz is required for best music reproduction.

3.7.3 Tempo

The speed of playing a sequence of notes is known as the *tempo* of the sequence. Tempo does not have to be nearly so precise as pitch; changing tempo makes the music play faster or slower without changing its pitch. In fact, many musicians introduce subtle variations of tempo while playing to add emphasis or feeling to the music. In a sampled digital audio system, tempo will be reproduced with the same accuracy as pitch (see also Section 3.9.3).

3.8 AUDIO NOISE REDUCTION

Noise in an audio pickup or recording becomes noticeable when the sound source is quiet or stopped. During these times the listener may hear noise as a hissing sound. Various systems have been developed to sense the loudness of the sound and modify the system during

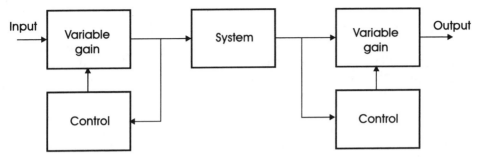

Figure 3.4 Companding.

quiet passages to make noise less audible. These have been widely used, especially with audio tape recorders.

The fundamental approach is called *companding* (see Figure 3.4). At the input of the system, the sound level is sensed and the system gain is adjusted so that lower-level audio is processed at higher gain, and at higher levels the gain is reduced so the channel will not overload. At the output end of the system, the reverse action must occur to restore the system dynamic range. The result is that channel noise is reduced for low-level signals by the amount that the compander increases the gain of these signals. Typically the noise reduction is 10 dB or more.

Simple companding has many problems, including the matching or *calibration* of the input and output processing and the choice of appropriate control dynamic operation. For these reasons, the design of noise reduction systems is an art and is highly competitive. There are products from several companies for both professional and consumer tape recording and for various transmission channels, including TV multichannel sound, satellite transmission, and digital HDTV broadcasting. Details of these systems are beyond the scope of this book, but they may be pursued in the references.

3.9 DIGITAL AUDIO

The audio Compact Disc (CD) was one of the first mass-market application of digital audio technology. ("Compact Disc" is the trade name for the system, which includes the spelling of disc with a 'c'.) It has swept the prerecorded audio market and has spun off the personal computer CD-ROM and other variations.

3.9.1 The Audio Compact Disc

Optical disc recording technology was developed in the 1970s and first appeared in analog form as the laser videodisc (LVD). This product never made it in the consumer market but it has been important in the education and training markets where the random-access capability of disc recording made it more suitable than tape recording.

The CD was developed by Sony and Philips and introduced in the early 1980s using the basic physics of the LVD for digital recording on a 12-cm plastic disc. The system is described fully in Chapter 11; here we will cover only the sampling parameters. The system choices of the CD-Digital Audio (CD-DA) standard are very conservative and provide a working bandwidth of at least 18 kHz and a SNR of over 90 dB. This translates to a sampling frequency of 44.1 kHz and 16 bits/sample. The encoding is straight two's-complement *pulse-code modulation* (PCM) with no compression. The channel coding for error protection includes Reed-Solomon block-error coding and interleaving (see Section 7.2.5.6).

The result of the CD-DA standards is a robust system for play-only audio distribution. Players today are available at prices under $100 (US) and deliver the full system performance at that price. This is one advantage of digital technology: if a system works at all, it works to full specification—there is no in-between performance.

3.9.2 DAT

Following on the success of the CD as a play-only medium, a digital magnetic tape system was developed and proposed as a record-play system that matched the performance of the CD. This is known as *digital audio tape* (DAT), but it has not been actively marketed for the consumer market because of industry concerns about the ability to make digital copies of audio CDs. DAT has been used primarily in the professional audio field or as a backup or archiving medium for personal computers, where the ability to store over 4 GB on a single tape is valuable.

3.9.3 PC Audio

Personal computers have the capability of storing and playing anything that is digital, so it is natural for them to handle digital audio. Early PCs did not have the hardware capability (ADC and DAC) to handle high-quality analog audio I/O and widespread use of digital audio did not occur until add-in boards were developed for this purpose. That happened in the late 1980s and now nearly every PC has audio I/O.

However, the data generated by CD-DA sampling (9 MB/min) is too much for the storage capability of most PCs, so special PC audio standards were developed to allow trading off sound quality for data size at several levels. The lowest quality choice offers 11.05-kHz sampling at 8 bits/sample—this is suitable for speech-only use at a data rate of 0.66 MB/min. The sampling rate and bits/sample are doubled for music use, and this standard can also be used in stereo, where the data rate grows to 4.5 MB/min.

PC audio standards also include a compression option, based on the ADPCM algorithm (see Chapter 9) that can reduce the data rate by a factor of four with minimal loss of quality.

Note that the unstructured character of an audio signal offers far less opportunity for data compression than video.

3.9.4 MIDI

The musical instrument industry embraced electronic technology early on in the form of electronic organs and synthesizers. Notes are produced electronically in these instruments and they are amenable to electronic control from computers or other controllers. This gave rise to the need for a standard for electronic control of musical instruments and the industry responded in 1984 with the *musical instrument digital interface* (MIDI) standard. The MIDI standards are distributed by the MIDI Manufacturers Association [3]. Nearly all electronic musical instruments, even at the low end of the price spectrum, now support MIDI. It allows keyboards to be separate from synthesizers or for one keyboard to control several instruments, providing what is known as *layered* sound.

Personal computer audio boards also all include a MIDI-controlled synthesizer chip that can be run from MIDI data stored on the PC. For music only, this is an important alternative to digitizing natural music because it can deliver high quality music at 100 or more times lower data rate. Of course, this is because the MIDI data only needs to store note representations rather than fully sampled sounds.

3.9.4.1 MIDI Data Format

The MIDI standard calls for a serial data interface running at 31.25 kbps. The protocol uses a message format that has a status byte followed by one or more data bytes. Data bytes are transmitted with two additional bits for system control, so the data rate can go up to 3,125 bytes/sec. Since most messages have three or more bytes, this means that the system can transmit a maximum of about 1,000 messages per second. In complex music, that can result in some noticeable delays.

The data format is shown in Figure 3.5. Codes are sent for each musical event, such as the start and end of a note. Each code begins with a status byte that is indicated by having its MSB equal to 1. The other seven bits of the status byte are a code, which in some cases may include the MIDI channel number. MIDI supports up to 16 channels, which may be independent musical instruments. Following the status byte, there are a variable number of data bytes, all of which are marked by their MSBs being zero. Thus, only seven bits are available for information in each data byte. The system exclusive (Sys. Exc.) event is basically an escape code; it allows any number of data bytes to be sent until the End. Exc. status code is received.

MIDI communication operates in real time, which means that the time of sending a message determines when the message will be acted upon. This is not an ideal situation, but it results from the heritage of the system, which was real-time control between keyboards and synthesizers. When MIDI data are stored for later playback, the file must contain a

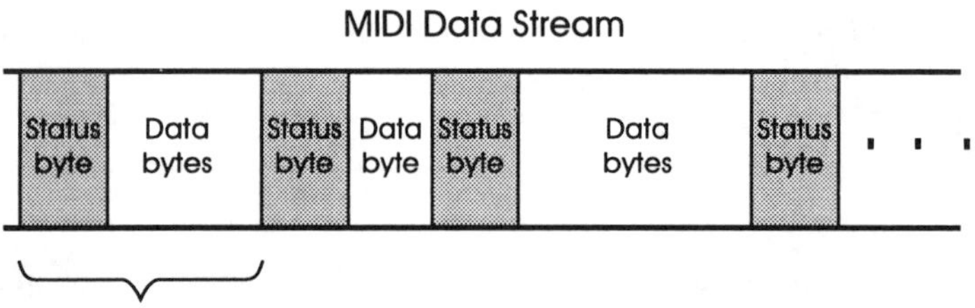

MIDI Data Stream

Status byte	Data bytes	Status byte	Data byte	Status byte	Data bytes	Status byte	▪ ▪ ▪

Event	Status Byte	Data Bytes	
	MSB-------	MSB-------	MSB-------
Note On	1 code chan	0 note No.	0 velocity
Note Off	1 code chan	0 note No.	0 velocity
Ctrl Chg.	1 code chan	0 ctrl No.	0 value
Pgm Chg.	1 code chan	0 Patch No.	None
Sys. Exc.	1 code	0 Mfr. Code	0 variable . . .
End Exc.	1 code	None	

Figure 3.5 *MIDI data format.*

representation of time so that the player software knows when to send each message. A later addition to the MIDI standards provides a file format for this purpose.

3.9.4.2 Music Synthesis

The technology of music synthesis is extremely well developed, and there are several types of synthesizers and PC audio boards available. There are two different objectives for synthesizers: one is to reproduce acoustic instruments as closely as possible, and the other is to create new and unusual sounds that are not found in nature. Both are important.

The best method for synthesizing natural sounds such as those from acoustic instruments is what is known as *wavetable synthesis.* In this method, actual instruments are digitally sampled playing one note at a time, usually at several points over the frequency range of the instrument. These samples are stored in memory in the synthesizer and when a note is to be played, the closest sample is chosen from the memory and shifted in frequency by digital processing. In a well-designed system, the result can be extremely realistic.

Many other types of synthesis are available but the most widespread one is called *FM synthesis*, where FM stands for frequency modulation. The principle of this method is that one or more oscillators are frequency modulated by another frequency to produce a rich spectrum of sidebands that are filtered to produce the output sound. This type of synthesis is very flexible in the sounds that it can produce, but programming the sounds is complex and nonintuitive, even to musicians. In spite of that it is popular because it delivers a lot of performance at low cost. However, it is not as good as sampling for synthesizing real instrument sounds.

3.9.5 Digital Audio Processing

Once audio has been digitized, many manipulations can be performed by digital processing, either in hardware or in software on a programmable system like a PC. In the digital form it is possible to modify the pitch of sounds without changing the playing time or do the opposite—change the playing time without changing the pitch. Digital reverberation has already been mentioned (Section 3.1.1) and other complex frequency or timing manipulations can be done.

Another audio processing task that is best performed in a programmable environment is that of editing—mixing and cutting. This is an art in itself that is covered in Chapter 12.

3.10 MULTICHANNEL AUDIO

Two or more audio channels reproducing sounds from the same source with a spatial distribution provide a more realistic reproduction because the listener can then sense the directivity of the sound. Although many systems multiplex the audio channels together for convenience of recording or distribution, the objective is usually to keep the channels independent of each other with the only mixing of the channels being that which occurred in the space where the sounds were picked up. This way, the listener's experience of actually being in that space is enhanced.

3.10.1 Stereo and Surround Sound

Two-channel audio is called stereo and it is widely used in recording and broadcasting of both audio and television. The channels are called left (L) and right (R), corresponding to the speaker locations for reproduction.

The spatial sound experience can be further enhanced by having one or more reproduction channels that deliver sound behind the listener. This is the principle of surround sound, which has been widely used in movie theater presentation and will soon become available for the home in digital HDTV. These systems provide up to "5.1" channels, that is five full-bandwidth channels and one subwoofer (0.1) channel. Some high-end TV receivers provide a simulated surround sound, which is effective even though TV broadcasting is only in stereo.

REFERENCES

1. Benson, K. Blair, *Audio Engineering Handbook*, Chapter 16, McGraw-Hill, New York, 1988.

2. ibid., p 16.11.

3. MIDI Manufacturers Association, PO Box 3173, La Habra, CA 90632-3173, http://www.midi.org.

Chapter 4

Audio-Video Systems

4.1 INTRODUCTION

Most applications of digital audio and video require a number of separate components to accomplish the functions that were shown in Section 1.4 and Figure 1.10. Such a group of units interconnected so as to perform a complete task is a *system*. However, systems are not necessarily packaged according to the functional elements shown in Figure 1.10. This chapter discusses real systems and their building blocks as used in various environments. The environments may be classified in terms of the user and the purpose of the system. For example, systems may be designed for home use, semiprofessional use, videoconferencing, broadcasting, professional program production, or other use. Most of this system discussion is independent of whether the system components are analog or digital—the discussion points out where that is not true.

4.1.1 Program Creation

Audio-video systems generally are used to create a *program*, which is a sequence of audio and/or video elements that will be viewed as a continuous event. A program can be created all at once by capturing the sequence as it occurs in real life or it can be built up by using a series of elements that have been captured separately and assembled at a later time into the program. The latter approach is called the *production-postproduction* style of program creation. Production is the process of capture to a recording medium and postproduction is the process of assembling the program from the captured elements. Production-postproduction allows material captured at different times and different places to be incorporated into the same program, a flexibility that is essential for all but the simplest of programs. Nearly all programs are created this way. Postproduction is the subject of Chapter 12.

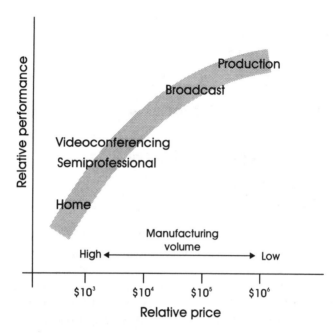

Figure 4.1 Price-performance curve for audio-video systems.

4.1.2 Standards

It is impossible to build systems unless the components can be connected together and those interconnections actually work. It is the purpose of standards to ensure such interoperability initially and over time. Cable connectors, signal formats, recording medium properties, and record formats—all must be specified for a system to work properly. The standards for this must be formally documented and made public so that multiple manufacturers are able to compete for the components of any system. Standards are discussed further in Section 4.7.

4.2 SYSTEM PERFORMANCE

It is common to equate system performance with audio or video quality, but there are other factors that should also be considered part of performance. For an extreme example, a videoconferencing system may deliver pictures and sound that most people would consider to be barely acceptable, but its performance is high because it is able to send them over a telephone line in real time. That purpose can justify a higher price than (for another example) a home video system that may deliver much better pictures and sound but it cannot transmit them at all.

Taking that broad view of performance, one can construct a price-performance curve as shown in Figure 4.1. The price range in this graph goes from thousands to millions of dollars. The performance scale does not cover such a wide range primarily because of the effect of *manufacturing volume*, which is the quantity of units manufactured per unit time. For example, components for home audio-video systems are manufactured in millions of units per year, while at the other end of the scale, professional system components are made, at most, in thousand quantities per year. The result is that a low-priced home unit delivers much more performance than its relative price might indicate.

High production volumes can justify a much greater investment in design and manufacturing facilities to reduce product cost, whereas low-volume products put most of their investment into the factors needed to obtain the highest product performance. This is also an example of *diminishing returns*—as more and more performance is required, the price increases disproportionately. Markets that demand the highest performance must pay for the privilege.

4.3 CLASSES OF SYSTEMS

This section defines classes of systems according to their purposes and discusses their performance requirements. These system classes are used throughout this chapter and the rest of the book. Although the term *video* is used for these systems, the reader will understand that audio is always an important ingredient. For the purpose of comparison, all systems are considered at the sound- and picture-quality level of NTSC or PAL standards. A similar comparison would result if systems were compared relative to HDTV standards, although, of course, the price scale would be higher. This discussion is summarized in Table 4.1, which is shown at the end of this section.

4.3.1 Home Video Systems

Video systems in the home are based on television signal formats because every home has one or more television receivers that can serve as displays for other video uses. Home video systems are used to play prerecorded media such as videotapes or video discs and to create home video programs.

The principal use for home video creation is recording of family events for archival purposes or for school projects. Most home-created video programs are captured all at once, but as lower cost and easier-to-use editing equipment becomes available, many home video users will use production-postproduction methods to organize their materials. However, price limitations will keep home video systems at a simple level.

The primary requirement of home video equipment is price—there is no market at all until the price per major component falls below about $1,000. Because of the inherent complexity of major video products, it requires a mass market—millions of units—before usable performance can be achieved at such a price point. A second major requirement is ease-of-use; most home users will not make the effort to master a difficult product that they only will use occasionally. Picture and sound performance are also important and are a basis for competition at any particular price point. Because of the use of television receivers as displays, there is no market yet for higher-than-TV picture quality. That will change once HDTV has penetrated the home.

Standards are extremely important for home use. The typical home user does not have the technical capability to deal with noncompatible formats or connections and will not invest in equipment until it is guaranteed to work in his or her environment and to do that over a long product life. A home user cannot afford for a video product to become obsolete in a few years. This is difficult for manufacturers who want to develop innovative products and compete on the basis of that innovation, but the public has learned to be very wary of any one-manufacturer system—they want standards and a choice of manufacturers. The industry has learned this, too, and today most standards battles now occur before products are actually offered for sale to the public.

4.3.2 Semiprofessional Video Systems

Video systems used for production of training programs, special event programs such as weddings and, in some cases, news programs are called *semiprofessional*. A full capability for production-postproduction operation with a good TV-level of quality is necessary for these uses. These requirements have created a market for products priced slightly above the home level with somewhat higher performance. The semiprofessional line includes a full complement of editing equipment to support the needed postproduction, although the necessary low pricing keeps these systems simple.

Since the output from semiprofessional postproduction will usually be viewed on TV equipment, the standards for the output format are the same as the home market (TV). Usually, TV standards are also used for semiprofessional production, although that is not mandatory as long as the postproduction can deliver the proper output format. This is an opportunity for semiprofessional production to be done digitally and it is an important market for the entry-level digital video products now coming available.

4.3.3 Videoconferencing Systems

Using video (and audio) for meetings between people who are at different locations is called *videoconferencing* (VC). This is a market that has existed for many years but has been limited by the cost of equipment and the communication channels needed. However, with digital technology and modern digital communications, costs of equipment and communication are coming down and the use of VC should explode over the next few years.

The system needs of VC are dominated by the communication task, which calls for the most sophisticated digital video compression technology available. VC is not alone in this requirement and the necessary developments are also being pursued simultaneously for personal computer video, home HDTV, and digital video discs (see Chapter 9).

Standards for VC are available for the communication part of the system, but they are less well developed for the origination and display parts of the system. However, even the communication possibilities are being confused by the slow emergence of widespread high-data-rate communication channels. This is partly due to the maneuvering of the telecommunications companies for position in this new market and also by the diversity of technology being considered.

To the extent that a company builds its own VC systems for all its different locations, it can develop its own internal standards and this is the way the market largely is today. However, this requires each company to have a good technical capability to custom design their system (which is costly) and precludes interoperability among the systems of different companies. In the long run, complete standards are needed for this market to develop to its full potential (see Section 4.5.3 for more about videoconferencing).

4.3.4 Video Delivery Systems

The term *video delivery* is used in this book to mean the task of assembling programs into a continuous stream to feed a transmitter, cable channel, or a satellite channel. This is done by broadcasters, networks, cable operators, and any others who deliver continuous video to a group of viewers. Server operations require lots of storage for video and audio, means for making smooth transitions between individual programs, and automatic operation to reduce labor costs.

A special class of video delivery operation is *interactive video* or *video on demand*. In this case, the video content is specified by each viewer and a system operator may deliver many different continuities at the same time to different viewers.

Video delivery viewers typically use TV receivers for display but an important new class of interactive video is the Internet, where most of the viewers are using PCs or other computer-based devices for viewing. This is not used much for video today because most users have telephone-based modem connections, which are too slow for good video. That will change as the use of higher speed communications becomes more widespread.

4.3.5 Production Studio Systems

Video and audio production is done either in a studio or on location in the field. The choice is a tradeoff between the ability to completely control the production environment (studio) and the availability of natural environments and events (field). Because studio production implies control of everything, it takes elaborate facilities manned by many more people than would be used in the field. Thus, studio production tends to be more expensive. Many programs combine both types of production.

Production studios require much flexibility in how their equipment can be arranged to support the production needs of a wide range of programming types. Audio and video quality should be very high so that any losses in postproduction will not bring the overall signal quality below acceptable standards.

Most production studios today operate within TV standards, although there is a trend to perform production in a higher standard (such as HDTV) and only convert to TV standards when they are needed for distribution after postproduction. This way, the investment made in the production can be applied to distribution in different media, including TV, motion pictures, computers, and even HDTV. However, such facilities are expensive and less well standardized. This also will change as a mass market grows for HDTV.

4.3.6 Production Field Systems

Field production as defined here is the use of portable equipment for news and other production that must be captured in the field quickly and without a large team of people. There is a special class of "field" production that does not fit this definition—that is pickup at major sporting events where a complete studio setup may be taken to the sports stadium. The systems used for such events are really just temporary studios. (Some are not even temporary; a broadcaster may have permanent installations in the local sports venues where most of the system remains in place all the time.)

Since studio- and field-produced material will often be integrated into the same program, the technical requirements for field production ought to be the same as for studio production. But two things make field equipment very different from studio equipment. They are (1) the need for portability and (2) the fact that the field environment cannot be controlled by the production crew as it can be in the studio. The result is that picture and sound quality sometimes may have to be compromised in the field.

One consequence of the portability requirement is that units that would be separate in the studio are often combined in the field. A good example is the camcorder, which is universally used in the field but rarely used in the professional studio. As convenient as a camcorder is, it involves performance and quality compromises to achieve a hand-held package. These compromises can be eliminated in separate (larger) cameras and recorders as are used in studios.

Field equipment must face much greater ranges of environmental factors such as lighting, temperature, and humidity than studio equipment. Cameras are often hand-held and therefore must deal with unstable mounting. These factors tend to make field equipment more expensive than might be indicated by its compromised picture and sound quality.

4.3.7 Postproduction Systems

The task of assembling previously produced audio and video into a finished program is *postproduction*. It is usually done in a facility designed specifically for that purpose and there are often separate facilities for audio and video. Postproduction requires precise synchronization of all operations so that audio and video can remain in sync and so that operations can be precisely repeated while previewing during the decision process. All input material must therefore contain *time code* to exactly identify every frame of video or audio. (Audio does not have frames, but it is customary to mark it into frames that match the video frames and to use the same time-code format as video.)

Computer control is an essential ingredient in postproduction and every unit in the system should be controllable from the central computers. Video recorders, video processors, switchers, graphics or titling equipment—all are remotely controlled. It is ideal for everything in postproduction to be digital and many new systems are built that way. Of course, the input and output formats may or may not be digital, so a digital post facility also must include the appropriate A-D and D-A units. Postproduction is covered further in Chapter 12.

4.3.8 Personal Computer Video Systems

Presenting, storing, and processing digital audio and video on personal computers is a recent development that has become so important that nearly every PC being sold today has some of this capability and many designs are in the works to make that even better in the near future. The PC is the ultimate audio-video system because it is inherently digital and theoretically capable of doing everything needed for a complete audio-video production and postproduction system except for the cameras and microphones. All this is in one box and is all controlled by software, which means that any capability or combination of what resides in the hardware can be accessed by any system.

As powerful as PCs are, they cannot process high-quality digital video in real time without some hardware assist, which presently comes in the form of add-in boards. However, PCs are now being designed with video-processing capability built into their microprocessor chips, which is a trend that will continue. The audio-video system of the future is a PC (or a box that may not look like a PC but has one hidden inside).

The programmable nature of PC video systems also means that they need not be locked into a single standard—a change of standard is simply a change of software. Although this does not eliminate the need for standards, it makes things much easier for upgrading when improved standards are introduced.

4.3.9 The Comparison Table

Table 4.1 is a comparison of some of the key requirements of the different classes of systems discussed above. Of course, it is impossible to condense the diversity of systems discussed (and their variations, which were not discussed) into one simple chart, so Table 4.1 takes some liberties. Each item is shown in the form of a bar graph, and the wider the bar, the more important the requirement is to the system. The most valid way to view the comparison is to look at the items within one column; this shows how the particular requirement differs among the systems. Although one can also look along the rows, that

Table 4.1

Comparison of Requirements for Different Systems

System class	Price	A-V quality	Ease of use	Flex- ibility	Expand- ability	Most important items
Home audio-video	███	██	███	██	█	Price and ease of use
Semi- professional	███	███	██	██	███	Quality and price
Video- conferencing	███	█	███	███	███	Video compression
Video delivery	██	███	██	███	███	Storage capacity
Studio production	█	████	██	████	█████	Quality and flexibility
Field production	██	███	██	████	████	Portability, ease of use
Post- production	█	█████	█	█████	█████	Quality and flexibility
Personal computer	████	██	███	███	███	All

comparison is less meaningful. The following paragraphs briefly discusses the column headings.

Price—The bars show the *importance* of price to the class, not the price itself.

A-V Quality—This refers to the signal performance parameters such as signal-to-noise ratio and bandwidth. Since the importance of quality and the quality itself go the same way, the bars can be interpreted in terms of either.

Ease of use—This refers to how important it is for the user to easily learn and use the system. This is very important for systems (such as home systems) that are used only occasionally. However, when the same user uses the system every day as part of his/her work, an investment is learning is justified. Professional systems, which are inherently more complex than home systems, require such a commitment to learning.

Flexibility—this refers to the importance of being able to adapt the system to different kinds of programs and programming situations.

Expandability—This item tells how important it is that the system can grow over time for either added functionality or added capacity.

4.4 SYSTEM COMPONENTS

A home user might like to have an audio-video capture and editing system in one box that he or she could connect to a TV, and it would do everything needed to create personal programs. At the other extreme, a broadcast station might like to have each part of their system be packaged separately so that the system could be configured dynamically to suit the immediate needs of the station's activity. Neither extreme is very practical, and audio and video product packaging has evolved to suit a more reasonable view of the market needs.

Some of the home camcorder manufacturers seem to be striving for the one-box-does-all scenario, but this makes an expensive package for which the price of entry is high and the flexibility and expandability are limited to what is designed into that box. This may attract some new users who can afford it, but as the market becomes more mature, even home users will migrate toward some separate system units that offer more flexibility, expandability, and convenience.

The following sections discuss some of the common system components for audio-video systems.

4.4.1 Capture

The process of acquiring audio and video from natural scenes to a storage medium is called *capture*. This is done with a video camera and a recorder, a camcorder, or and audio recorder with a microphone. These products are discussed in Chapters 6 (cameras) and 11 (recorders). Cameras and microphones are analog transducers; for digital systems, ADC must be performed, which may be done in either the camera or the recorder unit.

4.4.2 Storage

Programs captured for later editing or playback are stored on magnetic tape or computer hard disk. Storage units may be separate products, or they may be combined with other functions such as in the camcorder or PC.

4.4.3 Signal Processing

Signal processing tasks in audio-video systems include audio or video adjustments for frequency response, color, and so forth, or special effects and other means for combining signals. Most of these tasks are performed in postproduction systems and may be packaged as standalone products or combined with other products such as video switchers or editors.

4.4.4 Transmission

Transmission is the task of sending audio and video from one location to another and is accomplished by terrestrial broadcasting, cable, satellite, or computer network. This is covered in Chapter 7.

4.5 SYSTEM DIAGRAMS

The following sections describe a typical system in each of the system classes. It will be appreciated that there is a wide range of diversity even within one class. That is especially true with the larger systems that are designed to be highly flexible and expandable.

4.5.1 Home Video System

A high-end home video system is shown in Figure 4.2. It uses nonlinear digital editing on a PC to provide capabilities for home video production, editing, and display. Three different products are needed to accomplish this:

1. Camcorder, for original capture of video and audio. This is an analog format, such as VHS, VHS-C, or 8 mm.

2. PC with analog audio and video capture cards. It is used for nonlinear editing (see Chapter 12) of the video and audio captured on tape by the camcorder. To simplify the system, captured material is played directly from the camcorder into the PC,

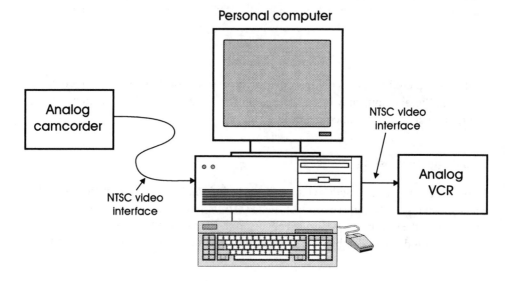

Figure 4.2 *Home digital video system.*

where it is digitized and stored on the hard disk for editing. The output from editing is analog NTSC or PAL.

3. Home video recorder, which is used to make videotapes from the output of the editing system for distribution to friends or family, who can play them on ordinary home equipment. Notice that this system produces edited output only in analog format, even though the signal is digital inside the PC.

All the components of this system are available today, and they cost less than $5,000 in total, which is high enough to limit such systems to only very dedicated home users. However, a large part of the cost of a home video editing system is the PC, which has many other uses. Prices are rapidly falling and such systems will become more popular in the near future.

4.5.2 Semiprofessional System

The semiprofessional system, shown in Figure 4.3, is similar in structure to the home system, but it uses the latest digital camcorders and VCRs to achieve significantly higher quality. However, the output is still analog videotape for the same reasons as the home system.

An additional digital VCR is added to the system to play tapes from the camcorder into the PC for editing. This is convenient in that the camcorder does not have to physically be brought into the editing room to input its material; only the tape needs to be brought there.

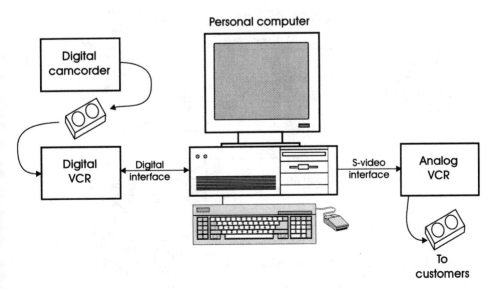

Figure 4.3 *Semiprofessional digital video system.*

It should be pointed out that although the digital system shown is available at this writing, there are very few in service simply because they are new and still a little expensive. Most semiprofessional systems today use analog videotape and perform editing with analog VCRs, typically using assemble or A-B roll videotape editing. These techniques are described in Chapter 12.

4.5.3 Videoconferencing System

Figure 4.4 shows a typical videoconferencing system coupling two locations. Each site is equipped with a camera that views the conference group and a second camera that can capture hard copy material produced by the group. There are two displays at each location to show the view of the other group and the hard copy from the other group. A digital processing and control box handles the manipulation of the data and the compression and multiplexing necessary to transmit between sites.

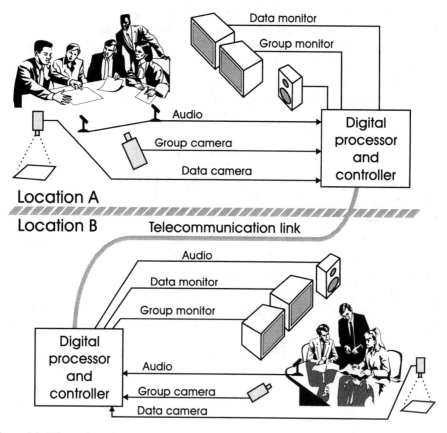

Figure 4.4 *Videoconferencing system.*

The group camera captures and transmits motion video, but the hard copy camera sends only still pictures (on demand) and it operates at a higher resolution than the group camera. The extent of this tradeoff depends on the available transmission data rate.

In spite of the apparent complexity of the figure, this is a fairly simple videoconferencing setup. Some systems have a camera and microphone for each speaker, and the system automatically handles camera switching depending on who is speaking. Usually, cameras would have remote positioners operated from the central controller and one or more of the participants may have remote controllers to manage the operation of the central unit at each location. Still other systems can handle more than two locations in a single conference. Another valuable feature is to integrate a PC into the system so that applications running on the PC can be viewed and operated from any conference location.

Another variation on videoconferencing is "desktop" videoconferencing—a PC performs all the operation of the entire system at each location. Because of the limitation on how many people can view and operate a PC, this approach is best when there are only one or two people at each site. A PC configured for this purpose would have video and audio capture add-in cards and probably another special card that handles the compression and multiplexing for transmission. Of course, all is controlled by software designed for the purpose.

4.5.4 Video Server Systems

In the early days of television, video delivery was based on live programming because there was no capability for recording of video. As video recording came into use, delivery was more and more simply the playback of prerecorded programs. Live programming was relegated to news and special events. A typical modern system for videotape delivery is shown in Figure 4.5(a). A bank of VCR players and a video switcher are computer controlled to provide automatic playback of prerecorded tapes. Operators are responsible to keep the VCR players filled with the currently required material and for proper programming of the computer. Once that has been accomplished, everything runs automatically on clock-time control.

In the digital era, the concept is the same, but the hardware is different. As shown by Figure 4.5(b), a bank of large-capacity hard disks stores the video library on a PC, and a computer program controls playback of the proper segments on time cues. The operator only has to make sure that the necessary program material is on the hard disks and that the correct computer program is running.

Such a computer-based video delivery system is called a *video server* and is also an element of other kinds of systems, especially a postproduction editing system. Large video servers are being developed to deliver several independent outputs simultaneously from a single video storage bank. This has application in cable TV systems to feed several channels and in systems for *video on demand* (VOD), which is the delivery of individually selected programs to a number of viewers.

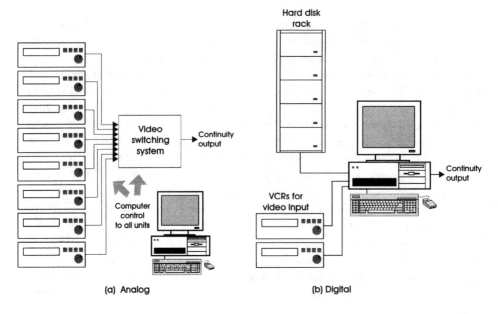

Figure 4.5 *Analog and digital video delivery systems.*

4.5.5 Production Studio System

A well-equipped production studio will have a number of cameras, a number of recorders, and a switching system that allows cameras to be connected directly to recorders or through a video effects to a recorder. There are many ways of doing this; Figure 4.6 shows one possibility.

This studio has four cameras, three VCRs, and a two-input effects unit. All units connect to a 9 × 6 switching matrix that allows different combinations of connection that an operator or a computer can change dynamically during production. The black dots on the switching matrix show active connections; all other switch points are open. Therefore, cameras 1 and 2 are going to the input of the effects unit, where they are modified or mixed. The output of the effects unit goes to the input of VCR1. Cameras 3 and 4 are connected directly to VCR2 and VCR3, respectively. Thus, at this moment in production, there could be three different shots being simultaneously recorded—two are single-camera shots and the other is a two-camera shot through the effects unit.

This studio could also be operated as a live studio by using the LINE video output. The switching matrix would also allow the LINE output to be recorded at the same time. An architecture such as this example, where all video sources and all video users are connected to the same switching matrix, allows a great deal of flexibility.

The figure skips over some of the details of systems like this. For the switching to work properly, all the inputs to the switcher must be synchronized precisely, which is a

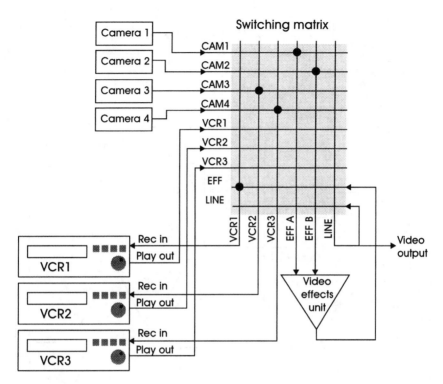

Figure 4.6 *Studio production system.*

nontrivial problem. Synchronization is discussed in Section 4.6. There are also several recursive connections that pose their own timing problems.

4.5.6 Field Production System

Obviously, the multiple units and many interconnections of Figure 4.6 would not be practical for field production. Usually switching is not used in the field and each camera is connected to its own recorder. This is ideal for the use of camcorders and a single modern high-quality camcorder can provide everything needed for field production. The one exception is that it is often desirable to use a separate audio recorder to accommodate multiple microphones or to facilitate separate audio postproduction. A portable multitrack audio recorder easily fills that need, but means must be provided for time-code matching with the camcorder if synchronized audio and video are being captured. Professional camcorders have their own time-code generators and can also provide an output to feed another recorder.

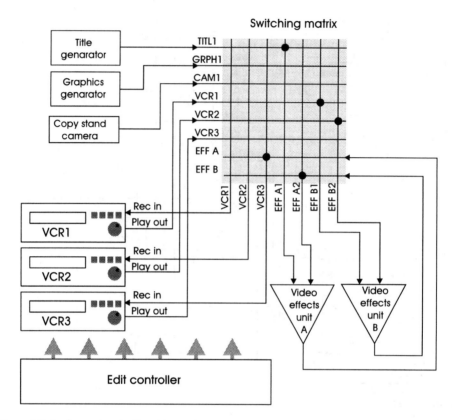

Figure 4.7 *Analog postproduction video system.*

4.5.7 Postproduction System

Figure 4.7 is a video block diagram for a moderate-sized analog postproduction editing suite. It operates on material that comes in on videotape or is generated locally by the title and graphics generators or from hard copy using a copy stand camera. There are two effects units, which would probably be different types to offer more flexibility. Three VCRs support A-B roll editing (see Chapter 12). An edit controller provides programmable control of all units.

The switcher setup shown is for the final stage of A-B roll editing, where the A and B tapes are already assembled on VCR1 and VCR2 and VCR3 will record the mix. The A- and B-channels are being switched or mixed in effects unit B, whose output goes through effects unit A for insertion of titles from the title generator. The switching matrix and the effects units provide many other possibilities for how the mix is done.

A digital postproduction facility would look quite different from Figure 4.7 because all the switching, effects, and mixing would be done in a single processor unit, controlled by

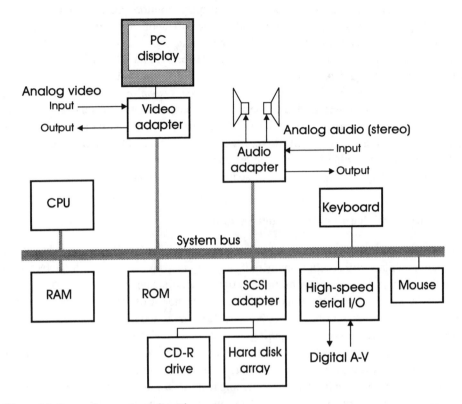

Figure 4.8 *Personal computer audio-video system.*

software. The resulting block diagram might look a lot simpler but, in fact, the capability would be much greater. This is described in Chapter 12.

4.5.8 Personal Computer Audio-Video System

The architecture of a PC was introduced in Chapter 1 and shown in Figure 1.13. Since the programmable nature of a PC means that it can do *anything* if it has the proper peripherals, this discussion covers a PC that will perform nonlinear video and audio editing (the operation of which is described in Section 12.4.2). For this purpose, the PC must have an array of very large and fast hard disks, analog video I/O with support hardware for compression, and analog audio I/O. Figure 4.8 is an expansion of Figure 1.13 showing such a system.

The figure shows capability for both analog and digital A-V input and output. This is necessary to support editing and delivery of material in either format. The video adapter for this system must support analog video capture and compression as well as driving an analog output and the PC display monitor. In some cases this might require more than one adapter card. Some editing software can use two display monitors (one, for control and one to show high-quality video), and that would also require another video display adapter.

Similar to the video, the audio adapter is capable of analog audio I/O, in stereo. For digital I/O of audio and/or video, a high-speed serial data port is required. This is not a standard feature of most PCs (at least, not yet) and requires another add-in card.

The mass storage capability uses a *small computer system interface* (SCSI) adapter, which is a high-speed interface that supports an external bus containing up to seven external devices. As shown in the figure, it is used here for an array of hard disks and a CD-R drive. The CD-R is a recordable CD drive, which is useful for creating output in the CD format or for archiving. Other mass-storage features might include a tape drive for the same purposes as the CD-R, or a second SCSI adapter with additional hard drives.

4.5.9 Large Broadcast or Production Facilities

The system examples given so far are for small, single-purpose facilities. A large broadcast or production plant will combine many of these subsystems into an overall large technical plant that can flexibly perform a multiplicity of production, video delivery, or postproduction tasks at the same time. It is important to maximize the use of the plant's major components, such as cameras, tape recorders, special effects units, and so forth, without requiring any physical connecting or reconfiguring for each task.

Usually, this is organized by providing a number of *control rooms*, which serve as the central control location for each separate task that is running at a time. A control room would contain remote control panels, switching panels, monitors, speakers, and any other things needed to control and monitor the task, but the major equipment itself would be located elsewhere, usually in a central room dedicated to that function. Of course, cameras would be located in studios, but they could be accessed from any of the control rooms.

This architecture is brought together by what is called a *routing switcher*, which provides all the connections of video, audio, and control so that any major component can be made available to any control room as if it were physically there. The routing switcher is a matrix like the one shown in Figure 4.6 but, in addition to video and audio, it switches control data. Since the purpose of routing is only to set up the system configuration, there are no dynamic functions like special effects in a routing switcher. Each control room has control over the part of the routing switcher that affects the things coming to or going from that room. Figure 4.9 is a very simplified diagram of how such a major facility is arranged. In this example, there are three studios with three cameras each, five VCRs, three effects units, one titler, and two communication lines to outside sources or users.

A common system design places the routing switcher and all video equipment except the cameras in a central equipment area. All video signals stay in this area and video goes to the control rooms only for monitoring purposes. This minimizes cable lengths in the main video paths. Although the same thing could be done for audio, most systems bring audio into mixing boards located in the control rooms, which does simplify the wiring.

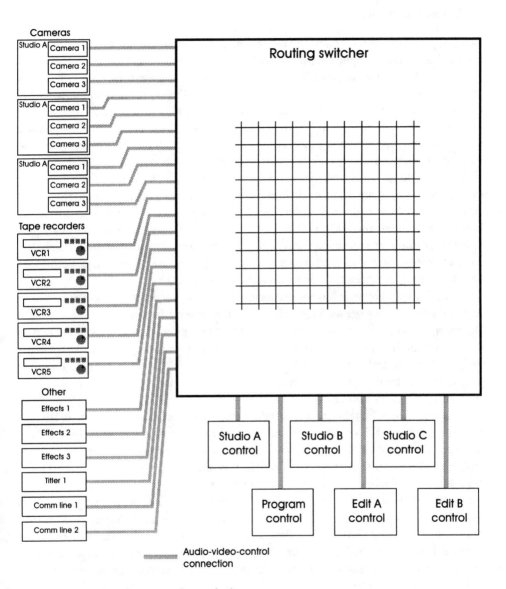

Figure 4.9 *Large broadcast or production facility.*

4.6 SYNCHRONIZATION

It is often necessary to switch or intermix the audio and video signals in a system. This requires *synchronization* of the signals at the point of switching or mixing. There are three
levels of synchronization needed: scanning (video only), modulation, and program time.
They are discussed below.

4.6.1 Scanning Synchronization

Switching among video signals without visible interruption requires that the horizontal and vertical scanning implied in each signal be accurately matched. Analog signals contain sync pulses for this purpose (see Section 2.5); these indicate the exact instants when horizontal and vertical retrace must occur for proper display of the signal in real time. In analog systems, the synchronization means must allow accurate alignment of the sync pulses in every signal for intermixing to be possible. That is normally accomplished by having a central source of sync pulses, a *sync generator,* that drives all the units of the system so their output signals are in sync. The output of a sync generator is usually a composite sync signal that includes horizontal, vertical, and color subcarrier components. Each unit in the system receives this signal and controls its internal operations so that its output signals accurately match the sync timings. In the case of horizontal and subcarrier timings, the delays between the system units and the switching point are significant and means is usually provided for adjustment to compensate for system delays. Since that may sometimes require advancing the timing at the signal source to be ahead of the sync pulse, phase-lock loops are usually provided because they are capable of such behavior.

Digital signals, however, do not necessarily represent the picture in real time because digital displays may store the signal for as much as several frames before presenting it. Digital signal formats contain codes that indicate the beginnings and ends of video data blocks for scan lines, fields, or frames. Although digital switching units could contain a variable delay capability to automatically match up the timings of incoming signals, it is usually simpler for the system to provide this in the same manner as is done in analog systems, using a sync generator.

Both analog and digital signals must deal with signals coming in from remote sources over communication lines, networks, microwave links, or broadcasts. In these cases, the approach of sending sync out to the sources will not work. There are two solutions to that problem. (1) The entire studio system may be slaved to the remote source, using a technique known as *genlock.* This works but it puts the entire system at the mercy of the integrity of the remote signal and, of course, it only works with one remote signal at a time. A much better solution (2) uses a device of the digital era, known as a *frame synchronizer.* This unit contains a digital memory that stores remote signals as they come in and reads them out in sync with the local system. This requires a memory size of at least one frame, but that is not much by today's standards. All digital systems contain frame synchronizers, and most analog ones do, too.

4.6.2 Modulation Synchronization

Proper mixing of composite analog or digital signals requires that the color subcarrier signals be precisely matched in frequency and phase at the mixing point. Of course, this is not an issue in a component system that has no color subcarrier. For analog signals, this is done via the sync generator as described in the section above. Digital composite systems, however, usually define the sampling pattern relative to the subcarrier phase of the analog signal being sampled. Once that has been done, the subcarrier phase is implicit in the sampling pattern and will not be affected by minor system delays. At a digital switching point, the switching circuits must simply match up the sampling patterns of the signals to ensure subcarrier phase alignment.

4.6.3 Program Time Synchronization

The final level of synchronization involves matching signals frame-by-frame according to *program time*. This is a critical issue in editing, where time codes are provided in all recorded signals for this purpose. Edit controllers are capable of controlling recording devices to deliver a specified frame number at a specified program time so as to match to another signal at another specified frame number. Time codes and editing are described in Chapter 12.

4.7 SYSTEM INTERCONNECT STANDARDS

All the units in systems must talk to one another for video, audio, and control purposes. Much industry effort has gone into standards for these signals, both in analog form and, now, in digital form. In addition, signals that are interchanged on magnetic tape or other recorded media also need standards. The following industry bodies work on standards for the audio/video industries:

ITU (International Telecommunications Union) is an international body that promulgates standards for telecommunications (ITU-T, formerly CCITT) and broadcasting (ITU-R, formerly CCIR.)

ISO (International Standards Organization) is an international standardizing organization in many fields. A related organization is the IEC (International Electrotechnical Commission.)

SMPTE (Society of Motion Picture and Television Engineers) is an organization located in the United States but with international membership and recognition of its standards.

IEEE (Institute of Electrical and Electronics Engineers) is another United States organization with worldwide membership and active in standards.

EIA (Electronic Industries Association) is a United States organization of electronics manufacturers.

EBU (European Broadcasting Union) is an organization of broadcasters in Europe that develops standards used there.

In addition, many standards are developed by individual manufacturers or groups of manufacturers, especially in the computer industry. They become accepted standards simply by being the most widely used approach (this is called *de facto* standardization.) However, most de facto standards usually are submitted to one of the industry standardizing bodies

Table 4.2

Worldwide Digital System Standards

Standard	Description	Parent organization
Rec. BT.601	Sampling and encoding recommendations for 525- and 625-line component video	ITU-R
274M	1920 × 1080 scanning at 16:9 aspect ratio	SMPTE
125M-1995	4:2:2 component bit-parallel interface	SMPTE
244M-1995	NTSC composite digital encoding	SMPTE
259M-1993	10-bit serial interface	SMPTE
H.261	Coding and decoding for audiovisual services at 64 Kbps or multiples of 64 Kbps	ITU-T
JPEG	Still image compression	ISO-ITU
MPEG-1	Motion video compression for CD-ROM and other low-data-rate (1.5–2 Mbps) storage devices	ISO-ITU
MPEG-2	High-quality motion video compression for data rates of 4–20 Mbps	ISO-ITU

once the market for it begins to grow. This allows other manufacturers to enter the market and cause it to grow even more.

Table 4.2 shows a list of the most important standards that are relevant to digital audio and video and their source organizations. The bibliography at the end of the book also lists the World Wide Web pages of these organizations.

Chapter 5

Analog-to-Digital Conversion

5.1 INTRODUCTION

The maximum signal quality of a digital audio or video system is almost completely determined at the point of analog-to-digital conversion (ADC). The digital system beyond that point can be capable of perfect reproduction of the signal but it cannot improve the sound or picture quality beyond what was digitized. (Digital processing that enhances or modifies the signals might be said to improve their quality, but the limitations from the initial conversion are still there.) A full understanding of the limitations of ADC is important to the design and use of digital systems and that is the objective of this chapter.

5.2 THE STEPS OF ADC

A generalized block diagram for ADC is shown in Figure 5.1. The steps consist of prefiltering to remove input frequencies that are too high to be correctly digitized, sampling to convert the time scale to digital, quantizing to convert amplitudes to digital, and encoding to specify how digital values are represented. Each of these is discussed in the sections below. At the end of a digital system, the original analog signal is recovered from a series of samples by a digital-to-analog converter (DAC) that converts the samples to amplitude-modulated pulses, and then low-pass-filters the pulses to remove components at the sampling frequency and above.

As can be seen from Figure 5.1, sampling and quantization operate on orthogonal properties of the signal (time and amplitude), which means that they are independent of one other. Therefore, these two steps can be done in either order, which is equivalent to doing quantization first instead of sampling first as shown in the figure.

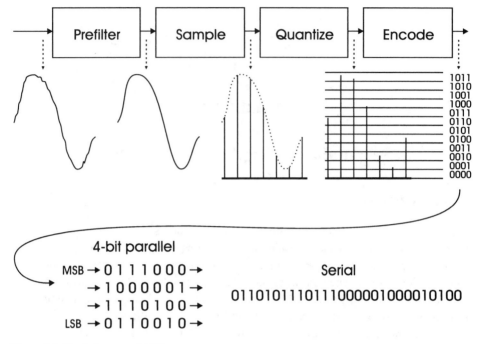

Figure 5.1 *Block diagram of ADC.*

5.2.1 Prefiltering and Sampling

For the sake of an orderly discussion, it is best to consider the sampling process first; the actual first step (prefiltering) will also be covered in this discussion. Sampling is the process of periodically taking readings of the value of a waveform. Usually, samples are intended to be *instantaneous*, which means that the sample is taken in a time that is short compared with the period of the sampling frequency. The *sampling width* is the percentage of the period of the sampling frequency over which the sample is averaged. Section 5.2.1.3 discusses the effect of sampling width on sampling performance.

The output of sampling is a series of analog values (samples) corresponding to the points on the waveform where sampling occurred. This is usually in the form of pulses at the sampling frequency whose amplitude represents the sample values.

Sampling is done at a constant frequency, f_S. As discussed in Section 1.4.2.1, the sampling frequency must be high enough to reproduce the highest desired frequency components of the input waveform. The Nyquist criterion says that

$$f_S = 2 f_{MAX} \tag{5.1}$$

where f_{MAX} is the highest frequency to be reproduced.

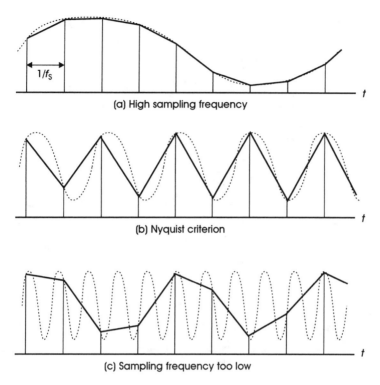

(a) High sampling frequency

(b) Nyquist criterion

(c) Sampling frequency too low

Figure 5.2 *Sampling frequency and the Nyquist limit.*

Input filtering is used to make sure there are no frequency components higher than f_{MAX}. Because of practical difficulties with sharp cutoff filters, f_S is usually set somewhat higher than the Nyquist criterion; sampling at 2.2 to 2.5 f_H is common. Some systems go much higher; this is called *oversampling* and is covered in Section 5.3.1.

The implications of the Nyquist criterion can be seen in the examples of Figure 5.2, which show sampling below, at, and above the Nyquist frequency. To a first approximation, the content of a series of samples can be estimated by connecting the peaks of the samples with straight lines. (See the discussion on DAC in Section 5.4.) The figure shows that the samples reproduce the correct signal frequency until the signal frequency exceeds one-half the sampling frequency, at which point the output frequency becomes the difference between the sampling and signal frequencies. This is a spurious and undesired result that is called *aliasing*. The extent to which this is objectionable depends on the application. For example, in audio systems, aliasing frequencies will be heard as unrelated frequencies in the sound and should therefore be eliminated. In the case of video, aliasing causes patterns in the reproduced pictures that may or may not be objectionable (see Section 5.2.1.2).

The Nyquist criterion can also be viewed in the frequency domain. A series of samples may be considered as a periodic impulse function at the sampling frequency whose

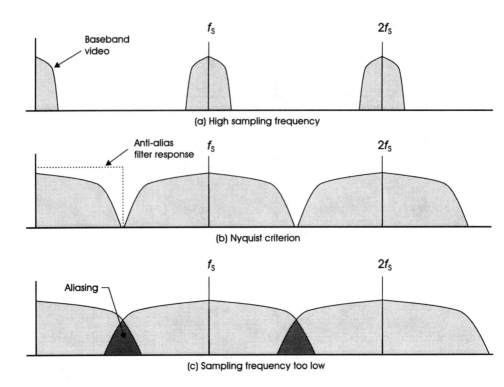

Figure 5.3 *Spectrum of sampling corresponding to Figure 5.2.*

amplitude is modulated by the sample values. The spectrum of a periodic impulse consists of a zero-frequency component plus equal-amplitude components at the repetition frequency and its harmonics. Each component has sidebands representing modulation by the signal frequencies. This is shown in Figure 5.3 at three conditions corresponding to the cases in Figure 5.2. Aliasing occurs when the sidebands of the sampling frequency component overlap the sidebands of the zero-frequency component. If this overlap occurs, there is no way to remove it after sampling—it must be prevented by input filtering. It is obvious from the figure that overlap will occur whenever the maximum signal frequency is higher than one-half the sampling frequency, so this is just another way of expressing the Nyquist criterion.

When it is necessary to operate with signal frequencies close to the Nyquist limit, the requirements of the input filter become difficult. As can be seen in Figure 5.3(b), the filter cutoff must be sharp to avoid distorting the desired signal while removing frequencies that would cause aliasing. Some ADCs employ *oversampling* to help this problem (see Section 5.3.1).

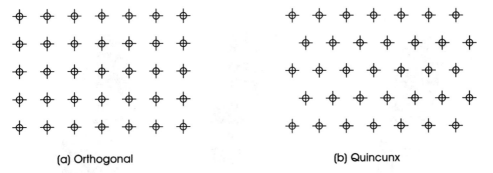

(a) Orthogonal · (b) Quincunx

Figure 5.4 *Spatial sampling patterns.*

5.2.1.1 Sampling in Two Dimensions

An analog video waveform resulting from scanning already has been sampled at line rate (vertical detail—see Section 2.3.5). Sampling this in an ADC represents a second dimension (horizontal detail). This may be viewed in terms of the image as shown in Figure 5.4. To avoid certain disturbances, sampling frequency is usually synchronized with line-scanning frequency If that is an exact integral relationship, sampling will be at identical points in each line (called *orthogonal* sampling) as shown by Figure 5.4(a). Figure 5.4(b) shows *quincunx* sampling, which is achieved by having the sampling frequency be an odd multiple of twice the line-scanning frequency. Different sampling patterns would occur with more complex frequency relationships, but these are usually undesirable because they repeat over larger spatial areas, and any disturbance caused by the pattern will be more visible in the picture.

Quincunx sampling is advantageous in that it provides better resolution in all directions (including diagonally), but it is not much used because it makes digital processing of signals more difficult.

5.2.1.2 Aliasing in Two Dimensions

Figure 5.5 shows what aliasing looks like in an image of a diagonal black line on a white background. Figure 5.5(a) shows a line image overlaid by an orthogonal sampling pattern, and Figure 5.5(b) shows the result of sampling when the output is based simply on whether the signal is black or white at the instant of sampling. It is the familiar jagged line that is often seen on computer displays when displaying near-horizontal or near-vertical lines or edges.

Figure 5.5(c) shows the effect of anti-aliasing, where the output value is based on how much of the sampling area (a rectangle one sample period wide in each dimension and

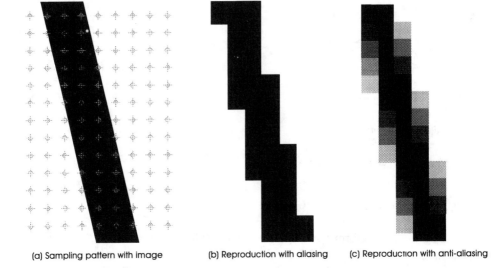

(a) Sampling pattern with image   (b) Reproduction with aliasing   (c) Reproduction with anti-aliasing

Figure 5.5 *Aliasing. This figure should be viewed from a distance of about 20 ft to see the effect.*

centered on the sampling point) contains the line. If the figure is viewed from a distance, one can see that the anti-aliased line looks smoother than the jagged line.

Using a proper prefilter ahead of the sampler actually achieves the result in Figure 5.5(c). Since the filter removes frequency components above the Nyquist limit, the edges of the signal waveform will become sloped at a rise time approximately equal to one cycle of the sampling frequency. Instantaneous sampling of this sloped edge will automatically produce the correct intermediate amplitudes for the pixels at the edges of the line.

5.2.1.3 Sampling Width

Averaging the sampled value over a significant percentage of the period of the sampling frequency causes a loss of sample amplitude at high frequencies, as shown by Figure 5.6. The sampling width is represented by the shaded area in the figure; averaging over this width gives the value shown by the dotted line, which is slightly less than the value that would be read by an instantaneous sample taken at the peak of the signal waveform. This is known as the *aperture effect,* which occurs in many video processes. The actual loss is of the form $\sin(x)/x$ and is shown in Figure 5.7. The width parameter, W, is given as a percentage of the period of the sampling frequency. The loss is significant for full-sample width ($W = 100$); at the Nyquist limit, the response is down to 63.6%. However, Figure 5.7 shows that for sample widths less than 20%, the loss is negligible. This aperture effect is a factor contributing to MTF loss in the sampling process (see Section 2.5.2.1).

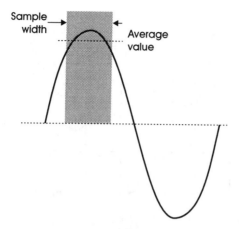

Figure 5.6 *Sample width.*

5.2.1.4 CCD Sampling

A charge-coupled device (CCD) camera (see Section 6.4) has rectangular areas (cells) of sensitivity as shown in Figure 5.8. Each cell is independent of its neighbors. Usually a cell equates to a single pixel in the final digital signal.

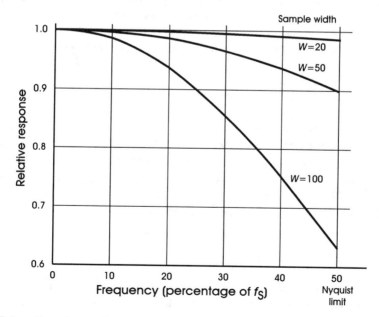

Figure 5.7 *Sampling aperture effect.*

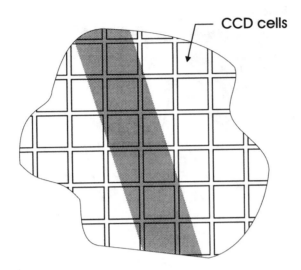

Figure 5.8 *Enlarged view of CCD imaging surface.*

Light falling on the CCD is averaged over the area of each cell to determine the cell's output when the CCD is scanned. Since the cell spacing determines the sampling frequency of the CCD both horizontally and vertically, this is close to a $W=100$ condition in two dimensions. The $W=100$ loss can be corrected by aperture correction in the camera processing circuits, but the necessary prefiltering to eliminate aliasing must be accomplished optically since the CCD is directly sampling the optical image.

5.2.1.5 Sample and Hold

When sampling is done before quantizing, a *sample-and-hold* circuit is usually employed to store (hold) the sample values long enough for the quantizer to operate on them. This circuit, shown in Figure 5.9, captures the sample by closing the switch for a short time to charge a capacitor up to the sample value. When the switch opens, the capacitor holds the sample value until the next sampling pulse. Thus, the quantizer circuits have almost the full period of the sampling frequency to perform their logic.

5.2.2 Quantization

Quantization (or *quantizing*) is the process of converting a continuous range of analog values to a limited set of discrete values. With this definition, sampling can be viewed as quantization in the time dimension because the samples represent signal values only at the discrete time points where sampling takes place. All input signal values between the sampling points are eliminated in sampling. As was shown in Figure 5.5, this time-

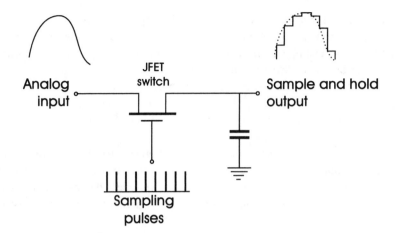

Figure 5.9 Sample and hold circuit.

quantization produces distortions that result in jagged lines. In spite of this, the word "quantization" is generally used to mean making the signal discrete only with respect to *amplitude*. That is the usage in this book.

The output of a sampler is a train of pulses that are discrete in time but still analog in amplitude. The amplitude values must be quantized so that they can be expressed digitally in a specified number of bits. Figure 5.10 shows the effect of quantization without sampling. (Remember that sampling and quantizing are independent and do not have to be performed together or in any specified sequence.) Figure 5.10(a) shows that the amplitude range is divided up into regions (quanta) and the quantizer applies the same value to any amplitude

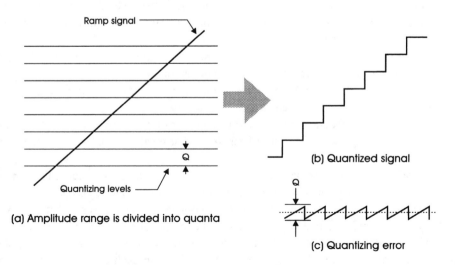

Figure 5.10 Quantizing.

falling within each region. Thus, for a linearly rising input, the output of a quantizer (Figure 5.10(b)) steps from one quantum value to the next. All intermediate values of the input signal are lost. This example is *linear* quantization because all quanta are the same size. Nonlinear quantization is discussed in Section 5.2.2.7.

For quantization, the number N of bits per sample and thus, the number of quantization levels or quanta (2^N), is chosen large enough that the discreteness of the levels will not be seen or heard. Typical values are 8 bps for video and 16 bps for audio, although other values are used in specific situations.

The nature of quantization errors may be seen in Figure 5.10(c). The error is the difference between the ramp of Figure 5.10(a) and the step waveform of Figure 5.10(b), which is a sawtooth kind of waveform whose peak-to-peak amplitude is the width Q of one quantization level. Note that this error reduces linearly as the number of quantizing levels is increased.

5.2.2.1 Quantizer Circuits

Quantizers are based on the *comparator* circuit, which compares the signal value of its input to a *reference voltage*. It outputs digital 0 when the signal is less than the reference value and 1 when the signal is above the reference. The reference value is sometimes called the *threshold* of the comparator. Comparators must be very stable and accurate (on the input side, they are analog devices) and must switch from 0 to 1 for a very small change of the input.

Figure 5.11 shows one way how comparators are used for quantization. There is one comparator per quantum level, the input signal is applied to all comparators, and a resistance ladder sets the reference value of each comparator to successively higher levels. Because this approach takes 2^N comparators, it is practical only up to about $N = 8$ or 10 bits. (Of course, all the comparators are on the same integrated circuit, so it is not as though they were individual devices that someone had to connect.)

There are 2^N outputs from the comparator ladder in Figure 5.11; all outputs are 1 up to the quantum level of the input signal and higher quantum levels output 0. Further logic is necessary to reduce that to the N output lines. This logic is called *priority encoding* and also is included on the ADC integrated circuit.

The comparator architecture of Figure 5.11 performs quantizing ahead of sampling—the sampling occurs in the priority encoder. This is called a *flash ADC*, which is one of the fastest types of ADCs.

Different architectures are used in quantizers of more than 10 bits because the number of comparators for a flash ADC becomes prohibitive. One popular approach is the *successive approximation* quantizer, which contains only a single comparator that compares the output from an internal DAC to the input voltage. The digital input to the DAC is adjusted by a feedback loop until the comparator gives zero output. Thus, the digital input to the internal DAC becomes the output for the ADC. This approach is very accurate at high

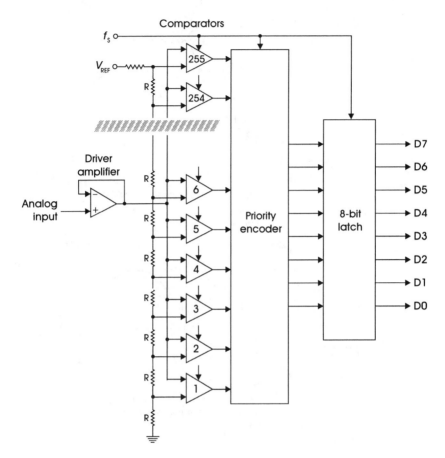

Figure 5.11 *The flash ADC.*

bit numbers (like $N = 16$), but it is slow because the feedback loop must go through N iterations to reach the output value for each sample. It can still be fast enough for audio but not video.

5.2.2.2 Setting the Amplitude Range

A quantizer cannot provide a higher (or lower) output than that specified by the limits of its range of quantizing levels. If the input signal exceeds this range, the output value should saturate at the maximum (or minimum) value. In analog terms, this is *clipping*, which represents severe distortion and should be avoided. This may take extra circuitry because most digital devices will simply *wrap around* to zero when the maximum digital value is exceeded, which is even worse than saturation.

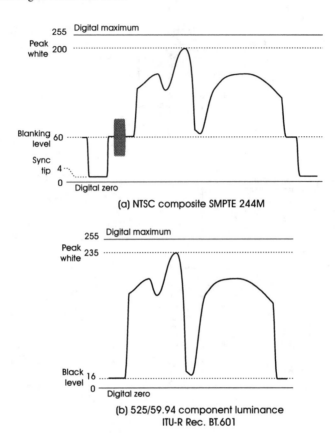

(a) NTSC composite SMPTE 244M

(b) 525/59.94 component luminance
ITU-R Rec. BT.601

Figure 5.12 *Levels for quantizing video.*

Because signal-level control is never exact, most digitizing standards specify that signal levels should be set so that the full quantizing range is not used. This allows some tolerance for levels to be slightly off. For example, Figure 5.12 shows the level standards for SMPTE 244M composite digitizing and SMPTE 253M component digitizing. Note that in most video circuits, the absolute level of sync tip or picture black will shift around with average picture brightness because the dc component of the signal is not present in the circuit. To maintain the sync tip or signal black levels at a fixed digital level, the dc component must be restored in the ADC, which is done by *clamping* the signal. This is simply a circuit that monitors the level of the sync tip or picture black and adjusts the system to hold that constant.

In the case of audio digitizing, the perceptual effect of clipping is even worse than it is with video, and audio levels are more difficult to control. As a result, digital audio systems usually contain automatic level control or limiting means to prevent overload from occurring and they may still operate with a 3-dB or so margin against overload. Since audio signals inherently do not have a dc component, no clamping is required.

5.2.2.3 Signal-to-Noise Ratio

When the signal fills the quantizing range, quantizing error can be considered as noise added to the signal, where the noise is random with a peak-to-peak (p-p) value of one quantizing step and a uniform *probability density function* (pdf). The signal-to-noise ratio (SNR) can be estimated easily for the case of sine wave signals by the following analysis: Assume that a sinusoidal signal fills the full quantizing range, which has L levels ($L = 2^N$, where N is the number of bps.) Since quantizing error has a p-p value of one quantizing level or $1/L$, the SNR based on p-p values equals L. For audio purposes, SNR is measured as the ratio of rms (root-mean-square) signal to rms noise, and the above analysis would be correct only if the pp-to-rms ratio for the signal and the noise were the same, which they are not. For a sine wave signal, the rms value is $0.354\,S_{p\text{-}p}$, but for the quantizing noise (assuming the uniform pdf) it is $0.29\,S_{p\text{-}p}$. Thus, the SNR is higher than L by 1.22:1 (1.76 dB). Converting everything to dB:

$$\text{SNR (dB)} = 6.02N + 1.76 \tag{5.2}$$

This is for audio. For video, SNR is the ratio of p-p signal to rms noise, so the 0.354 factor above should be eliminated. The result for video is

$$\text{SNR (dB)} = 6.02N + 10.8 \tag{5.3}$$

Equations (5.2) and (5.3) apply only to the large-signal case, where the signal fills the quantizing range. As the signal becomes smaller, the effect of quantizing noise increases because the signal occupies fewer quantizing levels. The "noise" becomes signal-dependent, which is distortion, not noise. For either audio or video, low-signal distortion with a uniform quantizer as described above is severe and unacceptable. Fortunately, this problem can be eliminated by proper application of *dither* (see Section 5.2.2.5).

5.2.2.4 Quantizing Artifacts

In audio, quantizing noise is apparent in low-level passages of a sound track, where it sounds like a sort of "granular" distortion. It definitely does not sound like random noise. The use of dither converts this granular distortion to a random noise sound, which is more acceptable.

In video, quantizing noise can be seen in areas of the picture that have smooth shading from one color or one brightness to another. Lines become visible in the picture where the signal value passes from one quantizing level to another. This is not very evident at 8 bits/pixel, but it becomes severe at 6 bits or fewer per pixel. Since there is correlation between adjacent lines in the picture, quantizing transitions appear as wavy lines in smooth-shaded areas, much like the altitude lines on a contour map. From that metaphor, the distortion is called *contouring*. Figure 5.13 is an example of contouring, caused by displaying the image at only 2 bits/pixel (4 levels).

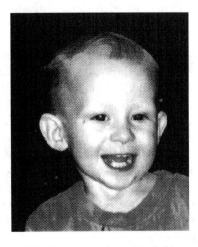 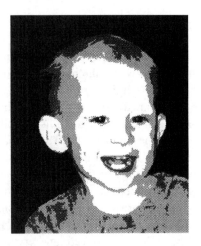

Figure 5.13   *Contouring, (a) original, (b) quantized at 2 bits/pixel.*

5.2.2.5 Dither

The contouring in Figure 5.13(b) does not look as bad as it might because the original image contained some noise. The effect of the noise is to break up the contour patterns so they are harder to see. In fact, most ADCs deliberately add a carefully specified amount of random noise ahead of quantizing—this is called *dithering* and causes quantizing errors to appear as random noise instead of signal-related effects such as contouring or granular noise. Figure 5.14(a) shows a quantizer without dither, Figure 5.14(b) shows how the dither modulates the quantum levels, and Figure 5.14(c) shows how (on the average) dither linearizes the transfer characteristic. The dither signal must have a specified amplitude and, for best results, should have a pdf that is triangular or gaussian. A uniform pdf could also be used, but this causes the resulting noise in the signal to be modulated as the signal level changes, which is objectionable. The triangular or gaussian pdfs do not cause noise modulation with signal level. Figure 5.14(d) shows these possibilities.

Dither causes a slight loss of SNR, but the improved behavior of quantizing noise is worth it. For example, triangular pdf dither requires a p-p amplitude of 2 quantizing levels, and the resultant SNR on a p-p/p-p basis is:

$$SNR \text{ (dB)} = 6.02N - 3 \tag{5.4}$$

Incoming audio or video signals may have an inherent noise level that accomplishes the same result as dither. However, it is unlikely that such signals will provide the optimal noise amplitude and pdf under all conditions, so it is customary for ADCs to include their own optimized dither.

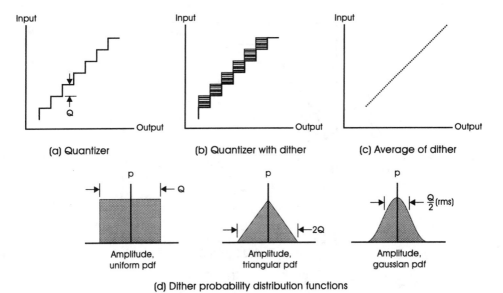

(a) Quantizer

(b) Quantizer with dither

(c) Average of dither

(d) Dither probability distribution functions

Figure 5.14 *Quantizing with dither.*

5.2.2.6 Requantizing

Sometimes, it is necessary to reduce the number of bits per sample. This happens often in signal processing involving multiplication because that process extends the bits per sample. At the end of the process, the samples must be reduced to the original bits per sample. If that is done by simple truncation of the least-significant bits, the effect of dither in the original quantization is lost and a new quantizing error is introduced. This can be corrected by digital dithering followed by rounding to the desired number of bits. Digital dithering is simply the addition of suitably random digital numbers to the bits to be removed. After this, rounding takes place based on the most significant of the bits to be removed. If that bit is 0, the extra bits are simply truncated; but if it is 1, rounding up is done by adding 1 to the remaining bits.

5.2.2.7 Nonlinear Quantizing

As mentioned above, quantizing distortion increases at low-signal levels that do not occupy the full range of the quantizer. This feature can be exploited by making the quantizer nonlinear; that is, using finer quantization at low levels and coarser near maximum level. This has been widely used in digital telephony. It is similar to the analog process known as *companding*, where the amplitude range of the signal is compressed ahead of a transmission channel and expanded after transmission. Because of the

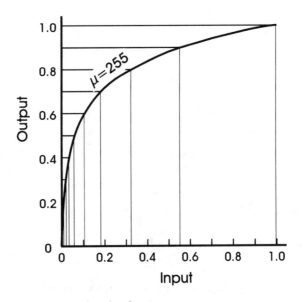

Figure 5.15 *Nonlinear quantizing—the μ-law function.*

similarity, nonlinear quantization is also called companding. It has the effect of keeping the average signal levels higher in the channel and thus, better overcoming the channel noise.

Nonlinear quantization is used in speech audio at low number of bits per sample, such as 8 bps. It is usually accomplished by quantizing at higher bits per sample first, such as 12 bps, and then using a lookup table to drop down to the nonlinear 8 bits. The result of this is shown in Figure 5.15. The shape of the nonlinear curve must, of course, be carefully specified because it has to be reproduced in both the ADC and the DAC. The most common function is known as the *μ-law* [1], which is specified as

$$y = \frac{\log(1+\mu x)}{\log(1+\mu)} \tag{5.5}$$

Where:

x is the input to the μ-law device.

y is the output.

μ is a parameter, usually set to 255.

Notice that this approach lowers the SNR for large signals but increases it for smaller signals. The idea is that the presence of the large signal will mask the higher noise for the listener, but the better SNR at low signals will be heard as an improvement.

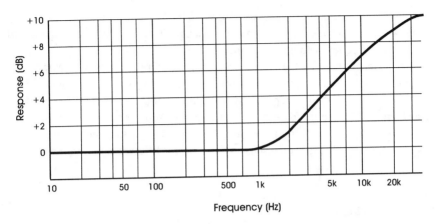

Figure 5.16 *Preemphasis curve for audio.*

5.2.3 Preemphasis

Another technique that is often used in audio systems is *preemphasis*. This exploits the fact that higher signal frequencies usually have lower amplitudes, so their amplitudes can be increased without overloading the system. An analog filter is inserted at the input of the system to emphasize the high frequencies, and a complementary filter is used after the DAC at the end of the system. A typical preemphasis function is shown in Figure 5.16. Because preemphasis reduces the overload margin of the system, it must be carefully used. Preemphasis is not used with digital video.

5.2.4 Encoding

The process of assigning digital numbers to the quantizing levels is called *encoding*. This can be a simple process, such as pure binary or two's-complement; a nonlinear process, such as μ-law; or a very complex process intended to accomplish data compression. The latter choices are the subject of Chapter 9.

5.3 CHOOSING SAMPLING FREQUENCY

Sampling frequency determines the system bandwidth that can be achieved without aliasing and also determines the basic bit rate of the system according to

$$\text{bit rate} = (\text{sampling frequency}) * (\text{bits/sample}) \tag{5.6}$$

To minimize bit rate and cost, most systems employ various compromises and compression techniques. Sampling frequency plays an important part in these tradeoffs. For example, it would be desirable to operate as close to the Nyquist limit as possible to get the lowest bit rate, but that calls for expensive anti-alias filters. It usually pays to use a slightly higher sampling frequency to have reasonable filter specifications.

In video systems, there is also the requirement that sampling be synchronized with the line-scanning rate in a certain way to achieve the desired sampling pattern (see Section 5.2.1.1) and to achieve the desired number of samples in the active line period. This reduces the choice of frequency to certain specific values. Additional considerations, such as having a frequency that will work for both NTSC and PAL sampling, can narrow the choices even further. This section discusses some of the different situations and their considerations.

5.3.1 Oversampling

An alternative to working very close to the Nyquist limit is to actually work very far from it. This is known as *oversampling* and is very advantageous in cases where hardware for the necessary higher-frequency sampling is available. It is widely used in audio, where signal frequencies are low, and it is sometimes used in video as well. The idea is to sample at a multiple of the desired rate, such as 2×, 3×, 8×, or even as much as 64× (only for audio.) The analog prefilter needed to remove aliasing is easier to implement because the sampling frequency and the desired passband are farther apart. After sampling and quantizing, the digital signal is filtered down to the desired final bandwidth using a digital filter (see Section 8.3.2) and the sampling rate is then reduced to the final value by *decimation*, which is the process of removal of unwanted samples. Sometimes these two steps are combined in a *decimation filter*.

A digital filter, which contains multiplication, increases the number of bits per sample. The inherent action of the filter trades bandwidth for increased amplitude resolution, and some of the increased bits are valid and can be kept. The remaining extra bits must be removed by requantizing (see Section 5.2.2.6).

Figure 5.17 is a block diagram of an oversampling ADC. The advantages of oversampling are:

1. The analog prefilter only has to remove frequencies higher than half the oversampling frequency. It can easily have flat response in the desired band and then roll off slowly up to one-half the oversampling frequency.

2. Because the digital filtering process actually increases the number of bits per sample, the original quantization does not have to have as many levels as desired in the final result.

3. The final frequency response (and alias removal) is determined by a digital filter, which is readily implemented in an integrated circuit for almost any response specification. The digital filter response is precisely reproducible and stable over time.

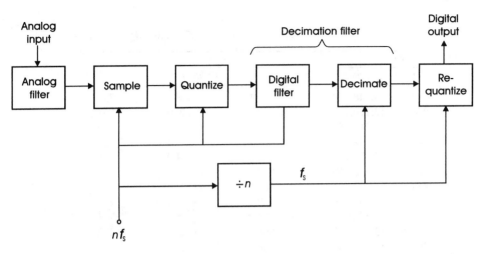

Figure 5.17 *An oversampling ADC.*

5.3.2 Audio Sampling Frequencies

Because there is no inherent structure in an audio signal that requires synchronization at various points in a system, audio sampling frequencies are chosen based only on bandwidth considerations. That, of course, could lead to a tremendous diversity of audio sampling rates, which is a problem that is solved by standards. However, different industries have adopted different standards, so there are still a considerable number of standards in use. Table 5.1 lists audio standards for the Compact Disc, audio production recorders, personal computers, and telephony.

Table 5.1

Audio Sampling Frequencies

Frequency (Hz)	bps	Audio bandwidth (Hz)	Data rate (bps)	Use
48,000	16	20,000	192,000	Audio production (stereo)
44,100	16	20,000	176,000	Compact Disc (stereo)
22,100	16	9,000	88,400	PC WAV stereo—music
10,500	8	4,000	10,500	PC WAV mono—speech
8,000	8	3,500	8,000	Telephone

Table 5.2

Choice of Video Sampling Frequency for ITU-R Rec. BT.601

525/59.94		625/50		
n	Frequency	n	Frequency	Dif.
842	13,248,250	848 *	13,250,000	1,750
844 *	13,279,719	850	13,281,250	1,531
846	13,311,187	852 *	13,312,500	1,313
848 *	13,342,656	854	13,343,750	1,094
850	13,374,124	856 *	13,375,000	876
852 *	13,405,593	858	13,406,250	657
854	13,437,061	860 *	13,437,500	439
856 *	13,468,530	862	13,468,750	220
858	13,499,999	864 *	13,500,000	1
860 *	13,531,467	866	13,531,250	217
862	13,562,936	868 *	13,562,500	436
864 *	13,594,404	870	13,593,750	654
866	13,625,873	872 *	13,625,000	873
868 *	13,657,341	874	13,656,250	1,091
870	13,688,810	876 *	13,687,500	1,310

* Divisible by 4

5.3.3 Component Video Sampling

ITU-R Rec. BT.601 specifies the sampling frequency for component digital systems using 525/59.94 or 625/50 scanning standards. A single frequency is recommended for all uses, which also provides for subsampling (see Section 8.3.3.2) by 2:1 or 4:1 for color difference components. The choice of this frequency, 13.5 MHz, is interesting in that the same frequency operates in both 525- and 625-line scanning systems. Because the bandwidths are different, a lower frequency could have been specified in 525-line systems than in 625-line systems, but the advantages of having a single frequency worldwide were important enough to drive the choice of one frequency.

A major requirement is that the sampling should be orthogonal (see Section 5.2.1.1) in both systems. This is because component digital systems are widely used for image processing and special effects where it is highly desirable that samples are located at the same points on adjacent lines. A further requirement is that the sampling should remain orthogonal when the sampling rate is divided down by 2:1 or 4:1.

Orthogonal sampling requires that the sampling frequency be an exact integer multiple of the line-scanning frequency. If this condition is to be maintained while subsampling by 2 or 4, the multiple of line frequency should also be a multiple of 4. The two line frequencies are 15,625 Hz for 625/50 and 15,734.26 Hz for 525/59.94. This quickly narrows the frequency choice; in fact, it makes it impossible. There is no single number that meets all these criteria.

Considering that 625/50 requires 5-MHz bandwidth, the sampling frequency must be higher than 10 MHz—maybe as much as 12 to 13 MHz—to allow some filtering margin. Without delving into all the combinations, Table 5.2 shows the even integer multiples of both line frequencies in the vicinity of 13 MHz. The asterisks show numbers divisible by 4. Note that the frequency values almost exactly match at the multiples 858 for 525 lines and 864 for 625 lines, and that magic frequency is 13.5 MHz. Unfortunately, 858 is not divisible by 4, which means that 4× subsampling will not yield an orthogonal sampling pattern for 525 lines. However, there is no better match of frequency than this, so the 13.5 MHz value was chosen for the single sampling frequency.

As mentioned above, Rec. BT.601 provides not only for full sampling of RGB components, but 2:1 or 4:1 subsampling of color difference components, which is consistent with the lower bandwidths that are acceptable for color-difference components. The different system choices are described by a notation where the basic sampling frequency is referred to with a "4," 2:1 subsampling is a "2," and 4:1 subsampling is a "1." Thus, RGB sampling is called 4:4:4, 2:1 color-difference subsampling is 4:2:2, and 4:1 is 4:1:1. Another choice in this notation is 4:2:0, which refers to subsampling color differences by 2:1 both horizontally and vertically. This is not part of Rec. BT.601 but is often used in compressed video systems.

5.3.4 Composite Video Sampling

Although it does not avoid the distortions of analog composite signals, digitization of NTSC or PAL signals is widely used in video systems that are mostly analog. Since digital technology is the only practical way to perform tasks like time-base correction, frame storage, or image-manipulation effects in a composite analog system, these devices must incorporate ADC and DAC to fit in the system.

Many image-processing applications require that the digital signal be in component format, which means composite-digital signals must be decoded to component format before any of these processes. This is an awkward step, which can cause signal distortion. It is a major disadvantage of composite-digital systems. However, composite-digital systems are fine if the only thing done in the system is storing or recording of the signal.

It is generally desirable to synchronize the ADC with the color subcarrier of the composite signal. Because the subcarrier must be somewhat below the Nyquist limit, the reasonable choices are 3× and 4× subcarrier and 4× is generally preferred. Thus, for NTSC conversion, the frequency is 14.318 MHz, and for PAL it is 17.72 MHz. Synchronization is achieved by extracting the color burst from the composite signal and using a phase-lock loop to generate the sampling clock.

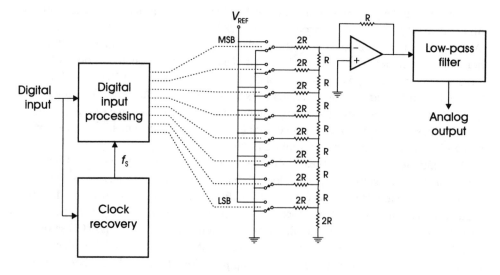

Figure 5.18 *The R-2R digital to analog converter.*

5.4 DIGITAL-TO-ANALOG CONVERSION

On first glance, DAC seems to be a simple process—reconstruct the samples as amplitude-modulated pulses and low-pass-filter them. It is simpler than ADC, but there are still some important considerations. Figure 5.18 shows a block diagram of a typical DAC design suitable for video. This structure is known as the *R-2R* architecture, for the two resistor values that are used.

The digital input is converted to a parallel format (if it is not already), and a stable data clock is extracted for reclocking the data to remove any jitter that may be present at the input. The input processing also includes a sample-and-hold circuit (see Section 5.2.1.5) for each bit. Each bit switches a node of the network from ground (0) to a reference voltage (1). When a switch is up (digital 1), a current flows that is divided down 2:1 by as many times as there are nodes between that switch and the input of the operational amplifier. For example, the LSB switch's current passes through seven nodes to get to the opamp, so it is divided by 128 (2^7). On the other hand, the MSB switch's current flows directly into the opamp, so it is not divided at all. Since the opamp input impedance is very low because of the feedback on it, currents from multiple switches that are up will sum linearly. Thus, the output current is

$$i_0 = \frac{V_{REF}}{2R}\left(\frac{bit0}{128} + \frac{bit1}{64} + \frac{bit2}{32} + \frac{bit3}{16} + \frac{bit4}{8} + \frac{bit5}{4} + \frac{bit6}{2} + bit7\right) \tag{5.7}$$

The output voltage from the opamp is i_0R. The resistors R and 2R must be very accurate to produce a linear conversion, and this limits this architecture to no more than 8 or 10 bits. For example, at 8 bits, one quantum level is 1/256 or 0.4%, and if the desired accuracy is

1/10 of a quantum level, an accuracy of 0.04% is required of the resistors. This is barely practical and DACs for higher numbers of bits require a different approach to achieve the accuracy requirements.

All the switches in this type of DAC can cause errors if there are transients (often called *glitches*) produced in the output waveform from the opamp due to the switching action. Many DACs perform a resampling process after the conversion to eliminate switching transients. This is called *deglitching*. The resampling is timed to start later than the switching in the converter but to end before the next switching period, so it occurs during a time when the output from the converter is at a stable value.

The output filter of a DAC running at f_S must meet the same requirements as the input filter of an ADC. If bandwidth is required close to the Nyquist limit, this filter is difficult to design and may be expensive.

The same technology that helps high-bit ADCs can help high-bit DACs—that is oversampling. In an oversampled DAC, the filtering requirements can be more readily met and the bit accuracy is easier to accomplish.

REFERENCE

1.   ITU-T Rec. G.711.

Chapter 6

Video Cameras

6.1 INTRODUCTION

The picture quality and artistic nature of a video production are largely determined at the time the pictures are captured using video cameras. This is true whether the camera is being used by a consumer in the home or in a professional production studio. Certain things can be changed or fixed later in postproduction, but the limits are still set at the time of production. The video camera has its own limits of performance and flexibility, which are the subject of this chapter.

To organize the discussion, a camera can be divided into functional areas that exist in all cameras. This is shown by Figure 6.1. A camera views a natural scene and must optically focus that into an image, much like a photographic camera. The subjects of light and optics are very important and will be considered first. This chapter assumes that all cameras have color capability, and the discussion of color theory that began in Section 2.4.1 will be continued here.

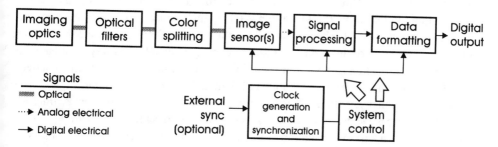

Figure 6.1 *Functional diagram of a video camera.*

Image sensors are the heart of any camera. Nearly all video cameras use solid-state charge-coupled device (CCD) sensors, which will be covered in depth. Since this book is about digital video technology, it assumes that all video cameras are digital. This is a trend that is not fully accomplished, but the statement will soon be true. Therefore, analog processing techniques will not be discussed, in order to give the maximum space to digital techniques

6.2 LIGHT AND OPTICS

The signal path of a video camera begins with an optical scene that is converted to an image by the camera optics. The camera transducer changes this optical image to a series of electronic images. This section discusses the aspects of optics that are important to cameras.

6.2.1 Illumination

The light falling on a scene and by which we (and cameras) are able to see the scene is called *illumination*. The reflecting properties of the various objects or surfaces in the scene modify the illumination and reflect back the light rays that actually reach our eyes and are perceived by the brain. Thus, the appearance of an object is a complex function of the illumination, the reflectance of the object, and the physical and psychophysical properties of human vision. The objective of a video camera is not to reproduce a scene exactly, but to reproduce it in a way that an observer viewing the video system's display will think he or she sees the same thing that would be seen when viewing the scene directly.

The most common natural illumination source is, of course, the sun, which radiates a broad spectrum of energy covering not only the visible spectrum but the entire range from infrared to ultraviolet. However, cameras must confine their response to only the visible range of illumination from 400- to 700-nm wavelength because the camera's response to light should match that of the eye to make the captured picture appear as a human observer would see it. Because of this, it is customary to express light values in ways that take the eye's *luminosity function* (see Section 2.4.4) into account. Many terms contain the letters "lum" to signify this; for example, luminance, lumen, luminosity, and so on.

There are also many artificial sources of illumination, such as incandescent or fluorescent lights. Figure 6.2 shows approximate spectral distributions for several sources. These also emit a broad spectrum of radiation so as to produce illumination that a human observer will see as white light. However, the eye tries to adapt to a source of broad-spectrum general illumination so that many different spectral distributions will appear as white to an observer (after adaptation, which may take a few seconds.)

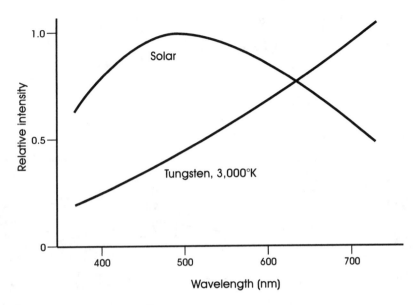

Figure 6.2 *Spectral distributions of illumination sources.*

6.2.1.1 White Balancing

A video camera does not have an adaptation characteristic like the eye does, and that capability must be provided in the camera electronics—it is called *white balancing*. In an RGB system, "white" corresponds to equality of the three component signals and, in a luminance-chrominance system, "white" corresponds to zero of both color-difference components. In either type of system, the "white" signal condition will produce a color on the display that a viewer will perceive as white under the specified viewing conditions *at the display*.

Ordinarily, the white balance of a display is also adjustable and it must be set so that the "white" signal condition will produce a color that a viewer perceives as white.

In setting up a video camera for white balance, the camera is pointed at an object that a viewer would see as white in the scene and the camera electronics are adjusted (either manually or automatically) to produce the "white" signal condition. By this process, the system will compensate for any viewer adaptation that might occur because the display viewing conditions are not the same as the viewing conditions at the original scene.

If the illumination at the camera changes during shooting, the camera white balancing procedure must be repeated, or the viewer may see different colors at the display.

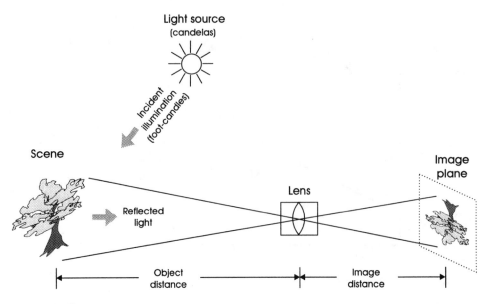

Figure 6.3 *Illumination.*

6.2.1.2 Quantification of Illumination

Figure 6.3 shows the situation of an object illuminated by a single source and viewed by a camera. The source, which could be the sun, emits light energy in all directions but only a portion of it falls on the scene. A source of light, such as the sun, can be characterized by its *energy density* (watts per square centimeter or other convenient unit) received at the scene, but it is more useful for illumination purposes to define a source by its *luminous intensity*, which accounts for the eye's spectral response. Since the intensity can vary with direction, it must be specified at the angle the scene makes with the source. This is accomplished by making observations by looking from the scene back at the light source.

Light is a flow of energy over time, so intensity is represented by the time rate of flow of light energy. The unit of flow of luminous energy is the *lumen,* and luminous intensity is expressed as lumens per unit solid angle. International standards exist that specify the lumen in terms of fundamental physical quantities.[*]

Since the energy in a given solid angle spreads out as one moves away from the source, the actual amount of energy falling on an area of the scene changes as the inverse square of the distance between light source and scene. Thus, it is still more meaningful to express the

---

[*] A light source emitting energy uniformly in all directions with an intensity of one *candela* emits one lumen per steradian (unit solid angle.) One candela is defined as the luminous intensity of 1/600,000 of one square meter of projected area of a blackbody radiator operating at the temperature of the solidification of platinum and at a pressure of 101,325 n/m^2.

light at the scene in terms of lumens per square meter (or other unit of area.) The unit *lux* has been defined for this purpose. One lux equals one lumen per square meter. An equivalent unit is the *foot-candle*, which is one lumen per square foot. The ratio between these two units is simply the ratio of a square meter to a square foot: For the same intensity, 1 lux = 10.76 foot-candles. Video camera sensitivity is usually expressed in terms of lux.

The brightness of a surface is the result of all the illumination falling on the surface and the reflectance of the surface. Because this is different from the illumination, it has its own unit of measurement, the *nit*, which is one candela per square meter.

6.2.2 Lenses

Geometrical optics is the science of propagation of light as rays. It articulates the properties of refraction and reflection that occur as light rays pass through or over different materials. Although this is the basis for the design of lenses, prisms, mirrors, and other optical components that may be used in video cameras, one can discuss the characteristics of these components without going deeply into geometrical optics. [1]

The lens is the optical element that focuses an optical image of the scene on the sensitive surface of the camera's sensor or sensors. The properties of lenses are discussed in this section.

6.2.2.1 Focal Length

Figure 6.3 shows that the distance from the scene to the lens (object distance) and the distance from the lens to the image (image distance) are geometrically related. However, the image will be in focus at only one point (or a small range of points) according to the equation

$$\frac{1}{S_O}+\frac{1}{S_I}=\frac{1}{F} \tag{6.1}$$

where

S_O = object distance
S_I = image distance
F = lens focal length

If the object distance is infinity, it can be seen that (6.1) reduces to $S_I = F$. Thus, the image distance equals the focal length for a scene at infinity. For a given size of the image plane, such as the size of a CCD's sensitive surface, focal length will determine the angle of view of the camera. Larger (longer) focal lengths will give smaller angles of view. A "normal" angle of view is about 50°, measured diagonally. Smaller angles of view are produced by *telephoto* lenses and larger angle of view are produced by *wide angle* lenses. For example, the normal focal length for a ½-in CCD would be about 12 mm.

Table 6.1

Speed versus f-numbers

f-number	2.0	3.0	4.0	5.6	8	11	16	22
Speed Ratio	128	64	32	16	8	4	2	1

6.2.2.2 Aperture

The light-collecting ability of a lens depends on its effective diameter (*aperture*[*]). Most lenses contain an iris mechanism that allows adjustment of the aperture. Aperture values are defined in terms of the ratio of the focal length to the diameter of the aperture. This is called the *f-number*. For example, a lens of 12 mm focal length with an f-number of f/4.0, has an aperture diameter of 3 mm. Larger f-numbers mean smaller apertures and thus less light-collecting ability. Since light-collecting ability depends on the *area* of the aperture, it changes as the inverse *square* of the f-number. The f-numbers are often referred to as *f-stops* or just *stops*. A stop is an f-number ratio of ($\sqrt{2}$ 1.4) and represents a change of 2:1 in light intensity through the lens. Table 6.1 shows typical f-stops and the light intensity ratios they represent with f/22 taken as 1.0. For convenience, some of the f-numbers are rounded off.

The *speed* of a lens can be defined by its ability to deliver luminous flux at the image plane. Speed is an inverse-square function of the f-number and is independent of focal length.

6.2.2.3 Depth of Field

For a given distance from the lens to the scene, there is a specific image plane where the image is focused at a distance behind the lens according to (6.1). Points in the scene closer or farther from the lens are progressively more out of focus at the image plane. This is shown in Figure 6.4. The point P is beyond the focused plane in the scene and would therefore be focused in the image plane closer to the lens as shown at P'. The diameter of the bundle of light rays from P as it passes through the focused plane is known as the *circle of confusion* (c-of-c) and represents the degree (relative to the scene) of defocusing of P at the image plane. It can be seen that the size of the c-of-c is a function of the lens aperture A, the object distance So and the distance D_1.

The significance of the c-of-c depends on how the resulting image will be used. For example, in a CCD camera, no defocusing is observable until the c-of-c diameter exceeds one

---

[*] The word "aperture" has a different meaning in the context of scanning (see Section 2.3.3). The scanning aperture of a CCD is usually taken as the size of one cell.

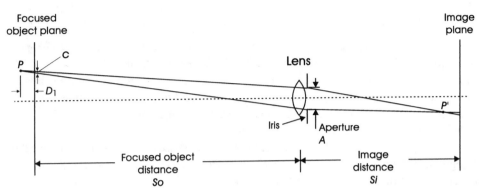

Figure 6.4 *Depth of field.*

pixel in size. Therefore, the depth of field represents the distance in the scene within which the c-of-c remains less than the size of one pixel projected into the scene. Using the geometry of Figure 6.4, the projected size c of one pixel in an image plane of height H and having L scan lines is

$$c = \frac{HS_0}{LS_1} \tag{6.2}$$

If we assume $D_1 \ll S_0$, the similar triangles give

$$\frac{c}{D_1} = \frac{A}{S_0} \tag{6.3}$$

eliminating c and solving for D_1

$$D_1 = \frac{S_0^2 H}{ALS_1} \tag{6.4}$$

S_1 can be eliminated using (6.1)

$$D_1 = \frac{S_0 H(S_0 - F)}{ALF} \tag{6.5}$$

A can be replaced by the f-number (F/f) and expressing D_1 as a percentage of S_0

$$D_1 = 100 \frac{S_0 f H(S_0 - F)}{LF^2} \tag{6.6}$$

finally, we can assume $S_0 \gg F$ and observe that $H/2F$ is the tangent of half the angular field of view q

$$D_1 = 200 \frac{f \, S_O}{FL} \tan(\frac{q}{2})$$

(6.7)

Equation (6.7) shows that depth of field increases with smaller apertures (higher f-numbers.) For the same f-number, depth of field increases with greater field of view, which implies shorter focal lengths. Also, depth of field reduces as the resolution of the image sensor increases because the pixels are smaller. Notice also that the depth of field increases with greater object distance (S_O), which means that to obtain the greatest depth of field, one will focus slightly behind the closest foreground object.

Great depth of field is not always desirable. In many cases, it is more pleasing for the foreground to be in good focus but the background to be out of focus. This helps the viewer concentrate on the object of interest and not be distracted by the background.

6.2.2.4 Aberrations

Imaging by a lens is not perfect, especially as the point of interest moves off-axis (away from the center.) Imaging distortions are called *aberrations* and fall into at least four classes—geometric, focus, color, and intensity. In general, aberrations increase with aperture size and with angular field of view.

Geometric aberration usually takes the form of magnification that depends on the view angle, which causes the corners of the image to be either compressed (barrel) or enlarged (pincushion) geometrically.

Focus aberrations are spherical, astigmatism, coma, and curvature of field. Spherical aberration is caused by the rays passing through the edges of the lens focusing closer than the rays going through the lens nearer the axis. Astigmatism is where the lens cannot focus to a sharp point but goes from an ellipse in one direction to a perpendicular ellipse as focus is adjusted. Coma is similar to spherical aberration in that the off-axis rays do not focus at the same place as on-axis rays. Curvature of field is where the plane of best focus is not a plan but a curved surface.

Color aberrations result when the lens behavior varies with wavelength. There are several types but the result is the same: different colors do not focus at the same points.

Intensity aberration is variation of the image intensity with view angle. It is sometimes called *vignetting*.

The challenge of lens design is to minimize aberrations while maintaining a large aperture. By using structures of multiple lens elements, many of the aberrations can be corrected.

Another form of lens problem is loss of contrast in the lens due to internal reflections that become part of the image. Although technically not an aberration, loss of contrast and internal reflection is an important lens performance parameter.

6.2.2.5 Resolution

The fundamental limit of lens resolution is caused by diffraction in the aperture of the lens, which becomes worse as the aperture size is made smaller. However, this limit is seldom significant in video lens applications and resolution performance is mostly determined by aberrations. Since CCD cameras will have aliasing if the optical image becomes too sharp (see Section 5.2.1), it is desirable for lens resolution to be somewhat limited anyway.

6.2.2.6 Zoom Lenses

The preceding discussion dealt primarily with the properties of fixed focal-length lenses, but nearly all modern video cameras have variable-length (zoom) lenses. Zooming a lens involves a lens system having a number of optical elements that are mechanically moved with respect to one another to achieve variable focal length. These designs can become extremely complex, involving 10 to 20 lens elements and several different mechanical motions. Some zoom lenses are adjusted mechanically by turning a ring on the lens, but most have some form of motor drive so that zooming can be controlled remotely and zoom speeds can be preprogrammed. A complete discussion of zoom lens design is beyond the scope of this book.

The most important parameter of a zoom lens is its *zoom ratio*, which is the ratio of the highest to the lowest focal length. Most video cameras have optical zoom ratios from about 6× to 15× although some lenses go up to 40× or more. Higher zoom ratios are accomplished electronically in some cameras, although this usually involves a trade off on resolution (see Section 6.6.3.2). In professional video lenses, the specification of minimum focal length and zoom ratio is combined. For example, a lens with a 12× zoom ratio that can zoom from 6.5 to 78 mm focal length would be referred to as a 12×6.5 lens.

6.2.3 Optical Filters

Filters are used to modify light intensity independent of wavelength (monochrome or *neutral-density*) or to modify the intensity according to wavelength (color). They can be constructed using materials that absorb light or by structures involving reflection or refraction.

6.2.3.1 Absorptive Filters

The light level over which a camera must operate has a range of 10,000 to 1 or more. This range cannot be accommodated by adjustment of lens aperture only, and that must be supplemented by other means of light adjustment. For example, Table 6.1 shows that the range covered by a lens that adjusts from f/2.0 to f/22 is only 128:1. Some adjustment at the low-light end is accomplished by adjustment of camera signal gain, maybe as much as 30

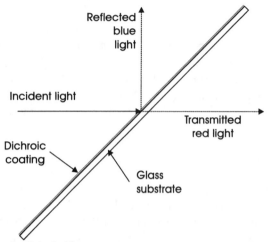

Figure 6.5 *Operation of a dichroic filter.*

dB (32:1), which is not enough for the necessary 10,000 range, and it means that at high light levels, the camera always operates with the lens nearly fully stopped down to f/22. That does not allow the lens aperture to be used for depth-of-field control (see Section 6.2.2.3). Therefore, cameras also have neutral-density (ND) filters. Professional cameras usually have a filter wheel that allows a choice of ND filtering (and sometimes other filters as well). ND filters are specified by the $\log_{10}$ of the reciprocal of their transmission factor. For example, adding an ND 1.0 (0.1 transmission) filter in the optical path will allow the lens to be opened up by about 3½ stops. Most cameras also have an ND 2.0 (0.01 transmission) filter.

Color-absorptive filters are created from optical materials that have a selective absorption of different wavelengths. Some cameras have one or more color filters intended to accomplish approximate white balancing for different illuminations. Although white balancing may be accomplished entirely by adjustment of signal levels, it is sometimes desirable to use a filter for approximate balancing so that light levels falling on the CCDs do not get too unequal with different illumination types.

Another use of absorptive color filters is for *trimming* the camera colorimetry (see Section 6.3). Because absorptive filters inherently cause some loss of light energy, they are not the best choice for the color filtering needed to establish camera colorimetry.

6.2.3.2 Reflective and Refractive Filters

Much of a camera's colorimetric filtering can be accomplished by the use of reflective and refractive techniques that divide the light without any absorption loss. An example of this is illustrated in Figure 6.5, which shows a *dichroic* reflective filter. The dichroic reflector uses a two-layer coating that has a ¼-wavelength thickness at the wavelength of color separation desired. The filter can be designed to reflect wavelengths either above or below the critical frequency, but not both at the same time.

6.2.4 Color Splitters

The dichroic technique described in the previous section is used for color separation in cameras that employ separate sensors for the R, G, and B primary colors. Although this can be done with dichroic mirrors of the type shown in Figure 6.5, a better design uses a cemented prism composed of three or more glass blocks as shown in Figure 6.6. The advantage of this is that the dichroic surfaces, which are very fragile, are contained within the prism, and the cemented glass pieces establish very precise and stable positioning of the optical elements.

The prism contains two dichroic surfaces for reflecting blue and red light; light not reflected at either surface passes on to the green sensor. Air gaps in the prism provide for total reflection at two surfaces to direct the blue and red light to their appropriate sensors. From the spectral response curves in Figure 6.6, it can be seen that the green channel response (see Section 6.3) is well approximated by the prism response but the blue and red require trim filters between the prism and the imagers to reduce their response at the edge of the visual range.

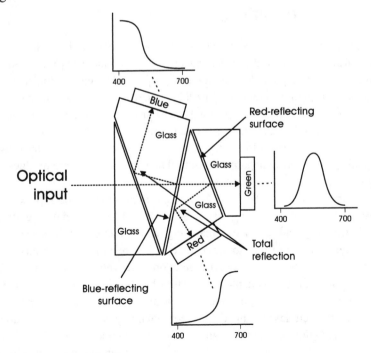

Figure 6.6 Prism optics for a color camera.

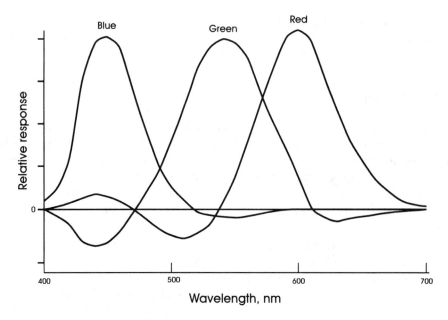

Figure 6.7 *NTSC color camera taking curves.*

6.3 CAMERA COLORIMETRY

The red, green, and blue signal components in a color camera are obtained by providing the proper spectral responses in the optical channels for the image sensors. Color video systems have standard response curves for this purpose. The curves for NTSC color TV (called *taking curves*) are shown in Figure 6.7. Notice that each color channel has a peak of response at the wavelength that corresponds to the primary color for that channel but notice also that the curves often go negative at other wavelengths. These *negative lobes* are important in obtaining correct colorimetry, but they cannot be produced by the sensors, which are incapable of delivering negative outputs. The negative lobes are produced electronically by a process called *masking* (see Section 6.3.1).

The primary objective of the optical filtering is to provide a good approximation to the positive lobes of the camera taking curves. Secondary objectives relate to getting the highest optical efficiency and reasonably matching the light levels on the sensors.

Further considerations relate to the accuracy of the resulting colorimetry. Small colorimetric errors in a video camera are difficult to observe when the camera signal is viewed by itself because of the eye's adaptation, but they become important in the situation where several cameras will be used together in the same program. This requirement is called *camera matching* and includes not only colorimetry but many other camera operating parameters. Professional cameras include many features to provide accurate colorimetry and to allow adjustment of the most important parameters for camera matching. Home cameras are seldom used in multicamera systems, so matching of home cameras is not an important consideration.

6.3.1 Masking

The trichromatic theory (see Section 2.4) states that any color can be reproduced by the appropriate combination of three primary colors, so it follows that primary colors can be modified by the same process. This is called *masking* and consists of a linear mixing according to equations of the following form:

$$E_{RM} = k_1 E_R + k_2 E_G + k_3 E_B \qquad (6.8)$$

$$E_{GM} = k_4 E_R + k_5 E_G + k_6 E_B \qquad (6.9)$$

$$E_{BM} = k_7 E_R + k_8 E_G + k_9 E_B \qquad (6.10)$$

where the coefficients k_n can be positive or negative. By this means, the camera primaries could be of any form, and masking could be applied to convert to the standard primaries at the output. However, masking often involves negative coefficients (required, for example, to achieve the negative lobes), which means signal subtraction. Small amounts of this are acceptable, but random noise always adds, whether the signals are added or subtracted, and severe masking will result in SNR degradation. This can happen if the optical spectral response is too different from the desired response and therefore requires too much correction.

Masking can be used to assist in matching camera colorimetry between cameras, but it is a difficult process that is impractical to perform manually because there is not a simple relationship between the coefficient values and the observable behavior in the picture. For this reason, most cameras have fixed masking used only to correct their primaries. In film-to-video cameras (see Section 6.7), there is an important need for adjustments to deal with color variations in film. A technique similar to masking, called *color correction*, is used for that purpose.

6.4 CAMERA SENSORS

Video camera sensor technology has a long history that goes back to the early twentieth century. That will not be covered here, but there are many references that do it justice [2]. Since nearly all modern cameras use CCD sensors, this section will cover them exclusively.

A camera sensor has to perform two tasks: (1) convert an optical image to an electronic image and (2) scan the electronic image and deliver an electrical (video) signal. Therefore, it is a transducer between an optical image and a scanned video signal.

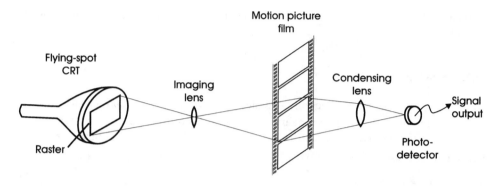

Figure 6.8 *Principle of a flying-spot camera.*

6.4.1 The Storage Principle

It is possible to scan an optical image directly by either mechanical or electronic means without first creating an electronic image. An electronic method of doing this is called a *flying-spot scanner* and it is sometimes used for video scanning of motion picture film (see Section 6.7).

In a flying-spot scanner (see Figure 6.8), the scanning raster from a CRT is focused on the film to be scanned and a high-sensitivity photodetector is arranged to collect the light that passes through the film. For color pickup, light splitting as described in Section 6.2.4 is used with three photodetectors. This is an instantaneous process where the light from the scanning spot is continuously collected as the spot scans over the frame. A very-high-intensity spot is required to obtain good SNR, and the technique is practical only for scanning a small area such as a film frame.

There is a major advantage to forming an electronic image before scanning, which is that the light coming from the optical image can be *integrated* in the form of electric charge over the entire time of a scanning frame. This is often called *storage* imaging. The process is not instantaneous—the electronic image builds up during the frame time and is read out as a video signal as the scanning means passes over each part of the electronic image. The result is a massive increase in sensitivity of the sensor, corresponding approximately to the number of pixels in the final image. For example, if scanning is performed using 640 × 480 pixels, the sensitivity is increased 307,200 times compared with that of an instantaneous scanning method at the same resolution. The development of storage-type image sensors was one of the breakthroughs that made electronic television practical.

6.4.2 Charge-Coupled Devices

The CCD is an integrated circuit device that performs the two steps of image sensing: storage and readout (scanning). It is based on a two-dimensional array of cells that may be thought of as pixels. Although is it not necessary that the CCD array match the final pixel format of the digital video signal, it may be convenient to do so. Each cell of a CCD array has two modes: (1) a storage mode where electric charge accumulates in the cell according to the light falling on the light-sensitive area of the cell and (2) a transfer mode where the charge in the cell can move to an adjacent cell, either horizontally or vertically according to the cell construction. The transfer mode of a whole line of cells or even of a two-dimensional array of cells can be operated together to accomplish the step-by-step transfer of the charge contents of lines of cells, rows of cells, or the entire charge image.

Most CCDs contain two arrays of cells: an *imaging area* where the optical image is focused and a *readout area* that is shielded from light. The transfer mode is used to move the electronic image from the imaging area to the readout area, usually during the vertical blanking period. During active picture time, the imaging area is placed into the storage mode and the readout area uses the transfer mode to move the parts of the charge image to a signal output port.

6.4.3 CCD Architectures

CCD architectures differ based on how the imaging and readout areas are arranged and how the transfer takes place. Figure 6.9 shows the three major architectures and how they work. There are also variations on the basic architectures that are not discussed here.

6.4.3.1 Frame Transfer Architecture

Figure 6.9(a) is the *frame transfer* (FT) architecture. The imaging area is placed above an identical readout area, which is masked so that light will not fall on it. (This explanation assumes that the optical image is upside down on the imaging area.) Storage takes place in the imaging area during active picture time. During the vertical blanking interval, the entire storage area is transferred vertically into the readout area. The cells of each line are transferred down simultaneously by one line and this process is repeated for each line of the image. If the image has 480 lines, there will be 480 transfers during one vertical interval.

During horizontal-blanking intervals that occur outside of the vertical blanking interval, one line at a time in the readout area is transferred vertically into a one-line horizontal readout array. (Notice that this requires transferring *all* the lines down each time.) During active line time, the horizontal array is clocked to transfer pixels to the right, delivering the video signal.

Because the charge accumulation in the imaging area cannot be stopped during the transfer to the readout area, and the transferring takes a finite amount of time (about 1 ms), a *transfer smear* effect occurs and is visible as a vertical trail above and below highlight areas of the picture. A mechanical shutter is required in the optical system of an FT CCD to

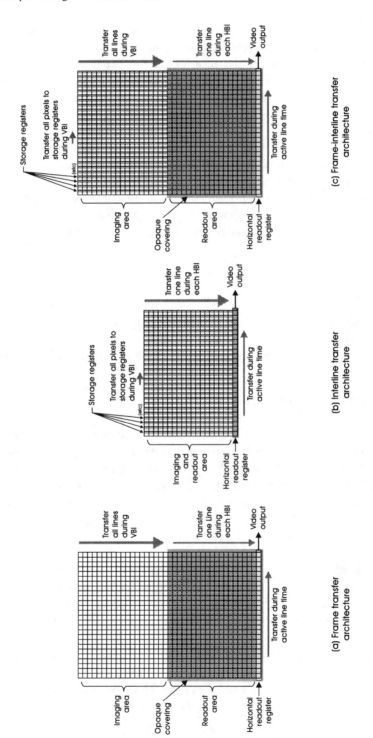

Figure 6.9 CCD architectures

eliminate transfer smear. Because of this, FT imagers are seldom used in high-performance video cameras.

6.4.3.2 Interline Transfer Architecture

Figure 6.9(b) shows the *interline transfer* (IT) architecture. This design interleaves the imaging and readout arrays horizontally next to each other on a pixel basis, resulting in a somewhat smaller chip size than that of the FT architecture. The optical image is focused on this entire area. The readout cells must be optically masked, and light from the image falling on these areas will be lost, reducing sensitivity. In some IT CCDs, a *microlens* array is placed over the CCD cells so that all the light hitting a cell is directed to the sensitive area, thus restoring the light sensitivity. The microlens is an expensive approach, but it does solve the problem.

Storage in an IT CCD occurs all the time but during the vertical blanking interval, the charge in all cells is transferred horizontally to the readout array. During horizontal blanking intervals, the readout array is shifted down by one line to deliver one line to the horizontal readout array that is then clocked during active line time, delivering the video signal.

An IT CCD does not require a mechanical shutter to eliminate transfer smear, but it does have a similar highlight problem because the optical masking of the interleaved readout cells cannot be perfect. This can cause vertical line artifact to appear on image highlights.

6.4.3.3 Frame-Interline Transfer Architecture

Figure 6.9(c) shows the *frame-interline transfer* (FIT) architecture, which combines the features of both FT and IT architectures. During vertical blanking, the entire image is transferred into the interleaved transfer registers and then further transferred down to the readout array. During active picture time, readout occurs in the same manner as the FT architecture. Since all transfers out of the imaging array occur in a small percentage of the time (vertical blanking) and occur in the optically masked registers, there is no need for a shutter to eliminate transfer smear nor any problem with highlights. This is the preferred architecture for professional cameras.

6.4.4 Interlaced Scanning in CCDs

The discussion of architectures above has assumed progressive scanning of the CCDs. If the CCD has a line of cells for every line of the interlaced picture, a FIT CCD can be clocked to transfer only the odd or even lines into the vertical-transfer registers and therefore produce an interlaced output for which the image integration time is a full frame time for every pixel. This provides high sensitivity and also means that the readout array only needs to hold half of the total lines. However, this method has the normal interlacing artifacts on fast motion and vertical aliasing will show up on sharp horizontal edges unless optical filtering is used.

It is also possible to operate the CCD in progressive-scan mode at the field rate and digitally process the signal to an interlaced form. There are two approaches. One is to drop every other line at the output of the CCD and expand the remaining lines to the correct timing using a line memory. This is fairly simple, but it essentially throws away half the signal and therefore causes loss of SNR.

The second approach is to digitally store two lines from the CCD and combine two adjacent lines to produce an interlaced signal. This achieves an SNR advantage but causes some loss of vertical resolution; at the same time, this improves aliasing in the same way that oversampling does (see Section 5.3.1). Motion artifacts are improved in this method because the exposure time is shortened by 2:1 compared with that of direct interlacing. Both methods of using progressive scan in the CCD require that the horizontal registers of the CCD operate at twice the speed required for direct interlacing.

6.4.5 CCD MTF

Because a CCD is a sampling device with a finite sampling width in each direction (the width and height of the sensitive area of a pixel), there is an MTF loss due to the sampling (see Section 5.2.1.4). The frame transfer architecture, which has most of the pixel area devoted to sensitivity, comes close to the $W = 100$ condition in each direction and thus will have nearly 3-dB MTF loss at the Nyquist frequency. However, the interline-transfer structures may have better horizontal MTF just because the sensitive area is reduced in that direction. When microlenses are used to increase the sensitivity of interline-transfer CCDs, the effective sampling width is also increased, bringing the device back to the $W = 100$ condition.

There can be other MTF losses in CCDs due to charge spreading or transfer losses. Although these were important limitations in early CCDs, they have been pretty much eliminated in modern devices.

Another MTF loss factor in CCD cameras is caused by the need for an optical low-pass filter to reduce aliasing due to sampling. None of these losses is large enough to cause any problem and, if necessary, they can be corrected in the camera signal processing.

6.4.6 Spatial Offset

The inherent sampling by the cell structure of a CCD will limit the device's maximum resolution. This creates a demand for a large number of cells in a device and the more cells, the more cost due to larger silicon area and smaller production yield. Improved resolution can be obtained by combining the outputs from two CCDs that have their optical images offset horizontally by one-half the pixel width. This is shown in Figure 6.10. The CCDs in the figure are IT or FIT types, and the reproduction shows a full-width pixel being

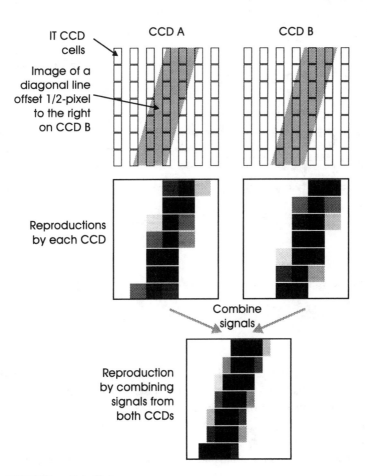

IT CCD cells

Image of a diagonal line offset 1/2-pixel to the right on CCD B

CCD A

CCD B

Reproductions by each CCD

Combine signals

Reproduction by combining signals from both CCDs

Figure 6.10 *CCD spatial offset.*

produced from the intensity value of the half-width sensitive area. By combining signals 50/50 with a delay between them equal to a half-pixel period, a double-resolution reproduction is obtained.

In most three-CCD cameras, spatial offset is accomplished by shifting the red and blue devices horizontally by half a pixel width compared with the green device. Since the luminance signal combines 59% of green with 41% of red and blue, the effect (for the luminance) is approximately that of sampling at twice the spatial frequency of one CCD. Because the signal combination is 59/41 instead of 50/50, there will be some output at the double-sampling frequency and the luminance bandwidth must cut off before this frequency. However something like a 50% improvement in resolution is still achievable without serious aliasing.

With interline-transfer CCDs, where the sensitive area of a pixel is 50% of the width or less, there is no overlap of the effective pixels when offset. The result is that the MTF

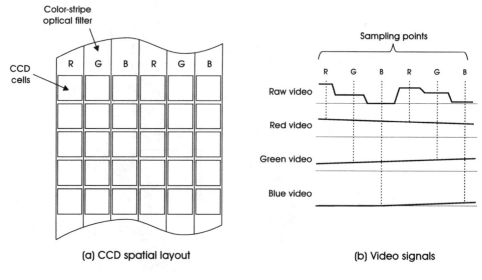

(a) CCD spatial layout   *(b) Video signals*

Figure 6.11 *Single-CCD color camera.*

corresponds to $W = 100$ at the half-pixel width. However, if microlenses are used to in-crease sensitivity, the offset pixels now overlap and the MTF loss at the half-pixel fre-quency would correspond to approximately $W = 200$, meaning that the MTF would go to zero at the half-pixel Nyquist frequency. Since the response must be cut off there anyway, this is not too serious.

For HDTV, resolution is at a premium and some cameras have been designed with four CCDs so that two CCDs can be devoted to the green channel. This eliminates the 59/41 compromise and the full 2× resolution improvement can be realized for green. It is said that the cost savings of using lower resolution CCDs in an HDTV camera is more than the extra cost of the fourth chip and its optics.

The offset technique depends critically on the physical positioning of the CCDs relative to the optical path. The resolution and aliasing improvement deteriorates rapidly as the de-vices shift from their optimal position.

6.4.7 Single-Sensor Camera

The discussion so far has been based on RGB cameras having one CCD for each color. This type of camera dominates in the professional fields but is too expensive for the home and semiprofessional markets because of the cost of optical light-splitting and three CCDs. Single-CCD cameras have been developed for these markets. The basic approach is shown in Figure 6.11.

A color-stripe optical filter is placed over the cells of the CCD so that adjacent cells respond to different colors (Figure 6.11(a)). In the signal-processing electronics, RGB colors are retrieved by sampling the video signal at three phases as shown in Figure 6.11(b). The rest of the camera processing can then proceed the same as a three-CCD camera.

The approach shown in the figure gives one-third of the pixels to each primary color, reducing the resolution per channel by a factor of three. This can be improved by providing half the pixels for green and then assigning the remaining pixels alternately to red or blue. This complicates the signal retrieval but improves the green resolution to one-half the bare CCD resolution.

6.4.8 CCD Signal-to-Noise Ratio

The noise component in a CCD imager comes mostly from the shot noise of the electronic image. Signal levels out of the chip are high enough that thermal noise in amplifier circuits is not an issue. SNR performance of a CCD depends on the area of a pixel—the larger the better. However, larger pixels require a larger chip, larger optics, and more light, all of which mean higher cost of chip and camera. Actual CCD chip designs are thus a tradeoff between pixel size, number of pixels, chip size, and cost.

Another factor in the design is consideration of dynamic range, which is the ratio between the highest possible output from the CCD and the noise level. Normally, the maximum operating signal level (peak white) is set considerably below the saturation point of the CCD itself, leaving the top end of the dynamic range for highlight protection. This is done to avoid CCD saturation on highlights as much as possible because there can be spurious effects such as spreading, blooming, or tailing when the CCD is overloaded with a highlight. It also makes possible deliberate overexposure of some parts of the scene without concern for any spurious effects beyond the fundamental effect of overexposure.

In professional cameras, it is common to allow for protection of highlights that go 600% over peak white; this represents 15.6 dB of the dynamic range [3]. The camera signal processing compresses any highlights that go into the protection region according to an algorithm that suits the end use of the camera (see Section 6.5.2). CCD dynamic range can approach 80 dB and, for 525-line or 625-line cameras, SNRs of 60 dB are possible and for HDTV, SNR can be about 52 dB.

6.5 DIGITAL CAMERA SIGNAL PROCESSING

The signal output from a CCD device is sampled by the pixel and line structure of the CCD but is analog in amplitude. An ideal "digital" camera will linearly amplify the CCD video signal up to a level suitable for ADC, convert, and then proceed in the digital domain. Any signal manipulation or nonlinear processing will be avoided in the analog domain for reasons of stability and performance. However, camera designers are not always rigorously holding to this philosophy, and some of today's "digital" cameras still have some analog

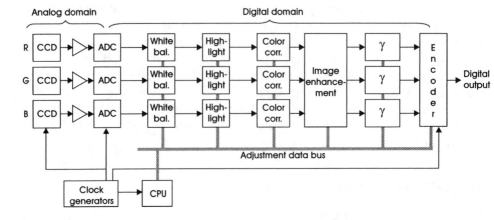

Figure 6.12 *Block diagram of signal processing for a typical digital camera.*

processing. In the discussion below, it is assumed that this is not the case and all processing is digital.

Figure 6.12 is a simplified block diagram of the signal processing in an all-digital RGB camera. The sequence of processes shown in the figure is one possibility but it may differ in some camera designs.

6.5.1 ADC Considerations

The two ingredients of ADC are *sampling* and *quantizing*. The pixel structure of the CCD has already performed the time sampling process, and the video signal flows smoothly from one pixel value to the next. But the quantization process still must be done on the signal. This requires resampling of the video waveform at the pixel frequency to extract stable pixel values from the smoothly changing analog signal. Such a process of sampling the pixel values was shown in Figure 6.11 where it was used to extract the R, G, and B components from a single-CCD camera. However, for complete digitization, this must be followed by quantizing.

As was discussed in Section 5.2.2 and shown by (5.3), quantizing introduces its own component of noise. For quantizing noise to not degrade the camera SNR, the number of bits of quantizing should be set high enough that quantizing noise is 6 dB or more below the analog noise level of the CCD. For example, if the full CCD dynamic range is to be digitized so that digital highlight compression of 600% can be done and the CCD SNR is 60 dB, the quantizing SNR should be

$$SNR = 60 + 15.6 + 6 = 81.6 \text{ dB} \tag{6.11}$$

or higher. Using (5.3), this requires linear 12-bit quantizing. Even after processing, if the 60 dB CCD SNR is to be preserved, quantizing SNR should be 60 + 6 = 66 dB or higher. This requires at least 9-bit quantizing at the camera output. This is the reason that ITU Rec. BT.601 provides a 10-bit quantizing option.

Another important ADC consideration is the clamping (see Section 5.2.2.2) of the video signal going into the ADC to maintain black-level stability of the camera. Any black-level instability at the ADC will become part of the digital signal and may be difficult to correct later.

6.5.2 Highlight Compression

In Section 6.4.8, it was pointed out that professional cameras allow up to 600% highlight overload to occur before the CCD saturation limit is reached and that this must be handled by the signal electronics. The usual approach for highlight compression is to provide a transfer characteristic that is linear up to the 100% level and then breaks to a lower slope that is adjustable to compress actual highlights to fit within the overload capability of the recorder, transmission, or display equipment. This is shown in Figure 6.13.

Highlight compression should be done early in the signal chain so that most of the processing will not have to handle highlights. However, it must be done at a point where signals have been color balanced and level standardized or there will be color effects introduced

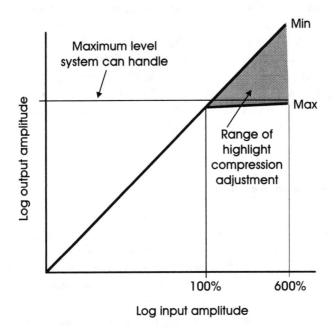

Figure 6.13 *Highlight compression.*

by the highlight compression. This is accommodated in Figure 6.12 by the white balance circuits being the first operation in the signal chain. White balance is accomplished by multiplying the signal by constants that are determined at the time of white balancing. This can be done with a lookup table consisting of a digital RAM memory that holds the output values for every possible input value. In operation, the input signal is used to address into the lookup table memory and the appropriate value is read for the output signal. It is a fast, stable, and economical approach for gain control or nonlinear operations such as gamma (see Section 6.5.5).

With 12-bit samples, the lookup table memory must hold 4,096 12-bit values for each of the three color channels. During the white balance procedure, the system CPU calculates the points for the gain values and iterates until balance is obtained. Then the constant values remain in the white balance RAM until another white balancing procedure is invoked.

The same RAM memory lookup approach is used to modify the transfer characteristic for highlight compression. It would be possible to perform both white balance and highlight compression in the same lookup table; that just means the computer has to calculate the proper combinations of values when either function is adjusted.

6.5.3 Digital Color Correction

Color correction has two purposes: (1) to perform masking to trim the camera colorimetry to standard and (2) to make other adjustments of color for artistic purposes. Many cameras employ color correction only for colorimetry and do not provide means for other adjustment. However, adjustable color correction is a feature that is widely used in film-to-video cameras to correct for color variations of the film. In any case, color correction is done by linear mixing of the signals in a matrix as described in Section 6.3.1. Again, multiplication is by constants and can use lookup tables, but signal addition also is required to combine the three components needed in each channel. The computer is very important to the control of this process. Adjustment of color correction in an RGB system may affect color balance, unless the computer calculates the coefficient changes appropriately to maintain balance.

6.5.4 Digital Image Enhancement

Image enhancement features of cameras range from aperture correction to noise reduction and special processing of flesh tones. The aperture response (MTF) of a CCD camera is determined primarily by the number of pixels and the sampling width. CCDs often approach the $W = 100$ sampling width condition both horizontally and vertically, and this can be corrected with a digital filter (see Section 8.3.2) of appropriate characteristics. However, much more processing is done, both linear and nonlinear, to achieve a flexible image enhancement capability. A block diagram of one type of camera image-enhancement processor is shown in Figure 6.14.

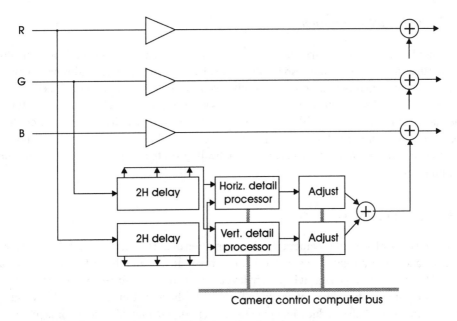

Figure 6.14 *Block diagram of one type of digital image enhancement system.*

Two "detail" signals are developed from the contents of the red and green channels, using tapped digital delays of two line periods. Detail signals are created both horizontally and vertically. The detail signals can be adjusted for their frequency content, amplitude, and nonlinear characteristics. The latter can, for example, reduce the correction signals at low levels to avoid enhancement of noise and clip the correction signals at high levels to prevent overshoots on high-amplitude transitions in the video. After adjustment, the detail signals are added back into all three color channels to introduce the enhancements.

6.5.5 Digital Gamma Correction

The video amplitude transfer characteristic of a CCD is strictly linear over most of the dynamic range but, as explained in Section 2.2.2, this usually must be modified for gamma correction. Gamma is easily introduced digitally by the use of a RAM lookup table as was described in Section 6.5.2.

Adjustment of the gamma characteristic is done by changing the values held in the memory. A camera that provides for manual adjustment of gamma must use writeable gamma memory and have a means to reload the memory from other permanent storage or from computed values.

6.5.5.1 Contrast Compression

It is possible that the scene may have a contrast ratio between bright and dark areas that is higher than the video system (especially the display) can reproduce. Additional gamma correction can help this situation. This is called *contrast compression*. Some cameras have separate circuits for this purpose, but nearly the same effect can be achieved by modifying the main gamma circuits. With computer control, the operator can have a separate control for contrast compression but the computer will calculate the correct curve that combines gamma and contrast compression and automatically load the proper coefficients into the gamma memories.

6.5.6 Exposure Control

Exposure control in a video camera involves operation of the lens iris, neutral-density filter wheels, and, at low-light levels, video-gain increase. Increasing the video gain causes a loss of SNR, so it is only used at low-light levels where the iris is already wide open and all filters are removed from the optical path. Because of the reduction of SNR at high gains, many cameras will also reduce image enhancement or even unenhance the image under these conditions.

The exposure functions are adjusted to maintain the proper video output level from the camera. This can be done either manually or automatically. In the automatic case, video level is sensed in the signal processing chain and a computer decides what adjustments to make. There are various algorithms used for this purpose, principally to achieve good response under conditions where the light levels may be changing rapidly or the camera is panned from highlights to dark areas or the reverse. Because even with the best algorithms the automatic behavior may not be what is desired, most cameras provide for turning off the automatic exposure control.

Automatic exposure control is an important feature in home cameras but is less important in other markets. In professional studio operations where lighting is controlled, automatic exposure would almost never be used.

6.5.7 Automatic Focusing

Home cameras and some others provide automatic focusing, where the camera monitors an area in the scene and adjusts the lens to keep that area in focus. Focus sensing is usually based on looking for high-frequency detail in the area being monitored—this component will maximize when the image is in best focus. A maximizing feedback loop involves some sort of dithering so as to sense the point where the high-frequency energy reduces on either side of the present setting. This point is the maximum; at all other points, the high frequencies will increase on one side and reduce on the other side of the present point.

There are some limitations to the sensing of high-frequency energy for a focus servo because the scene may not always have enough of such energy to operate the automatic focusing. In this case, the focus servo may slew back and forth and will not stabilize anywhere. Such considerations make the design of an automatic-focusing system tricky.

6.5.8 Encoding in Cameras

The encoding section of a camera converts its internal signal format to the external signal format of the system that the camera will be used in, or it may convert the internal format to the format of the video recorder connected to the camera. Many cameras will be used in NTSC or PAL analog composite video systems—their encoders convert the digital signals of the camera to standard composite video. In other cases, encoding may be digital for feeding a digital transmission circuit or a digital video recorder. There is nothing special about the camera in this regard and the format conversions are done the same way they might be done anywhere in a system.

6.6 CAMERA PACKAGING

Camera designs range from the familiar home camcorder to the professional studio system camera with full remote control over distances measured in miles. The fundamentals of camera technology covered above apply to all these cameras but differ greatly in implementation. Most differences can be covered by considering only two classes of camera: the system camera, which operates in a real-time system with other cameras and signal sources, and the portable or standalone camera, which operates by itself.

6.6.1 System Cameras

The governing application of a system camera occurs when the camera's output will be switched, mixed, or otherwise integrated in real time with other signal sources. This gives rise to requirements for synchronization and matching. System cameras are usually designed to be mounted on a tripod or pedestal, although that is not a fundamental requirement and hand-held system cameras also exist.

Another feature of system cameras is that they often provide for the separation of the artistic and technical aspects of camera operation. This requires remote control features where a camera cable connects a camera head to a base unit. The person who operates the camera head is the cameraperson, and he or she is responsible for the artistic aspects of camera positioning, image framing, and camera motion. There is one person per camera head, and he or she concentrates on the artistic aspects and is not concerned with technical matters.

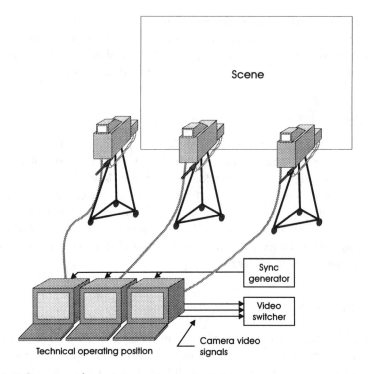

Figure 6.15 *Multicamera video system.*

Usually, if there are multiple cameras, all the base units are located together and one technician deals with technical operation of all cameras (see Figure 6.15). He or she has access to all camera technical adjustments through remote control.

Since the multiple-camera setup just described involves several operators, there is also a communications need that is supported by voice intercom facilities built into all the cameras and base stations. This usually provides at least two separate circuits so that there can be separate direction of technical and artistic matters.

6.6.1.1 Camera Size

System cameras for nonportable use are generally larger than portable cameras because there are advantages to a larger size. The most important one is that a larger optical format can be used. This allows somewhat improved picture performance and allows for larger lens options. The latter is particularly important for sporting events where the cameras often must be far from the action, and the option of a 40:1 or higher zoom ratio is important. Of course, all this comes at a price, and larger-format cameras are more expensive. Another large-camera feature is a larger viewfinder, which offers more flexibility in camera operation.

6.6.1.2 Synchronization

Multiple cameras operating with a real-time video switching system must deliver signals that are synchronized in frequency and phase. A *sync generator* provides a source of signals for synchronization of scanning and color subcarrier for analog composite systems.

In an all-digital system, it is possible to operate without exact synchronization of signal sources by providing a frame memory with appropriate read and write controls (a *frame synchronizer*, see Section 4.6.1) for each source. However, if the system is all at one location, it is less expensive and more convenient to synchronize at least the scanning process of all sources. Sources that are coming from other locations can still use frame synchronizers. Frame synchronizers are also available for analog systems—they employ the same concept as in digital systems, with the addition of ADC and DAC units to interface to the analog system.

6.6.1.3 Camera Matching

The subject of *camera matching* was introduced in Section 6.3. All system cameras provide features for this purpose and (at least) a test of match is carried out by the technical operator of the system before each use of the system. Special test charts are placed before the cameras, and the results are compared by means of waveform monitors and picture monitors at the technical operating position. Camera parameters that are important in matching are video levels (black and white), gray scale linearity (gamma), white balance, enhancement settings, and colorimetry.

6.6.1.4 Remote Control

In the days of vacuum-tube image sensors, cameras often had literally hundreds of adjustments to maintain registration and camera matching. *(Registration* is the matching of scanning parameters so that the red, green, and blue images precisely superimpose one another. Poor registration causes color fringes around objects in the picture.) Remoting all these controls to a technical operator's position required complex and expensive multiwire camera cables or a multiplex system that used a smaller cable. Analog circuit stability was not good enough to avoid regular adjustment and system camera design always faced the tradeoff between placing circuits in the camera head and providing remote controls or placing circuits in the base unit where they could be adjusted directly.

Most of the complexity involved with registration has disappeared with CCD cameras because they do not have electron beams to drift over time, and the registration setup can be mechanically fixed in the optical assembly. The video signal parameters of CCDs are also much more stable than tube imagers were and digital signal processing is more stable than analog processing. However, in a system with camera-matching requirements, some controls still require regular adjustment

Table 6.2

Color Camera Operating Controls

Control	Mode of use
Video master gain	Operation
Iris	Operation
Filter selection	Setup
Black balance	Setup
White balance	Setup
Contrast compression	Setup
Highlight compression	Setup
Color correction	Setup
System Mode Selection	Setup or operate

Table 6.2 shows a typical list of camera adjustments and also shows whether a control is used for setup (adjusted before shooting and left alone during shooting) or operation (adjusted during shooting to achieve best pictures). In an ideal system, all these controls should be available at the technical operating position. Some systems may even provide the option of a special operating position for the artistic controls so that their use can be more under the control of the program direction people.

With digital signal processing, the trend in professional cameras is to place all the processing circuits and the camera computer in the camera head and to provide a digital signal path and a control data bus between the remote operating position and the camera head. This can be implemented with a simple cable or with a fiber-optic cable. In the latter case, the cable must still carry a few wires to send power to the camera head because, for convenient operation, there should only be one cable going to a camera.

6.6.2 Camera Viewfinders

The operator handling a camera must be able to see the picture being captured by his or her camera to set camera position and focus. There also may be need to see the picture from the camera after it has been mixed or composited with other signal sources, This requires a video feed from the system switcher back to the camera viewfinder.

Camera viewfinders have generally been high-resolution monochrome CRTs of small size—3 to 5 inches in system cameras, approximately 1 inch in hand-held cameras. The small-size viewfinders require the use of an eyepiece that the operator must look into, whereas larger viewfinders do not require an eyepiece.

The availability of LCD displays has started a trend to use color LCDs in camera viewfinders. This is happening in home and semiprofessional cameras but is still not too widespread in professional cameras because the color LCD resolution is not good enough for critical focusing of a high-performance camera. As color LCD resolution improves, they will surely be used in more cameras.

6.6.3 Portable Cameras

Nearly all home cameras are designed to be hand held or shoulder held, and special designs of professional cameras are also available for this use. The overriding requirement is lightweight, especially for hand-held, less so for shoulder-held. Hand-held means the camera will be held up in front of the eyes and an eyepiece viewfinder is provided so the camera can be steadied against the head. An appropriate weight for this service is about 2 lb but higher weights up to 4 or 5 lb are workable. As the weight increases, the camera-mounting stability is improved, but the operator fatigue factor from holding the camera increases.

Shoulder-held cameras are rested on the operator's shoulder, and the viewfinder is mounted to the side of the camera near the front to account for the eye-to-shoulder distance. Again, most have eyepiece viewfinders. Most professional portable camera operators prefer the shoulder-mounted configuration because it allows much better camera stability. With the camera resting on the shoulder, the entire upper body of the operator helps in maintaining camera stability. Shoulder-held cameras are inherently larger than hand-held cameras and they cover a weight range from about 6 to 15 lb. The heavier cameras are somewhat more stable in use but, of course, they are heavier to carry.

The advent of LCD viewfinders for portable cameras has allowed a larger viewfinder screen that does not have to use an eyepiece. However, the viewfinder must be far enough away for the eye to focus yet not so far that the operator cannot see the full resolution of the viewfinder. This is an impractical configuration for normal shoulder mounting because the viewfinder would have to be somewhat ahead of the camera. However, it does add flexibility for hand-held use, because the camera can be held low or high, and most LCD viewfinders are swivel mounted so that they can be seen at any angle to the camera. The camera cannot be held against the head for stability, but it can be held against other parts of the operator's body.

6.6.3.1 Image Stabilization

Hand-held or shoulder-held cameras produce picture stability that is a function of the operator's skill in holding the camera. The more the operator tries to move about by walking, or moving the camera for panning, the less stable the picture. Several systems are available to deal with camera instability. Mechanical devices are available that hold the camera in a gimbal mount that moves independently from the operator. These units can provide good stability of a professional-sized portable camera even when the operator walks up stairs or runs on level ground. Similar devices (at lower cost) are available in the home market. Because of the lower price and the lower weight (mass) of home cameras, the stabilization performance is somewhat less than the professional units.

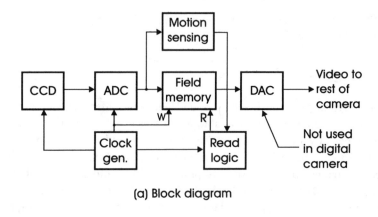

(a) Block diagram

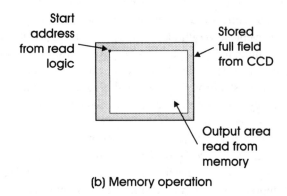

(b) Memory operation

Figure 6.16 *Digital image stabilization.*

Stabilizers are also available within a camera as either a mechanical system in the optics or an electronic system using digital techniques. In either case, the stabilization performance depends on the method of sensing the camera motion. This can be done with a gyrolike mechanical sensor in the camera or by electronically extracting camera motion from the picture itself. Both types have limitations, not only of the sensor, but in the logic for dealing with deliberate camera motion such as panning. However, these systems are popular in the home market.

Figure 6.16 shows a digital electronic stabilizer using a field memory in the camera. This is for a single-CCD camera and operates on the signal before the color-stripe pattern has been decoded. All the pixels from the CCD are stored in each field scan and, based on signals from the motion sensor, a central window of the field is read as the output signal. As the camera motion is sensed, the control signal moves the area taken from the field memory to compensate for camera motion.

An electronic motion sensor is shown in Figure 16.6 that divides the frame into four segments and separately computes a motion vector for each segment by comparing the values in consecutive frames. The four motion vectors are then compared by a fuzzy logic circuit to control the positioning of the read-out field. To the extent that the four vectors contain a component of identical motion, the sensor interprets it as camera motion that should be compensated. Additional logic deals with what to do at the limits of correction (when the output window tries to go beyond the input field) or when there is motion that is determined to be the operator's deliberate panning or tilting.

Since the output window from the field memory must contain fewer pixels than the CCD does to provide room for motion correction, this approach loses some resolution compared to the best that the CCD could otherwise provide.

6.6.3.2 Electronic Zoom

Some home or semiprofessional cameras have an electronic zoom feature that also uses a field or frame memory in the camera. The full output of the CCD is stored in memory, and only a portion of the stored image is read out. Interpolation processing (see Section 8.3.3) allows the smaller image to be expanded to full-screen size. This is a zoom. The operator controls the size of the small image to set the zoom factor. Of course, resolution is lost in proportion to the degree of zooming, but the result can still be valuable as a special effect.

6.6.3.3 Camcorders

A video camera and a video recorder together are the equivalent of a film camera. Such a combination is called a *camcorder* and can operate from batteries and while recording. It requires no connections to any other hardware or system. Camcorders today generally use videotape recording, although camcorders using digital disk drives (see Section 11.2.5) are beginning to appear and will surely be important in the future. The signal output is taken by removing the recorded medium and putting it into a player or by taking the entire camcorder to a monitor and connecting a playback cable between camcorder and monitor. All cameras in the home market and nearly all portable cameras for the semiprofessional market are camcorders.

In the professional market, there are both standalone cameras and camcorders. Professional camcorders sometimes have a *docking* feature, where the "cam" and the "corder" can be separated. This provides flexibility to use different combinations of hardware, to update either part separately in the future, or to use the camera by itself in a system. This latter option requires a system adapter that plugs into the docking connector of the camera.

6.7 VIDEO FROM FILM

In professional fields, there is a vast amount of program material on motion picture film, and more is being produced all the time. Bringing this material into a video system could be

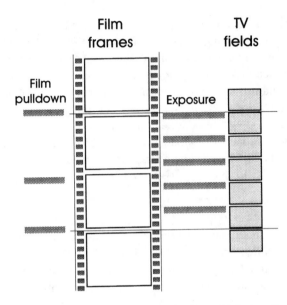

Figure 6.17 *Operation of 3:2 pulldown for capture of 24-fps film on 30-fps interlaced TV.*

done simply by projecting the film on a screen and viewing the screen with a video camera. A video signal is generated but is not very good for a number of reasons. Much better results are obtained by using a video camera called a *telecine* camera that is specially designed for converting film programs to video.

6.7.1 Frame Rate Conversion

Most motion picture film is 35 mm and the frame rate is 24 frames per second (fps). The biggest challenge of film-to-video conversion is the conversion of the film frame rate to video field and frame rates. Many systems have been developed for film frame rate conversion for television. In 60-Hz field rate television systems, there is a 4:5 relationship between the frame rates (24:30), and it was an early development to use what is called *3:2 pulldown* in television film systems. This is illustrated in Figure 6.17. One film frame is exposed to a storage-type television camera for three video fields, and the next film frame is exposed for two video fields. The pulldown of the film frames and the exposure times are carefully timed to not interfere with each other. An intermittent mechanism is needed for film pulldown between the television camera exposure periods. Thus, after two film frames or five video fields, the cycle repeats. Although this process has some strange artifacts in moving images, it has been the best available approach for many years. In 50-Hz television systems, the approach was simply to run the film at 25 fps and expose one film frame for two television fields. This requires a 4% speedup of the film, which makes motion slightly faster (not much of a problem) and increases the audio pitch by 4% (a bigger problem).

Fortunately, digital video technology offers much better ways to do frame rate conversion. All approaches involve a digital video frame memory that is read out at the video system frame rate. The film runs at its normal 24 fps and the video camera also runs at that frame rate. The video camera output is written into the frame memory as an independent operation from the reading of the frame memory. This is the frame synchronizer principle that is covered in Section 4.6.1.

6.7.2 Scanning the Film

Two methods are currently available for film scanning—flying-spot and CCD line-scan devices. Each is briefly described in this section. There are also many vacuum-tube film scanners still in use. These generally employ vidicon tubes but, since new equipment of this type is no longer manufactured, they will not be covered here.

6.7.2.1 Flying-Spot Film Scanners

The flying-spot principle was briefly described in Section 6.4.1 and diagrammed in Figure 6.8. Most flying-spot film scanners do not use a standard raster scan but instead use a modified raster that takes into account the motion of a continuously moving film. This way, the film transport does not have to have an intermittent pulldown. The output of the pickup cells is stored in a digital memory, and a standard TV scan is developed by the proper readout of the memory image. This is another application of the frame synchronizer principle that is used for many purposes in digital video.

The flying-spot scan could actually be a single-line scan but that would quickly burn a line on the flying-spot CRT. Therefore, a small raster scan is used and the operation of the digital memory write circuits compensates for the extra motion.

6.7.2.2 CCD Line-Scan Film Scanners

The same general idea described above for flying-spot scanning of film can be used with CCD line-scan devices. Instead of the flying-spot CRT, a continuous light source illuminates a small horizontal area of the film. The light passes through the film and the film image is focused onto a CCD device that has a single line of sensors. The film moves continuously and the CCD reads lines continuously into a frame memory. Again, the control of the read clocks allows any standard scan format to be produced at the output of the memory.

Some line-scan systems have more than one line in the CCD device, but the CCD is designed to read out all its lines simultaneously to separate output circuits. This offers the possibility of doing some image processing in real time as the scanning is taking place.

6.7.3 Film-to-Video Signal Processing

The basic steps of video processing for telecine cameras are the same as live-pickup cameras, but there are some important differences in implementation that arise from the optical properties of motion picture film. Color in film is a subtractive color process (see Section 2.4.2)—colored dyes in the film absorb part of the light passing through the film to produce the color picture. To produce intense (saturated) colors, the dyes must be built up to a high density, which means that intense colors are inherently dark. This is the opposite of what happens in an additive-color video system and the result is a fundamental incompatibility between film and video.

Telecine cameras must deal with this incompatibility by processing the video in several different ways. The most important step is to provide increased gamma correction to bring up the color information in the low-light areas. Because increasing gamma also brings up the noise in the video signals, it is important to begin with the highest possible SNR from the camera devices. It also is desirable to add nonlinear filtering that will reduce the bandwidth in the low-light areas to further reduce noise expansion.

The second factor that is important in telecine cameras is that the colorimetry of film is quite variable, especially as film ages. This creates a need for special color correction that allows a film-to-video operator to readily adjust the color correction. On some old films, it is even necessary to adjust the color correction as the film plays and sophisticated systems have been developed to preprogram color correction dynamically during film transfer.

Because of these difficulties, film-to-video transfer is somewhat of an art, and companies that specialize in this field have developed their own equipment and techniques to get the most out of the system. It is common practice to transfer old films to videotape before they are used for broadcasting or other purposes. The difficult transfer process is done once and, after that, videotapes can be played with consistent results every time.

6.8 CAMERA SPECIFICATIONS

The camera field is moving rapidly, and any listing of specifications has to be a snapshot and an average of all the products available. Table 6.3 shows typical current specifications for home, semiprofessional, and professional (broadcast) cameras designed for standard TV formats. In addition, the current performance of a high-end HDTV camera is listed—this area is where the most change is occurring.

Table 6.3

Color Camera Specifications

Item	Camera type			
	Home	*Semi-prof.*	*Broadcast*	*HDTV*
Scanning standard	525/60i	525/60i	525/60i	1125/60i
Architecture	1-CCD	3-CCD	3-CCD	3-CCD
Packaging	Camcorder	Camcorder	Dockable	Camera
Spatial offset	N.A.	Yes	Yes	No
CCD optical Size	1/4 in	1/3 in	1/2 in	1 in
Max. optical Speed	f/1.2	f/1.6	f/1.4	f/1.2
CCD resolution (pixels)	270,000	270,000	380,000	2,000,000
Aspect ratio	4:3	4:3	4:3	16:9
Max. horiz. resolution	275 TVL	530 TVL	750 TVL	1,000 TVL
Video SNR	40 dB	50 dB	60 dB	50 dB
Normal illumination	>100 lux	1,400 lux @ f/5.6	2,000 lux @ f/8	1,000 lux @ f/4
Minimum illumination				
Normal gain		8 lux	60 lux	
High gain	2 lux	1 lux (+18 dB)	2 lux (+30 dB)	
Remote control	No	No	Yes	Yes

REFERENCES

1. Benson, K. B., and Whitaker, J. C., *Television Engineering Handbook*, New York:McGraw-Hill, 1992

2. ibid., Chapter 11.

3. Hamalainen, J., et al., "Facts and Fiction," International Journal of Imaging Systems and Technology, Vol. 5, 314–322, 1994.

Chapter 7

Digital Transmission

7.1 INTRODUCTION

From the smallest camcorder to the worldwide Internet, all digital systems face the problem of transmission—getting data from one place to another. Recording and storage are another kind of transmission application—getting data from one time to another. This chapter discusses the technologies and systems for digital data transmission.

7.2 DIGITAL TRANSMISSION TECHNOLOGY

There is no such thing in nature as a truly *digital* transmission medium. All real transmission media (called *channels* in this discussion) have the familiar analog limitations of bandwidth, noise and interference, time-base instability, and amplitude nonlinearity. These analog impairments can cause errors in digital transmission and thus disrupt the basic advantage of being digital—perfect reproduction. This section discusses some of the technologies used to deal with these analog problems in digital transmission.

Figure 7.1 is a block diagram of a typical digital transmission system showing all the possible elements that it may include, although not every system will have all of them. The discussion in Sections 7.2 and 7.3 will define and use the terminology of this diagram.

7.2.1 Encoding

In most cases, the original binary data generated by ADC is not suitable for transmission and must be formatted before transmission. This is known as *encoding* or *coding* and is a process that converts or adds to the data without losing any of the information content. Encoding may be done and undone (*decoded*) several different ways as digital signals pass through a system. The encoding techniques discussed here are specific to transmission;

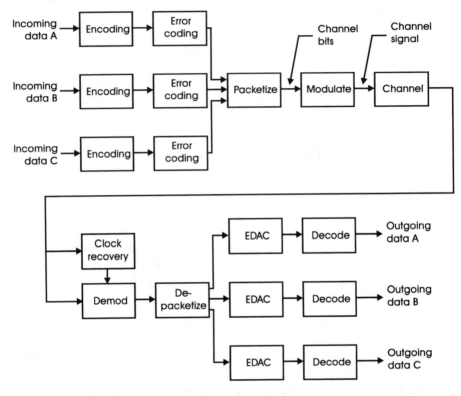

Figure 7.1 *General block diagram of a digital transmission system.*

additional encodings may be applied, for example, to accomplish data compression, which may lose some unimportant information content in the interest of better compression (see Chapter 9).

In the telecommunications industry, it is customary to view the steps of communications processing as a series of "layers" of protocol. The *Open Systems Interconnection* (OSI) model was developed by the ISO as standard IS 7498 (1984) and defines seven layers between the user and the physical circuit. This standard is widely used in Europe for computer interconnection over communications channels; in the United States, OSI is also used but the TCP/IP standard (see Section 7.5.2.1) that is the basis for the Internet is more common. The OSI layers are shown in Figure 7.2[1]. A brief description of the layers is

1. Physical layer—this layer includes the actual physical hardware and software for communication. It includes everything necessary to establish a physical connection and transmit a bit stream over it.

2. Data-link layer—this layer controls the actual physical link, and it may provide additional error management functions.

User

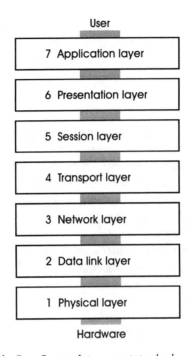

Hardware

Figure 7.2 *Protocol layers of the Open Systems Interconnect standard.*

3. Network layer—this layer handles routing of communication through a network.

4. Transport layer—this layer provides the bridge between application-related functions and communication-related functions. It also performs error protection, flow control, and multiplexing functions.

5. Session layer—this layer establishes, manages, and releases the communications connection.

6. Presentation layer—this layer specifies how sessions are established and terminated.

7. Application layer—this highest layer is the user interface between the data communication service and the user.

Simple systems, of course, do not employ all the layers. The OSI model terminology will be used where it applies in the rest of this discussion.

In this chapter, the word "encoding" refers only to the binary digital processes that are involved in preparing data for transmission. The output of encoding is still a binary bit stream. Although such a bit stream may sometimes be passed directly to an analog transmission channel, it is usually desirable to perform further digital or analog processing to make the signal more suitable to the channel. The output of such processes is no longer a *binary* digital signal—it may now have analog features as well. In this chapter, this channel-specific processing is called *modulation* or *channel coding*. Note that some of the steps of encoding as defined here are commonly referred to as "modulation" in the industry; for example: frequency modulation. This is confusing, but there is no attempt here to change general industry terminology.

7.2.2 Serial and Parallel

Digital data for audio or video are usually structured into groups of bits that represent a single piece of information, such as a video pixel or an audio sample. Many times, the hardware generating the information outputs its data on a number of parallel circuits, one circuit per bit of the basic data structure. Thus, an 8-bit ADC would have eight output wires. This *parallel* organization is convenient for sending data over short distances and has the advantage that the data rate per wire is lower than the total data rate by an amount n equal to the number of parallel wires.

However, the handling of parallel signal wires is awkward when transmitting data outside of a single box and becomes completely impractical when long distance or radiated transmission is required. In such cases, the data must be *serialized* so that it can all be transmitted over a single channel.

7.2.2.1 Parallel-to-Serial Conversion

The task of conversion between parallel and serial connections is ubiquitous in digital systems. The hardware for this purpose is simple—a *shift register* (see Figure 7.3). Shift registers are available as separate packages, or they may be built into more complex integrated circuits that contain additional functions.

To make a shift register, a group of register circuits (see Section 1.3.5) is connected so that data move from each register to the next by means of the Q, $\overline{Q}$ to R, S connections, every time the registers are clocked by a shift clock signal. (In the figure, shifting is to the right.) The registers can also be loaded or read in parallel by means of a separate set of connections and another clock. To function as a parallel-to-serial converter as shown in Figure 7.3(a), the parallel data are loaded into the shift register under control of the load clock and then clocked to the serial output by means of the shift clock. Thus, for continuous data flow, the shift clock is n times higher than the load clock for a shift register of n stages supporting a parallel data path of n bits per word.

7.2.2.2 Serial-to-Parallel Conversion

A shift register functions as a serial-to-parallel converter by connecting it as shown in Figure 7.3(b). In this case, the serial data are shifted into the registers using the shift clock and the contents of all registers are captured periodically using a set of latches driven by the read clock.

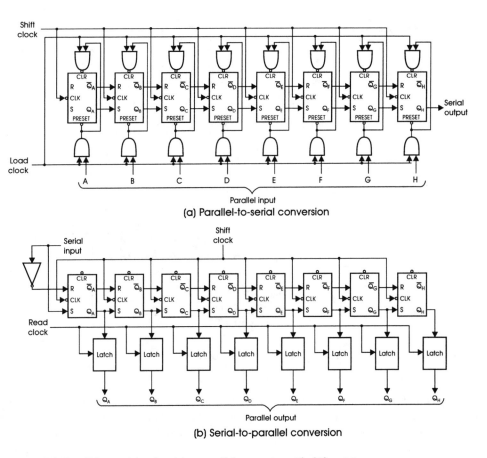

Figure 7.3 *Parallel-to-serial and serial-to-parallel conversion with shift registers.*

7.2.3 Synchronization

There are two parts to data synchronization: (1) extracting a clock that allows reliable reading and latching of the data stream and (2) synchronizing to the data format so that the content can be recognized and decoded.

7.2.3.1 Clock Extraction

In a parallel-data system, a separate wire is usually provided for clocking, so there is no clock extraction problem. However, serial systems must inherently contain the clock signal within the data so that the receiving equipment can reliably identify the data bits. This is called *self-clocking*.

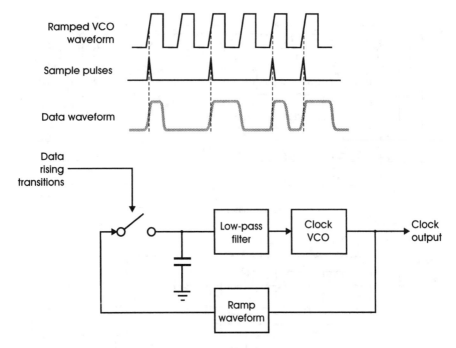

Figure 7.4 *Clock synchronization by means of a phase-lock loop.*

A serial data stream can be characterized as a random sequence of ones and zeros. Typically, there will be a significant signal component at the data-repetition frequency, which can be extracted by a phase-lock loop (PLL) operating at the expected data-repetition frequency. One objective of encoding and modulation is to insure that clock extraction can be reliably accomplished for any possible pattern of the data bits.

Figure 7.4 is a block diagram of a phase-lock loop. A *voltage-controlled oscillator* (VCO) operates at approximately the expected clock frequency. It is controlled by the output of a phase detector made by sampling and holding a ramped VCO waveform with pulses derived from the leading edges of the data signal. The output of the sample-and-hold detector is a voltage that changes the frequency of the VCO in a direction that will move toward lock. At lock, the detector will end up sampling the VCO signal at approximately the center of each positive transition. Since there may be time jitter in the incoming signal, and, for some formats, there may not be a positive transition at every clock period, a low-pass filter in the PLL slows the operation so the extracted clock remains stable. Some encoding methods are better for clock extraction than others.

The output of the PLL's VCO becomes the data clock. However, this may not be reliable with generalized data because there can be extended sequences of all ones or all zeros, during which there is no clock-frequency component and the PLL will drift out of lock.

For clock extraction to work reliably, the data must be conditioned during encoding to make sure that sequences of the same value do not become too long. This characteristic of a

Table 7.1

Parameters for Several Common Encodings

Name(s)	Acronym	T_{min}	T_{max}	DR	DC component	Self-clocking	Waveforms 1 0 0 1 1 0 1 1 1 (
Nonreturn to zero	NRZ	T	∞	1	large	no	
Frequency modulation biphase-mark code	FM	T/2	T	0.5	zero	yes	
Phase encoding Manchester code	PE	T/2	T	0.5	zero	yes	
Modified FM delay modulation Miller code	MFM	T	2T	1	small	yes	
Eight-to-fourteen code	EFM	1.41T	5.18T	1.41	zero	yes	(see text)

data stream is called its *run length* and the technique of controlling it is called *run-length limiting* (RLL). RLL is quantified by specifying the minimum (T_{min}) and maximum (T_{max}) times between transitions of the data states in the transmission channel. The T_{min} value relates to the maximum frequency component in the data stream (it is approximately one-half cycle of the maximum frequency,) and the T_{max} value relates to the longest time that the clock-recovery circuit must hold without any input.

A further parameter is the data *density ratio* (DR), defined as the ratio of T_{min} to the minimum time T between transitions of the incoming data stream before encoding. The larger the DR, the more information is transmitted by a given channel. If T_{min} is given as a fraction or multiple of T, then DR = T_{min}.

7.2.3.2 DC Component

Another important feature of a data stream is its *dc component*, which is the long-term average of the bit values in the stream. This is important because most transmission media cannot transmit a dc value. Loss of the dc component of a data stream will cause errors or, at least, it will reduce the system's margin for errors. Good encoding schemes eliminate or minimize the dc component.

Table 7.1 lists some encodings and their properties. The first entry in the table, *nonreturn to zero* (NRZ), is when the ones and zeros of the signal are transmitted directly one after another. This is the way we usually think of a bit stream. In NRZ, a positive-going transition indicates a one and a negative-going transition indicates a zero. Strings of repeated ones or zeros generate no transitions. NRZ is simple but impractical because the infinite T_{max} and large DC component make clock extraction impossible.

A variant of NRZ is NRZI (NRZ-inverted). In NRZI there is a transition (in either direction) for every one but no transitions for zeros. This coding is polarity insensitive but is the same as NRZ in that $T_{min} = T$ and $T_{max} = \infty$.

The FM encoding scheme (also called *biphase mark* coding) transmits two channel transitions for a 1 and one transition for a zero. This eliminates the DC component but cuts T_{min} in half, so the DR is only 0.5. It is self-clocking.

The PE or Manchester code has a transition for every bit, located in the center of a bit cell. A zero has a positive transition and a one has a negative transition. When consecutive values are the same, extra opposite-direction transitions are added between bit cells. This achieves the same results as FM encoding: no DC and DR = 0.5.

In the MFM code, also known as delay modulation or Miller code, a one is coded by a transition of either direction at the center of a bit interval, whereas there is no transition at that position for a zero. A string of zeros will have a single transition at the end of each bit interval. This gives a DR of 1 with a probability of a small DC component.

7.2.3.3 Group Encoding

More elaborate codes based on groups of data bits are possible and are widely used. This generally takes the form of adding a certain number of extra bits to the data in a way that allows control of the data stream properties independent of what data come into the encoder. For example, one popular method, called *eight-to-fourteen modulation* (EFM), breaks the data bits into groups of eight and adds six additional bits to each group, meaning that fourteen bits are actually transmitted for every eight data bits.

The insertion of extra bits in EFM is accomplished by using a lookup table that outputs fourteen bits for every incoming eight-bit value. (The contents of such an encoding table is called a *code book*.) The table has 256 14-bit entries. Since a 14-bit word can represent up to 16,384 values and only 256 are needed, the actual 14-bit values to use can be selected to control T_{min}, T_{max}, and the DC component. Different ways of making this choice lead to different modulation systems. Of course, the method must be standardized because the decoder must know the exact code book that is used.

One possibility for EFM selects 14-bit values that always have two or more like bits together. Since two output bits correspond to $(2 \times 8)/14 = 1.14$ input bits, $T_{min} = 1.14$ (T_{min} is calculated in terms of the input bits.) The DR has the same value, so by adding six bits for every eight bits, we have been able to transmit 14% more data! This happens because the choice of EFM 14-bit values has avoided all single-bit transitions, thereby halving the required channel bandwidth. This EFM encoding limits the maximum sequential output bits to seven, so calculating in terms of the input bits, $T_{max} = (7 \times 8)/14 = 4$.

In practice, the EFM process is more complex than described above because there are not enough 14-bit values that meet all the conditions when considering the concatenation of adjacent 14-bit codes. To make sure that the bit patterns produced at the joining of sequential 14-bit codes will not violate the system conditions for T_{min}, T_{max}, and DC

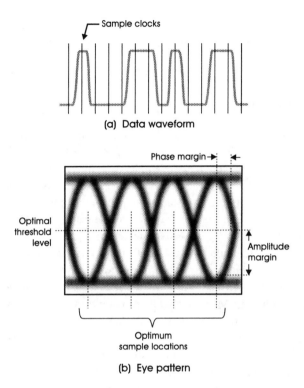

(a) Data waveform

(b) Eye pattern

Figure 7.5 *The eye pattern.*

component, the EFM encoder also examines that situation and chooses the appropriate one of four alternate 14-bit values. Thus, the lookup table actually must store 1,024 14-bit values.

The list in Table 7.1 also shows parameters for the particular EFM coding used in the D-3 magnetic video recorder.

7.2.3.4 The Eye Pattern

A typical digital signal in a transmission channel will have noise added as shown in Figure 7.5(a). A clock extracted from this signal may also have time jitter relative to the signal. For system testing, both of these properties can be viewed on an oscilloscope by displaying the signal with the horizontal sweep synchronized to the extracted clock. This is known as an *eye pattern* display and is shown in Figure 7.5(b). The pattern shows the jittering signal surrounding an open area (the eye), the center of which would represent the ideal sampling point on the signal, where the most reliable *data separation* is obtained. When the transmission performance becomes poorer, the eye gets smaller and more critical positioning of the sampling point is necessary to maintain low error rates. As shown in the figure, the height and width of the eye represent amplitude and phase margins, respectively.

7.2.3.5 Recognizing the Data Format

Being able to detect the ones and zeros of the encoded data is only part of the process of synchronization. One must also locate the unique features of the data format so that the actual information can be recovered. For example, decoding of the EFM format described is Section 7.2.3.3 requires location of the exact bit where each 14-bit pattern begins. This is usually accomplished by defining a unique bit sequence (sync word) that is inserted into the encoded data. On recovery, finding the sync word means (in EFM, for example) that the data bit immediately following is the start of a 14-bit encoded word. In other cases, the bit following the sync word could be the start of a header that defines the first level of the data format. Of course, the encoding must be designed so that the sync word is unique—it must be impossible for random data to produce the sync word. Some of the more advanced encoding schemes such as EFM automatically provide for unique sync words.

A hardware approach for finding a sync word is simple—a serial-to-parallel shift register configuration as was shown in Figure 7.3(b) is used. The encoded data containing sync words at unknown positions passes continuously into the serial input of the shift register. The parallel bits are latched during every serial clock period, and all bits of the parallel output are compared with the expected sync word. If all bits compare, the sync word has been found. This process can also be accomplished in software although, especially for video data, that may require too much processing speed and hardware support will still be required.

7.2.4 Modulation

As explained in Section 7.2.1, the process of configuring an already-encoded data stream for optimal transmission over a given analog channel is *modulation*. This section discusses such channel-specific processes.

7.2.4.1 Channel Properties

A transmission channel can be characterized by its analog transfer characteristic, which includes the properties of frequency response, SNR, time-base stability, and amplitude linearity. Examples of transmission channels are telephone lines, fiber-optic cables, coaxial cables, magnetic recorders, satellite broadcast channels, and terrestrial broadcast channels. Each of these has its own specific properties that demand different modulation means to achieve the best digital transmission. The channels are compared in more detail in Section 7.3.

7.2.4.2 Symbols

In the discussion so far, it has been assumed that a channel signal consists of a stream of bits having values of one or zero, or it is a stream of transitions between binary values. To support discussion of more advanced methods of modulation, it is useful to define the concept of a *symbol*, which is the basic unit of data carried at one moment of time by the channel signal. Each symbol may carry a number of bits determined by the modulation method used in the channel.

Modulation may be thought of as the process of converting data bits into symbols. *Demodulation* is converting the symbols back into bits. The best modulation method for a specific channel will transmit the most bits per symbol; practical values of bits/symbol range from about ½ to 4. Larger values, though possible, are usually not practical because they require too high a channel performance for SNR and linearity.

There is a minimal period of time needed for the channel signal to transmit one symbol independent of adjacent symbols. This determines a maximum *symbol rate* for the channel, which obviously depends on the channel's bandwidth. Data transmission rate is bits per symbol multiplied by the symbol rate.

Most channels are inherently analog and approximately linear. Such channels are thus capable of handling more than just two values. Depending on the SNR and other properties of the channel, it may be a waste of channel capacity to transmit digital data as only two values. When symbols support more than two values, the possibility exists for transmitting more than one bit per symbol.

7.2.4.3 Multilevel Symbols

At the receiving end of a transmission channel, the signal contains noise introduced during transmission. A symbol clock is recovered that can be used to sample the signal to recover symbol values. However, these values must be quantized to convert them to true digital values. In the case of a system that has just two symbol levels, each symbol quantizes to one bit. Of course, more symbol levels will quantize to more bits. For example, if the system is designed for four levels, then each symbol quantizes to two bits.

More symbol levels require higher channel SNR for quantization to be successful. However, the system's data rate for a given bandwidth increases according to the power of two represented by the number of levels. It also should be obvious that multilevel operation based on signal amplitude places high demands on the amplitude linearity of the channel. For example, magnetic recorders, which have a highly nonlinear channel, cannot use multilevel symbols.

Multilevel symbols make possible an effective tradeoff between SNR and bandwidth. A good example of multilevel symbols is the Grand Alliance HDTV transmission system (see Section 7.4.3) that transmits a net data rate of 19.3 MB/s over a 6-MHz TV channel.

7.2.4.4 Modulation Methods

Symbol values can be transmitted over an analog channel by modulation of the amplitude, phase, or frequency of the channel signal or by combinations of these parameters. Often, a carrier frequency is modulated with the encoded data, which results in the data spectrum being shifted up to the vicinity of the carrier frequency.

Using combinations of methods (such as amplitude and phase modulation) is a means for increasing the symbol levels. For carrier-based systems, this can be seen by looking at a vector diagram of the carrier waveform. Figure 7.6 shows some examples of modulation methods and their vector diagrams. The name for these diagrams is *signal set* diagrams but, because of the appearance of the vector diagrams, they are sometimes called *constellations*.

The figure shows four types of modulation. AM stands for *amplitude modulation*, and 2-AM is amplitude modulation by a binary signal. PSK is *phase-shift keying* or phase modulation. 4-PSK is a 2-bit multilevel modulation and 8-PSK is 3-bit multilevel. QASK is *quadrature amplitude-shift keying* or *quadrature amplitude modulation*, which is a combination of amplitude and phase modulation that conveys 4 bits per symbol.

7.2.5 Error Protection

All real digital transmission channels will occasionally produce bit errors. This is characterized by specifying a channel's *bit error rate* (BER), which is the probability of occurrence of a single bit error. BER is usually specified as a power of ten, so, for example, a channel that on the average produces one bit error in every million bits has a BER of 10^{-6}.

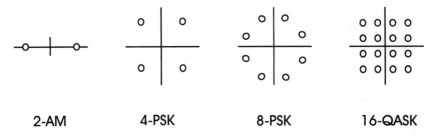

| 2-AM | 4-PSK | 8-PSK | 16-QASK |

Figure 7.6 Signal set diagrams for several modulation methods.

Depending on the type of data involved, bit errors can have more or less significance. Practical systems are designed to tolerate a certain level of channel errors by using the techniques of *error protection*. This ability of digital systems to detect and correct errors is a major advantage over analog systems. It is the reason why transmission errors do not cause significant data errors and errors do not accumulate as the system is extended.

Errors are a consideration at all points in a digital system and error protection is a factor in all processing, not just transmission. In transmission systems, there are usually error protection features built into every step of the encoding and, with the combination of several techniques, it is possible to have a truly robust (low BER) system that operates successfully over a very poor (high BER) transmission channel.

7.2.5.1 Error Statistics

Statistics of the errors are important in designing error protection systems. Errors may occur as isolated single-bit errors or as *burst errors* of any length. Detecting and correcting single-bit errors is much easier than handling long bursts of errors. When burst errors are expected, it is effective to *interleave* the data (see Section 7.2.5.7) before applying other error protection methods. Interleaving effectively spreads out burst errors into a number of separated single-bit errors, which are then easier to correct.

7.2.5.2 Principles of Error Protection

The basic concept of error protection is to build *redundancy* into the data stream. This redundancy, which takes the form of extra bits, is specially configured to facilitate error detection and correction at the receiving end of a transmission system. Figure 7.7 is a block diagram of the concept. Redundant bits are calculated from the data and inserted into the data stream before transmission. At the output of the transmission system, the redundant bits are tested for indication of errors and appropriate action is taken. In some cases, errors can be detected but not corrected; it may still be possible to *conceal* the errors. This requires knowledge of the redundant properties of the original signals and is described in Section 7.2.5.8.

It is interesting to compare the performance of analog and digital transmission channels. In most analog channels, the channel impairments directly affect the signal and, as the channel degrades, the signal performance degrades similarly. This is known as *graceful degradation*. In a digital system that has error protection, channel degradation does not affect the signal until the channel performance becomes so bad that the error protection system is overloaded. This means that a digital system maintains its performance until a point is reached where performance abruptly degrades or even completely fails. This is known as the *cliff effect*.[*]

Analog systems that use frequency modulation (FM) have a similar characteristic. The cliff occurs when the FM carrier level falls below the limiting level.

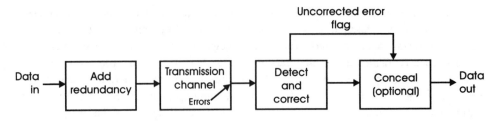

Figure 7.7 *General block diagram of error protection.*

7.2.5.3 Parity

The simplest form of error detection uses a single extra bit that is added periodically to a bit stream. For example, an extra bit may be inserted after every eighth bit in the bit stream. This bit has a value that will make the number of ones in the eight bits plus the extra bit always have an even value. This is known as even parity and the extra bit is the *parity* bit.

To test the bit stream for errors, one simply adds up all the one-bits in every nine-bit group; if the result is an odd number, one or more errors have occurred. It will also be apparent that this scheme can only detect an odd number of errors in a group—even numbers of errors will not affect the parity test. Because simple parity only really works for a single error in a group and it only detects the presence of an error but cannot tell which bit is in error, it is only used in special circumstances such as in random-access memories or simple communication systems, such as RS-232.

7.2.5.4 Product Codes

The parity concept can be made more powerful by applying it to a block of data. For example, 64 bits of data can be thought of as a two-dimensional array of 8 × 8 bits. If a parity bit is assigned for each row and each column of the array, it becomes possible to detect an error and its position in the array. Then, the error can be corrected by simply reversing the bit at the indicated position. This is the simplest case of what is known as a *crossword* or *product code*. Figure 7.8 shows how it operates. Parity must be checked for each row and each column; when an error is detected in one row and one column, the bit at the intersection of the row and column is the one in error. This scheme is still only capable of detecting one error per block, but the concept can be extended to accomplish more correction as explained below.

In the product code example of Figure 7.8, sixteen parity bits are generated for each 64-bit block of data. The usual way of handling this for transmission is to send the data block unchanged and append or prepend the parity bits to the bit stream. This is called *systematic coding*. Most error protection applications use systematic codes.

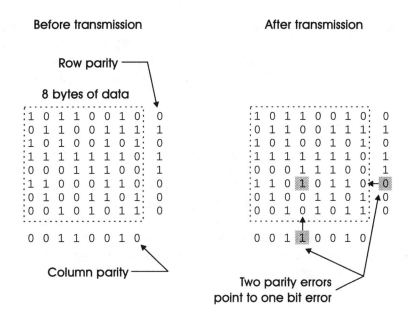

Figure 7.8 *Two-dimensional parity for correction of single-bit errors.*

7.2.5.5 More Advanced Codes

The theory of error-protecting codes becomes extremely complex and very mathematical and is well beyond what can be reasonably presented here. However, some key concepts will be described to give some understanding of what is behind the more popular approaches.

The previous example of the 8×8 block with two-dimensional parity can be viewed as eight 8-bit data words plus two 8-bit redundancy words, where the redundancy words are calculated as row-and-column parity. But there are other ways to calculate redundancy words and additional words can be added. This offers many options for tailoring error performance to suit different applications.

7.2.5.6 Reed-Solomon Coding

A widely-used error protection code is the *Reed-Solomon* code [2]. It is used in audio and video recorders, the audio Compact Disc, the Grand Alliance HDTV system, and many others. It is a block code system that can correct multiple errors per block. For example, a block that contains 20 bytes of R-S error protection overhead is capable of correcting up to 10 error bytes in the block. The choice of correction capability is made in the design of the system. The processing is exceedingly complex, but with the available integrated circuits, practical implementation has become very easy and inexpensive.

R-S codes are identified by giving the number of bytes in the total block and the number of bytes in the data field. For example, the code used in the Grand Alliance transmission system (see Section 7.4.3.4) is called a (207,187) code because the total block size is 207 bytes and there are 20 bytes of R-S parity codes, leaving 187 bytes for the data.

7.2.5.7 Interleaving

None of the error algorithms can deal directly with bursts of errors, but the *interleaving* technique can be use to convert burst errors into single-bit errors. Figure 7.9 shows this.

A block of data is read into rows of a memory that is organized as a two-dimensional array. The data are then read out from the memory by columns. The reverse process is done on recovery. If a burst of errors (shown by X's in the figure) occurs while the signal is in the interleaved format, it will be converted to single-bit errors when the data are de-interleaved upon recovery. This technique is widely used in systems such as magnetic recorders that are susceptible to burst errors.

7.2.5.8 Crossinterleave Coding

Still further improvement is possible by placing the interleave process between two instances of error protection coding such as Reed-Solomon. This is called *crossinterleaving* and is shown in Figure 7.10.

The input data are divided into Reed-Solomon blocks with redundancy coding (called the *outer* coding) and then read into an interleave memory. The memory has one row per R-S block. The interleaved output from the memory is then given another R-S coding (the *inner* coding.) On recovery, these processes are reversed.

The inner coding can correct for single-bit errors occurring in the channel but it cannot correct the burst errors, which are corrected by the outer correction. Crossinterleaving is used in nearly all magnetic and optical recording systems.

7.2.5.9 Error Concealment

In some cases, an error protection system can detect errors but cannot correct them. If the existence of an error in a block of data is known, there may be techniques that will make the error less visible or less audible in the reproduction. This depends on an error being a fleeting thing and psychophysical factors that affect how one sees or hears such one-time anomalies. The considerations differ for audio or video.

At the point of error detection, a flag may be generated by the error-protection processor that indicates a particular block of data may contain an uncorrected error. The significance of an error to the reproduction will depend on the digital encoding of the audio or video at the point of the error. For example, if we are dealing with audio that is encoded in straight

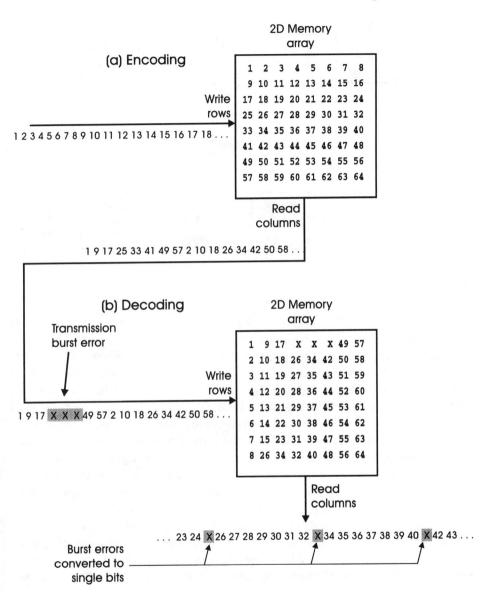

Figure 7.9 *Interleaving converts burst errors to individual bit errors.*

PCM, a single-bit error will be an error in a single sample value that may be heard as some kind of click in the reproduction. The magnitude of the click will depend on the significance in the sample word of the bit that is in error. However, if the audio is encoded in a compressed format, a single-bit error may be much more damaging and may require a different concealment technique.

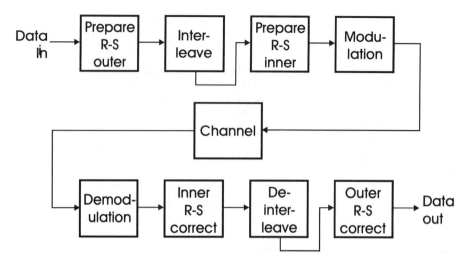

Figure 7.10 *Crossinterleaving.*

Continuing with the PCM-encoded audio case, there are several possibilities for concealment of a single sample known to be in error. Figure 7.11 shows an input waveform being sampled and three cases of the output waveform with a single sample error. The first case (b) is with the error uncorrected. The next (c) is to replace the faulty sample with the value of the previous sample, and the last (d) is to interpolate between the previous and the next samples to create a concealment value. Both of these operate on the assumption that a sampled audio signal usually does not change abruptly from one sample to the next.

A burst error that takes out a number of successive audio samples is a more difficult case. Here the assumption that there will be little change in the signal during the error is probably not valid. In this case, a better concealment strategy may be to replace the samples damaged by the burst with zero values. This may cause a brief interruption in the sound, but it will be far better than a burst of random noise (if no concealment is used) and may also be better than what either of the single-bit strategies will sound like.

Concealment strategies for video offer more choices because of the redundancy inherent in scanned video. Again, consider straight PCM encoding of video. A single-sample error will appear as a dot of wrong brightness or color in the picture. The techniques described for audio will work well to conceal such an error in video. However, burst errors are a different story.

They can be concealed by replacing the faulty area with information from the previous line or previous frame of the picture. These strategies depend on the thought that video images usually do not change very much from one line to the next or (at the same pixel locations) from frame to frame. Of course, either of these approaches requires that the system contain memory to store previous lines or frames for concealment purposes. Most systems will have such memories already for other reasons and concealment can be added without great expense.

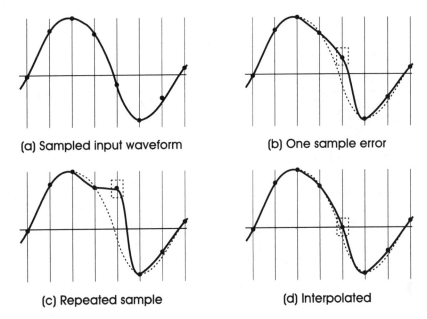

(a) Sampled input waveform

(b) One sample error

(c) Repeated sample

(d) Interpolated

Figure 7.11 *Error concealment (dotted lines show the original waveform.)*

The discussion above has been specifically for PCM encoding. When more elaborate encoding is used and especially when compression is employed, concealment becomes encoding-specific and must be a consideration of the encoding design.

7.2.6 Packetizing

The previous discussion of error protection presented many techniques that are based on dividing a bit stream into blocks. There are other advantages of blocks of data throughout the communication channel—these persistent blocks are usually called *packets*. The use of packets is widespread in telecommunications systems and in computer networks and it is coming into use in video and audio systems as well [3].

The idea of packets is that the data stream is divided into a series of blocks, where each block contains a header that identifies the packet and a specified amount of data. Packets may be all the same size or they may be different sizes with the packet headers specifying each packet's size. Several bit streams may be packetized and merged sequentially into the same channel. Figure 7.12 shows a diagram for a "packet video" system. Encoded video frames are processed into packets for transmission over a packetized network. At the receiving end, the packets are decoded back to the compressed video format, which is then decoded to video for display.

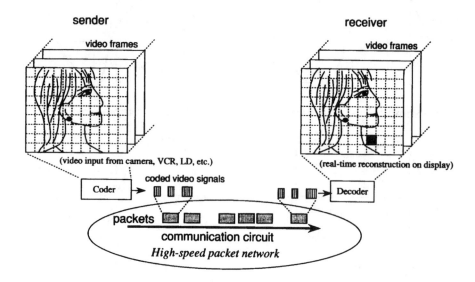

Figure 7.12 *Packet video (From Ohta, N.,* Packet Video Modeling and Signal Processing, *Boston:Artech House, Inc., 1994).*

7.2.6.1 Advantages of Packetizing

The advantages of packetizing are:

1. Packet transmission provides a flexible way to allocate a transmission channel dynamically to multiple bit streams. An example is the transmitting of audio and video on a single channel—each has its own specifically-identified packets, which are interleaved as necessary to support the different bit rates of the audio and video streams.

2. Many bit streams of different data types can be transmitted concurrently over the same channel. For example, video, several audio streams, supporting data streams, user command streams, and the like may coexist in the channel. It is not necessary to preallocate for all the bit streams; their packets can simply be "slipped into" the packet stream whenever they occur. This works as long as the total channel capacity is not exceeded.

3. In addition to any error protection that may already be in the incoming bit streams, packets can contain their own error protection coding.

4. Packet headers can contain destination information in addition to identification so that systems can be designed with the capability to route individual packets to

different destinations. This is the basis for the packet switching telephone networks now in use and also for the Internet.

Since packetizing involves the addition of overhead in the form of packet headers, it is appropriate only in situations where the advantages listed above are important. For example, packetizing offers no advantages to video and audio recorders and is not used there. However, for long-distance transmission over telecommunications networks or for broadcasting, it is an important technique.

One major application of packets is in the Grand Alliance HDTV system that is described in Section 7.4.3. Another is the *asynchronous transfer mode* (ATM—not to be confused with the banking industry's use of the same acronym) packetizing system used in telecommunications networks.

7.3.6.2 Asynchronous Transfer Mode

Packet size is an important characteristic of packetizing systems that must be chosen at the time of system design. It can be either variable-sized or fixed-sized. Although variable-size offers more flexibility, it is more complex than fixed-sized and most system designs have a fixed packet size. Then it is a matter of choosing the fixed size. Because there is a certain amount of overhead required in a packet header regardless of its size, the impact of the overhead is less as packets are made larger. However, smaller packets offer more flexibility in system performance. Because of the flexibility and because it takes the same amount of processing to manage packetizing regardless of packet size, most system designs have packet sizes that are small—in the range from 50 to a few hundred bytes.

The ATM system is at the low end of this range; its packets are called "cells" and have a size of 53 bytes as shown in Figure 7.13. Each cell has a data capacity of 48 bytes and a 5-byte header. The figure shows the structure of the cell header as it appears coming out of an ATM network. (The header is different going into the network.)

There are five parts to the ATM cell header plus 8 bits of error protection code for the header. The five parts are

1. Flow control—4 bits that can be used for controlling flow of information from the user's network interface hardware.

2. Virtual path identifier (VPI)—12 bits that identify the destination for the cell. Many cells of different types may have the same VPI.

3. Virtual channel identifier (VCI)—12 bits that identify the channel for a specific stream.

4. Payload type (PT)—3 bits that the user may use to identify the information type. These bits are ignored by the network hardware and software.

5. One reserved bit.

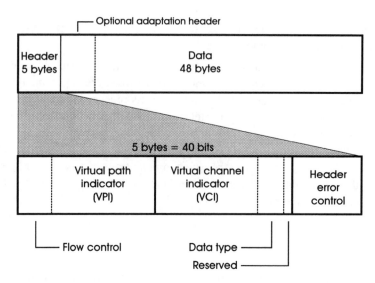

Figure 7.13 *Asynchronous transfer mode packet structure.*

In addition to the 5-byte standard header, the ATM protocol provides for an additional user-defined *adaptation header* that may occupy the first four bytes of the data field.

7.3 TRANSMISSION MEDIA

Transmission requires some type of connection between the data source and the user. This is either a physical connection such as copper or fiber-optic cable, telephone line, and so forth or it is a radio-frequency connection as used in terrestrial broadcasting or satellite transmission. These media are discussed here.

7.3.1 Coaxial Cable

Coaxial cable connections range from the small flexible video cables used in broadcasting or home systems to the semirigid cable used for cable TV trunk lines. All these have the property that signals are attenuated over distance and more so at higher frequencies. For analog service, it is customary to *equalize* the cable over the intended working bandwidth by means of filter circuits placed at one or both ends of the cable. As more equalization is used, the cable SNR degrades and that becomes the limit on how long a cable circuit is practical. This can be overcome by periodically amplifying the signal with a *repeater* unit. These are widely used in cable TV systems.

All these approaches are valuable in digital systems, but there is the additional opportunity of choosing the digital encoding and modulation to suit the characteristics of the cable.

Table 7.2

Digital Performance of Different Cable Types

Media	Data rate (Mb/s)	Distance (km)	Rate×distance (Gb-km/s)
Twisted pair	1	2	0.002
Coax cable (small)	10	1	0.01
Coax cable (cable TV)	2,000	1	2
Multimode fiber	600	2	1.2
Single-mode fiber	2,000	100	200

Digital transmission can take place over any type of cable with any type of encoding, but the practical operating length will be limited. The limit can be extended by choice of proper encoding and the use of analog techniques such as equalization. Table 7.2 lists some typical cables and their properties for digital transmission.

7.3.1.1 Cable-TV Systems

The equalized analog bandwidth of cable-TV systems is 300 to 500 MHz and is divided into TV channels, giving 50 to 80 6-MHz channels. As with terrestrial TV broadcasting (see Section 7.3.4), it is possible to mix both analog and digital services on the same cable by defining certain channels to be analog and others to be digital. Using the Grand Alliance HDTV forms of modulation, each 6-MHz channel on cable is capable of about 38 Mb/s data rate. If 50 cable channels were digital, this would be an aggregate data rate of 1.9 Gb/s. With MPEG-1 video compression, a single cable-TV system could transmit up to 1,000 video and audio channels at modest resolution. The capacity is prodigious, but the real challenge is to learn how to use it. It is unlikely that any cable system would try to deliver 1,000 different programs all the time, but applications such as video on demand may be able to use that capacity (see Chapter 14).

7.3.2 Fiber-Optic Cables

Fiber-optic cable has much greater bandwidth and length properties than copper cable. It requires electronic-to-optical transducers at each end of a link, which means that taps or branch connections are more difficult. However, it offers nearly complete immunity from electrical or magnetic interference. Digital signal properties of fiber-optic links are also listed in Table 7.2.

7.3.3 Telephone Lines

The worldwide telephone network was originally built for analog voice communication at a bandwidth of about 3.5 kHz. It provides *full-duplex* (two-way) communication through a circuit-switched dialup network. Connections are established through dialing and, once established, they are dedicated to the users until one or the other hangs up. Even though the telephone network provides a basic analog service, a lot of the circuits within it are digital, which is because digital techniques facilitate multiplexing of many voice circuits on a single trunk cable.

Today, the digital capability that exists within the telephone network is slowly being made available to subscribers. This is both in the form of permanent leased lines, which are available at data rates of 1.5 Mb/s (called *T1*) and up and as dialup service under the name of *Integrated Services Digital Network* (ISDN), which provides a basic data rate of 128 kb/s. ISDN is available at most locations in the United States, but the various local telephone companies have implemented their interfaces for this service differently, so it is still somewhat confusing to install and the pricing varies widely. The ISDN data rate is still not enough to do much with video, and a still newer service, called *broadband ISDN* (B-ISDN) is being developed. This will provide data rates up to 1.5 Mb/s, which will prove very useful for video.

7.3.3.1 Telephone Modems

In the meantime, users have adapted the existing analog connections to digital transmission by the use of modems. This is widespread in the computer field and is, so far, the basis for the wide use of the Internet and the World Wide Web. Current telephone modems use multilevel modulation at up to 4 bits per symbol and sophisticated systems of automatic configuration and equalization. These latter features are necessary because the performance of individual telephone connections varies widely, and the high data rates are only possible when line conditions are good and analog impairments are corrected. If a particular connection delivers poor performance, most modems will automatically reduce their data rate until adequate error performance is achieved. International standards for telephone modem modulation are established by the ITU-T.

Unfortunately, the narrow bandwidth and limited SNR performance of analog voice connections has so far limited the data rate of telephone modems at about 33,000 bps. Such rates are effective for text communication, but they do not support video, audio, or graphics very well. At the time of this writing, the industry is introducing "56,000-bps" modems, which are capable of delivering that data rate only in the downstream direction (server to client). This is possible by exploiting the ability for servers to use direct digital connections to the telephone network.

The long-range potential of digital communication over telephone lines requires far greater data rates to be available to subscribers. The phone companies are working on this, and there are a number of offerings, but the industry has not yet settled on a standard approach that will deliver high data rates at reasonable cost. Since the future of the much-touted Information Superhighway depends on this, one expects that it will soon happen. Meanwhile, we wait.

7.3.3.2 Telephone Cables

The cable used for analog voice communication is twisted-pair copper wire, which has surprising capability in digital transmission. Table 7.2 lists digital performance of twisted-pair connections. Parts of the telephone network that are digital also use coaxial cables and fiber-optic cables for longer distances.

7.3.4 Radio-Frequency Transmission

Radio-frequency (RF) communication can be point-to-point or one-to-many (broadcasting). A dedicated point-to-point (p-p) link is expensive, and the number of such links is limited by available frequency spectrum space.

7.3.4.1 Cellular Radio

Most p-p communication today is over RF networks, such as cellular telephones. These systems spread their cost and share their spectrum space over many users. The cellular network was originally analog, for voice use, but it is now becoming digital. Although cellular telephones can be used for digital transmission with modems, the cellular switching makes this unreliable. As the cellular network becomes digital and appropriate encoding to deal with its characteristics becomes available, data transmission use will grow.

7.3.4.2 Broadcasting

Video and audio broadcasting is ubiquitous around the world. Tens of thousands of radio and television transmitters are broadcasting every day to a billion or more receivers. Essentially all these services are analog, but digital services are being developed and should begin deployment in the near future. An important one of these new developments is the Grand Alliance system that has been developed in the United States. This system is described in detail in Section 7.4.3. Other systems are under development in most major countries of the world.

7.3.4.3 Satellite Broadcast

Geosynchronous satellites are in use for both broadcast and point-to-point communication [4]. These involve a receiver-transmitter combination called a *transponder* in the satellite to receive a signal source from the ground (the *uplink*) and retransmit it at a different frequency and through a different antenna (the *downlink*) to one or more receiving stations on the ground. Because the power on a satellite is from solar cells, the transmitted power of a satellite is limited, and microwave frequencies and narrow-beam dish antennas must be used to achieve satisfactory performance. In spite of the limitations, broadcasting to a large area such as the entire continental United States has been achieved.

Early satellite transponders used analog FM modulation but newer designs use digital modulation. Various types of end-user service are available for video, audio, or data uses.

7.4 TRANSMISSION SYSTEMS

The definition of a transmission system must include its encoding and modulation. When a specific medium is required, the definition will also specify physical media, connectors, and the like. Several widely-deployed (or potentially so) systems are described here.

7.4.1 Bit-Parallel 4:2:2 Component (SMPTE 125M)

The SMPTE has created several digital interface standards for NTSC, PAL, and HDTV signals in both parallel and serial formats. SMPTE 125M is a 10-bit parallel interface for 525/60 systems operating with ITU-R Rec. BT.601 digitizing in the 4:2:2 format. A special cable is used containing 12 twisted-pair circuits with DB-25 connectors. Ten pairs are used for the data, the eleventh pair is a clock path, and the remaining pair is used for additional grounding. Cable length up to 50m is possible without equalization; lengths up to 300m may be possible with equalization. Note that these parallel interfaces require careful matching of the individual circuits in the multiwire cables so that the timing of each bit path remains within the clocking tolerances. This ultimately limits the performance of parallel interfaces.

The signal encoding on each data line is NRZ, and the 10 data lines transmit PCM samples in parallel. There is no provision for error protection of the video data, which is reasonable for a hardwired cable connection. The three color components are Y, C_R, C_B, and they are multiplexed in the sequence: C_B Y C_R [Y] C_B ..., where the three C_B Y C_R values correspond to samples taken at the same image position (cosited) and the [Y] value is the inbetween Y sample that has no cosited C_B and C_R samples. This multiplexing of the subsampled C_R and C_B components means that the data rate on the cable is twice the sampling rate of 13.5 MHz, or 27 MHz.

The Rec. 601 format does not require sampling of the horizontal and vertical blanking intervals but that time remains available for transmission of ID signals and other

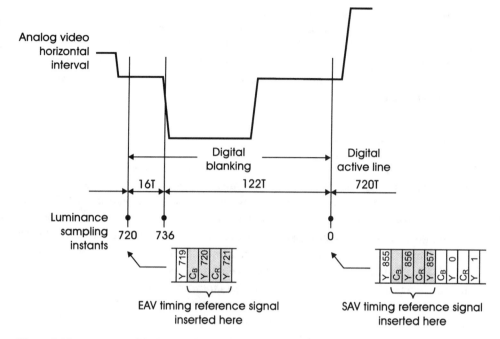

Figure 7.14 *Assignment of the horizontal blanking interval samples in SMPTE 125M (NTSC).*

information. For example, there are 858 total samples in one line period but only 720 active samples are specified. Figure 7.14 shows how the rest of the horizontal blanking interval is specified.

Two four-word synchronization blocks are placed at the start of active video (SAV) and the end of active video (EAV). The sync blocks consist of one word that is all ones, two words that are all zeros, and a fourth word that identifies vertical blanking and field-sequence number. Since at the 27-MHz interface clock frequency there are 276 clock periods in the digital horizontal blanking interval and eight are used for synchronization, there remain 268 clock periods that may be used for transmission of ancillary data.

If ancillary data are used, each block requires its own three-word header that has one word all zeros and two words all ones. (Note that the Rec. 601 format requires that video data must never contain the all-zero or all-one words—these are reserved for synchronization purposes.)

If all the horizontal blanking intervals of the composite digital standard were used for a single ancillary data stream, there would be a maximum of 262 10-bit words in each HBI, which gives a data rate of 41.2 Mb/s. This is plenty of capacity for several audio channels with a lot to spare.

This basic design of a parallel interface has also been extended to a format for a digital version of the SMPTE 240M analog HDTV production format. This digital interface is described in SMPTE standard 260M. At the higher sampling frequency of 74.25 MHz required for this format, it is not practical to multiplex the color components with the luminance as was done in 125M. Therefore, additional data pairs are added to the cables for this service. For Y, C_R, C_B transmission, a 21-pair cable is used and for R, G, B transmission, 31 pairs are needed. Even so, the high clock frequency limits cable lengths to a maximum of 20m without equalization.

7.4.2 10-Bit Serial (SMPTE 259M)

Although the hardware for the parallel interfaces is simple, the multiwire cables are expensive and awkward and are limited in length. Further, they are totally new to existing analog facilities, which means that none of the existing cabling can be used with parallel digital interfacing. It is very desirable to have a digital interface that can use the standard RG-59 coax already existing by the mile in analog video systems. A serial interface solves these problems but with more expensive terminal hardware. SMPTE 259M is a serial interface for 10-bit transmission of 525/60 or 625/50 component or composite digitized signals. This standard is also referred to as *serial digital interface* (SDI).

Coaxial cable is used with BNC (IEC 169-8) connectors. The bits of each sample are arranged serially with the LSB transmitted first and the encoding is scrambled NRZI. (The scrambling alleviates NRZI's problem of $T_{max} = \infty$.)

Synchronization of the format for component signals is accomplished using the SAV and EAV signals that are already in the parallel input format as specified in SMPTE 125M.

In the case of composite encoding, synchronization of the format is provided by the use of a timing reference and identification (TRS-ID) signal placed in horizontal blanking intervals right after the normal location of the horizontal sync leading edge. This signal consists of one word of all ones, three words of all zeros, and a fifth word that contains bit flags for field identification and five bits for line number identification. Note that five bits only allows 31 values, so all lines cannot be uniquely identified. The line ID begins with line 1 at the start of vertical blanking on odd fields and line 264 (525/60) or line 314 (625/50) in even fields. Lines are numbered until the 5-bit value reaches 31 and then the remaining lines of the field are all numbered 31.

7.4.3 Grand Alliance ATV

Development of the world's first comprehensive digital television standard was begun in the United States by a consortium of research and commercial organizations called the Grand Alliance (GA) that was formed in 1993. The basis for this was development work around the world over the past ten or more years that was originally under the name of HDTV. However, the GA standard is much more than that because it can be used to broadcast (or otherwise distribute) TV signals at standard resolutions (525-lines or 625-lines) as well as HDTV. Therefore it is now called the advanced TV (ATV) standard. The transmission features of the ATV standard are covered here; other features are covered elsewhere in this book.

7.4.3.1 Objectives for ATV

Much of the earlier work on HDTV was based on analog technologies, but by the time of the formation of the Grand Alliance in 1993, there was consensus that the new standard should be all-digital. The objectives for the system [5] were:

- High-quality digital HDTV pictures and sound,
- A system that could coexist with analog TV broadcasting without interfering either way,
- Cost-effective equipment should be possible for consumers, producers, and all users at the time of introduction and over the life of the standard,
- Interoperability with other transmission media and applications,
- The potential for a worldwide standard.

The last objective was fulfilled in the eyes of the developers, but we will have to see what the impact will be in international standards circles. The other objectives are all met by the final system design.

7.4.3.2 Layered Architecture

The GA system architecture is shown in Figure 7.15, which also shows how it relates to the OSI layers described in Section 7.2.1. The other standards and technologies that apply in each layer are shown.

The GA defined four layers:

1. Picture layer—the GA system provides multiple formats and frame rates, all of which could be decoded and presented by a GA ATV receiver. This approach allows different services to have different scanning standards as suits their purposes (see Section 10.6).

2. Compression layer—the video compression of the GA system is based on the ISO-MPEG-2 standards (see Section 9.4.3), and the audio system uses Dolby AC-3 audio compression (see Section 9.4.5) that provides 5.1 channels of surround-sound in a data rate of 384 kb/s. The video data rate for HDTV picture formats is approximately 18.9 Mb/s and for standard-definition picture formats it is 3 to 5 Mb/s.

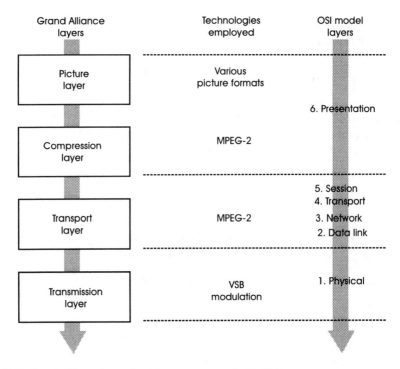

Figure 7.15 *Grand Alliance layered architecture compared with OSI layers.*

Transport layer—the GA system used packetized transport based on the MPEG-2 packet structure. Any number of separate audio, video, or data streams can be multiplexed into the transmission bit stream.

4. Transmission layer—this layer performs forward error correction processing and modulation using multilevel symbols.

Only the transport and transmission layers are discussed further here.

7.4.3.3 The GA Transport Layer

The transport layer receives separate audio and video bit streams and multiplexes them by means of packetizing. Any number of streams can be handled; multiple streams of video, audio, or other data types can be sent over the same channel, limited only by the total data rate capability of the system.

The GA packet is a 188-byte fixed-length block shown in Figure 7.16. Each packet contains a 4-byte header with a 184-byte data field that may also contain an optional "adaptation header" of variable length. This packet design offers several possibilities for interoperability with the ATM packet structure (see Section 7.3.6.2).

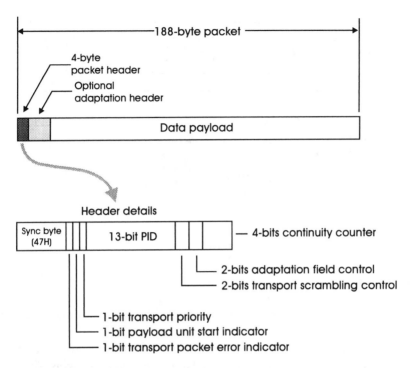

Figure 7.16 *The GA transport packet structure.*

In addition to the a one-byte synchronization field, the packet header provides:

1. A 13-bit field for packet identification, which is used for demultiplexing the packet bit stream. For this purpose, the packet ID (PID) value of 0 is reserved for a special packet that contains an index to the multiplexing structure. This index is in the form of a *program association table* that specifies one or more complete programs and the number of the PID for a *program map table* for each one. The program map table specifies the PID and the type for each data stream in the program. By reading these tables, a receiver can select the packets containing the data streams that it needs.

2. A 4-bit *continuity counter* field, which the transmitter cycles sequentially from 0 to 15 for each packet with the same PID. This allows the receiver to recognize when complete packets have been lost in transmission.

3. The rest of the bits in the packet header are bit flags for specific purposes as shown in Figure 7.16. They provide some packet management functions, indicate the use of optional scrambling to control end-user access, and indicate whether an adaptation header is present in the data payload.

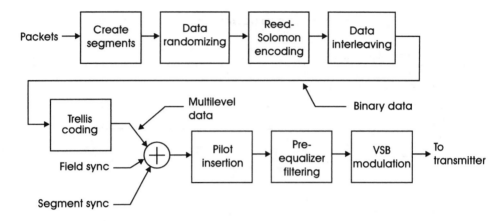

Figure 7.17 *Processing in the GA Transmission layer.*

7.4.3.4 The GA Transmission Layer

The output of the transport layer is a single bit stream containing multiplexed packets for all the data types to be sent down the channel. The transmission layer performs the modulation that allows this stream to be transmitted over a 6-MHz quasilinear analog channel. It uses *vestigial sideband* (VSB) modulation of multilevel symbols. This is called 8-VSB or 16-VSB modulation, where the number indicates the number of symbol levels transmitted. Broadcast systems use the 8-VSB format that has better error protection capabilities whereas cable-TV systems can use the 16-VSB format that offers higher data rates but also requires the higher SNR that cable can provide. The transmission processing is shown in Figure 7.17.

The transmission layer processing converts each packet into a *segment*, to which Reed-Solomon error coding is applied. The segment includes the contents of a packet less the sync byte, which is replaced later in the processing. First, the data are randomized by XORing it with a pseudorandom sequence. (In the receiver, the data are again XORed with the same pseudorandom sequence, which restores the data.) Then, R-S processing is done and 20 bytes of R-S error-correction codes are added to each packet, so the 188-byte packet grows to a 207-byte segment (without the sync byte).

Segments are then grouped into data *fields*, which have 313 segments. The first segment of each data field is a *data field sync* pattern that is used at the receiver for purposes of automatic equalization at the receiver, help the receiver to select the appropriate filtering to use, for system diagnostics, and to let the receiver configure its tracking loops. Thus, the receiver is able to readjust its setup periodically to compensate for dynamic changes in the transmission path.

The next step of transmission processing is data interleaving by a convolutional interleaver, which spreads the data over a 52-segment region. This allows the error protection coding to correct for burst errors up to 193 µs. That time period contains approximately

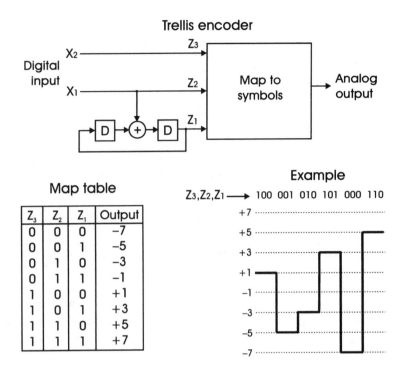

Figure 7.18 *Trellis coding.*

3,600 data bit errors, all of which could be corrected! Interleaving is performed only on the data bytes of the segments; the segment sync and the field sync do not get interleaved because they are added later in the processing, as shown in the figure.

The next step departs from binary encoding and creates multilevel symbols, so this is the start of the modulation process. For broadcasting, 3-bit symbols are used, and for cable transmission, 4-bit symbols are used. In the broadcast case, each two bits of the encoded data are converted into a 3-bit (8 level) symbol using *trellis coding*, which is an error protection technique that improves the system error performance without increasing the bandwidth.

The idea of trellis coding is that in an environment that supports n symbol values but there are only $n/2$ valid values (1 bit less), symbol errors will create sequences containing invalid values. However, a suitable detector can often correct an erroneous sequence by looking for the most likely correct sequence to one that is in error. This is called a *soft decision detector*, sometimes called a *Viterbi* detector [6]. It is most effective when the modulation system is designed to produce the greatest distance (on the constellation diagram of the modulation—often called a Euclidean *distance)* between valid symbol states. A diagram showing these distances appears similar to a garden trellis, which gives the method its name.

VSB carrier

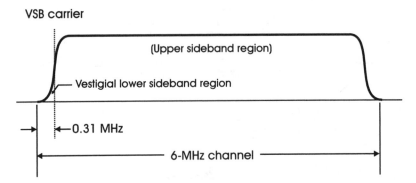

Figure 7.19 *Frequency spectrum of the GA transmission signal in a 6 MHz bandwidth.*

To achieve this concept, the trellis coder for 2-bit data creates the extra redundant bit and maps the resulting 3-bit values to the modulation constellation. Figure 7.18(a) and (b) shows these two steps.

Because of consideration of filters that are introduced in the system to reject interference from NTSC signals that may be on the same channel or on adjacent channels, there are actually 12 trellis coders that are interleaved in a 12-symbol sequence. This prevents the filters from interfering with the trellis coding.

After trellis encoding, the signal is now an 8-level analog format. However, the segment sync and the data field sync patterns are not trellis coded but are inserted as two-level (binary) signals going between modulation levels +5 and −5. The resulting complete signal with sync is amplitude modulated on the channel carrier using suppressed-carrier vestigial-sideband modulation. *Suppressed-carrier* means that for zero-level input, the output carrier is at null and the carrier phase shifts 180deg between positive and negative input levels. *Vestigial sideband* means that one sideband (the lower) of the amplitude-modulated spectrum is partially canceled as shown in the spectrum diagram of Figure 7.19.

As mentioned above, for operation in a cable TV environment where there will be less interference and better SNR, the modulation is 16-VSB and no trellis coding is used. This allows twice the data rate to be transmitted in each 6-MHz channel on cable. The overall performance parameters of several options of the ATV transmission systems is tabulated in Table 7.3.

7.4.4 The AES3 Audio Interface

Many video formats, such as MPEG or Grand Alliance, provide for sending of audio data along with video. However, in an audio-only production or postproduction facility, there is need for separate audio transmission. The AES3 format is widely used in professional audio and a number of other organizations have adopted similar formats [7].

Table 7.3

Performance Parameters of the ATSC ATV System at Several Resolution Levels

Parameter	HDTV-1	HDTV-2	SDTV
Active pixels	1920×1080	1280×720	720×480
Total samples	2200×1125	1600×750	858×525
Frame rate	60 Hz interlaced	60 Hz progressive	59.94 Hz interlaced
	30 Hz progressive	30 Hz progressive	29.97 Hz progressive
	24 Hz progressive	24 Hz progressive	23.97 Hz progressive
Chrominance sampling	4:2:2	4:2:2	4:1:1
Aspect ratio	16:9	16:9	4:3
Video compression	MPEG-2	MPEG-2	MPEG-2
Payload data rate	19.3 Mb/s	19.3 Mb/s	6.0 Mb/s
Audio channels	5.1	5.1	2
Audio bandwidth	20 Hz–20 kHz	20 Hz–20 kHz	20 Hz–20 kHz
Audio sampling freq.	48 kHz	48 kHz	48 kHz
Audio data rate	384 kb/s	384 kb/s	128 kb/s

AES3 is a serial digital interface that supports two audio channels and certain nonaudio data. It uses a single twisted-pair cable that can cover distances up to 100m without equalization. It can also be used with coaxial cable, which allows the length to be increased up to 1 km.

The format is self-clocking and self-synchronizing and can be used at any sampling frequency. Sixty-four bits are sent for each sampling period, in a subframe, frame, and block format as shown in Figure 7.20. For example, with an audio sampling frequency of 44.1 kHz, the data rate of AES3 is 2.822 Mb/s. Audio data can be up to 24 bits/sample and is linearly quantized and encoded in two's-complement format. The channel modulation is the biphase mark code (see Section 7.2.3.2).

A frame corresponds exactly to one sampling period at the source rate, it contains 64 bits and one audio sample for each channel, plus headers. A block is 192 frames. The *channel status data* bit of the frames in a block are accumulated to become a 192-bit (24-byte) data field that provides for channel status, time code, and many other features. This is also shown in Figure 7.20.

The AES3 two-channel standard has been extended to multiple channels in the AES10 standard, which provides for up to 56 audio channels. This standard has a fixed data rate of 125 Mb/s.

7.4.5 IEEE 1394 Firewire

The IEEE 1394 standard [8, 9] addresses the need for an inexpensive, real-time, high data rate network for use in interconnecting audio and video devices as well as computers. It has many options, only a few of which are described here. Using a double twisted-pair cable

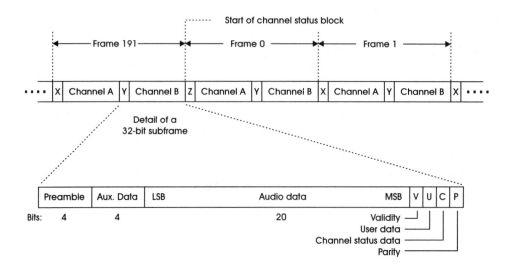

Figure 7.20 *The AES3 64-bit frame structure.*

(four signal wires) with two additional wires for power, 1394 can achieve data rates up to 200 Mb/s over distances of 4.5m between devices. Future 1394 systems will support higher data rates.

The protocol is based on packets, and the two twisted pairs are operated as two channels that may be either isochronous, asynchronous, or both at the same time. The isochronous mode is of most interest to audio/video applications because it allows a connection to be established for a guaranteed data rate. This is possible because the bus runs at a fixed cycle and allows a number of packets to be transmitted on each cycle. Each active connection reserves a packet in each cycle. Connections can be of two types—point-to-point, which cannot be changed by another user, or broadcast, which can be terminated by any user.

The asynchronous transmission mode operates more like a conventional computer network, where all users vie for the bus capacity in real time and no reservations are possible. However, asynchronous operation is also possible on an otherwise isochronous bus by utilizing unused packet spaces in each bus cycle. The 1394 bus is managed by users sending asynchronous control packets to set up registers in each unit connected to the bus. This must be done to establish any type of connection.

The 1394 standard is new, but it is already being proposed for interconnection between digital video cameras, digital VCRs, video effects processors, and computers having video capability. It should become an important feature is many future video systems.

7.5 COMPUTER NETWORKS

Computer networks comprise an important class of digital transmission systems. They differ from the other communications methods discussed so far in that they service a multiplicity of users "simultaneously" through time-sharing. The time-sharing may be tightly managed to control each user's access to the network or it may be managed on a "collision" basis, where users have to wait until they see that no one else is using the network before sending. This latter operation results in a variable delay in going through the network, which is unacceptable for real-time audio or video transmission.

A network may be a *local area network* (LAN), which connects a group of computers at a single location, such as within one building; or a *wide area network* (WAN), which connects a group of computers over long distances—even worldwide. An important form of WAN is the *internetwork*, which connects a group of networks. The *Internet* is the most important member of this class.

7.5.1 Network Properties

Most LANs consist of a bus that connects all computers. There are also ring and star architectures but these are more expensive and are used mostly for high-end business installations. Still more expensive and less common is a switched network. However, switching capability is accomplished in low-cost networks by packetizing, using a variety of protocols to control who uses the network at any given time. There is not space here to cover the details of networks and their protocols, but table 7.4 gives a comparison of some properties for several popular network types. More information can be found in the references [10, 11].

7.5.2 The Internet

In the 1960s and 1970s, the United States military, defense contractors, and academic communities developed an internetwork to aid researchers in sharing information. This

Table 7.4

Computer Networks

Parameter	Ethernet	100-Mb Ethernet	ATM
Length (m)	500	200	100
Clock rate (MHz)	10	100	155
Switched?	no	no	yes
Nodes	<255	<255	~10,000
Standard	IEEE 802.3		

was known as the ARPANET, named for the *Advanced Research Projects Agency* (ARPA) of the U.S. Department of Defense. Without going into all the history, this evolved into what is known today as the Internet, a worldwide public network linking tens of thousands of networks and tens of millions of users and it is growing as much as 100% a year. All this is based largely on a single protocol that allows diverse networks running diverse computers to communicate effectively. That protocol is known as *Transmission Control Protocol/Internet Protocol* (TCP/IP), which uses two levels of packetization to handle network addressing and routing. Other protocols also exist on the Internet; they are accessed through interfaces called *gateways*.

The physical structure of the Internet consists of *hubs* where several networks are brought together. Hubs are connected to other hubs until one reaches certain key hubs that are connected to the *backbone*, which is a high-speed communications path between key hubs. Hubs are equipped with *routers*, which are a combination of hardware and software that controls the flow of packets between specific hubs based on the addressing scheme provided by IP.

7.5.2.1 TCP/IP

The packet structure of TCP/IP (called a *datagram*) is shown in Figure 7.21. TCP is the first layer of protocol when sending a message. TCP uses a variable-length packet that can contain up to 65,516 bytes of data. Larger data objects are sent in multiple datagrams. The TCP header structure is a 20-byte group that includes fields for identifying source and destination for the datagram, a sequence number that allows the receiving TCP to reorder the datagrams if they arrive out of order, and various other fields and flags for management

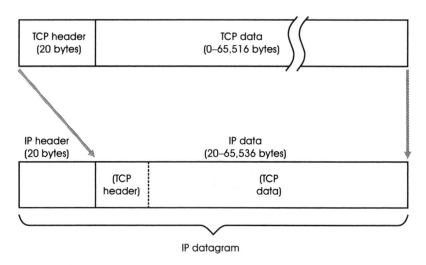

Figure 7.21 TCP/IP packet structure.

of transmission. A checksum field provides error detection for the contents of the datagram.

An IP header is appended to each datagram generated by TCP. It provides fields for control of the routing of the datagram through the networks. IP adds additional source and destination information and also provides fields that support IP processing later in the path to divide the datagram into several pieces if that will provide best transport. The *lifetime* field provides for the case where a datagram might be routed around endlessly and never find its destination. It provides for a maximum number of hops, after which IP will destroy the datagram.

TCP/IP provides an acknowledgment back to the sender for the successful reception of each datagram. This allows lost datagrams to be sent again or, after an appropriate timeout, for the sender to know that a message was never received.

The preferred mode of operation of the Internet is that one connects to the net only long enough to send or receive a single transmission and then logs off. The network is not held connected while waiting for a user to do something. This uses the minimum of network capacity but has the problem that any dynamic activity that is required at the client end should run on the client's computer. Strategies for doing that have been developed for the World Wide Web (see Section 13.5).

7.6 CONCLUSION

This chapter has shown the tremendous diversity of digital transmission technology and has given a few examples of transmission systems. Digital transmission is indispensable in modern systems and is also rapidly replacing analog technology in telecommunications. The opportunities for digital transmission are still coming into view and are the basis for many new system proposals.

REFERENCES

1. Bodson, D., McConnell, K.R., and Schaphorst, R., *FAX: Digital Facsimile Technology and Applications,* 2nd ed., Artech House, Boston, 1992, pp. 94–100.

2. Reed, I.S., and Solomon, G., "Polynomial Codes Over Certain Finite Fields," *J. Soc. Ind. Appl. Math,* 8:300–304, 1960.

3. Ohta, N., *Packet Video Modeling and Signal Processing*, Artech House, Boston, 1994.

4. Inglis, A. F., *Satellite Technology: An Introduction*, Focal Press, Boston, 1991.

5. *Grand Alliance HDTV Signal Specification,* ver. 2.0, Grand Alliance, Dec. 1994.

6. Viterbi, A.J., "Error Bounds for Convolutional Codes and an Asymptotically Optimum Decoding Algorithm," *IEEE Trans. Information Theory*, vol. IT-13, Apr 1967, pp. 260–269.

7. Pohlman, K. C., *Principles of Digital Audio*, 3rd ed., McGraw-Hill, New York, 1995.

8. http://www.ti.com/sc/docs/msp/1394/1394.htm

9. *IEEE Standard 1394-1995, Standard for a High Performance Serial Bus*, IEEE Standards Press, 1-800-678-IEEE.

10. Hennessy, J. L., and Patterson, D., *Computer Architecture: A Quantitative Approach,* 2nd ed., Morgan Kaufmann, San Francisco, 1996.

11. Lu, G., *Communication and Computers for Distributed Multimedia Systems*, Artech House, Boston, 1996.

Chapter 8

Digital Signal Processing

8.1 INTRODUCTION

Although the advantages of digital transmission may justify many digital audio or video systems, the reason that most of the first digital audio and video devices came into use in otherwise analog systems is because of the capabilities of digital signal processing. Tasks such as time-base correction and video special effects have been done digitally for nearly 20 years—these are things that are not practical at all with analog signals. Other, more mundane processing tasks such as gain control, mixing, and filtering, which are part of all systems, are now routinely done digitally. This chapter discusses the digital signal processing techniques employed in audio and video and gives some system-level examples of their use.

8.2 PROCESSING ENVIRONMENTS

Signal processing involves performing mathematical operations on the basic samples or pixels that make up an audio or video bit stream. Samples must be directly accessible to the processing hardware or software without complex decoding.

8.2.1 Signal Formats

The accessibility of the signal elements means that any compression applied to the signal must be removed by decompression before processing. Ordinarily, a straight PCM format of audio samples or video pixels is the best for processing. Because decompression-recompression may cause loss of signal information if performed repeatedly, it is desirable for all processing to be performed before compressing the signals. Once a signal has been compressed, it may be impossible to perform processing without some signal degradation.

8.2.2 Hardware or Software

In a signal origination environment such as a video camera or audio digitizer, it is likely that signals will be in a parallel format. However, once a signal is prepared for transmission, it is more likely that it will be in a serial format. Processing can be done in either format, but parallel processing hardware is usually going to be more complex. Since parallel-to-serial or serial-to-parallel conversion is lossless and inexpensive, the choice of processing format is usually based on a different consideration—speed.

The system parameter that tells the most about processing speed is the number of processing steps that the system can complete in the time of one pixel or one audio sample. For example, if a system has a 100-MHz processor dedicated to video and is processing 640×480-pixel images at 60 frames per second, the pixel rate is 640×480×60 = 18,432,000 pixels per second. Thus, there are only about 5.4 processor clocks per pixel available to this system, which would limit it to extremely simple processes, such as truncation or decimation. More elaborate processes, such as interpolation or resizing an image, can easily require thousands of process steps per pixel.

In the case of audio processing where the sample rate is hundreds of times slower that video, processing with a 100-MHz processor is more reasonable. For example, at 44.1 kHz audio sampling, the 100-MHz processor has 2,267 clocks per sample available for processing, which would support many types of process.

Until general-purpose processors become about two orders of magnitude faster than they are today, the solution to the video processing speed problem is to design dedicated processing hardware. Custom integrated circuits—*application-specific integrated circuits* (ASICs) are capable of extremely complex processes, even in parallel formats, and they are economical when there is a large enough market for the functionality involved. This is particularly relevant in the case of complex compression or decompression processes. For a particular compression standard to succeed, there must be a low-cost decompression chip available and compression hardware must be produced at reasonable prices for that market.

8.2.3 Pipelining

In a complex processing unit, the rate of handling input data (pixels or samples) is determined by how long it takes the hardware to perform the entire process on a single element of data. If the maximum processing time is T, then the maximum data rate capability is $1/T$ elements/second. This can be speeded up by breaking the process down into stages and operating all of the stages in parallel, an architectural technique called *pipelining*. It is like a traditional manufacturing assembly line. Figure 8.1 shows pipelining for a process made up of four steps, A, B, C, and D. Each data element enters process A and then proceeds through the other processes just as if they were in series. What is different is that the next data element enters processor A as soon as it has finished the first data element instead of waiting for the entire process to finish. The maximum data rate that can be handled is $1/T$

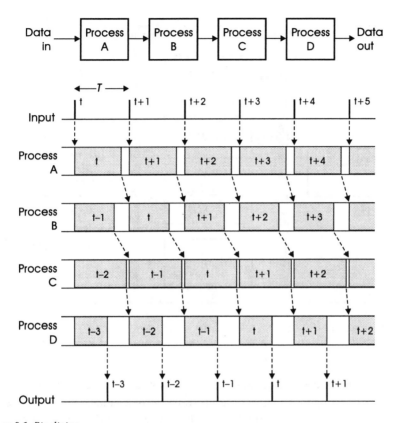

Figure 8.1 *Pipelining.*

where T is now defined for the slowest section of the process, which is process C in the figure. Pipelining has been developed to a high art in modern microprocessor design.

8.2.4 DSP Chips

Digital signal processing (DSP) can be performed in dedicated hardware that contains just the logic needed for a specific task or in a microprocessor controlled by software. The latter approach is much more flexible and cost effective but may be limited in performance by the speed of the processor because samples must be processed in real time at whatever rate they arrive. A special class of microprocessors that are designed to facilitate high-speed signal processing are called *digital signal processors* (DSPs). These chips have an architecture that supports rapid moving of data and often contain special processing features that perform common DSP operations that would be very time consuming in a general purpose microprocessor. Typical of such operations are fast multipliers with accumulators

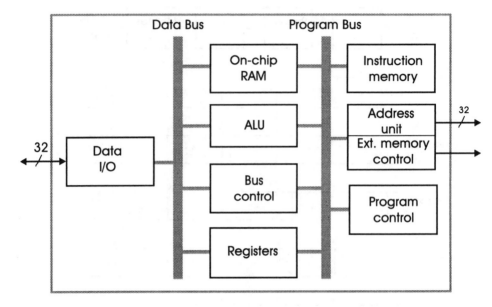

Figure 8.2 *Block diagram of a digital signal processing (DSP) microprocessor.*

(used in digital filters), separate memories for instructions and data (general speedup), and various pixel-processing functions, such as interpolation or decimation. Figure 8.2 shows a block diagram of a typical DSP chip. This can be compared with the typical PC computer shown in Figure 1.12. It shows the basic two-bus architecture with on-chip and external RAM capabilities. Most DSPs are RISC designs, with instructions executing in one machine cycle, and they are heavily pipelined.

Since DSPs are software controlled, they can perform different tasks simply by changing their software and, if there is enough speed, one DSP can perform several different functions that would otherwise require separate chips in a hardwired architecture. The ability to update software means that a system can be kept up to the latest standards without replacement of hardware.

8.3 GENERAL TECHNIQUES

Typical audio or video signal processing uses not only the digital techniques covered in Chapter 1, but also some of the more advanced techniques covered here.

8.3.1 Multiplication

A key ingredient of most digital processes that modify sample values is multiplication. As explained in Section 1.3, the number systems used in digital audio and video are pure binary, offset binary, or two's complement, which are integer representations of the sample values. Integer multiplication is easily accomplished with addition by adding copies of the multiplicand a number of times equal to the multiplier. This is simple, but the number of operations required grows exponentially with the number of bits per sample and quickly becomes impractical because of speed.

In Section 6.5.2, it was also shown that, for the case of multiplication by a constant, a lookup table memory could be used to multiply. This is a fast approach that is quite practical for 8- or 10-bit data, but it becomes impractical for longer data words. It also is not applicable when the multiplier must be changed rapidly because it takes significant time to calculate and reload the multiplier memory.

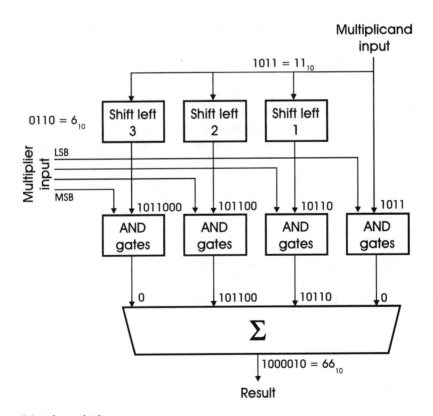

Figure 8.3 *A fast multiplier.*

A better fast multiplier approach is that shown in Figure 8.3, which is a 4-bit example. The numbers shown are for multiplying 11×6. Ascending powers of 2 of the multiplicand are created by shifting bits to the left and the bits of the multiplier are used to control which powers of the multiplicand must be added for the result. This is equivalent to the way one multiplies decimal numbers with paper and pencil. It is fast, but it becomes extremely complex for long word lengths. However, it is not too complex for an integrated circuit and fast multiplier chips are available for the word lengths required in digital audio and video.

Multiplication of two n-bit values can produce an output word with up to $2n$ bits. Since the subsequent hardware may not be able to handle $2n$ bits per sample, it is usually necessary to requantize after performing processes involving multiplication. This was described in Section 5.2.2.6.

8.3.2 Digital Filtering

Analog filtering can be characterized as a frequency-domain process (frequency- and phase-response) or as a time-domain process (transient-response). The same can be said for digital filtering. Most analog filters are specified and designed based on frequency-domain characterization, and many techniques are available for going from frequency-domain specifications to filter design specifications. A significant problem in analog filters is control of the phase response, and many filter designs require a separate phase equalizer section to compensate for phase distortion in the filter itself. The phase characteristic of a filter will contribute distortion unless the phase curve is linear with frequency (called *linear phase*). Since delay is the derivative of phase versus frequency, nonlinear phase means that the filter's delay changes with frequency, which will cause signal frequency components to be shifted with respect to one another. This shows up as asymmetry of the transient response of the filter.

These considerations are different in the digital world. Digital filters are usually designed based on their transient response and achieving linear phase performance (if required) is easy. However, it is still most convenient in system design to define filter specifications in terms of frequency-phase response, so digital filter design usually requires first deriving the analog impulse transient response implied by the frequency-domain specifications. This comes about because a digital sample is essentially an impulse in analog terms. As shown in Figure 8.4, the relationship between the time domain and the frequency domain can be readily characterized for simple signal forms. For example, Figure 8.4(a) shows that an impulse has a flat frequency spectrum to infinity. However, when that frequency spectrum is truncated to a rectangular shape [shown in Figure 8.4(b)], as required in a low-pass filter, the transient response becomes a $(\sin x)/x$ shape. Thus, a digital filter that produces a $(\sin x)/x$ transient response will have a rectangular low-pass frequency response. One method of designing a digital filter is to reproduce the desired transient response by summing a series of appropriately delayed and scaled copies of the input samples.

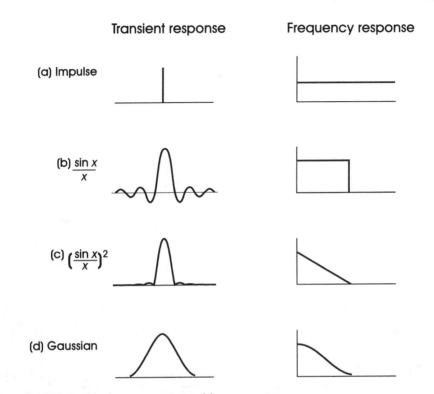

Figure 8.4 *Relationships between transient and frequency responses.*

This process is illustrated in Figure 8.5. Incoming samples pass through a series of delay elements, each delaying by one sample interval. This can be achieved with a shift register architecture (see Section 7.2.2.1), one register for each parallel bit of the incoming samples. The shift registers are clocked at the sampling rate. Outputs are taken from each stage of the shift registers and passed through multipliers that modify the sample amplitudes in accordance with the coefficient values that will produce the desired transient response. The outputs of the multipliers are summed to produce the output from the filter. This type of digital filter is called a *finite impulse response* (FIR) filter because its impulse response is determined by a finite number of samples, equal to the number of stages in the shift registers.

The development of the coefficient values from the transient response is shown in Figure 8.5(a) for a filter having 21 points. Figure 8.5(b) shows a block diagram for this filter example. Note that no multipliers are required for the coefficients that are zero.

Samples must be created symmetrically on both sides of the impulse response to produce a linear phase response and the number of samples used will determine how accurately the filter reproduces the desired response. Thus, the main output sample comes from the center stage of the shift register, so the main pulse has a delay equal to one-half the

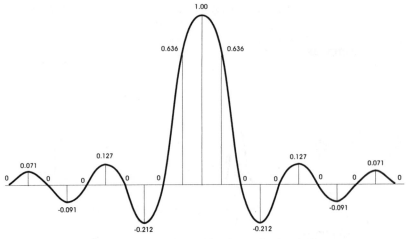

(a) Derivation of values for a 21-point filter from a $\frac{\sin x}{x}$ transient response

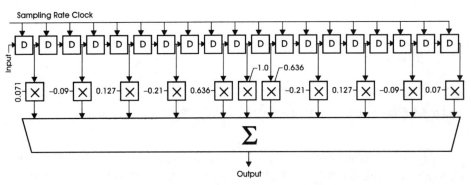

(b) Block diagram for the 21-point filter

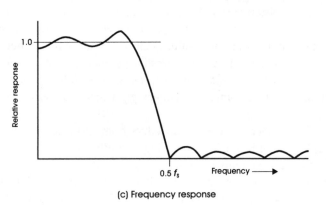

(c) Frequency response

Figure 8.5 *Example of a FIR digital filter.*

delay of the entire shift register. The symmetry requirement means that a filter will always have an odd number of stages. Filters that have such symmetry can be simplified to use the same multipliers for the samples on each side, an architecture called a *folded* digital filter.

An ideal impulse response is infinite in extent—the response extends both ways in time from the main output. To limit the number of stages, a practical filter must truncate the response at some point and this causes some errors in the filtering. For example, the frequency response will contain ripples as shown in Figure 8.5(c) for the 21-point filter. These errors can be reduced by applying a *window function* to the coefficients, rather than just abruptly ending the filter. For example, a triangular function may be used to linearly reduce the coefficient values proportional to their distance from the main response. The use of more points in the filter will also reduce rippling; some audio filters have more than 100 points.

Digital filters have important advantages over analog filters. The easy achievement of perfect linear-phase was already mentioned. Another advantage is that complex filters can be built as integrated circuits and deliver highly precise and reproducible filtering performance.

A digital filter can also be built in a recursive configuration, shown in Figure 8.6. It is called an *infinite impulse response* (IIR) filter. The filter shows the response of a filter with a rather long delay; shorter delays will cause the impulse responses to begin overlapping.

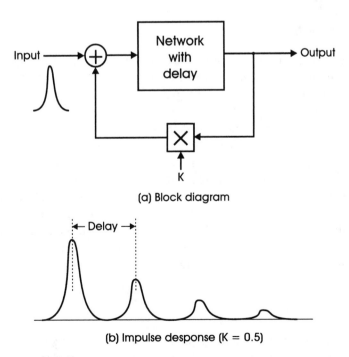

(a) Block diagram

(b) Impulse desponse (K = 0.5)

Figure 8.6 *An example of an IIR digital filter.*

Such a filter will become unstable if the feedback factor K exceeds unity. Because the response of an IIR filter is not symmetrical, it has nonlinear phase, although there are some design techniques to correct the phase distortion. IIR filters are used primarily in audio noise-reduction applications and are generally not used in video.

8.3.3 Interpolation and Decimation

Audio samples represent the values of the input waveform at discrete points defined by the sampling clock signal. Similarly, video samples represent the color values of the image at the discrete scanning locations that occur at the times of the video sampling clock pulses. In either case, it is often necessary to create samples representing the input signal or the image at different times or locations. This is done by *interpolating* from the existing sample points. It is a vital ingredient of time-base correction, video effects, audio pitch changing, and other tasks.

The opposite task is also often required—the elimination of certain samples. This is called *decimation*. Because interpolation or decimation result in different numbers of samples per unit time, they are also called *sample rate conversion*. Processes that increase the sampling rate can be done without regard for aliasing, but reduction of sampling rate can cause aliasing unless proper filtering is used.

8.3.3.1 Sample Interpolation

Given two data points on a curve, intermediate points are determined by interpolation. The simplest case of this is linear interpolation, which assumes that the curve values change linearly between points as illustrated in Figure 8.7. The calculation is performed with a one-sample delay and a single multiplier, in a structure that is similar to a digital filter. A more advanced form of interpolation is done with a special interpolating filter, which require taking additional points of the curve into account. An example is shown in Figure 8.8. The figure shows an example of double-rate conversion. Figure 8.8 (a) shows a superimposition of the impulse responses resulting from 11 adjacent samples. It can be seen that the curves are one for the samples itself but they are zero at all adjacent samples locations. To interpolate samples between the incoming ones, a filter must sum up the values that the adjacent samples contribute at the position of the interpolated samples. The filter must apply these coefficients to the interpolated samples, but the original samples are transmitted unchanged to the output by the center multiplier.

8.3.3.2 Sample Decimation

When the sampling rate is reduced by dropping samples, aliasing becomes a problem unless proper filtering is used before the dropping of samples. It is common to combine the

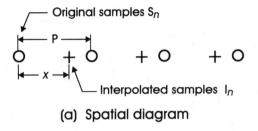

(a) Spatial diagram

$$X = \frac{x}{P} \qquad I_n = S_n + (S_{n+1} - S_n) X$$

(b) calculation

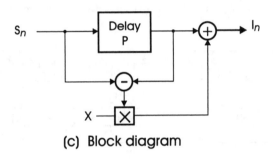

(c) Block diagram

Figure 8.7 Pixel interpolation (linear).

two tasks—filtering and decimation—into a structure called a *decimation filter*. This avoids the inefficiency of filtering (calculating) samples that will subsequently be dropped in decimation. A FIR filter structure as shown in Figure 8.5(b) is used, but the multipliers and the accumulator are clocked at the output (decimated) sample rate. The output impulse response is broader due to the narrower output bandwidth, so there must be more points taken on the sin(x)/x curve.

Sometimes a fractional sample rate conversion must be performed. An example is to convert video samples created at $4 \times f_{sc}$ to $3 \times f_{sc}$ samples. This is done by performing interpolation to raise the sampling rate followed by decimation to lower the rate. In the 4:3 example just quoted, the input samples would be interpolated up 3× and then decimated 4×. If this were done in the reverse order, the intermediate sample rate would be lower than the output and bandwidth would be lost.

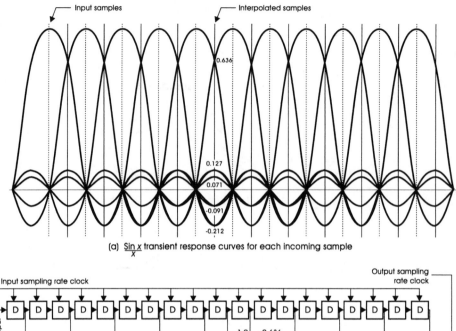

(a) $\frac{\text{Sin } x}{x}$ transient response curves for each incoming sample

(b) Block diagram for the interpolating filter

Figure 8.8 *An interpolating filter for 2× interpolation.*

8.3.3.3 Video Line Interpolation

Interpolation between video lines to create a new line is basically the same as sample interpolation except that the calculations must be performed on samples at equivalent horizontal positions in two adjacent lines. A memory is used to store an entire line of information and then the interpolation calculation is done between the current samples and the output of the line memory, which is from the immediately previous line. The architecture is the same as in Figure 8.7(c). Sometimes it is necessary to do both sample and line interpolation. This can happen, for example, when a video object must be moved by a distance that is less than one pixel. Such is needed in video compression that employs motion compensation, where one-pixel jumps between frames would be too great (see Section 9.3.2.8).

8.3.3.4 Video Frame Interpolation

Frame interpolation is important in standards converters that must convert frame rates, such as between 50 and 60 Hz. Although the approaches described for sample and line interpolation could be applied to frame interpolation by interpolating pixel values between adjacent frames using a frame memory, the result is unsatisfactory when motion occurs between the frames. This can be seen by considering a scene containing a small object that moves a distance of several pixels from one frame to the next. Interpolating pixels at the same screen location in each frame causes distortion at the edges of the moving object as shown in Figure 8.9. This appears as a jumpy effect on moving objects known as *judder*.

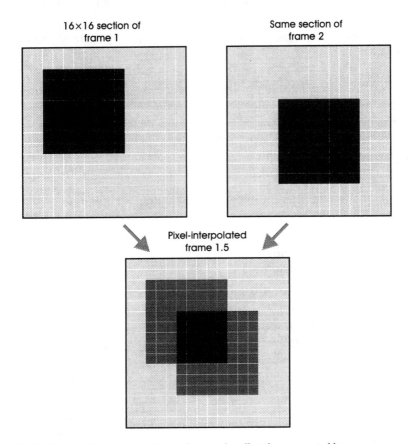

Figure 8.9 *Pixel-by-pixel frame interpolation showing the effect that causes judder.*

What is required is for the interpolation to process related pixels of the moving object, not just pixels at fixed locations on the screen. That can be accomplished by the use of motion compensation, which is described in Section 9.3.2.8. Motion compensation is a very complex process, but has become common in standards converters, effects processors, and video compression processors.

8.3.4 Memory Techniques

Video processors that involve line or frame storage use RAM for the storage. This poses design choices for memory organization and write and read address generation. All video memories use a component parallel data format because of speed considerations and convenience in the processing that follows the memory.

Some memory word structure possibilities are shown in Figure 8.10. The memory may be organized with 8-bit words, which requires interleaving of the color-difference components. However, this readily accommodates subsampled color differences, as in the 4:2:2 format. Alternatively, the memory may have 24-bit words, which would be consistent with 4:4:4 components. The advantage here is that a single memory address writes or reads a complete pixel, whereas an 8-bit format will require separate writing or reading of the three components at different (though related) addresses.

Although RAM chips internally have an x-y array structure with separate row and column addressing, most memory hardware is designed to hide that in favor of a single memory address that external circuits use to find a location in the memory. Thus, the memory becomes a one-dimensional structure. Since scanned video data also has an x-y structure, one might think the memory chip's x-y addressing could be used for picture horizontal and vertical, but this is usually inefficient because memory chips are organized around powers of 2 (256, 512, etc.) and video scanning standards are not usually powers of two. The result would be that memory capacity gets wasted. In fact, the address calculations for one-

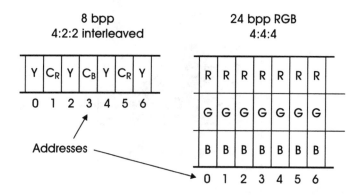

Figure 8.10 *Some frame memory word structures.*

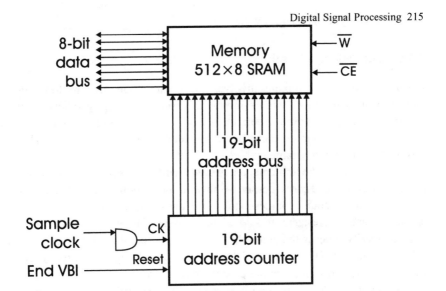

Figure 8.11 *A frame memory to store the luminance component of Rec. BT.601 component video.*

dimensional addressing are very simple, and the added flexibility of this organization is highly advantageous.

Figure 8.11 shows a frame memory and address generator for storing the luminance component of ITU-R Rec. BT.601 format video at 8 bits/pixel. The total memory required for NTSC (if blanking intervals are also stored) is 858×525×8 = 3,603,600 bits or 450,450 bytes. Since there is one byte per pixel, the 450,450 number indicates the number of separate addresses that are needed in the memory. This can be achieved with 19-bit (524,288) addressing, although it is probably convenient to round this off to 20 bits (1,048,576). This memory could be built with a single 512k × 8 (4 Mb) static RAM memory chip, which would still have 73,838 addresses available for other uses.

Addressing for writing is in linear fashion, produced by a counter operating from the sampling clock of the input data. Assuming progressive scanning, the counter is reset at the end of the vertical blanking interval, so the first word written to memory (address 00) is the first active pixel of the frame. Different strategies may be applied with interlaced scanning, depending on whether the two fields are to be stored separately or interlaced into a frame in memory. This would be accomplished by modifying the write addressing procedure.

8.4 PROCESSING EXAMPLES

With modern ASICs, extremely complex processors can be built at moderate cost. Usually the limit of sophistication is what is practical to design. Within this limit, digital processors delve into very fine points in the interest of quality performance. This section shows some examples of real-world digital processing design.

8.4.1 Audio Mixing Console

Postproduction audio mixing involves the combination of a multiplicity of inputs (sources) into one or more outputs (mixes). A mixer has capability for level control, equalization, and effects such as reverberation or ambiance processing for each channel. Channel outputs are combined into the mix outputs under control of an edit decision list that specifies times and mixing parameters.

Audio mixers can be implemented in either hardware or software. Most personal computers that have sound cards (nearly all) have an application program that controls the mixing of the various sound sources available in the PC such as microphone, compact disc, music or voice synthesizers, and stored digital audio. These mixer control applications do not necessarily process the audio directly in software, rather they control the hardware mixing capability of the sound card. However, audio editing applications are available for PCs that do accomplish the entire process in software.

Professional audio mixing consoles can require up to 100 channels. A channel consists of a signal source with its associated settings for level, equalization, and effects. In a digital environment, the concept of a *virtual channel* refers to a channel that is described in software but is not coupled to physical hardware until it is used in the mix. This means that far less physical hardware is required than in an analog environment where every channel would have its own hardware for all the mixing functions. A digital mixing console thus consists of an array of DSP-based physical channels coupled to a computer system that manages storage on hard disks for audio data, virtual channel descriptions, and mixer control information. The interface to the user consists of either a physical control panel or, more flexibly, a computer display screen with mouse, keyboard, or touch controls.

Figure 8.12 shows a typical digital audio mixing console that follows this design philosophy. All internal connections are parallel, serial-parallel converters are not shown. Audio data for mixing may be live (directly from external sources) or stored internally on hard disk, accessed under control of the central computer, and routed to the appropriate channel processor unit through the router module. The router has its own CPU linked to the system control computer and is capable of connecting any signal source to any input and any output to any input. One router architecture would have a central data bus, where all the audio signals coexist. Each signal-using device in the router would have an address and signals would be selected from the bus by addressing, similar to the way a computer defines its signal routing (see Section 1.6.3). Thus, the operating configuration of the system is entirely under computer control.

There are multiple channel processors that can be assigned to different parts of the system by the router. Each channel processor contains its own DSP chip with RAM and I/O for data and control. All channel processing is defined in software on the DSP. Software for the channel processor DSPs comes from the system computer over the control bus. The channel processors are capable of performing gain control, equalization, and other processes depending on the software installed. Channel processor outputs are returned to the router module for assignment.

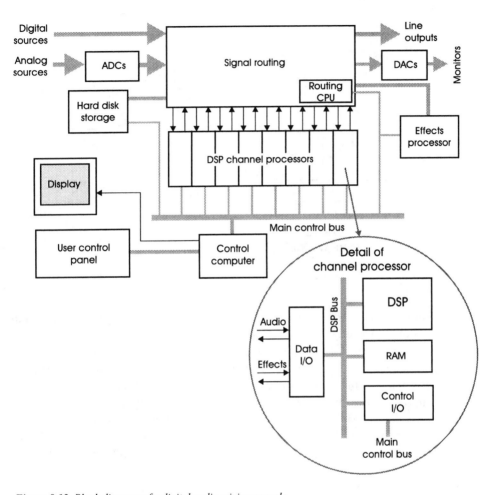

Figure 8.12 *Block diagram of a digital audio mixing console.*

User control is through a control panel and display connected to the system computer and monitoring outputs are provided from the router module.

8.4.2 Video Mixer

The basic purpose of a video mixer is the same as an audio mixer—to combine multiple sources into a program or mix. However, the hardware is quite different and the number of effects possibilities is far greater than with audio. The different hardware occurs because the data rates for video are 100 or more times higher than audio and the concept of performing all processing in software will just not work at such rates. Most of the video processing has to be done in dedicated hardware but still under software control, of course.

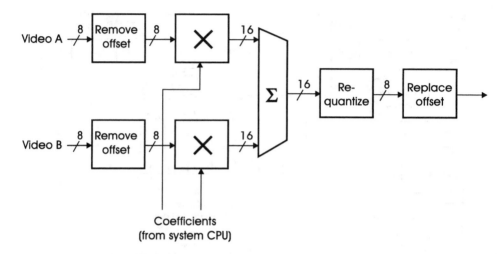

Figure 8.13 *Block diagram of a video mixer for Rec. 601 components.*

Video mixers become dominated by their effects capabilities, which are described in the next section. However, the outputs of effects processors must be combined by conventional mixing or keying. Figure 8.13 shows how video mixing is accomplished for Rec. 601 component video. The diagram applies to each component of the signal. Since the inputs are offset binary, the offset must first be removed so that mixing is respect to black level, not the offset. For the luminance, the offset is 16 and the signal should never go below that level, but for color-difference components, the offset is 128 and the signal goes both ways from there. Removing an offset of 128 is accomplished by reversing the MSB, which converts offset binary into two's complement. Note that the offsets are replaced at the output of mixing.

Mixing is done by multipliers and an accumulator; the multipliers are given coefficients that specify how much of each signal is to be included in the mix. The central computer calculates these values to assure that output overload will not occur after the mix. The multiplication process can extend the bpp, and this has to be removed after mixing by requantizing the signals back to 8 bpp.

8.4.3 Video Effects Processor

Television viewers are very familiar with dynamic video effects such as pans, zooms, windowing, rotation, skewing, perspective, three-dimensional mapping, and many others. These effects are all produced digitally, even if the rest of the video system is analog. They depend on frame memory and signal processing techniques.

A video screen is a two-dimensional array of pixels and all effects can be achieved by processing only the two dimensions. This is true even if the effect is a three-dimensional

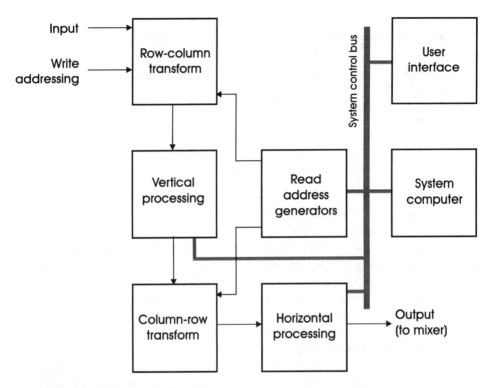

Figure 8.14 *Block diagram of a video effects processor.*

one—the resulting presentation is mapped to two dimensions to display it on the screen. Because the two dimensions of the screen (horizontal and vertical) are orthogonal, it can be shown that all two-dimensional effects can be produced by processing the two dimensions separately, one after the other in either order. Effects processors use this principle; a typical architecture is shown in Figure 8.14.

The frame buffer is logically configured as a two-dimensional array of pixels (horizontal rows) and lines (vertical columns). By writing in the row configuration and reading in a column configuration, a process that is controlled by the address generators, a picture can be transformed from horizontal to vertical organization. In the vertical organization, successive pixels coming from the memory are actually from adjacent lines in the original picture. Thus, the same process that one would use on pixels in a horizontal line (e.g., interpolation) operates vertically after this transformation. This transformation by a two-dimensional memory array is the same thing that is done for interleaving in error protection for transmission (see Section 7.2.5.7).

Notice that an entire frame must be written into the memory before the memory can be read by columns. This means the transformation has an inherent one-frame delay. Such a delay may cause errors in lip-sync, especially if the video signal passes through the effects

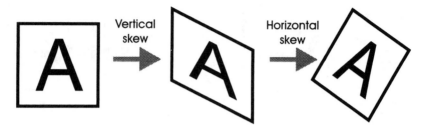

Figure 8.15 *Rotation produced by separate vertical and horizontal skew operations.*

unit more than once. It also means that there must actually be two frame memories so that one can be loaded while the other is being read.

The vertical processor usually contains a high-speed DSP and supporting hardware and is programmable from a central computer to establish the type of effect and its parameters. After vertical processing, the picture is again transformed to return it to the horizontally oriented format, and horizontal processing is done. The horizontal processor is similar to the vertical one and is also programmed by the central computer. As an example of how separate horizontal and vertical processes are combined, Figure 8.15 shows how separate horizontal and vertical skew operations produce a rotation.

The user interface is an important part of a video effects system. That is provided by the central computer and may involve either or both dedicated control panels and graphical computer screens.

8.4.3.1 Windowing

Inserting one picture into a rectangular area of another picture is called *windowing*. This is often used in news programs where a window area appears over the shoulder of a newscaster. The news clip currently being discussed appears in the window. At times, the window may be zoomed to full screen to present the news clip with the newscaster being voice-over. This effect requires the horizontal and vertical processors to perform interpolation and decimation to shrink the news clip video to the size of the window. The small video rectangle is then keyed into the video of the newscaster to assemble the effect. The processing is shown in Figure 8.16.

The video for the window is reduced in size to fit the window by decimation and interpolation. As the figure shows, this is performed in two separate steps—vertical first and then horizontal. The keying into the background occurs by replacing pixels in the background frames with the pixels of the reduced window frames. This can be done by writing them into the background frame memory at addresses that correspond to the location of the window on the screen. Then, the composite scene is displayed by reading from the background frame memory.

Figure 8.16 *Processing for video windowing and zoom.*

8.4.3.2 Zooming

Zooming of the video window up to full screen requires the same processing as the windowing; the shrink factor and keying coordinates are simply changed with time to produce the zoom. The effect is controlled by the central computer, which computes coordinates for each frame and sends them to the effects processors and keyer.

8.4.4 Graphics

Computer screens are generally built with *graphics* objects—text and drawings. The same capabilities are available in video systems by means of digital devices called *character generators* or *paint* tools. However, computers and video have different considerations regarding graphics.

In an analog video system, the introduction of digital graphics can cause a problem because the graphics characters or lines have sharp edges or transitions from one pixel to the next, whereas analog video changes smoothly from one level to another. The graphics represent an excessively wide bandwidth, which will become distorted within the finite-bandwidth analog system. This is especially serious with analog broadcasting or recording, where modulation is employed, because the sharp edges can cause overload artifacts from the modulation system. The solution is that the digital graphics signals must be filtered before introducing them into analog video. The mixing must be by means of a multiplier rather than a keyer. This is not a problem when graphics are introduced into digital video signals because the reconstruction filter of the DAC will remove out-of-band components before they can enter the analog system.

8.4.4.1 Text

Early computers used a lookup table approach to produce text on the screen. The pixels for each line of each text character were held in a memory array and at display time, the proper pixel data were read from the memory as the scanning progressed. This approach is inexpensive but it is quite inflexible in terms of the size, style, and color of the text. Modern computer displays store only an outline of text characters, which may be in the form of pixels or as a mathematical description. Such text character definition files are called *fonts*. The actual pixels for the screen characters are rendered in real time from the font data. Examples of outline characters are shown in Figure 8.17. Video character generators use this same approach except that the generated character pixels are merged with the video bit stream in real time.

Because the characters are rendered at the time they are displayed, with enough processing power, it is also possible to perform dynamic effects on text. Modern video character generators are capable of moving, rotating, skewing, or even projecting text onto three-dimensional objects.

8.4.5 Chroma Keying

An important class of effects uses the video itself to instantaneously control what is displayed on a pixel-by-pixel basis. This is known as *chroma keying* because the control of display is taken from color values of one of the videos. Chroma keying is valuable when it is desired to replace part of one image with another image.

A common example is the use of a keyed background behind an announcer or other performer. In this effect, the actor or actors who will be in the foreground actually perform in front of a solid color background, usually a saturated blue. (This color is appropriate because it does not reflect too well from skin or hair.) The scene is lighted so there will be no shadows on the background and the lighting of the background is as uniform as possible. Of course, it is important that the actors do not wear anything that is the same color as the keying color. In the effects processor, the video pixels from the foreground video are tested against the predetermined keying color; if there is a match (or a close match), the foreground video pixel is replaced by a corresponding pixel from a separate image, which will

Outline	Filled	Rotated	Sized

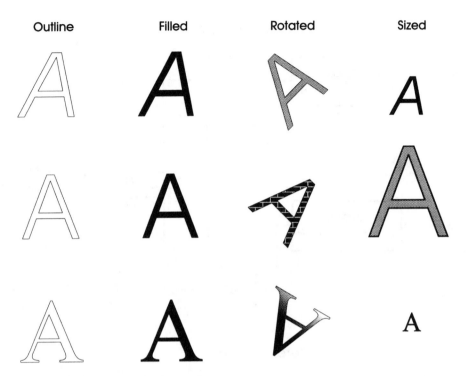

Figure 8.17 *Character generation from outlines.*

be the final background. Thus, a newscaster in the studio can appear as if he or she is standing in front of the news scene at some remote location.

Figure 8.18 shows one method of key signal detection for Rec. 601 4:2:2 component digital video. The color-difference signals C_R and C_B are interpolated up to the luminance sampling rate of 13.5 MHz so the key signal generator will be able to output a key value for every luminance pixel. Then two comparators are used in each color-difference channel to determine when those signals fall in the specified ranges that contain the background color. Although it will work to test only the color-difference signals as shown in the figure, many chroma-key units also test the luminance value with one or two more comparators; this provides further discrimination against noise, especially at low luminance levels. The outputs of all the comparators are ANDed together to produce the key signal. The reference levels are set by the user (through a control computer) to determine the proper values for the key color used.

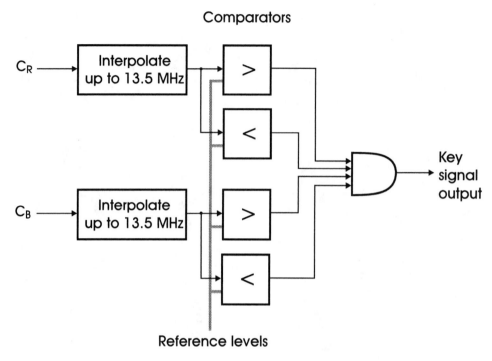

Figure 8.18 *Chroma keying.*

There are many variations of chroma keying based on how the key signal is detected and on what happens to keyed pixels. The keying signal generated by chroma detection may be processed to smooth its edges and then applied to the two video signals in a multiplying mixer. This produces a "soft edge" effect.

Chapter 9

Data Compression

9.1 INTRODUCTION

The amount of data generated by ADC of audio and video signals is so great that digital audio and video would be impractical if that data could not be reduced for use. In fact, the ability to *compress* audio and video data is one of the features that allows digital systems to use less bandwidth or storage capacity and at the same time deliver higher performance at a lower cost than analog systems. This chapter discusses data compression in general and focuses on the methods used for audio and video.

9.2 COMPRESSION ATTRIBUTES

As shown in Figure 9.1, data compression always involves two complementary processes—a *compressor* and a *decompressor*. Compression is usually only used in parts of a system that have inherent data capacity or data rate limitations, such as communication channels or storage devices. The compressor operates at the input of the compressed part of a system, and the decompressor operates at the point where the data have to be put back into its original format. The compressor and decompressor may be located in the same box or

Figure 9.1 *The compression process.*

they may be at a distance, such as when data are compressed for broadcasting to many users at other locations. Each user must be able to perform decompression before he or she will be able to use the data.

9.2.1 Algorithms

The detailed technical description of a specific compression technique is called its *algorithm*. An algorithm is often described mathematically, but other means, such as block diagrams or timing charts, may also be used. Although there are a limited number of general compression methods, they may be combined in almost unlimited ways, leading to a vast number of possibilities for algorithms. Since the compressor and the decompressor must both use equivalent processing for the system to work, the matter of standardization of algorithms becomes very important.

9.2.2 Lossless and Lossy Compression

A major advantage of a digital system is that perfect reproduction of data (and the information it represents) is an option available to system designers. Encoding and error protection methods allow large systems to store, process, and transmit data essentially without error no matter how many times it is done. This is the basis for our worldwide financial computer systems that handle billions of dollars with never an error of even one cent. Even in those systems, it is possible to have data compression, but it must be of the *lossless* type. That means the compression method will not cause any loss of data or errors. This is possible because nearly all real data contains repeating patterns of some sort that a compression processor can search out and then arrange to transmit more efficiently. In general, a lossless compression algorithm does not depend on knowing anything about the data being processed—it will work on any kind of data, but the performance (degree of compression) may depend on certain statistics of the data.

Lossless compression is used for audio and video but its capability is limited. Most audio and video compression techniques are of the *lossy* type, which means that some data are changed or lost. However, the name of the game is to find data that can be removed by the compression processor but will not materially affect the appearance of a picture or the sound apparent to a listener when the signal is reconstructed for display. Lossy compression works because digital audio and video signals may contain information that contributes little to the reproduction of audio and video as seen and heard by a real observer. Lossy compression schemes inherently depend on knowledge of the type of data, their format, and their use.

The above criterion for lossy compression is not the only consideration; the acceptable degree of degradation depends on where in a system the compression is being used. For example, in production and postproduction, very little loss can be tolerated before it begins to interfere with the processes of program creation. Many producers will not accept lossy compression at all. At the other end of the system—delivery to a viewer—the criterion of "apparent to a viewer" is good enough, and lossy compression is widely used for delivery. Even there, however, what will be apparent to a viewer depends on the viewing conditions, and that must be taken into account in the design of the compression system.

9.2.3 Symmetrical versus Asymmetrical Compression

Compression techniques involve a certain amount of processing to initially compress the data and, then, more processing to decompress the data at the end of the system. These processes are often very significant in terms of the amount of hardware and software that may be involved and in the amount of time required to perform each process. *Symmetrical* compression means that the compression and decompression processes are approximately equal regarding their hardware and software requirements and their processing time. For example, if it is desired to compress video in real time on a personal computer and then play back on the same system, a symmetrical algorithm is preferable.

However, a symmetrical algorithm that must run on a small system places a limit on the complexity of the algorithm that can be used. As will be seen in the discussion later in this chapter, compression efficiency can be improved by using more complex algorithms, even when the decompression will be performed on a small system. This leads to the *asymmetrical* algorithms, where compression requires a very large, dedicated system and may not even run in real time, but the decompression is done in real time on a small, inexpensive system. Asymmetrical compression is important especially in systems of mass distribution such as broadcasting or CD-ROM. Many times, compression can be done ahead of time on a large system, stored, and copied later to the distribution medium that goes to the end user.

9.2.4 Degree of Compression

It is often desired to quantify the degree of compression that is obtained by a particular system and to compare different systems that way. People like to speak of the *compression ratio*, which is the ratio between the data coming in to the data going out of the compression process. With lossless compression techniques, this is a very valid approach, since the information content of the data is, by definition, unchanged. However, compression ratio is a dangerous term to use with lossy compression unless it is qualified with additional information about the amount of signal degradation caused by the compression.

A better way to compare lossy compression schemes is to quote the signal performance of the system at a given data rate or the data rate for a given level of performance. However, even this becomes problematic because compression can introduce performance artifacts that are difficult to quantify themselves. In the end, there is a lot of subjective evaluation required to compare lossy compression systems, but simple quotation of compression ratio should be avoided.

Many situations require digital video systems to operate at a constant data rate. For example, a transmission system may have a fixed data rate, or a fixed-rate medium such as a CD-ROM may be the means of distribution. Lossy compression algorithms can be designed for a constant data rate by allowing the amount of picture quality loss to vary. The opposite is also possible—constant picture quality with varying data rate. In either case, the decisions must be made during the compression process.

9.3 GENERAL METHODS

There are a number of general compression methods, but few algorithms use only one of them. Most practical algorithms for audio or video use a combination of these methods. This section describes some of the general methods.

9.3.1 Lossless Methods

Although lossless compression is not often used for audio or video, its methods are often used as part of a lossy algorithm. All lossless methods depend on certain statistics about the data, although they do not need to know what the data represent. Depending on their application, lossless methods sometimes may be made lossy by introducing approximations into their calculations.

9.3.1.1 Run-Length Encoding

General data may contain values that repeat a number of times. This happens, for example, in a bitmapped image that has an area of solid color. Adjacent pixels in that area will have the same value. Such data can be compressed by recognizing when a string of repeated values occurs and transmitting the value once along with a second code that represents a count of the number of times to repeat the value—this is called *run-length encoding* (RLE). RLE must have a means whereby the decompressor can recognize when an RLE value occurs. This is usually done by having a reserved value that rarely or never occurs in data values. For example, the value 255_{10} in an 8-bit system might be reserved for this purpose. Such a reserved value is called an *escape code*. When the escape code is encountered, the decompressor will know the next two values represent a pixel value and the number of repeats for it. This is illustrated in Figure 9.2.

Thus, a single repeated object takes three data words to transmit, so there is no gain in using this method until there are more than three repeated words. Note that it is unnecessary to prevent the input data from containing the reserved escape code value; if that happens, two escape codes can be transmitted together to indicate that the data word has the escape value.

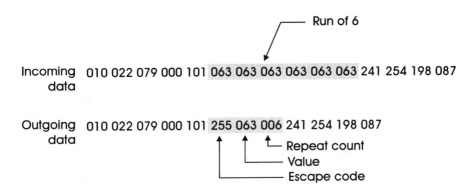

Figure 9.2 *An example of run-length encoding.*

9.3.1.2 Pattern Matching

The concept of RLE can be improved by recognizing repeated *patterns* rather than just words. This takes more processing at the compression end, but the decompression is simplified by sending a lookup table (a code book) that contains the patterns for the current signal block. Thus, whenever a pattern is encountered, the compressor will send an escape code followed by the lookup table index of the pattern to insert in the reproduction. Thus, each pattern takes only two data words but, of course, patterns may be much longer than two words if the compressor cares to go to the trouble of finding them. An example of pattern-matching compression of text is shown in Figure 9.3. Unlike RLE, patterns can be matched even when they are located at different places in the data. Pattern-matching is also called *dictionary-based* compression.

The overhead of the code book must be considered in determining the degree of compression. With the nonaudio or -video data types found in a typical personal computer, this type of compressor delivers about 2:1 compression. It is often less efficient than that with audio or video signals.

Pattern-matching compression is an asymmetrical technique. Several well-known algorithms using this approach are available on the market for generalized data, such as *Lempel-Ziv-Welch* (LZW), PKZIP, and others. However, they are not very useful with audio or video because both data types contain random noise that precludes effective pattern-matching. Note that pattern-matchers are looking for an *exact* match of patterns because they are intended to be lossless. One might also do lossy pattern-matching based on approximate matches, but this is difficult to design so that it properly recognizes the psychophysical considerations about what is important in the data. Other compression methods do a better job of that.

Incoming
text

The concept of RLE can be improved by recognizing repeated
patterns rather than just words. This takes more processing at
the compressing end but the decompression can be simplified
by sending a lookup table . . .

Compressed
text

^2 concept of RLE can be ^5d by recognizing ^6ed patterns
rather than just words. This takes more ^4ing at ^1 ^3ing end
but ^1 de^3ion can be simplified by sending a lookup table . . .

Pattern
table

Index	Pattern
1	the
2	The
3	compress
4	process
5	improve
6	repeat
. . .	

Note: The ^ character
is the escape code.

Figure 9.3 *An example of pattern-matching in text.*

9.3.1.3 Statistical Coding

General data compression can also be performed by considering the statistics of the input data. If it is known that certain word values will be used more often than others, a coding system can be set up to transmit the high-occurrence values with a short (few bits) code, whereas less frequently occurring values can use longer bit codes. A well-known system that uses this principle is the Morse code of telegraphy. In digital systems, the most common method for this is *Huffman* coding [1], which is widely used in video compression algorithms. Huffman coding operates at the bit level; an example is shown in Figure 9.4. The effectiveness of coding depends on prior knowledge of the probability of occurrence P_S of each data value. A binary tree is made from the values arranged in descending order of probability. The codes are created by reading from the output of the binary tree (point "A") back to the input, taking bit values from each branch. As with pattern-matching, a table of parameters or code book must be constructed by the compressor and sent with the data to the decompressor. Statistical coding is also called *entropy coding*.

9.3.2 Lossy Methods

Lossy compression methods must inherently know about the data format and the signifi-cance to the application of every bit or word in the data. It is also necessary to know about the viewer of the data and what he or she may be able to see or hear under the specified viewing conditions. For example, if video is only to be viewed at a large viewing ratio, some of the fine detail information can safely be removed because the viewer will not be

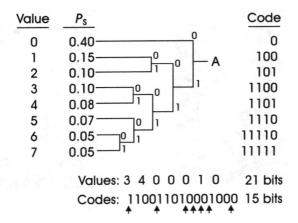

Values: 3 4 0 0 0 1 0   21 bits

Codes: 110011010001000 15 bits

Figure 9.4 *An example of Huffman coding of 3-bit values.*

able to see it anyway. On the other hand, if the viewing or listening conditions are more demanding, little information can be lost without it being noticed. In that case, more sophisticated compression methods are necessary.

9.3.2.1 Truncation

In the category of removing unnecessary data are truncation and subsampling. *Truncation* is the deletion of some of the least significant bits from the samples. This is what has been called requantizing elsewhere in this book and has to be done properly to preserve as much information as possible (see Section 5.2.2.6).

Under ideal viewing conditions, video component samples should have at least 8 bpp, but under less-than-ideal viewing conditions, that might be reduced to 6 bpp without too much noticeable degradation. Because the quantizing SNR degrades 6 dB for every bit removed, truncation is not a very good tradeoff in terms of data reduced versus performance reduced.

High-quality audio sampling requires at least 16 bps. However, many audio systems can operate successfully with as low as 8 bps, especially for speech only, where the bandwidth can be limited and the main criterion is intelligibility.

9.3.2.2 Subsampling

Fewer samples are widely used for color-difference video components compared with the luminance component. This technique is based on the fact that the human eye has poorer acuity for colors than it has for brightness (luminance) information, so the color bandwidth (sample rate) can be reduced without viewers seeing the loss. This is *subsampling* or

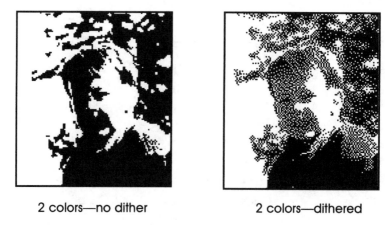

2 colors—no dither   2 colors—dithered

Figure 9.5 *Image reproduction using dither to create gray scale with only two colors.*

sample rate reduction and, as in analog television, it is part of most digital video compression systems (see Section 2.4.4). Subsampling reduces the Nyquist limit to the value represented by the subsampled rate and proper filtering is required to avoid aliasing.

9.3.2.3 Color Tables

For some purposes with video, it is possible to reduce the number of bits/pixel by making the pixel value itself be an index into a table of color values that are selected from a larger number of bits/pixel. For example, the PC VGA standard provides an 8 bpp mode that selects 256 colors from an 18-bit palette. Other systems use different numbers of bits.

It might appear that having only 256 colors would give poor reproduction of natural images but, under appropriate conditions, the reproduction can be surprisingly good. This is particularly true if the table colors are custom selected for each image. Further improvement is possible by using a dithering technique to achieve nontable colors by varying the colors of adjacent pixels. An example of this is shown in Figure 9.5 for an image reproduced by only two color values—black and white. If the viewer is far enough back so he or she cannot see individual pixels, the eye will blend adjacent pixels into combination colors (or, for the example, gray scale levels.)

However, color tables have serious limitations when applied to motion video because the motion of natural images will make the artifacts (such as contouring) more visible. For motion video, it is better to go to a direct color technique with more bits/pixel (such as 16) and use other methods of compression.

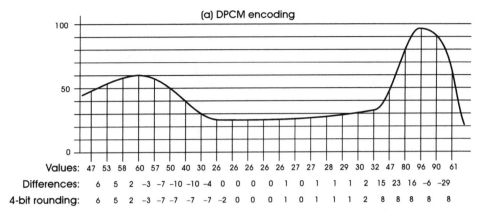

Values:	47	53	58	60	57	50	40	30	26	26	26	26	26	27	27	28	29	30	32	47	80	96	90	61
Differences:	6	5	2	−3	−7	−10	−10	−4	0	0	0	0	1	0	1	1	1	2	15	23	16	−6	−29	
4-bit rounding:	6	5	2	−3	−7	−7	−7	−7	−2	0	0	0	1	0	1	1	1	2	8	8	8	8	8	

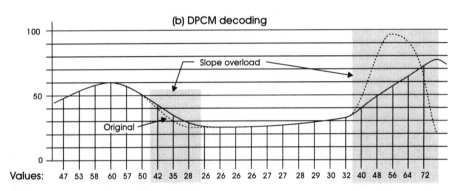

Values:	47	53	58	60	57	50	42	35	28	26	26	26	26	27	27	28	29	30	32	40	48	56	64	72

Figure 9.6 *Differential PCM.*

9.3.2.4 Differential Coding

For both audio and video, the amount of change in amplitude from one sample to the next has a probability distribution that falls off with amplitude. Taking this into account, one can compress by coding differences between samples rather than the samples themselves. If it can be expected that large-amplitude differences will be rare, the difference values may be transmitted with fewer bits than the original samples contained. This coding process is called *differential PCM* (DPCM) and is a member of a larger class called *predictive coding*. In simple DPCM, prediction of a sample is based on the previous sample plus an increment.

In DPCM, when a large difference value occurs, the DPCM system will be overloaded (called *slope overload*), which can cause momentary severe distortion. Figure 9.6(b) shows an example of slope overload. Note that some of the difference values have been corrected to cause the system to recover from moderate slope overload. This is accomplished by the prediction architecture described below.

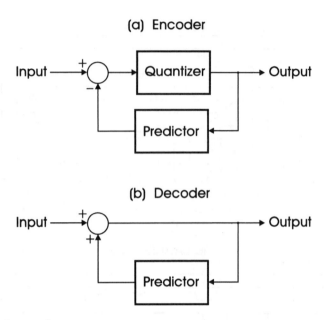

Figure 9.7 *Predictive coding.*

A more advanced form of DPCM has been developed to improve the performance with varying difference values—the relationship between the bits of the difference value and the actual difference they represent is adjusted dynamically based on how large the difference values of the signal are. For example, a typical system may have 4 bits for difference values, which is capable of only 16 steps of difference reproduction. However, if signal differences are running a low levels, the 16 steps of difference reproduction would be made small. If the differences in the signal increase, the adaptive mechanism will increase the step size so the 16 levels can transmit the large difference. This is called *adaptive* DPCM (ADPCM) and is often used for audio compression. ADPCM can achieve about 4:1 compression on general audio signals. There still can be some distortion as the adaptive mechanism shifts the step size but, considering the degree of compression, it is acceptable for many purposes.

9.3.2.5 Predictive Coding

Figure 9.7 is a block diagram that shows how DPCM may be generalized as a predictive coding mechanism. A predictor block performs a process to predict the next sample from the previous sample or samples. The result of the predictor is then compared with the next sample and the difference is transmitted. The receiver can then reproduce the samples using the difference values and an identical predictor module. In the case of DPCM, the predictor is simply the previous sample and the comparison with the next sample generates the difference value, which is transmitted. However, it can be seen that more elaborate predictors can be built, such as a slope predictor that estimated the next sample based on the slope between the previous two samples, and so forth. The success of this approach depends on developing a prediction algorithm that matches the properties of the data being compressed.

9.3.2.6 Speech Coding

With the impetus of telephony many methods have been developed specifically for digital coding of voice or speech. The standard for telephony is straight PCM with μ-law quantizing at 8,000 samples per second and 8 bps, giving a data rate of 64 kbits/s (see Section 5.2.2.7). However, more advanced compression methods are sometimes used to reduce that data rate for specific purposes. The best methods for speech coding are based on modeling the human voice tract in electronics. Such techniques can work well with speech, but they are not very effective for general sounds. These methods are covered in the literature of telephony [2].

9.3.2.7 Transform Coding

Dealing directly with the original signal samples is not necessarily the best way to expose signal redundancy that might be eliminated for compression. This is particularly the case with video, which is inherently a two- or three-dimensional signal (horizontal, vertical, and temporal.) This is the realm of *transforms*, which are simply alternate representations of the information that may be achieved by mathematical processing. Every transform must have an *inverse* transform—the transform is performed during compression and the inverse transform is performed during decompression.

In pictures, it is useful to consider a two-dimensional block of pixels as a unit. A common choice is to take 8 pixels in each direction—a total of 64 values. Looked at spatially, an 8×8 block is just a tiny piece of an image that may not even be recognizable as anything but, by transforming it to the frequency domain, components are seen that are much more readily evaluated for their importance to the final reproduction. This is based on the fact that high spatial frequencies are less visible than lower ones.

The prime transform that exploits this idea is the *discrete cosine transform* (DCT), which is related to the Fourier transform often used to extract the frequency components of an arbitrary waveform. The Fourier transform operates on continuous (analog) waveforms, but a version that operates on a group of samples taken on a continuous waveform is also available. Such sample-based transforms are given the prefix: *discrete*. The Fourier transform, whether discrete or not, delivers a set of sine and cosine frequency components, which can also be viewed as a set of frequency components having amplitude and phase values. A simplification is possible when the discrete Fourier transform is performed on a set of data samples followed by their mirror images in time. The sine terms of the Fourier transform will cancel, leaving only cosine components. This is the discrete cosine transform. It has the property that an 8×8 block of 64 samples is transformed to an 8×8 block of cosine terms, representing spatial frequency in two dimensions. Mathematically, it is expressed as

$$F(u,v) = \frac{1}{4}C(u)C(v)\sum_{x=0}^{7}\sum_{y=0}^{7} f(x,y)\cos\left[\frac{(2x+1)u\pi}{16}\right]\cos\left[\frac{(2y+1)v\pi}{16}\right] \tag{9.1}$$

where

x and y are indices into the 8×8 block of pixels.

u and v are indices into the 8×8 block of output coefficients.

$C(w) = \dfrac{1}{\sqrt{2}}$ for $w = 0$

$C(w) = 1$ for $w > 0$

Putting (9.1) into words, each DCT coefficient is calculated by summing all the input samples with a cosine-based weighting function that depends on the coefficient's position in the output array and the position of each sample in the input array. This is a massive calculation and, even with simplifying assumptions, is usually done in a custom IC. Some features of DCT are shown in Figure 9.8. The output from DCT processing is an 8×8 array of values representing the amplitudes of the spatial frequency components (Figure 9.8 (b)) in

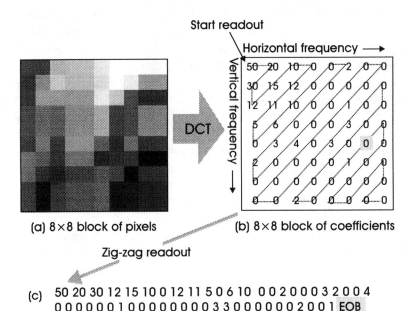

Figure 9.8 *The discrete cosine transform.*

the 8×8 block that was processed. At this point, the DCT processing has produced no compression—there were 64 pixels in the block and now there are 64 DCT coefficients. However, the coefficients are amenable now to considerable compression by further processing.

It is useful to put the coefficients into ascending-frequency order as shown in Figure 9.8(c), which is called *zigzag ordering*. As can be seen, the higher frequency components tend to zero or small values. Because these components are not too important anyway, they can be quantized coarsely without much loss of information in the picture. Therefore, it is only necessary to transmit the components that have nonzero values, thus achieving a considerable data reduction. Beyond a certain point, all coefficients will be zero. An end-of-block (EOB) marker is placed there and no further values are used. The remaining coefficients are usually encoded with RLE and entropy coding.

9.3.2.8 Motion Compensation

Motion video has considerable redundancy from one frame to the next. Much of a frame may not be new information at all—some parts may be stationary and others may simply be parts of the previous frame that have just moved a little. In principle, anything that already exists in the previous frame need not be transmitted again—it can just be copied by the receiver from a stored copy of the previous frame. The task of figuring out what is new or old in a frame is *motion compensation*. It is one of the most complex tasks of video compression, in fact, the effectiveness of motion compensation is always constrained by computational and speed limitations.

As with transform coding, motion compensation is based on processing the images in blocks. Given one complete (first) frame as a starting point, blocks from the next (second) frame are taken and compared with areas of the first frame to determine if there is a match at any position in the first frame. (The block may have moved between frames.) If a match is found, a *motion vector* is created for the receiver to use to predict that area of the second frame by copying it from the first frame. Recognizing that the amount of motion between frames is usually not too great, it is only necessary to search a small area surrounding the location of the block being tested. Even so, the amount of computation represented here is prodigious and it may be necessary to restrict the search range more than might be desired in the interest of practicality. Blocks that are not found in the previous frame must be coded by other means and transmitted in full.

Figure 9.9 is a diagram of this process that shows it in action with a scene that contains only a small moving object (bird) but with the camera tracking the object. That means that the scene is undergoing a pan effect, but most blocks of the new frame do exist at different locations in the preceding frame. Only the blocks of the new frame that could not be found in the preceding frame (the residual) have to be transmitted, so a high degree of compression is possible for this type of scene.

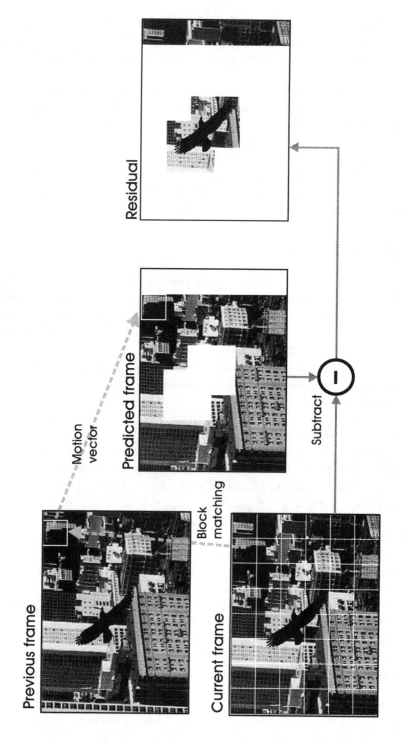

Figure 9.9 *Motion compensation. From A. F. Inglis and A. C. Luther, Video Engineering, Second Edition, McGraw-Hill, 1996 with permission of The McGraw-Hill Companies.*

9.4 PRACTICAL ALGORITHMS

The principles discussed in the preceding section are generally used in combination in practical algorithms. This section describes a number of algorithms to show how that is done.

9.4.1 JPEG

Motion video is nothing more than a series of still pictures transmitted at a high enough rate that the viewer sees them as a continuously moving image. One approach to motion video compression is to compress the still images one by one and transmit the result in a single bit stream. Any approach to still-picture compression could be used, but one of the best ones was developed by the *Joint Photographic Expert Group* (JPEG) of the ISO/IEC and is called JPEG compression [3].

The JPEG image compression standard is not a single algorithm but rather a "tool box" of compression techniques; it has modes and options covering a wide range of "continuous-tone" still-picture compression applications. There are choices for both lossless and lossy compression, different bits/sample, different resolutions, and several different algorithms. Four modes of operation are provided:

- Lossless—the image is reproduced exactly. All other modes are lossy.

- Sequential—this mode encodes in the order that the image was scanned. It is the normal way in which images are processed.

- Progressive—this is a multipass encoding method that first transmits a coarse image that can be rapidly displayed at the receiver. That is followed by repeated encodings at progressively higher resolutions, which can be displayed to give the viewer a progressively better image.

- Hierarchical—in this mode, the image is encoded at multiple resolutions. The user may choose the resolution for displaying the image.

The provision of configurable options in JPEG means that the standard can fit many different applications and can be readily upgraded in the future to keep track with the ongoing research and development of image compression technology. This is a very important and desirable feature in compression standards.

Figure 9.10 is a diagram of the JPEG architecture. The source image is encoded under the control of one or more tables of specifications. The encoded data are placed into the JPEG *interchange format* for delivery to the user. This is the format that would be stored or transmitted. At the receiving end, the tables of specifications and the encoded data are separated and the inverse processing is done to recover the original image.

All encodings except the lossless mode are based on DCT. Figure 9.11 shows the processing in more detail for the sequential mode of operation. Each component of the source image is partitioned into 8×8-pixel blocks, to which the forward DCT processing is

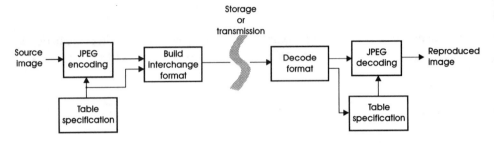

Figure 9.10 *The JPEG architecture.*

applied. This results in one dc coefficient and 63 higher frequency components, which are each quantized according to a table of 64 quantizing values.

This quantizing table is the first table specification of the algorithm; it must be supplied by the user and will become part of the data stream that is transmitted to the receiver. The user can control the tradeoff between degree of compression and image quality by how he or she specifies this table. The contents of the quantizing table are the step sizes that will be used; the DCT coefficient values are simply divided by the corresponding step size and the result rounded to a specified number of bits. Thus, a larger quantizing value results in coarser quantization and it means that larger values will be rounded off to zero.

Following quantization, the DC coefficient is differentially encoded against the DC co-efficient of the preceding block of the image. The other 63 quantized coefficients are then placed in the zig-zag order and statistically encoded according to either the Huffman method or to an arithmetic coding method that is described in the standard. In either case, a second table specification is required to define the statistical coding. Again, the user may vary this table to control the performance of compression.

The last step of encoding is to assemble the compressed data and table specifications into a one-dimensional bit stream according to the interchange format, which is shown in Figure 9.12. The various parts of the interchange bit stream are delineated by *marker*

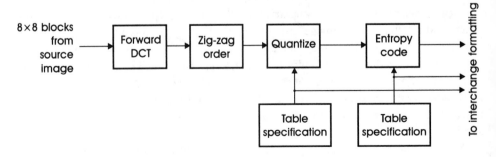

Figure 9.11 *JPEG processing for sequential mode.*

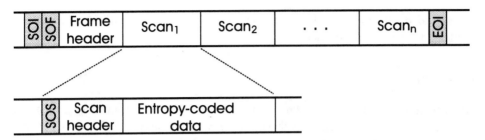

Figure 9.12 *The JPEG interchange format.*

codes, which consist of two bytes—the first is all ones (0xFF in hexadecimal) and the second is any value other than zero or 0xFF. (Note that if an 0xFF occurs in the data of the bit stream, it is encoded as 0xFF00 to prevent its being seen as a marker.) Markers are just like the escape codes that were described for RLE in Section 9.3.1.1.

The second byte of a marker defines the type of marker and some types of markers have additional parameters that follow. In this latter case, the first two bytes after the marker always specify the length of the parameter block that follows. So, for example, a frame header has a special marker defined and then a length parameter that tells how many more bytes are in the header. This is a very common approach in defining bit stream headers.

As Figure 9.12 shows, the encoded image data for a single picture (frame) is sent in a block called a scan, which (for sequential DCT formats) contains all the components of the image in an interleaved form. The table specifications are sent first so they are available for the decompression of the scan data that come later. The frame header and the scan header contain details of the image format and its decompression.

JPEG compression is typically capable of compressing the image data of a high-resolution natural image by 10:1 or more with barely noticeable degradation. Some images can be compressed more and some less and, of course, the viewing conditions will also govern how much compression is acceptable.

9.4.2 Motion-JPEG

The JPEG interface format supports multiple scans within a frame and, if the scans correspond to the frames of a motion video stream, the motion video is compressed. Since a motion stream usually can stand more image degradation than a still image because of the averaging effect of the multiple frames, more than the 10:1 compression ratio stated above is achievable in many cases. This approach is sometimes used because significant compression is possible with simpler processing than a more advanced motion compression system such as MPEG. It is called *Motion-JPEG* or M-JPEG. Because the JPEG standard was intended for images only, it makes no provision for the audio component required with motion video. There are a number of versions of M-JPEG, resulting as different companies tried to add audio to the standard.

9.4.3 MPEG

JPEG compression takes care of compressing the spatial redundancy in images, but it does not consider any of the redundancy that exists between the successive frames of a motion video stream. Another working group of the IEC/ISO, the *Motion Picture Expert Group*, (MPEG) was formed to address this problem and they have standardized two formats so far: MPEG-1 and MPEG-2. The difference between the two has to do with data rate and image quality—MPEG-1 was designed for transmission data rates up to about 1.5 Mb/s and works within that limitation to achieve the best possible pictures. MPEG-2 supports data rates up to about 20 Mb/s and provides for higher quality pictures; it is used for HDTV pictures as in the Grand Alliance ATV system standardized by the ATSC (see Section 7.4.3), and in digital broadcasting from satellites. That version of MPEG-2 is discussed here.

MPEG compression uses all the concepts of JPEG including DCT, quantizing, and entropy coding, and it adds motion compensation to compress interframe redundancy. As with JPEG, this is done in a flexible way that allows the user to tailor the compression to suit specific applications and scene content.

MPEG-2 uses 2:1 subsampling of color-difference components both horizontally and vertically. This is different from the 4:2:2 subsampling of ITU-R Rec. BT.601, which subsamples only in the horizontal direction. For that reason, and also to recognize that the chrominance data rate is reduced by another factor of 2 compared with 4:2:2, the MPEG-2 subsampling is called 4:2:0. The spatial sampling pattern is shown in Figure 9.13. C_R and C_B samples are cosited (meaning they are in the same spatial location), but they are displaced by half a line pitch from the luminance samples. This is done so that the chrominance sampling locations will be the same for either progressive- or interlaced-scanned sources; however, it requires that the sample values be interpolated from samples taken at the same times as luminance samples.

Because of the need to reduce the sample patterns to 8×8 blocks for DCT and motion compensation processing, the 4:2:0 subsampling requires the generation of another block concept: the *macroblock*. This is a 2×2 group of four 8×8 luminance blocks (thus, 16×16), which relates to two 8×8 color-difference sample blocks, one for C_R and one for C_B. Most MPEG-2 processing deals with macroblocks, since they are the smallest spatial unit that can be represented by an integral number of 8×8 blocks for all signal components together.

With motion compensation, each frame is based on differences from the previous frame, but there must be a way to get a first frame to begin the process. Therefore, MPEG-2 provides for frames that are entirely self-coded (*intracoded*) similar to JPEG images. These are called I-frames. Frames that are predicted from the previous frame by motion compensation are called P-frames. A third type of frame is also provided, based on

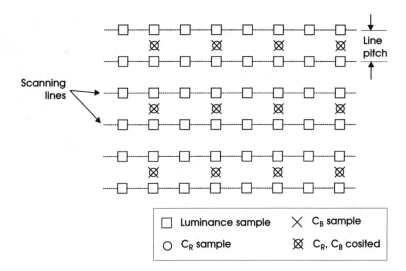

Scanning lines

Line pitch

Luminance sample	$\times$ C_B sample
$\bigcirc$ C_R sample	C_R, C_B cosited

Figure 9.13 *MPEG-2 spatial sampling pattern.*

prediction from both the previous and the next frame, which is called *bidirectional* prediction. These are B-frames. A B-frame can be compressed even more than a P-frame but requires the existence of a future frame at the decoder before the B-frame can be decompressed. This calls for sending frames out of order in the transmission stream, which is not a problem except that it calls for more storage at the receiver and it adds delay to the compression and decompression processes. The standard provides for this feature and its use is specified at encoding time.

Figure 9.14 is a diagram of a frame sequence, showing how I-, P-, and B-frames are used and the transmission order that results. Since I-frames are the least compressed frames, their use ought to be minimized for the lowest data rate, but they are required periodically for the video stream to recover itself after channel switching or an error outage. The standard specifies that I-frames should occur at least every 132 frames[*]—most systems provide them more often than that. This is determined at the encoder.

Figure 9.15 is a block diagram of the MPEG-2 compression processing embodying the principles discussed so far. Processing is done on an 8×8 block at a time. If the frame or the macroblock is to be intracoded, the pixels go directly to DCT processing. For intercoded blocks, the first step is to perform motion compensation using stored anchor frames from previous or future frames. The result of this is compared with the incoming pixels and the differences for the block go to DCT processing. At the output of DCT, the coefficients are quantized according to the quantization tables. There are different tables depending on

---

[*] The system actually provides for the choice of I or P processing to be made at the macroblock level and the "every 132-frame" requirement applies to macroblocks.

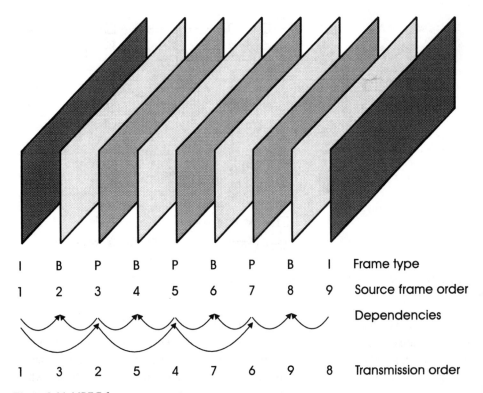

Figure 9.14 MPEG frame sequence.

whether intracoding or intercoding is used. The result of quantization is ordered and entropy coded for transmission.

An additional loop decodes the DCT differences so that the stored frames used for future motion compensation are degraded by the quantization just like they would be in a receiver. This keeps the distortion caused by quantization from accumulating as frames are predicted one from the other.

The encoding process must make choices regarding the type of frame prediction mode and the quantization. These choices may be made on a macroblock basis, if necessary. Thus, it can become quite an art to operate an encoder to achieve the best possible compression for a given data rate. Encoders can also include sophisticated automation to assist this process.

9.4.4 Personal Computer Video

Although MPEG video is used on personal computers and delivers excellent performance, it requires dedicated hardware except on the very fastest PCs. A number of other

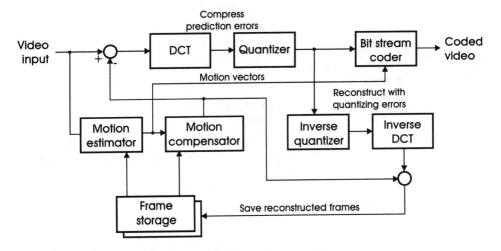

Figure 9.15 *MPEG compression processing.*

compression algorithms have been developed specifically for PC use. These make a different trade between degree of compression and picture quality to reduce the computational requirements for decoding. Most of these are inherently designed as asymmetrical systems. Some of the available standards are Intel *Indeo*, Microsoft *Video for Windows*, Apple *QuickTime* (for Macinstosh and Windows computers), and SuperMac *CinePak*. In each case, decode software is generally available but encode software (and hardware) is usually proprietary and must be bought. Because of the intense proprietary environment of these algorithms, details cannot be discussed here.

9.4.5 Audio AC-3

The audio system of the ATSC ATV system is a good example of high-end digital audio compression [4]. The system provides up to 5.1 channels of surround-sound stereo high-fidelity audio in a total data rate of 385 kb/s. (The 0.1 channel is a low-frequency subwoofer channel.) The AC-3 encoder produces a composite bit stream that can be packetized and merged with video packets in the ATSC transport system.

As in the MPEG video compression system, AC-3 audio compression is achieved by transforming audio data to the frequency domain where it is subject to coarse quantization. However, the time-frequency transformation is done differently for audio. The incoming audio samples at 48 kHz are grouped into 512-sample overlapping blocks. Each input sample is represented in two of the blocks and by using a kind of dissolve between the blocks, the audibility of blocking is diminished.

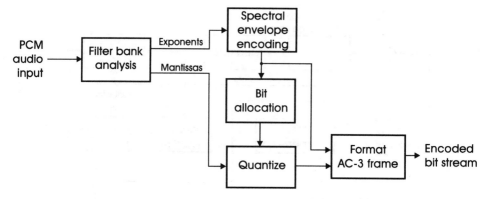

Figure 9.16 *Block diagram of AC-3 encoding.*

Figure 9.16 is a block diagram of the AC-3 encoder. The sample blocks are converted to frequency coefficients by the analysis filter bank processor. The output from this is a series of coefficients in a special floating-point format. The exponents represent a coarse view of the signal spectrum and are encoded separately from the mantissas of the floating-point format. The output bit stream for each six audio blocks are grouped into an audio frame representing 1,536 audio samples before compression or 32 ms of audio. The frame structure is shown in Figure 9.17. The frame begins with a sync word followed by a bit stream information (BSI) header that describes the audio service. After that comes the compressed audio data for the six blocks of samples and a CRC error protection code is at the end. The frame also provides for optional auxiliary data.

In addition to the compression, the AC-3 system provides several other interesting features that facilitate high-quality sound reproduction. One feature is a configurable system of dynamic range compression. In many services, it is customary to compress the dynamic range of audio to improve channel loading and the ability of the sound to be heard in poor listening environments or with reproduction equipment of limited power. If this is done at the transmitting end, it forces all viewers to the same limited range, regardless of the

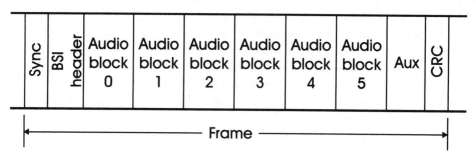

Figure 9.17 *AC-3 frame structure.*

quality of their reproduction equipment and environment. With AC-3, dynamic range compression occurs at the receiving end by means of compression codes that are transmitted with the signals. Thus, the receiver has the option of choosing how much compression to apply and the full original dynamic range is available to systems that are capable of reproducing it.

Another AC-3 feature is *loudness normalization*. When switching between different signal sources or channels, one often encounters variation in the loudness of the dialog component of the audio. This is difficult to control because different applications may require different amounts of headroom above the dialog level to allow for other sounds. The AC-3 standard requires that a parameter be sent along with the audio to identify the level at which dialog is set in the total audio dynamic range. This value can be used at the receiver to normalize all channels so that dialog always has the same loudness.

9.5 CONCLUSION

Digital video and audio compression is an enabling technology that is supporting the rapid growth of digital methods in video and audio applications. It makes possible transmission and delivery systems that surpass analog technologies in terms of signal performance and bandwidth utilization. It is also an excellent example of how complex processes become practical by the use of custom integrated circuits. Digital data compression processing is so complex that it would be unthinkable without ICs.

REFERENCES

1.   Huffman, D., "A Method for the Construction of Minimum Redundancy Codes," Proc. IRE, pp. 1,098–1,101, Sept. 1952.

2.   Jayant, N. S., and Noll, P., *Digital Coding of Waveforms*, Prentice-Hall, Englewood Cliffs, 1984.

3.   ISO/IEC Standard 10918-1, *Digital Compression and Coding of Continuous-Tone Still Images*.

4.   ATSC Standard A/52 (1995), *Digital Audio Compression AC-3*, http://www.atsc.org.

Chapter 10

Video Displays

10.1 INTRODUCTION

The final result of any video system, whether analog or digital, is the display of the picture for viewers to see. The success of any display depends on the displaying hardware including the display device and its supporting circuits, and the environment in which it is viewed. This chapter covers all those aspects of video displays.

10.2 DISPLAY REQUIREMENTS

The application of a display determines its requirements. Applications range from small hand-held units to large-screen television or HDTV displays to projection displays for meeting rooms, theaters, or arenas. Table 10.1 lists some applications and their technical requirements. General parameters used for specifying requirements are defined in this section. The subsequent section will discuss the display technologies and their capabilities versus the general requirement categories.

10.2.1 Display Size

The size of a video display is usually stated as the diagonal measurement of its active screen. However, some display sizes get exaggerated in the interest of marketing hype—this is especially prevalent in computer displays, where the display size number usually refers to the overall size of the display device, not its active screen area (which is a little less.) Display sizes range from the less than one inch of camera viewfinder displays to tens of feet in theater projection displays. Generally, the application will specify a size or a range of sizes.

Table 10.1

Display Applications and Their Requirement

Application:	Television		Computer	
Parameter	SDTV	ATV	Desktop	Portable
Display size (in.)	9–32	21–60	14–21	10–12
Max. resolution	720×480	1920×1080	1600×1200	800×600
Brightness (nits)	200	150	60	30
Angle of view	Wide	Wide	Wide	Narrow
Colors	16M	16M	256–16M	256
Interlace	Yes	Optional	No	No
Projection	Suitable	Suitable	NA	NA

10.2.2 Resolution

In the digital era, display resolution is specified in terms of horizontal and vertical pixel counts. CRT display devices do not have actual pixels, and their resolution has tradition-ally been specified in TVL, although computer CRT displays do specify pixels.* A pixel specification is appropriate for flat-panel displays that are generally based on arrays any-way. A pixel-based display device has a fixed resolution, whereas a CRT display can oper-ate at different resolutions determined by its driving circuits but, of course, limited by the electrooptical capabilities of the tube.

10.2.3 Brightness

Image displays are either *emissive*, which means they produce their own illumination; or they are *nonemissive*, meaning they control either the transmission or reflection of illumi-nation from a separate source. These choices are shown in Figure 10.1. In addition to the maximum brightness that the display can produce, the *contrast ratio* is also an important brightness parameter. This is the ratio between the maximum and the minimum brightness as seen by a viewer. Contrast depends on the properties of the display and the amount of ambient illumination falling on the display surface. A low-contrast display will appear washed out and unsatisfactory no matter how bright it is.

10.2.3.1 Emissive Displays

Emissive displays produce their own illumination and are thus responsible for the power required by that illumination. However, the display surface may reflect ambient light even when the display's illumination is turned off, so their minimum brightness cannot be zero;

---

* The pixel specification usually only refers to the scanning capability of the display. Actual resolution may be different (see Section 10.3.1).

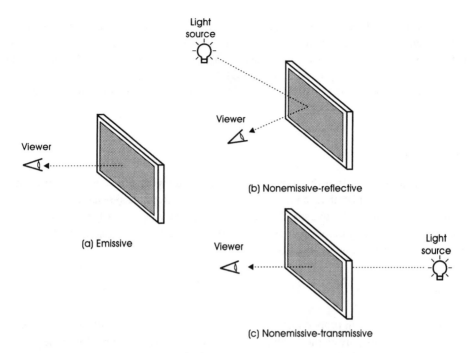

Figure 10.1 *Emissive and nonemissive displays.*

it is determined by the ambient light level and the reflectance of the display surface. Emissive displays are usually designed to have a low-reflectance (dark) surface. Another strategy to improve the contrast ratio of an emissive display is to place a neutral-density filter (see Section 6.2.3) over the display screen. Since all light from the display passes through the filter, the maximum brightness of the display is reduced by the transmission factor of the neutral-density filter but reflected ambient light is reduced by the square of the filter's transmission factor because it passes twice through the filter.

A second source of dark-area illumination can be light from bright areas of the display being reflected internally onto the dark areas. This is called *halation* and usually is a function of the distance from the bright area to the dark area. An external ND filter does not reduce halation.

10.2.3.2 Nonemissive Displays

Nonemissive displays depend on an external light source for their illumination, so they theoretically may require less power to operate. Instead of controlling the light produced, they control either the transmission or the reflection of external light. The contrast ratio of these displays depends on the ratio of transmission or reflectance they can produce between bright or dark areas of the scene. Reflective displays use ambient light for their illumination, so their contrast ratio is determined directly by their capability to modulate the reflection of ambient light. However, the contrast ratio of a transmissive display will depend not only on its ability to modulate the light passing through it, but on the reflection of any ambient light from the display surface. Thus, it is also important for these displays to have a non-reflective surface.

10.2.4 Angle of View

Another display property is the appearance of the display when the viewer is looking at it from an angle. A display that can be viewed successfully from the side has a wide angle of view, whereas a display with a small angle of view must be viewed nearly straight-on, or its brightness, contrast, or color will deteriorate. Such displays are suitable only for viewing by a single user at a time.

10.2.5 Color

Color is not an inherent property of most display technologies, and color displays need to have three sets of display elements for three primary colors. The proper color properties are obtained with colored phosphors or optical filters.

10.2.6 Gamma

An image reproduction system generally requires an overall linear transfer characteristic for proper reproduction of scenes. In the case of color systems, each of the color channels must be linear as explained in Section 2.2.2. However, systems that have been designed for CRT displays often have correction for the CRT gamma included in the signal standards so receivers or displays do not have to perform gamma correction. This is true for the NTSC, PAL, and SECAM television standards.

The newer display devices do not have the same gamma as a CRT and will not correctly display a signal that has CRT precorrection in it. Therefore, when viewing TV signals on LCD or plasma displays, gamma precorrection must be undone. Fortunately, as described in Section 6.5.2, this is easy to do in digital systems using a memory lookup table.

10.2.7 Persistence

Section 2.2.3 explained that the human eye responds to slow periodic variations of brightness with the sensation we call flicker. Most displays are scanned in some manner, and their light output (or transmission or reflectance) may vary according to the scanning frequencies. Thus, the scanning rates must be high enough to avoid flicker. In digital systems, the scan rates of the display need not be the same as the signals being displayed, so it is practical to run a display faster or slower than the signal depending on the needs of the display.

At the other extreme, some displays (LCDs, especially) are inherently slow to change their output, and this can cause smearing of moving objects in the scene. The early LCD panels used with portable computers were especially poor for this. The effect was easily observed as the screen cursor would disappear while it was being moved around the screen.

10.2.8 Projection Displays

All display technologies run into practical limitations if they are made too large. This restricts the application of the technology. For example, the weight and cost of a CRT increases rapidly as the screen size increases. The current practical limit for CRT displays is thus about 35 inches diagonal. However, displays of almost any size can theoretically be obtained by optically projecting the image from a smaller display.

In projection, screen brightness reduces as the square of the diagonal of the projection screen, so brightness of the display device is at a premium to achieve large screen sizes. CRT, DMD, and LCD devices are currently used in projection systems; they have different characteristics, but the LCD and DMD technologies are still undergoing improvement whereas CRT technology is quite mature. The result is that LCD and DMD projection systems are overtaking CRT-based projectors.

10.3 DISPLAY DEVICES

The CRT display has been around for more than sixty years and is still the technology to beat in most display applications. However, portable computers is a display market that cannot accept the size and power limitations of CRTs and has been the breeding ground for flat-panel technologies. The current leader in that field is LCD technology, which is reaching also a high state of development.

A future market is HDTV displays, which inherently must be in large-screen sizes to achieve the low viewing ratios that the system is designed for. A small-size HDTV display will limit the size of room in which the display can be effectively viewed. For example, a 32-inch HDTV display has a screen height of about 18 in, which, for a 3:1 viewing ratio, means that viewers must sit no more than 4.5 ft from the display. That would not be practical in most living rooms, where viewers usually sit 8 to 10 ft from the TV screen. Thus, a living-room-sized HDTV display ought to be in the range of 50 to 60 in. Such a screen size is not practical with a direct-viewed CRT and its performance is marginal using current projection methods. This problem may be solved with flat-panel displays or with the new DMD projection displays.

The leading technologies for full-color video displays are discussed in this section. Table 10.2 is a comparison of properties, which summarizes this discussion.

Table 10.2

Comparison of Display Properties

Property	CRT	AMLCD	PDP	DMD**
Type	Emissive	Nonemissive	Emissive	Nonemissive
Type of scanning	Analog	Digital	Digital	Digital
Type of input	Analog	Analog	Digital	Digital
Max. resolution*	1600×1200	800×600	1920×1080	800×600
Max. screen size (in)	35	12	>40	Projection
Max. brightness (nits)	>200	20	60	10–100
Contrast ratio	100:1	25:1	200:1	100:1
Viewing angle	Wide	Narrow	Wide	Medium
Display thickness	0.75(screen)	0.5 in	2 in	
Display weight	Heavy	Light	Light	Moderate
Cost	Lowest	Highest	Future	High

* These figures are for mass-produced devices. All types have been produced experimentally or custom-manufactured at significantly higher resolutions.
** Typical for a 50-inch projection display.

10.3.1 Cathode-Ray Tubes

Upwards of 100 million CRTs are manufactured worldwide each year. It is by far the most widely used display technology. A color CRT is an emissive display; its basic principles are shown in Figure 10.2. A large glass enclosure holds three electron guns at one end and a phosphor screen structure at the other (viewing) end of the tube. The tube must of necessity be evacuated to allow the electron beams from the guns to pass across the tube. A set of

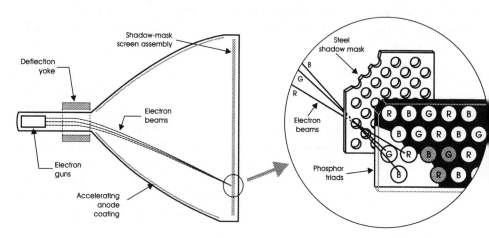

Figure 10.2 *A color cathode-ray tube.*

focusing fields are arranged with a high accelerating voltage (usually in excess of 20,000 v) to cause the electron beams to cross the tube space and impinge on the screen structure at high velocity, which causes the phosphor to emit light of a characteristic color that depends on the chemistry of the phosphor.

The screen structure includes a phosphor plane on which a three-color array of phosphor dots is placed in front of a metal mask, such that the electrons from only one gun will impinge on the dots of each color. Modulation is accomplished by controlling the intensity of each electron beam with a signal for the appropriate primary color, usually R, G, and B. Scanning is accomplished by deflection of all three electron beams, usually by a set of magnetic coils placed around the neck of the tube.

This explanation of color CRT technology may seem simple, but it is the result of years of development, and all the features have evolved as the result of much engineering and market testing. It is a mature technology.

Some of the design considerations of CRTs are

- A significant limitation of a CRT is that there must be a certain distance between the electron gun and the screen to provide for the deflection of the beam. CRTs are categorized according to their deflection angle 60, 90, 110 deg, and so forth. That will govern the depth of the display cabinet. Of course, a larger angle gives a smaller depth, but it also can make the deflection design more difficult to maintain focus and geometry over the full screen. Everything else being equal, a larger deflection angle gives poorer picture performance. Computer displays, which usually have more demanding specifications, use smaller-angle CRTs than TVs.

- The resolution of a color CRT will be limited by its color dot pattern, which is a sampling structure and has the usual Nyquist limit. The resolution is specified in terms of *dot pitch*, which is the distance between dots of the same color on the screen. Dot pitch is given in millimeters, 0.28, 0.4, and so forth.

- There are several general ways that the color dot pattern of a CRT can be constructed. Figure 10.2 shows what is called the *triad* or *shadow-mask* pattern, which requires the electron guns to be arranged in a triangle as shown. This is the original color CRT configuration and it offers good performance. However, other designs have evolved offering different tradeoffs between manufacturing considerations, cost, and performance. The Sony *Trinitron* design uses stripes of colors instead of dots—this is called a *line-screen* color CRT. Another design that combines some of the features of triad and line-screen tubes is the *in-line* design, which has the electron guns arranged side-by-side in a line and uses a series of oblong color dots on the screen, with the long axis of the dots perpendicular to the line of the electron guns. All configurations can give good performance. It should be noted that the dot pitch has different meaning for triad screens versus the others. This is because the width of the color dots or stripes in line-oriented screens is one-third of the pitch, whereas the width of a dot is one-half of the pitch for a triad screen. The result is that a triad screen will have slightly better resolution than a line-oriented screen of the same dot pitch. This is generally accounted for by line-oriented screens specifying smaller dot pitches, which does not necessarily mean better resolution.

- The brightness of a CRT display depends on the electron gun design, the accelerating voltage, the phosphor efficiency in converting electron energy to light, and the fraction of the electrons from the guns that actually reach the phosphors. This latter limitation comes because some of the electrons will fall on the shadow mask or the dividers in the line pattern. This varies between the different designs discussed above. A second brightness consideration is a limitation of electron optics that causes an electron beam to spread as its intensity is increased. This comes from the natural tendency of electrons to repel each other—there are more electrons in a stronger beam and thus more spreading. The result is that resolution deteriorates with increased brightness because the scanning spot becomes larger due to beam spreading. A typical CRT design will try to optimize the resolution loss due to the dot pitch and the beam spreading.

- Most CRTs have a somewhat curved screen surface, either spherical or cylindrical. This is due to the mechanical considerations of the atmospheric forces on the glass and also the deflection and focusing considerations of the scanning. As CRT design has matured, manufacturers are learning how to make flatter screens—some tubes used in computer displays have actually flat screens, but they are more expensive. A curved screen will pick up more ambient light from the surrounding room and reflect it toward the viewer, reducing contrast. A truly flat screen reflects light only from one place in the room, depending on the angle that the viewer sits from the screen.

- The matter of reflected light from the screen is also an important design consideration. Most CRTs have some treatment of the glass surface to reduce reflection and some tubes go further by making the internal structure as nonreflecting as possible. One approach is to fill the space between the phosphor dots with a black material—this is called a *black matrix* tube.

- The screen phosphors emit light when the scanned electron beam hits them, and the light output persists for some time after the beam has passed. However, the light will eventually decay and the result is that the screen may flicker if there is too much decay between passes of the scanning beam. This is a function of the phosphor material but, for given materials, the amount of flicker observed depends on the vertical-scanning frequency, the screen brightness, and the viewing conditions. Television CRTs are designed to give acceptable flicker performance when operated with the existing TV standards and in normal TV viewing conditions. Computer displays, which have much lower viewing ratios, are more susceptible to flicker and often are operated at higher vertical-scanning rates for this reason.

- The merging of the three electron beams at the proper dots on the screen is something that does not happen automatically. It requires the maintenance of specific conditions in the electron optics, which may vary as the electron beams are deflected to the edges of the screen. This is provided for by circuitry in the monitor or receiver for *convergence*, which is the process of insuring that the three color images merge over the entire screen area and color fringes do not appear on the edges of objects anywhere in the image. Convergence is usually a factory adjustment for TVs or monitors.

Another type of distortion in a color CRT depends on the local effects of earth's magnetic field or other stray fields, which may cause magnetization of some of the internal parts of the tube. This is usually provided for in receivers or monitors by a *degaussing* means. Modern units usually accomplish degaussing automatically whenever the unit is powered up but, in some cases, there is a button provided for a manual degaussing procedure. That would be used if the screen did not produce a uniform white color (called color *purity*). Convergence may also be affected by stray fields and degaussing should always be used before testing or adjustment of convergence.

- A CRT display device requires a lot of power and high voltages, which is an important consideration with regard to heat and reliability. It is also a cost factor because this power and voltage must be provided within the equipment. These requirements are also the reason why CRT displays are not suitable for portable equipment. A CRT display of even modest size can require between 25 and 50 W of power, which is too much to get from batteries in small, portable units.

The design considerations above may make it seem that CRTs are difficult to design and use. However, these problems and limitations have been overcome to the extent that CRTs are still the most widely used, highest performing, and cost-effective type of display device for all applications except portable equipment.

10.3.2 LCD Panels

Portable computers require lightweight, low-power displays in sizes suitable for one-on-one computing. The leading technology in this market is the *liquid-crystal display* (LCD), which is a nonemissive display technology based on the properties of a class of materials known as liquid crystals. This section discusses LCD technology and its design considerations.

The particular type of liquid crystal used in displays is known as *nematic*, for its elongated rod-shaped molecules. These crystals have the property that, when placed into a container that has its interior surfaces slightly grooved, the nematic molecules will naturally align themselves with the pattern of the grooves. Furthermore, if an electric field is applied to the liquid crystal in this situation, the molecular alignment will shift to be more or less parallel to the field. A display can be produced from this effect by viewing the crystal material with polarized light—the alignment of the crystal molecules is capable of rotating the

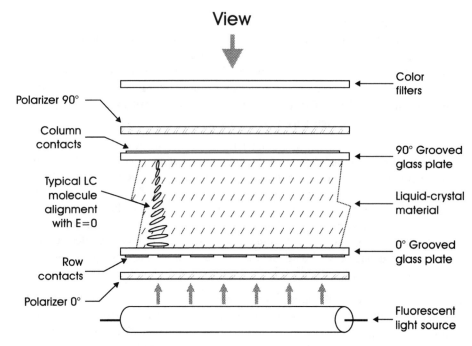

Figure 10.3 *Structure of an LCD panel. From A. F. Inglis, and A. C. Luther,* Video Engineering, *Second Edition, McGraw-Hill, New York, 1996, reproduced with permission of The McGraw-Hill Companies.*

light's polarization. Figure 10.3 shows a typical LCD display structure, called a *twisted nematic* display.

The twisting comes about because the grooves in the top and bottom plates of the liquid-crystal cell are placed at 90 deg to each other. This causes the crystal alignment to twist as one moves through the cell from top to bottom. If polarized light is applied to the cell with the polarization parallel to the top grooves, the polarization will rotate by 90 deg going through the cell. A second polarizer orthogonal to the first one is placed at the bottom of the cell, so that the light rotated by the cell will pass through it. However, if an electric field is applied to the cell in a direction normal to the cell surfaces, the molecules will align with the field and the twisting effect is destroyed. The result is that there is no rotation of polarization and light therefore will be blocked by the bottom polarizer.

Orthogonal patterns of electrodes are placed on the top and bottom surfaces of the cell as shown in the figure to control the effect locally for an array of pixels. Since there is a threshold field below which there is no effect, switching of individual pixels can be accomplished by using the combination of voltage applied to row and column electrodes to select the pixel at the intersection of the electrodes. Below are some of the considerations about this structure:

- The matrix of row and column electrodes shown in Figure 10.3 is what is known as a *passive-matrix* LCD architecture. Each pixel is addressed in sequence by appropriately pulsing the row and column electrodes and the pulse amplitude is modulated to control the density of each pixel in the display. Because the LC material decays slowly to the unexcited state, the pixel values can be set during the short pulse interval and they are held for some time so a steady picture without flicker is obtained. However, because of this operation, the response of a passive-matrix LCD is slow and moving objects on the screen have a tendency to smear. Also, the display has a low contrast ratio. Even so, passive-matrix displays are used widely because they are the lowest cost type of LCD.

- The limitations of passive-matrix operation are overcome by what is known as the *active-matrix* LCD architecture. In this design, a transistor switch is integrated on the bottom glass of the panel behind every pixel. The transistors set the voltage on each pixel of the panel and, because they can be individually addressed and they switch rapidly, the response speed and the contrast ratio are greatly improved. Adding the switching transistors is costly and active-matrix LCDs can cost as much as twice the price of passive-matrix units. However, users readily pay this price to have the performance advantages of an active-matrix LCD.

- LCDs can be produced in the transmission mode, as shown in Figure 10.3, or they can be made in a reflective mode by placing a mirror below the display. Ambient illumination passing through the display is reflected by the mirror. The contrast ratio of this mode is limited by the direct reflection from the display surface, not by the modulation in the display itself. The advantage of this is that no power is required for illumination, but most portable computer displays have a light source anyway so that they can be operated in the dark.

- Color in an LCD requires separate pixels for red, green, and blue with color filters to produce the color. Thus, color LCDs have three times the pixels in the horizontal direction—a 640×480 display actually has 1920×480 pixels.

- The angle of view of LCDs is limited because of their use of polarized light. Most LCDs are usable only over a field of view of about 30 deg, which is adequate for single-user application but not for multiple viewers.

- LCD panels are difficult to fabricate in larger sizes—the portable computer market is satisfied with 10 to 12-inch displays, but the television market requires much larger sizes.

10.3.3 Plasma Display Panels

A leading contender for a television flat-panel display is *the plasma display panel* (PDP). This is an emissive display that uses the radiation produced by an electronic discharge in a gas, such as xenon. In a color display, the plasma emits ultraviolet rays that excite normal

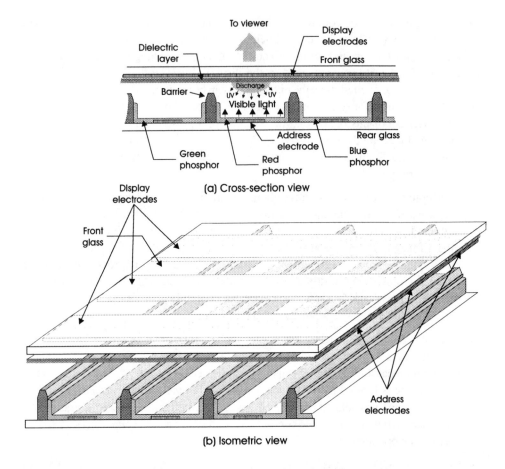

Figure 10.4 *Structure of a color plasma display panel (only the red cell is excited).*

color phosphors. There are many designs of PDPs that have been used for more than 25 years in special military and industrial applications. Now, they are emerging as a most promising technology for large-screen color television displays for HDTV, which is the only type of PDP discussed here.

Figure 10.4 shows a diagram of one type of color PDP. A sandwich of two glass plates contains a mixture of inert gases that are excited locally by electric fields set up by arrays of parallel, but orthogonal, electrodes on the inner glass surfaces. When sufficient voltage is applied to a pair of horizontal and vertical electrodes, a discharge occurs at the intersection of the electrodes. Ultraviolet energy is emitted, which excites the color phosphor located nearby and creates a spot of light at the color of the phosphor. The characteristics of this discharge result in a truly digital display device. A PDP has a digital input and performs its own DAC!

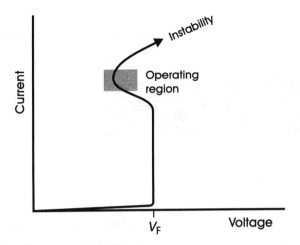

Figure 10.5 *Voltage-current characteristic of a PDP cell.*

Figure 10.5 shows the voltage-current characteristic for one cell of the display. The voltage scale represents the combined voltages of the two control lines that intersect at the cell. The significant feature is the extreme nonlinearity that occurs at the firing voltage V_F. The cell abruptly begins drawing current, which will increase rapidly until it is limited by some means outside of the cell. Thus, there is no practical way to control the brightness of a cell by conventional analog means. The cell is either on or off.

There are two general ways to limit the discharge current—the DC method where an external resistor is used and the AC method where an internal capacitor does the current limiting. This latter approach is the most popular because it also facilitates a memory feature that allows the pixel-on time to be increased. In an AC PDP, a dielectric layer is placed over the top electrodes of the panel to form a capacitor as shown in Figure 10.4. This capacitive coupling means that the cells can only be accessed by transient changes in the voltages applied to the electrodes. It also means that when a cell is fired, a charge begins to accumulate on the dielectric layer above that cell. The effect is to reduce the effective voltage of the discharge; when enough charge accumulates, the voltage drops and extinguishes the discharge. However, the charge on the dielectric, called the *wall voltage*, remains and it allows the cell to refire on the next transition of the applied (AC) voltage. Thus, the cell remembers whether it was fired on the last cycle and continues to refire and give out a pulse of light for every successive cycle until a special procedure is performed to erase the wall voltage.

This memory feature can be utilized to control the cell brightness digitally by a time-modulated technique shown in Figure 10.6. The frame-scanning interval is divided up into separate time periods for each bit of the digital signal being applied. For example, if 8-bit signals are to be applied, the field interval is divided into eight periods. Each period consists of a short time to erase the wall voltage in all the cells, followed by a longer interval to scan all the cells and specify whether they are to be on or off, followed then by an interval

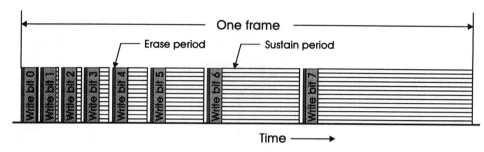

Figure 10.6 *Timing diagram for PDP operation.*

called the *sustain* interval. During the sustain interval, an AC voltage is applied to all cells to cause the ones who have wall voltages set to fire repeatedly. The sustain intervals of each period are lengthened by a factor of two from the previous period, corresponding to the significance of the signal bit that determines whether the cells will light for that period or not. For example, if the sustain interval of the first period is 1, the second period's sustain interval would be 2, then 4, 8, and so on. Thus, the light output from the eight sustain periods during each frame adds up with power-of-two weighting just like the currents sum up in a conventional DAC.

Some of the design considerations of PDPs are

- Because of their rapid response and the time-modulated nature of the light output, PDPs are not suitable for interlaced scanning—there is too much flicker. However, a frame memory is required anyway because signals are passed to the display one bit at a time for all pixels, followed by the next bit for all pixels, etc. Since most video signals are delivered as a series of complete pixels (all bits for a pixel, followed by all bits for the next pixel, and so on), a full-frame memory is required to reorganize the data for the display. Thus, the conversion from interlaced to progressive scanning can be accomplished in this same memory.

- The angle of view is very wide for PDPs making them suitable for almost any viewing situation.

- Although the principles of PDPs are the same as fluorescent lamps, which have high luminous efficiency (80 lm/W), present PDPs have not achieved high efficiency, being closer to 1 lm/W. This is expected to improve with further development, but at present it means that PDPs require more operating power than even CRTs of equivalent brightness. Much of the cost of a PDP display is in the power source and the ICs that deliver that power to the display panel itself.

PDPs have been built with HDTV resolution, high brightness, and large sizes (40–50 inches.) They may well fulfill the dream of the "picture on the wall" television display. Because of their inherent digital nature, they are equally suited for computer displays of large-screen sizes. At computer display screen sizes below about 15 inches, active-matrix LCDs will probably continue to prevail.

10.3.4 Digital Micromirror Displays

The *Digital Micromirror Display* (DMD) is an integrated circuit display device for projection use. It consists of a static RAM (SRAM) array overlaid by a structure of mirrors, one mirror for each SRAM cell. Each cell and its mirror forms one pixel of the display. The mirrors have the unique feature that they are capable of physical rotation through an angle of ±10 deg from their rest position under control of the data stored in their SRAM cells, which makes possible an optical switching mode of operation to produce an extremely bright, high contrast display. They are nonemissive displays.

The DMD technology was developed by Texas Instruments, Inc. Devices are being marketed for TV and computer projection displays, which are produced by several manufacturers. Some details of the structure and operation are shown in Figure 10.7. An integrated circuit substrate has a two-dimensional array of SRAM cells, one for each pixel of the desired display. Above that, a structure of moving parts is created using *microelectromechanical* technology, which allows moving parts to be fabricated using ordinary integrated circuit manufacturing techniques. In the DMD, each pixel has a 16×16-μm aluminum mirror mounted to a yoke structure that is supported on a torsional hinge. Electrostatic forces created by the SRAM signals are capable of rotating the yoke and mirror approximately 10 deg in either direction.

Figure 10.7(b) shows how this is used optically to produce a projection display. A source of illumination impinges on the pixels from an angle such that light is reflected from the mirrors to a projection lens when the mirrors are in one of their two states. Switching a mirror to its other state (shown dotted in the figure) causes the light to be reflected away from the projection lens entrance pupil, making the pixel dark on the screen. Better than 100:1 contrast ratio can be achieved by this optical switching. However, no gray scale capability is possible this way, but that can be achieved by digital pulse-width modulation in the same way as was described for the PDP in Figure 10.6. Thus, the DMD is also a true digital display device. The mirror switching time is less than 20 μs, which is more than fast enough to support 8 bpp at progressive-scan frame rates.

The DMD is basically a monochrome device—it reproduces in the color of the light source provided for it. Full-color reproduction may be achieved with a single DMD by a rotating color wheel or by using three devices, one for each primary color. In the case of the color wheel, the frame repetition rate is increased by a factor of three and the color wheel has filters that change the color of the light source at the same rate. Thus, frames of each color are displayed in rapid sequence and the viewer's eye merges them into a full-color image.

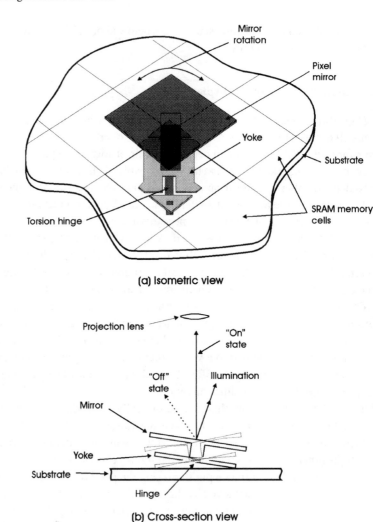

Figure 10.7 *Diagram of one pixel of a DMD display.*

10.4 DISPLAY SYSTEMS

A display device must have driving circuits and data interfaces to be usable in a system. The following sections discuss the concepts of display systems for computers and television.

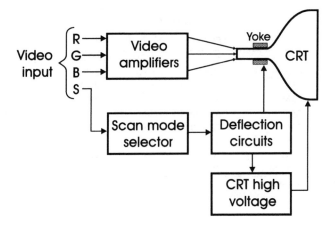

Figure 10.8 *Block diagram of a computer monitor.*

10.5 COMPUTER DISPLAY SYSTEMS

Present-day computers use CRT devices for desktop or other fixed-position use and LCDs for portable use. Both cases require significant hardware and software to connect into the computer and process the information for display. In the case of desktop use, the CRT and its driving circuits are packaged as a *monitor* unit, which is interfaced to the computer using a *video display adapter*. Some computers have the display adapter as an integral part of the motherboard, but in others (most) it is a separate plug-in board. The latter approach allows choice of display parameters on initial purchase or upgrade of the display later, without replacing the rest of the computer.

10.5.1 Computer Monitors

Desktop monitor units contain a CRT device, synchronization and deflection driver circuits, and a video interface. Figure 10.8 shows a block diagram of a typical computer monitor. The video interface between a computer and monitor is usually analog RGB video with a separate sync wire. One widely used standard is the VGA interface, which specifies a DB-15 connector. Since the monitor interface is analog, the DAC is contained in the video display adapter.

Computers usually provide for several choices of pixel resolution and scanning standards, which may be selected by software on the computer. The video display adapter and the monitor therefore have multiple scan modes. Table 10.3 shows some of the most common standards that are used, along with the scanning frequencies and video bandwidths they represent. Sometimes, there are several choices at the same resolution; this particularly involves the vertical-scan frequency, where some users may prefer higher frequencies to avoid flicker. Not all systems support the higher vertical-scan modes.

Table 10.3

Some Computer Display Scanning Standards

Resolution (active pixels)	Colors	f_H * (Hz)	f_V (Hz)	Pixel clock ** (MHz)	Memory size MB
640×480	256	31,500	60	24.2	0.307
640×480	16M	36,750	70	28.2	0.922
1024×768	256	58,800	70	72.0	0.786
1280×1024	256	78,400	70	121.0	1.310
1600×1200	256	91,900	70	175.7	1.920
1920×1080	16M (4:4:4)	70,900	60	162.3	6.220
1920×1080	16M (4:1:1)	70,900	60	162.3	3.110

*   Based on 9.4 % vertical retrace time.
**   Based on 20% horizontal retrace time.

Synchronization of computer monitors is automatic—the monitor senses the scan frequencies and appropriately adjusts its circuits. This includes adjustment of scan sizes, because computer displays are operated slightly underscanned so the picture is visible all the way to the edges. That requires precise adjustment compared with the way scan size is handled in television receivers (see Section 10.6).

10.5.2 Video Display Adapters

The video display adapter handles the interface from the display system to the computer bus and to the monitor. A block diagram for a display adapter is shown in Figure 10.9. The key item in the display adapter is the display memory, which stores a digital image of the current screen. Refresh of the display is handled by reading the memory at the pixel clock frequency to output pixel values in real time to the display. Having this separate memory and read circuits means that display refresh does not involve the system CPU at all. The display adapter must also provide an appropriately timed sync signal to the monitor so that the monitor scanning matches the memory read process.

The display memory can be standard dynamic RAM or may be a special *video RAM* (VRAM) that provides a separate output for the display. This has the advantage that the CPU accesses for updating the display do not have to be time-shared with the memory accesses for refresh. It is accomplished by having an onchip shift register that can be loaded in parallel from the RAM in a single memory cycle. As a separate operation, the shift register is then clocked at the pixel clock frequency to output the data for display.

Of course, when the display contents change, the CPU will access the display memory to make the changes. Most display adapters provide additional features to help the CPU in this task also. A coprocessor called a *display accelerator chip* is included to allow the CPU to issue high-level commands for which the accelerator chip will execute the low-level details. Thus, the CPU is free to perform more important operations with the result that the whole computer is faster.

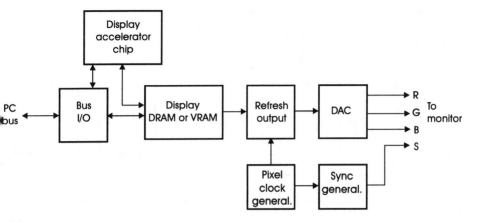

Figure 10.9 *Block diagram of a computer video display adapter.*

Typical tasks performed by display accelerators are drawing of graphics primitives, management of overlapping onscreen windows, video decompression, interpolation of subsampled U,V formats, and scaling of video or graphics windows.

10.5.3 Display Software

Special driver software running on the CPU is required for a display adapter. This software must handle the specifics of accessing the display memory, control of display modes, and any display accelerator that is present. The driver will present an API to the operating system that gives access to all the features of the display adapter. The overall display performance is controlled by the driver software; the best adapter in the world will not perform well unless it has good driver software.

10.6 TELEVISION RECEIVERS

The television display system is usually called a *receiver* and includes means for receiving video signals from broadcast or cable delivery. Present analog television receivers are not discussed here. The only digital TV receivers are the ones being developed for the new ATV service. These are covered here.

The ATV receiver display portion has an architecture similar to a computer video display adapter. Frame memories are required by the MPEG-2 motion-compensated decompression and they are put to good advantage to allow the display scanning to be independent of the scanning implied by the input signal. This is done by having separate write and read operations on the display frame memory running at the two scan rates involved. There is a scan converter inside of every receiver.

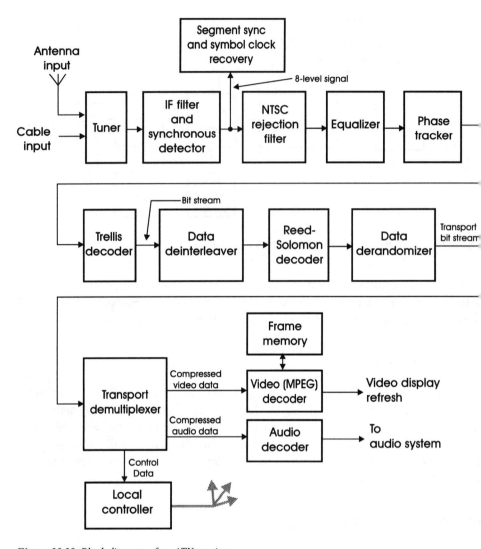

Figure 10.10 *Block diagram of an ATV receiver.*

To avoid the requirement for precise adjustment of scan sizes, present analog television receivers employ *overscanning*. The nominal scan size is set about 10% larger than the visible display area, both horizontally and vertically. The idea is that variation of scan size with time, temperature, and so forth. will never be enough for the edges of the raster to become visible—the picture on the screen is defined by the screen mask over the face of the tube. This has worked well, but it is a significant waste of system bandwidth because 10% horizontally and 10% vertically more signal is transmitted than is usually seen by the viewer. This has also led to program directors taking heed to a *safe title area* and *safe viewing area* specification that makes sure that all significant program content remains within the portion of the picture that most viewers will be able to see. It would be unfortunate if this practice is continued in the digital era. Digital CRT displays should be handled like computer monitors are or, if the edges of the picture are not to be seen, a small amount (few percent) of overscan might be specified. Pixel-oriented display panels, such as the PDP, should not require any overscan at all.

Figure 10.10 is a block diagram of an ATV receiver for the ATSC ATV standard that was described in Section 7.4.3. Signals are received into a tuner that selects the channel from either cable or antenna input. The intermediate-frequency (IF) circuits provide the necessary selectivity to reject adjacent channels. Next, the symbol clock is recovered and additional filtering, equalization, and phase tracking are done. Then the baseband signal is trellis-decoded to recover the original bit stream modulation.

The bit stream must then be deinterleaved, error corrected through the Reed-Solomon decoder, and derandomized to recover the transport bit stream. The transport stream is demultiplexed to separate video, audio, and auxiliary data channels. The separated bit streams are then passed to the appropriate decoders to decompress audio and video for presentation. This looks like a lot of processing but, for mass production, it can be integrated in a few integrated circuits.

10.7 CONCLUSION

Video display technology is beginning the transition from CRT displays to flat-panel displays. As ATV systems come on stream, this trend will accelerate. Flat panel displays, especially PDPs and DMDs, are ideally suited to digital systems and represent the wave of the future.

Chapter 11

Digital Recording

11.1 INTRODUCTION

Now, forty years after the introduction of videotape recording, it is difficult to imagine how the television industry could have existed without it. Recording of video and audio is fundamental to the program production process for all types of video distribution. Numerous advances have been made over those forty years; the latest advance is digital recording, which is coming of age in all markets for audio and video recording.

Although the signal portions of digital recorders use much of the same technology as transmission systems (see Chapter 7), a recorder provides a very different function—translation in time. With a recorder, one can move audio and video signals from one time to another (as well as from one place to another). Another difference from transmission is that recorders are basically mechanical devices having high-precision moving parts that operate at high speeds. Although nearly all of the electronic content of a recorder can be built into integrated circuits and is thus subject to the ongoing improvement of Moore's Law, the mechanical components do not respond to that law. In spite of that, over the years, recorders have improved in performance by several orders of magnitude while dropping in cost by similar factors.

Digital recorders were used in computers for general data recording long before they became practical for audio and video. That is because of two requirements of audio and video recording that can often be ignored in data recording—(1) recording and playback must be in real time and, (2) the system must be able to record or play for an uninterrupted period of one hour or more. Real time recording means that the system must record whatever data rate is produced by the signal source; it cannot slow down the data for recording or break it into pieces to record separately. Thus, if a digital video signal needs 100 Mb/s, the recorder must support that data rate and it must deliver it without interruption for the duration of the entire program. Early data recorders reached such data rates only by running tape at high speeds, which limited play times to only a few minutes. Digital recording

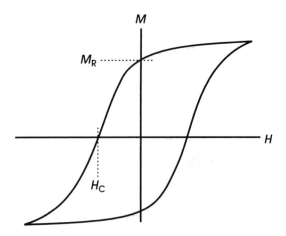

Figure 11.1 *Magnetic material's hysteresis loop.*

of video had to wait until techniques were developed to record high data rates for long playing times.

Two basic recording methods have dominated the last forty years and show no signs of giving up the markets to others—magnetic recording and optical recording. These are discussed below, followed by descriptions of some of the leading recording systems.

11.2 MAGNETIC RECORDING FUNDAMENTALS

Magnetic recording of audio and video started with analog methods, which was only natural because analog signals were the only kind around. Now, however, we have digital audio and video signals and this section focuses on the use of magnetic recording for digital signals.

11.2.1 Physical Principles

Magnetic recording is based on the property of certain materials to become magnetized in the presence of a magnetic field and to retain some of that magnetization when the field is removed. Magnetic materials are referred to as ferromagnetic or ferrimagnetic, which signifies that they have properties similar to iron.

This property of magnetic *remanence* is shown in a curve of magnetization M versus magnetizing force H, shown in Figure 11.1. This curve exhibits a form of extreme nonlinearity known as *hysteresis*, where the behavior is different whether the magnetizing force is increasing or decreasing. If the magnetizing force is increased and decreased periodically, the curve traces a loop, called a *hysteresis loop*. Two key parameters of hysteresis loops are M_R, the remanent magnetization remaining when the magnetizing force is reduced to zero,

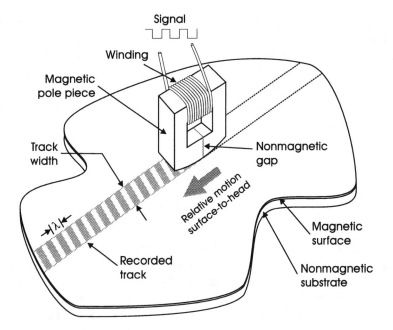

Figure 11.2 *Magnetic recording.*

and H_C, the *coercivity* or the magnetizing force needed to reverse the remanent magnetization to zero. Another important characteristic of magnetic materials shows as the flattening of the top and bottom of the hysteresis loop. This is called *saturation*, which means that there is a maximum amount of magnetization that can be produced in the material regardless of how much magnetizing force is applied.

Magnetic recording of information uses these properties to produce a pattern of magnetization on a surface that is usually a magnetic coating on a nonmagnetic substrate. The substrate is typically in the form of a tape or disk, although magnetic surfaces are used in other forms, such as the magnetic stripe on a credit card. The combination of a magnetic surface and its substrate is called the *medium*.

11.2.1.1 Recording

Recording is accomplished by producing relative motion between a recording *head* and the magnetic medium while applying information signals to the head. Signal current in the winding of the head causes the head to create a spatial magnetic pattern on the surface. The magnetic pattern is called a *track*. The recording process is shown in Figure 11.2. A magnetic head, consisting of a magnetic core with a nonmagnetic gap and a winding is positioned so that it passes close to or in contact with the magnetic medium. Signal current applied to the winding of the head produces magnetization in the core, which fringes out at the gap into the adjacent medium. As each part of the record medium passes through this fringing field, it is cycled through its hysteresis loop; the conditions pertaining at the instant it leaves the field of the head control the remanent magnetization of that part of the medium. The width of the track equals the active width of the head, but the size of the pattern details along the track depends on the signal frequency according to the relationship

$$\lambda = \frac{V}{f} \tag{11.1}$$

where

   λ is the wavelength of the pattern on the medium.
   V is the relative velocity between tape and head.
   f is the signal frequency.

Obviously, higher frequencies produce shorter wavelengths, and the bandwidth limit of a recording system is related to the shortest wavelength it can successfully replay. (There is no limit on the recording of short wavelengths, all limits occur in playback.) The considerations of this are discussed in the next section.

   Recording of wide bandwidth requires high-speed relative motion between tape and head so the wavelength will not be too short. However, high speed results in mechanical stresses and other difficulties. There are many ways of achieving the necessary motion between head and medium, such as linear motion of magnetic tape past fixed heads, rotating of a disk under fixed or moveable heads, or rotating heads scanning a linearly-moving tape. The shape of the track pattern depends on the type of motion: linear motion produces straight tracks along a tape, rotation of the medium produces circular or spiral tracks, and rotation of heads produces a pattern of short tracks repeated along the medium. These approaches are discussed in Sections 11.2.4 and 11.2.5.

11.2.1.2 Playback

A recorded track is read back by producing similar relative motion between the medium and a playback head. The playback head must pass accurately over the recorded tracks, a process called *tracking* that may often require servo control of the motion of medium or heads or both. In many cases, the same physical head is used for both recording and playback, although there are sometimes advantages to using different heads for each process. During playback, some of the fringing field from the medium is picked up in the head as the track passes under the gap region of the head. The coil on the head produces a voltage that is proportional to the rate of change of magnetic flux in the head core. Thus, the natural output of a magnetic head is the derivative of the flux on the tape and it rises in proportion to frequency.

   The gap length of a playback head acts as an aperture and it must be shorter than the shortest wavelength in the recording. The effect of the gap length is a sin(x)/x response

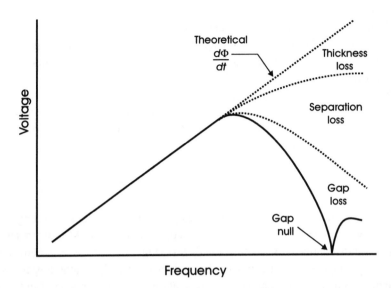

Figure 11.3 *Frequency response of magnetic recording (solid curve).*

function with the first null at the frequency corresponding to a wavelength equal to the gap length. In addition, there are losses due to the electrical and magnetic characteristics of the head, the separation between medium and head, and the thickness of the recording layer.

The separation effect is very significant and leads to operating the head as close as possible to the magnetic surface. *Separation loss* in decibels is

$$\text{Separation loss (dB)} = 54.6\frac{d}{\lambda} \tag{11.2}$$

where

d is the separation between head and medium.

For example, a typical minimum wavelength for video recording is 0.0001 in (100 μin.) If the separation is only 10 μin (10% of the wavelength), there is still 5.46 dB of signal loss. It is often difficult to achieve separations that small simply because the motion of tape or head produces an air film between them that causes larger separation.

Another response loss is caused by the thickness of the magnetic layer of the medium. For short wavelengths, a thick layer will direct some of the magnetization away from the surface, giving rise to *thickness loss*. This is not as serious as separation loss, but it cannot be ignored.

The result of all these playback response effects is shown in Figure 11.3. The natural rising response from the rate of change of flux is overcome at high frequencies by the gap effect, the separation loss, and the thickness loss. The electrical response of the head, which is a resonant circuit consisting of the inductance of the coil and its stray capacitance may further affect the total response.

The discussion so far has characterized the head in analog terms. Remembering the extreme nonlinearity of the fundamental magnetic process due to hysteresis, it can be seen that it will not be satisfactory to operate a magnetic head directly with a simple analog signal. Some form of modulation always must be used to achieve linearity for analog audio or video. One very useful form of modulation is digital—the subject of this book—which we focus on here. It should be noted, however, that analog tape recorders are very successful for audio and video. They employ either frequency modulation for video, or a high-frequency bias for audio [1].

11.2.1.3 Erasing

Before making a new recording, it is often necessary to erase previous recordings. An entire tape may be *bulk-erased* by subjecting a full reel or cassette to an AC field that is strong enough to saturate the magnetic coating and then slowly reduce the field to zero. This has the effect of cycling the magnetic material through progressively smaller hysteresis loops until both the magnetizing force and the magnetization go to zero. Erasing of an entire tape can also be done as it passes through a tape deck for recording by providing an erase head with a wide gap length and a gap width equal to the width of the tape. Erasing is accomplished by driving this head with a frequency that is higher than could ever be recorded by the erase head.

Alternatively, erasing can be done selectively on one or more tracks of the tape by using a special erase head driven by a frequency that is too high to be successfully replayed. This method is necessary when the recording must be selectively updated as in editing of audio or video.

Some digital recorders do not have separate erase heads; they simply overwrite previous recordings. This is widely done with digital disk drives where it would be impractical to have more than one head operating at a time. Some loss of recording efficiency occurs from this method because an allowance must be made for a certain percentage of residual signals from previous recordings, but the mechanical simplification is worth this loss.

11.2.1.4 Digital Recording

As with digital transmission, digital recorders employ encoding of the incoming bit stream to optimize the use of the medium. However, unlike transmission, multilevel symbols are not practical due to the extreme nonlinearity of the magnetic medium so digital magnetic recording is generally based on changing the state of magnetization in the medium from one polarity to the other. Therefore, intermediate levels of magnetization are not significant. Wavelength in digital magnetic recording is defined as the distance between magnetic flux transitions of like direction.

Due to the differentiation effect in playback, the recorded flux transitions are played back as pulses. As the wavelength is shortened, the replay pulses begin to interfere with

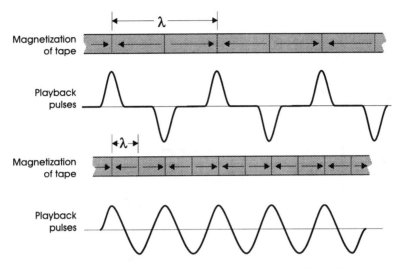

Figure 11.4 *Waveforms of magnetic recording and playback showing the effect of shorter wavelength.*

one another until the point is reached where they can no longer be reliably distinguished. This is shown in Figure 11.4. The process of extracting the data from these waveforms is called *data separation*. As with digital transmission, the eye pattern (see Section 7.2.3.4) is a good way to recognize the effectiveness of data separation.

11.2.2 Magnetic Media

Tapes and disks are the principal types of magnetic media. Both are area media, except that tape can be rolled up and thus is like a volume medium for storage, but it must be unrolled to record or play it. An important concept of recording on an area medium is the system's effectiveness in packing information into the area of the medium. That is called the *area density factor* and, in the digital world, it is expressed as bits per unit of area. Analog systems can also be characterized this way by converting from analog bandwidth by using two bits per cycle of the highest analog signal frequency. Since magnetic records are in the form of tracks, area density is the product of bits/inch along a track and tracks per inch in the orthogonal direction. Note that recorded tracks are not always placed directly next to one another; space (called a *guard band*) usually has to be left to allow for tracking tolerances in record and replay. In some helical recorders, the technique of *azimuth* recording allows guard bands to be eliminated (see Section 11.2.4.2).

As magnetic recording technology has advanced over the years since its origination, area density has shown steady improvement. Figure 11.5 shows that growth; although not as much as Moore's Law, it is still spectacular. Yet today's performance is still several orders of magnitude away from theoretical limits.

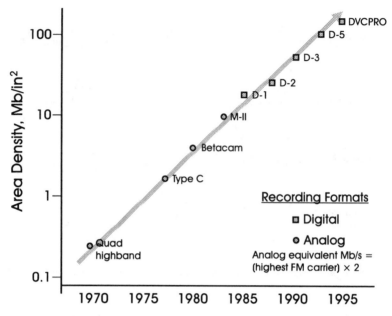

Figure 11.5 *Growth of magnetic recording area density performance. From A. F. Inglis and A. C. Luther,* Video Engineering, Second Edition, *McGraw-Hill, New York, 1996, reproduced with permission of The McGraw-Hill Companies.*

11.2.2.1 Magnetic Tape

Magnetic tape is usually based on a thin magnetic coating placed onto a plastic substrate having a thickness between 500 to 2,000 μin. Coating thicknesses range from 5 to 200 μin. Tape, as much as 5,000 ft long, is rolled onto a reel for handling in a recording deck. This limit in length is governed by the largest practical reel diameter and the maximum amount of tape pack that can be handled. Tape widths range from ¼ to 2 in, with most modern systems tending to the narrower widths because the mechanical components are smaller for smaller tape.

Magnetic coatings are made either as ferromagnetic particles embedded in a binder material or as a thin-film coating of a magnetic metal. In the case of particulate coatings, the particles are usually needle-shaped and are oriented by applying a magnetic field before the binder cures during manufacture to optimize recording in the direction the head and tape will move relative to each other. Because of the size of the magnetic particles, particulate coatings are limited in how thin they may be coated. The thinnest coated tapes are made with metal films. The coating must have uniform thickness, uniform distribution of the magnetic material, and mechanical properties suitable to withstand the stress of the head-to-tape interface.

Coercivity is an important magnetic parameter of tape coatings. Higher coercivity generally means higher performance and also better immunity to stray magnetic fields that might accidentally erase recordings.

11.2.2.2 Tape Cassettes

Early tape recorders stored their tapes on open reels that required manual threading into a tape deck and manually connecting to a takeup reel. However, all modern systems employ two-reel cassettes with the tape permanently contained in them. This not only provides better protection of the tape, but it makes possible fully automatic threading—usually all an operator has to do is insert a cassette into a slot.

Tape can be wound onto reels with the magnetic coating on either the inside or the outside. When the magnetic coating is inside, it is called *A-wrap*, and, when the coating is on the outside of the reel, it is *B-wrap*.

11.2.2.3 Magnetic Disks

Disks are made with flexible substrates (*floppy disks*) or with rigid substrates (hard disks). Coatings can be either particulate with a binder or metal thin films. Whereas the surface of tape is inherently protected when it is rolled up on a reel, a disk has its recording surface exposed and must be enclosed in some kind of protective container.

Floppy disks have mechanical properties similar to tape and are usually operated in a manner where the elasticity of the substrate provides the force to achieve head-to-tape contact. Floppies are generally provided in a plastic container that has a spring-loaded door that opens when the disk is placed into the recording mechanism (called a *disk drive*; see Section 11.2.5.)

Hard disks must operate in an entirely different mode because the substrate is rigid and the compliance needed to control head-to-tape contact must be part of the head design. Also, since both disk and head are rigid objects, it is very difficult to control the forces if any actual contact is allowed. Therefore, heads for hard disks are designed to "glide" on a thin film of air that prevents any actual contact while the disk is running at speed. Because of the head's gliding on a minute film of air (5 μin or less,) the mechanism is extremely sensitive to even the tiniest particle of dust or other contamination. Hard-disk drives are hermetically sealed to contain their own clean atmosphere (see Section 11.2.5).

11.2.3 Magnetic Heads

One must examine a magnetic head under a microscope to appreciate its sophistication. Built from exotic materials to dimensions measured in thousandths of an inch and with tolerances in the millionths of an inch, a magnetic head is an example of the finest engineering and manufacturing technique seen anywhere. At the same time, heads must withstand the

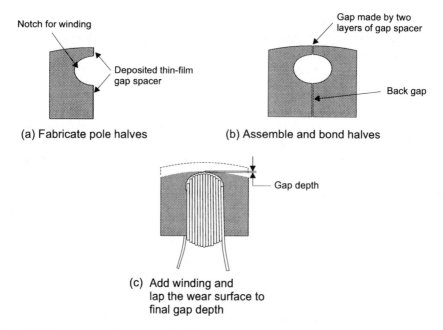

Notch for winding

Deposited thin-film gap spacer

(a) Fabricate pole halves

Gap made by two layers of gap spacer

Back gap

(b) Assemble and bond halves

Gap depth

(c) Add winding and lap the wear surface to final gap depth

Figure 11.6 *Construction of a magnetic head.*

stresses of scraping against an abrading surface at speeds up to 1,500 in/s for thousands of hours. And then they must be built at low enough cost that four of them can be included in a VCR that will retail (along with its thousands of other parts) for less than $200. What a challenge!

The basic ingredients of a magnetic head were shown in Figure 11.2—a magnetic pole piece including a surface that runs on the tape or disk and where there is a nonmagnetic gap for the fringing fields of recording or replay. The only other element is a coil of wire that handles the electrical signals.

Both the mechanical and the magnetic properties needed in head pole pieces are demanding. Because of this, many heads are designed to combine two materials in their pole pieces. A mechanically optimized magnetic material is used for the wear surface of the head, and a magnetically optimized material forms the rest of the pole pieces.

The gap area of the head is also a critical consideration from both mechanical and magnetic requirements. Since the gap must be nonmagnetic and of a precise length, possibly in the tens of microinches, pole pieces are often formed by depositing a thin film of nonmagnetic material on the surfaces of two pole-piece halves that are then bonded together to form the head and the gap, as shown in Figure 11.6. This technique causes a "back gap" to also be formed, but that is not a serious problem because the area of the magnetic path can be much greater in the back gap area. It is also important that the gap spacer material and the wear surface of the pole tips have compatible wear characteristics. If the gap spacer is too hard, it will become proud (stick up) as the pole tip material wears away, lifting the tape away from the active portion of the head. Similarly, if the gap spacer material is too soft, it will erode and again cause excessive separation loss.

As the figure shows, the magnetic circuit is deliberately narrowed below the wear surface at the gap. This dimension is called the *gap depth*, and the head is more sensitive the smaller it is. However, there is a tradeoff here because a head with too small a gap depth will fail prematurely as wearing causes the gap to begin opening. Of course, heads that do not contact the medium and thus theoretically have no wear, such as flying heads on disk drives, can have smaller gap depths, limited only by mechanical and manufacturing considerations.

Another consideration is that there should be a minimum of length around the magnetic circuit through the back gap. The opening for the winding is made as small as possible to achieve this and the winding is designed to entirely fill the opening.

11.2.4 Tape Decks

The mechanism of a tape recorder is called a *tape deck*. This name comes from the fact that many tape-handling mechanisms are built on a flat metal plate or "deck." Another common name is a tape transport. The basic objective of a tape deck is to bring tape and heads together in the correct way so that the heads can scan the tape according to a specified record format. In addition, the tape deck may provide different operating modes and rewinding of tape. Standards for recording are written in terms of the record format—the characteristics of the tape and the pattern recorded on it. This is because the medium that is taken from one tape deck to another is the tape and tape decks that write or read the same record format will be able to interchange tapes.

Proper handling of tape involves many considerations. The tape is an elastic medium that can be stretched or bent in the process of use but it is important that such operations be performed with care so as not to overstress the tape, damage its surface, or cause it to run off the guiding elements of the tape deck. Tape stretch is also a factor in specifying the record pattern when standardizing a tape format.

Tape is guided through a deck by its edges; however, the edges of tape can take very little force without damage, and a deck really has to be designed so carefully that tape will run through it with practically no force on the edge guides. This means that elements the tape runs around must be precisely perpendicular and tape reels and edge guides are precisely in plane. Any surfaces that the tape runs on must be smooth so as not to scratch the tape and they must be nonmagnetic so they cannot affect the magnetization of the tape's coating.

11.2.4.1 Linear Tape Deck

The simplest form of tape handling is a "linear" tape deck that records one or more longitudinal tracks on the tape. Figure 11.7 is a typical layout of such a deck, using a cassette that is

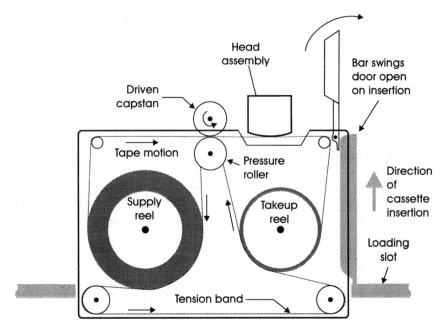

Figure 11.7 *Digital data cassette for linear recording.*

loaded into a slot. The slot shows at the bottom of the figure. This is the style of the familiar ¼-in tape data cassette used with PCs.

The tape on the supply reel of the cassette is B-wrap, so its magnetic coating is on the outside when looking at the edge of the cassette. As the cassette is inserted, a bar along the right edge causes a door over the tape to open so the head assembly can contact the tape. At the same time, a capstan drive roller presses into a slot in the cassette to drive the tape. This is backed up by a compliant pressure roller that is permanently in the cassette. The pressure roller provides enough force of the tape on the capstan that friction will drive the tape without slip. The cassette also contains a plastic band that runs against the tape on the reels and is driven by the tape being pulled from the supply reel. This provides drive to the takeup reel and maintains positive tension on the tape going over the heads.

This particular cassette design provides convenient loading—it is just pushed into a slot and then it is ready to go. However, that adds complication and expense to the cassette in the form of the incassette reel bearings, tape guides, capstan pressure roller, and the tension band mechanism. This is reasonable for the PC data cassette, but all those features can be eliminated for the lowest possible cassette cost. The analog audio cassette is an example of such a design. The cassette is cheap, but the drive is a little more complex and the cassette must be loaded by dropping it over some spindles or, for slot loading, the drive must move the spindles into place after the cassette has been inserted.

This example shows two important features that are required in every tape deck—a means to move the tape at a precise speed (capstan drive) and means for controlling tape tension (tension band). The capstan drive is widely used for driving tape. It consists of a rotating shaft or wheel that is driven by a motor and a means for pressing the tape surface against the capstan with sufficient force that friction will cause the tape to move at essentially the surface speed of the capstan. The capstan has a carefully roughened surface to add friction. The pressing means generally is a compliant roller mounted on a loose assembly that will allow the roller to align itself with the capstan. This is to make sure that the tape path is not distorted by the pressure roller. As mentioned above, it is very important that all the elements touching or guiding the tape be in precise alignment for the tape to run smoothly on the deck.

Tape tension control is important because a certain amount of tension must be held on the tape to control its motion. Since the tape is elastic, if it becomes loose, it becomes uncontrollable. The other reason for tension control is to determine the amount of stretching of the tape during recording and replay. This is especially important for helical-scan tape decks.

There are many different approaches for control of tape tension, but the tension band approach in the data cassette is an unusual one that is rarely seen. Most tape decks control tension by means of motors and/or friction-drag devices. The basic idea of tension control is to provide pulling force on the takeup end of the tape while holding back on the supply end of the tape. This causes the tape to move in the proper direction but the capstan, which is in between and is tightly coupled to the tape, adds or subtracts force to keep the speed constant. The important thing is that this action should never allow the tape to become loose.

Linear tape decks are limited in head-to-tape speed by the dynamics of rapidly moving tape. This problem results from the difficulties in guiding tape at high speeds and in obtaining adequate head-tape contact for short wavelength recording. Although linear tape decks have been built at speeds up to several hundred inches/second; for audio or video use, which requires a play time of one hour or more per tape; the practical speed limit is in the range of 10 to 20 in/s and this is caused by limits on reel size (see Section 11.2.2.1).

11.2.4.2 Helical-Scan Mechanisms

A basic approach to higher head-to-tape speeds is to place the heads on a wheel that rotates against the tape to produce a pattern of tracks that cross the tape. The first approach to this was developed by Ampex in the 1950s and used a wheel rotating about an axis parallel to the tape so heads on the wheel scanned tracks perpendicular to the tape edge. Four heads on the wheel required that a wide tape wrap 90 deg around the wheel for continuous recording without interruptions, which was accomplished by electronic switching of the heads so signal always came from the head that was contacting the tape. This system was called *quadruplex* and was the first successful video recorder. The quadruplex mechanism was complex and difficult to keep in good operation but it had little competition for more than 20 years. Later development focused on rotating-head mechanisms that scanned tracks at a small angle to the edge of the tape. This gave longer tracks on the tape and proved to be a more easily managed system that could be built at lower cost. These systems are called *helical-scan* systems because of the helical appearance of the tape going around the scanning drum. All present-day video recorders use the helical-scan principle.

Both quadruplex and helical scanning break the signal path up into a series of segments corresponding to the individual scans across the tape, a process called *segmentation*. If the system is designed for it, the segments can be reassembled electronically into a continuous signal path that has no interruptions. Alternatively, the gaps between segments can be positioned in time so that they do not affect the signal. For example, in analog helical-scan recorders, the segmentation gaps are usually positioned to occur within the vertical blanking intervals, where nothing has to be recorded since the correct signal can be reconstructed on playback. This implies that the rotation of the helical scanner must be synchronized to the incoming video signal. That is done by servo control of the scanner drum.

Figure 11.8 shows two basic approaches to helical scanning. The *alpha-wrap* configuration wraps the tape into a complete loop around the scanner. A single head on the drum can record continuously except for a slight gap when it crosses the edges of the tape where they meet on the scanner. In analog video recording, this slight gap can be controlled so it occurs during the vertical blanking interval. In digital recording, such a gap can be accommodated by the use of a memory to hold signals to fill the gap. Alpha-wrap systems were built and operated successfully but they have gone out of favor because it is extremely difficult to use alpha-wrap with tape held in a cassette. Today, everyone wants cassette loading of tape.

The *omega-wrap* approach does not require the tape to be made into a complete loop; essentially all present helical-scan systems are variations of this type. As shown in the figure, the amount of wrap required depends on how many heads per channel are on the drum. A single head requires a nearly full wrap of the tape but, if two heads per channel are used, as shown in Figure 11.8(c), a little more than 180 deg of wrap will give continuous recording. Since the track length wraps around only half of the scanner circumference, two heads per channel requires a scanner of twice the diameter of a one-head scanner. In spite of that, many systems use the two-head approach.

As can be seen from Figure 11.9, helical-scan mechanisms are built with two drums, one fixed and one rotating. However, they depart from the ideal of a flat tape deck with everything mounted in the same plane. Components are at critical angles to each other and not necessarily in the same plane. As the tape goes around the scanner, it changes height and angle; this is a problem because the two reels in a cassette need to be in the same plane. The problem is solved by setting the scanner at an angle to the tape deck and using tilted tape guides to level out the tape path to meet the cassette. These features complicate the design and manufacture of helical-scan decks, but the problems have been effectively solved and such decks can be built at extremely low costs. Helical-scan mechanisms are sold for a few

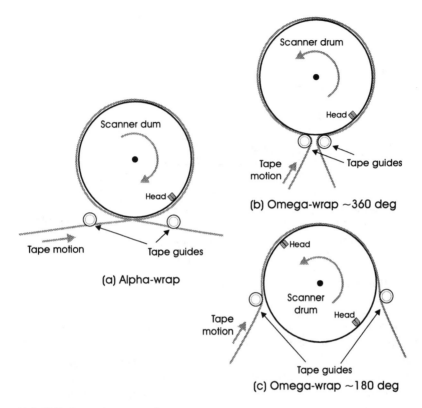

Figure 11.8 *Helical scanning approaches.*

hundred dollars in the consumer market and higher performance versions are made for professional markets.

There are important design considerations in helical-scan mechanisms:

- The *helix angle* is the angle between the edge of the tape and the plane of rotation of the heads. In the tape deck of Figure 11.9, the scanner is set at the helix angle relative to the deck. The angle of the recorded tracks on the tape is slightly different than the helix angle because the linear motion of the tape subtracts or adds to the track length, depending on whether the tape motion and the head motion are in the same direction or opposite, respectively.

- Ideally, the recorded tracks should be straight lines when the tape is laid on a flat surface. However, this may not be so unless the tape stretches uniformly as it goes around the scanner. This is difficult to maintain because there can be varying friction on the tape around the scanner and the tension distribution across the tape may not be uniform. Various scanner and tape deck designs address these problems differently.

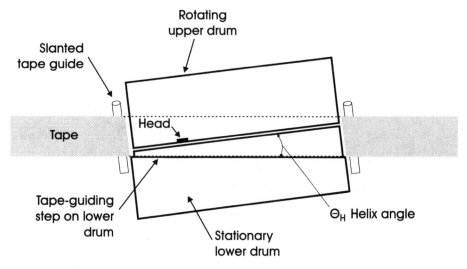

Figure 11.9 *Helix angle.*

- Some helical-scan systems have a servo-controlled mounting of the replay head that is capable of dynamically moving the head during scanner rotation to follow a distorted track. This is called *automatic scan tracking* (AST); it provides the additional feature that tracks can be followed even when the tape speed is incorrect and the track angle has changed. AST is also used to provide slow motion or stop-motion playback.

- In addition to the helical scanning, most video recorders also have longitudinal tracks, usually at the edges of the tape, for audio, control, and time-code recording. Because these are completely distinct from the helical tracks, they can be separately edited. It is important that the scanner be designed so that the helical tracks will not overwrite the longitudinal tracks. This is accomplished by choosing the scanner dimensions so that the helical tracks do not use the full width of the tape. This often results in the video heads not entering and leaving the tape at the edges, which is an advantage because the shock of heads hitting the edge of tape at high speed can be very damaging to both heads and tape.

- In helical-scan machines with two or more heads on the drum, a special technique can be used to eliminate the guard bands that are usually necessary between magnetic tracks. Heads are usually designed with the gap at an exact 90 deg angle to the edges of the track. This angle is called the head *azimuth* and must be precisely maintained or there will be a signal attenuation effect caused by reading different parts of the track at slightly different times. The azimuth angle becomes more critical the shorter the wavelength is. In a recorder where adjacent tracks are recorded by different heads, the azimuth angle of each of the heads can be deliberately offset in different directions

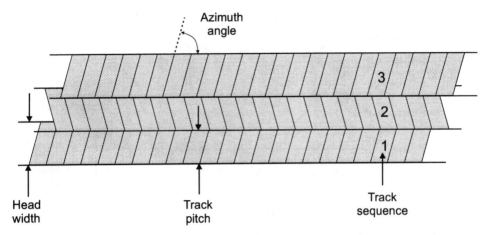

Figure 11.10 *Track pattern produced by azimuth recording.*

from the 90 deg value. Typical offset angles are ±15°. Then, if one head reads some of the adjacent track, there will be little or no output from the adjacent track because of the azimuth cancellation effect. This is shown in Figure 11.10, where odd-numbered tracks are recorded by a head with azimuth offset in one direction and even-numbered tracks are recorded by a head offset in the other direction. The figure shows that recordings can be made with heads that are wider than the desired track pitch. Each successive track overrecords a little of the previous track, reducing it to a width exactly equal to the track pitch. Of course, the offset azimuth angles must be precisely controlled.

- Tape tension control is very important for helical scanning because the track length, straightness, and angle depend on how much the tape is stretched while being scanned. Helical tape decks usually have some tension control means controlling the tension at the supply and takeup reels. This usually takes the form of a spring-loaded *tension arm* that has a pin riding against the tape. If the tape wraps around the pin to some degree, a force is exerted on the arm by the tension in the tape. In higher priced tape decks, this is used in a servo that monitors tension according to the position of the tension arm and controls tension using the reel motors.

Additional helical-scan features are mentioned in Section 11.4 for specific systems.

11.2.4.3 Cassette Mechanisms

The problem of cassette loading of tape is complicated in helical recorders because the tape generally has to be drawn out of the cassette to be wrapped around the scanner. Figure 11.11 is a diagram of how this is done. The cassette is loaded into a slot that is above the

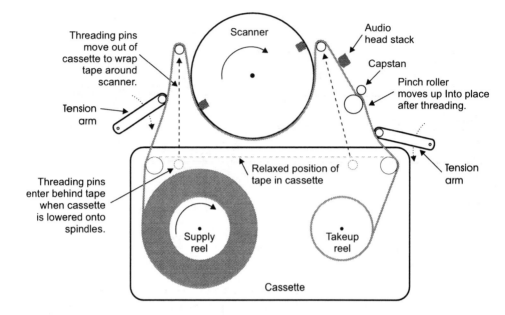

Figure 11.11 *Cassette loading of a helical-scan tape deck.*

final tape path of the deck. Once the cassette is in the slot, a mechanism lowers the cassette into the plane of the tape path, reel spindles enter the cassette to pick up the reels and a pair of fingers enter behind the tape. In a subsequent operation, the fingers are drawn from the cassette to wrap the tape around the scanner.

11.2.5 Disk Drives

The use of a disk instead of tape for a recording surface has the advantage that the entire surface can be accessed by a single motion of a head along a radius of the disk. No tape reels have to be unrolled to get at the recording. *Access time* is a parameter that becomes important with disk recording. It is defined as the time from the issuance of a command to retrieve data until the first bit of data returns. With a disk drive, access time is made of three parts: (1) *head stepping time*, which is the time to move the head to the desired track; (2) *rotational latency*, which is the time for the desired data in that track to rotate around to the head; and (3) *processing time*, which is the time for the data to be decoded for use. The first two of these components are statistical in that they depend on how far the head must move from the track where it was and where the desired data are located along the track when the correct track is reached by the head. For that reason, access time is usually specified as an average value. Values in the tens of milliseconds or less are typical for hard disk drives.

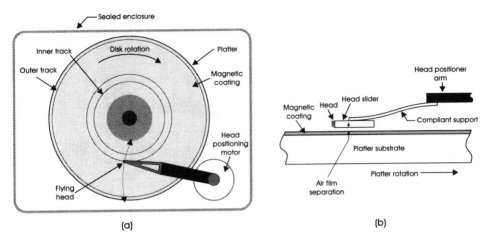

Figure 11.12 *Computer hard disk drive. From A. F. Inglis and A. C. Luther,* Video Engineering, Second Edition, *McGraw-Hill, New York, 1996, reproduced with permission of The McGraw-Hill Companies.*

Of course, the amount of area that can be accessed rapidly is limited to the usable area of one disk or to the area of a group of disks mounted on the same spindle, so the available recording area is severely limited compared with a roll of tape. This has restricted disk recorders to computer mass memory or to still pictures in video. However, as recording density has increased and digital video compression has been developed, the day of recording an hour or more of high-quality video on a single disk surface is here and the disk drive is an important video or audio recording device. Disk drives can use rigid (hard) or floppy disks.

11.2.5.1 Hard Disk Drive

Figure 11.12 is a diagram of a typical computer-style hard disk drive, also called a *fixed disk* drive, if the disk is nonremovable. One or more disks are mounted to a rotating spindle that is driven at a constant rotational speed. A head for each disk surface is mounted from an arm that can rotate through an arc across the disk surface in an approximately radial direction. Concentric tracks are recorded by stepping the heads quickly from one radial position to another. The brief interruption required to move the heads between tracks (a few milliseconds) is readily handled in a digital system by appropriate data buffering in RAM. The heads are mounted at the ends of the arms on a compliant structure that is designed to trap an air film so the head does not contact the disk surface but "flies" at a constant small separation, such as 5 μin. This mode of operation makes the head-to-disk interface very susceptible to dirt or dust particles and it must operate in a sealed, clean environment.

With multiple disks (platters), a single PC hard drive can store up to about 10 GB of data. With compressed video, such as MPEG-2, this could hold as much as one hour of

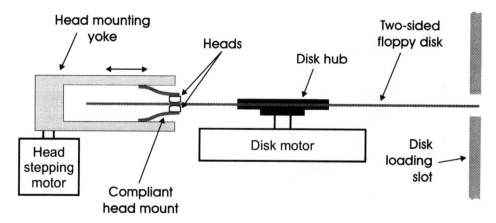

Figure 11.13 *Cross-section view of a floppy disk drive.*

standard-definition video. The disk drive access time of a few tens of milliseconds provides essentially instantaneous random access to any frame of the video—this capability is the basis for the popular nonlinear video editing systems now on the market (see Section 12.6).

Random access of data on a disk requires knowledge of where the data are physically located in the tracks of the disk. This is usually handled by maintaining an index, called a *directory*, of physical locations versus logical names of data objects. The directory is stored at a specific location on the disk. When a particular data object is accessed, the system first looks it up in the directory and then seeks to the physical location indicated to actually retrieve the data. There are thus two accesses on the disk to get data—one to the directory and a second one to the data. Software for managing this process is called a *file system*.

11.2.5.2 Floppy Disk Drive

A floppy disk drive is similar to a hard disk drive except that there is only one disk platter and the head mounting mechanism is different to account for the different properties of the head-to-disk interface (See Figure 11.13). In a floppy disk, the compliance of the disk partially controls the head contact pressure. Most floppy disks operate at slower speeds than hard disks so the heads can be placed in actual contact with the record surface without having too much wear of disk or head. The disk is coated on both sides and heads press against each side at the same location. A stepping motor drives a mechanism that moves the heads along a radius of the disk to change tracks. Operating this way, the storage capacity of a single floppy drive is only a few megabytes. This magnitude of storage is not particularly useful for audio or video, but the advantage of floppy disks is that they are removable and many different things can be stored on separate disks.

A new generation of floppy disks has been introduced offering much higher capacities—up to hundreds of megabytes. That is still small for video, but this is just today's point on a curve that will grow further in the future.

11.3 OPTICAL RECORDING FUNDAMENTALS

The advent of solid-state lasers has made possible optical recording technologies that exploit the properties of monochromatic light. Record patterns with submicron dimensions can be reliably detected with these means. Raw record densities of more than 1,000 Mb/in^2 are possible before error correction is added. With error correction, density can still exceed 400 Mb/in^2 with error rates less than 10^{-15}. In addition to high density, optical recording has other important advantages:

- Because optical reading is by means of a beam of light, there is no contact between the record medium and the reading head. Mechanical wear is eliminated and reliable performance can be achieved over many years.

- The recorded pattern can be embedded in a plastic substrate that makes it impervious to dirt or scratches. Damage to the plastic surface is unimportant because the surface can be out of focus for the reading light beam.

- Recordings are not affected by electric or magnetic fields.

- Read-only recordings can be made that cannot be changed after creation, which is excellent for maintaining data integrity for archival or security purposes.

- Records can be in the form of mechanical patterns that can be replicated inexpensively by pressing.

11.3.1 An Optical Read Head

The reading of optical records is based on the diffraction of monochromatic light. One implementation of this is shown in Figure 11.14(a). A solid-state laser provides a light source that passes through an optical system to the recorded surface, where it is reflected directly back into the optical system. By the use of a quarter-wave plate and a polarization beam splitter, the reflected beam can be directed to a photodetector that extracts the data from the recorded patterns.

The laser light first passes through a diffraction grating, which is a pattern of slits spaced a few wavelengths apart for the laser light. Light passing through the slits diffracts and causes an interference pattern that, when focused, shows up as a bright center spot with successively less intense spots on either side. The center spot is used for data recovery and automatic focusing, and the first secondary spots on either side are used for automatic tracking, a system called the *three-spot* architecture. Automatic focusing and tracking is

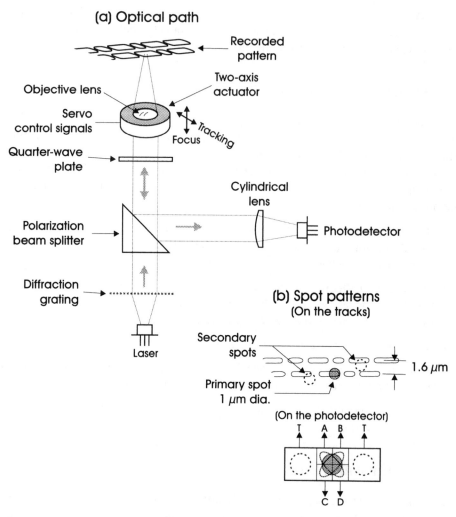

Figure 11.14 *(a) Typical components for playback of an optical recording using the three-spot method, (b) spot patterns.*

necessary because the high data density requires far tighter mechanical accuracy than can be achieved by even the best mechanical rotating parts.

The beam passes through the polarization beam splitter and then to a quarter-wave plate that rotates the plane of polarization by 45 deg. It is then focused by an objective lens onto the recorded pattern. The objective lens is mounted in an actuator that can be electrically moved in a direction perpendicular to the recorded surface for focusing and in a direction transverse to the recorded tracks for tracking.

The focused light is reflected at the recorded pattern and returns back the same optical path. A second pass through the quarter-wave plate adds an additional 45 deg rotation of polarization, with the result that the polarization beam splitter reflects the return beam over to a photodetector instead of passing it back to the laser.

There are several ways that the return beam can be modulated by the recorded pattern. One method is where the recorded pattern is a series of shallow pits in an otherwise smooth, reflective surface. When the focused spot is over a pit, the optical path length is slightly longer than when it is on a land. If the spot straddles slightly over pit and land, the path length difference causes a phase shift of the beam that results in partial cancellation of the return beam. Thus, it becomes amplitude modulated by the pattern. This effect is a maximum if the pit depth is a quarter-wavelength of the laser light. Another form of recorded pattern simply has different reflectances in the pattern instead of pits; this also produces amplitude modulation of the return beam.

The operation of the three-spot technique can be explained with the help of Figure 11.14(b). The center of the three spots reads the track for data recovery, while the other two spots are placed so they read a little to either side of the desired track. The three spots are imaged to three separate areas of the photodetector whose outputs are available separately. Because the secondary spots (dotted lines) read at the track edges, their outputs will be less than the main spot. Furthermore, as the tracking moves off center, the secondary spot outputs will become unequal. By comparing the outputs from the secondary spots, a servo error signal is developed to move the tracking actuator in a direction to correct the tracking.

Automatic focusing is accomplished by the use of the cylindrical lens in the optical path and the division of the center-spot photodetector into four quadrants. The effect of the cylindrical lens is to cause the spot on the photodetector to become asymmetrical when it is out of focus (a distortion called *astigmatism*) as shown by the dotted lines in the figure. By comparing the outputs from the four-quadrant detector, a servo error signal is created to move the objective lens actuator in the proper direction to correct focus. Of course, the outputs from the four quadrants are summed to obtain the data recovery signal from the center spot.

The servo of focus and tracking corrects for mechanical errors in disk flatness and rotation. The servo responses must be fast enough to correct errors that repeat several times in a single rotation of the disk. The example here shows only one method of accomplishing optical reading. Several other techniques are used in different players.

11.3.2 Optical Records

Optical recorders generally use a disk format. The optical read head is mounted on a mechanism that moves it along a radius of the disk to provide access to multiple tracks on the disk. Optical records can have either continuous (spiral) tracks or concentric tracks. The tracks can be placed very close together, up to 20,000 per inch or more.

Recording a number of concentric or spiral tracks on a disk results in a range of track diameters as the optical head moves across the disk surface. With a constant rotational speed, this would result in a variation of linear speed for scanning the track. Some disk systems vary the rotational speed to maintain a constant linear speed—this is called *constant linear velocity* (CLV) operation. CLV increases disk capacity somewhat compared to *constant angular velocity* (CAV) operation, but it has the disadvantage that the relatively massy disk must have a speed servo to adjust rotational speed as the tracking head changes radial position. This is costly and can lengthen access time.

11.3.3 Optical Formats

The most widely used optical format is the Compact Disc (CD), developed originally for digital audio but now used for computers (CD-ROM) and several other services. It is described in Section 11.5.1. The CD has a recording capacity of up to 750 MB on a single 12-cm optical disk. A new system, DVD (see Section 11.5.2), increases that density by about seven times.

Recording of optical disks can be done in several ways. Dimples (pits) can be pressed into the record surface. This was developed initially for the audio CD, which needs a low-cost high-quantity replication method. This method of recording requires the making of a master disc that is then used to produce stampers that can press multiple copies at very low cost (less than $1.00 per disc.) However, the making of a master costs about $1,000, so this method is reasonable only for large-quantity distribution of the same recording.

Another type of recording approach uses a similar head structure to the playback mechanism but with a higher power laser and an organic-dye recording surface on the disk that can be "burned" by the laser beam. The result is the same—a surface whose reflectance varies with the data. This method of recording is useful for small-quantity recordings that cannot justify the expense of mastering and pressing. Drives for CD recording (CD-R) are now available as PC peripherals at prices around $500. CD-R is described further in Section 11.5.1.3.

11.3.4 Magneto-Optical Recording

Another form of recording combines the properties of optical and magnetic technologies—*magneto-optical* (MO) recording. This depends on a property of magnetic materials called the *Curie point*, which is a temperature above which all magnetic properties of the material disappear. If, for example, a magnetic material is fully magnetized in one direction, and a laser beam is also focused on the material in the presence of a reverse-direction magnetic field, the material will become remagnetized in the opposite direction in regions where the laser beam is intense enough to move the surface temperature of the magnetic material above its Curie point. Such recording are replayed by a special optical pickup that uses the Kerr effect. This effect is a slight rotation of optical polarization by magnetic fields that can be detected with a sensitive detector. The advantage of MO is that recordings can be erased and rerecorded.

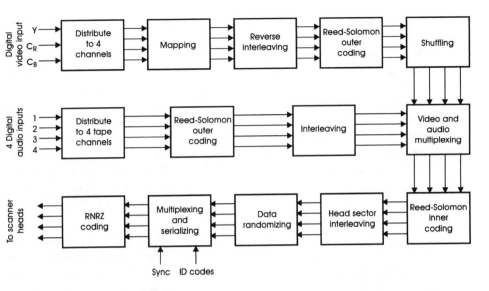

Figure 11.15 *Record-side signal processing of the D-1 tape system.*

11.4 DIGITAL MAGNETIC TAPE RECORDERS

This section presents several of the digital-tape recording systems and describes their record formats, mechanisms, and encoding methods.

11.4.1 SMPTE D-Series

The first digital video recorders were for broadcast or program production use, and they have been identified by SMPTE with the letter "D" and a number signifying the sequence. The actual standards documents have the usual SMPTE standards numbers. These standards are summarized in Figures 11.16 through 11.20. Specific matters are discussed below.

11.4.1.1 SMPTE D-1

The D-1 recorder was the first standardized digital recorder and operates with the ITU-R Rec. BT.601 4:2:2 component signal standards. Figure 11.15 shows the record-side signal processing of the D-1. The processing is quite complex but, of course, that can be manufactured in a few integrated circuits. The objective of the signal processing is to convert the incoming data into the format required by the recording channels and to introduce error protection coding. The signal system must deal not only with normal-speed operation but also with slow motion and fast shuttle playback. In the latter case, some information is inherently lost in scanning the tape, but the signal system is designed to still make the best possible picture from the remaining data.

Since the D-1 transport provides four recording channels for video data, the three component video samples are distributed to the four recording channels according to an algorithm that guarantees that all video components will use all four channels. This provides some playback capability even when one or two channels might fail. All remaining processing is done in four channels.

The next step is called *mapping*, which has the objective of making all the bits of the recorded samples have approximately the same significance as far as the video samples are concerned. Without mapping, an error in the MSB of a sample would be much more significant than errors in any of the other bits. Thus, a single-bit error will have approximately the same effect on the sample value regardless of which bit it is. Mapping is done with a lookup table.

Then a *reverse-interleave* process is done. This takes care of a problem caused by the distribution process; where the Y, C_R, C_B samples related to one pixel do not always end up in the same error-protection block. When blocks are lost in shuttle mode, it is desired that complete pixels should be able to be constructed from the remaining data. The reverse-interleave takes care of that.

Then, the Reed-Solomon outer coding is done. The blocks have 30 bytes of data and 2 bytes of error coding. Following this, a *shuffle* process is performed. This is an interleaving but with randomization added. Again, the consideration is for shuttle mode, where data are lost as the scanner heads cross tracks at the wrong angle due to the higher tape speed. With normal interleaving (see Section 7.2.5.7), lost data would appear in a regular pattern that would be highly visible to the viewer. The random shuffle breaks that pattern so it is less visible.

Video and audio are both recorded on the helical tracks. This is necessary because the digital audio data rate would be too high for longitudinal tracks as are used in analog recording. Also, with a digital system it is practical to multiplex the audio and video together and still retain the important feature that they be separately editable. This can be done because it is possible to rerecord the audio portions of the helical tracks during editing without degrading the video signals.

After multiplexing video and audio, the inner Reed-Solomon coding is done. Then, sector interleaving is performed—this is to further distribute the data among the four channels. Last, the data are randomized to create as uniform a pdf as possible for the modulation.

At this point, The sync and ID blocks are added to the data and the data in each of the four channels are serialized for RNRZ coding, which is the final modulation that is directed to the heads.

The audio processing provides for four input channels, but these are distributed to the four heads so that each audio channel shares all four heads. Then Reed-Solomon outer coding is performed, the data are interleaved to break burst errors and are multiplexed with the video. The audio is recorded in four blocks at the center of each helical track; in fact, each audio block is recorded twice for additional redundancy. The audio blocks have guard bands along the track to provide for erase switching during audio-only editing.

The D-1 record pattern and specifications are shown in Figure 11.16. D-1 is based on 3/4-in tape in a cassette design that is used by D-1 and D-2. There are four channels in parallel helical tracks on the tape, each written by a separate head on the scanner. The scanner also has erase heads and confidence-replay heads for each channel, giving a total of 12 heads. (*Confidence-replay* provides replay during recording to confirm that tracks have actually been written on the tape and it also is used during editing to replay right up to the point of recording.)

11.4.1.2 SMPTE D-2

Although the component format of D-1 is very successful, for many users it is unnecessarily expensive, especially where the recorders are being used in an otherwise analog composite system. Signals in such a system already contain the limitations of analog composite and the higher quality possible with component recording cannot be enjoyed. This creates an opening for a digital recorder that digitizes the composite signal for recording: the D-2 system.

Composite digital has slightly lower data rates than 4:2:2 component digital since there is only one signal that is digitized at 4fsc (14.3 MHz for NTSC; 17.7 MHz for PAL), so the recorder can be somewhat simplified to take advantage of this. Figure 11.17 shows the tape records and parameters for the SMPTE D-2 standard. The recorder uses the same 3/4-in tape cassette design as the D-1 but with slightly different tape in it. Two channels are sufficient for the video signal and azimuth recording is used. The result is that tape speed can be reduced by more than 2:1.

The signal processing for D-2 is similar in concept to that shown for D-1 in Figure 11.15 except, of course, there is ADC at the inputs and DAC at the outputs and the data are distributed to only two record channels instead of four. The channel coding is Miller-squared, which is a modification of Miller code (see Section 7.2.3.2) that completely eliminates the DC component.

11.4.1.3 SMPTE D-3

As ½-inch tape decks became available, it was desirable to design digital recorders using them to take advantage of their higher density performance and their smaller size. This is important particularly for portable applications. The D-3 composite ½-inch tape format was the result. D-3 uses two helical record channels with a slightly smaller scanner than that of D-2. Track width is reduced 2:1 and azimuth recording is used. The result is more than a 2:1 improvement in area density over D-2. This is possible primarily because of better tape.

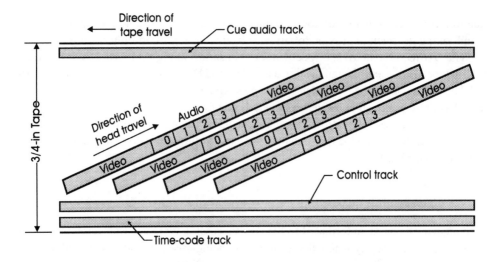

Parameter	Value
Video format	4:2:2 component
Tape width	3/4 in
Cassette	D-1 standard
Tape speed	11.3 in/s
Tape usage	8.48 in^2/s
Channels for video	4
Record heads/channel	1
Total heads on drum	12
Number of audio channels	4
Video track width	1.6 mils
Azimuth recording	No
Drum diameter	2.95 in
Drum rotation speed	150 rps
Video channel coding	R-NRZI
Video writing speed	1,404 in/s
Vide sample rate—Y	13.5 MHz
Video sample rate—chroma	6.75 MHz
Total video data rate	216 Mb/s
Area density	25.5 Mb/in^2
SMPTE standards	
Tape records	224M
Tape	225M
Cassette	226M
Signal content of helical records	227M
Signal content of cue & time-code tracks	228M

Figure 11.16 *D-1 records and parameters.*

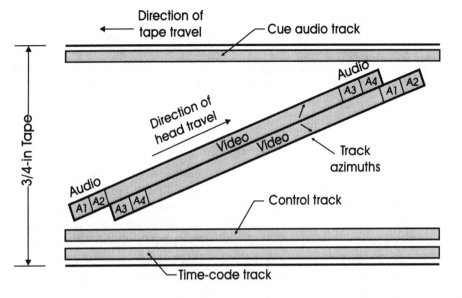

Parameter	Value
Video format	Composite
Tape width	3/4 in.
Cassette	D-1 standard (different tape)
Tape speed	5.2 in/s
Tape usage	3.9 in^2/s
Channels for video	2
Record heads/channel	2
Total heads on scanner drum	10
Number of audio channels	4
Video track width	1.6 mils
Azimuth recording	Yes
Drum diameter	3.8 in
Drum rotation speed	89.9 rps
Video channel coding	Miller^2
Video writing speed	1,080 in/.
Vide sample rate	4$f$sc
Total video data rate	115/142 Mb/s (NTSC/PAL)
Area density	29.5/36.4 Mb/in^2
SMPTE standards	
Tape records	245M
Tape	246M
Cassette dimensions	226M
Signal content of helical records	247M

Figure 11.17 *D-2 records and parameters.*

Audio is recorded in editable blocks at each end of the helical tracks. D-3 aligns the guard bands between audio and video blocks in each channel so that a single double-width flying erase head can operate on both tracks for independent editing of audio or video.

D-3 signal processing is similar in concept to Figure 11.15 except there is ADC at the inputs and DAC at the outputs, and the data are distributed to only two record channels. The channel coding is EFM (see Section 7.2.3.3).

11.4.1.4 SMPTE D-5

The component digital version of ½-inch tape recorders is the D-5. Sampling is 4:2:2 at 13.5 MHz and 10 bps or 18.0 MHz and 8 bps. The scanner and tape deck are the same as that of D-3 except that there are four helical channels and the tape speed has been doubled to accommodate that. The scanner rotational speed is unchanged. Audio is recorded in blocks at the center of the helical tracks. Editing guard bands between audio and video blocks are aligned in the four tracks so a single flying erase head is used for insert editing. D-5 machines can play D-3 tapes if the tape speed is reduced and the appropriate changes are made in signal processing.

Signal processing is similar to the D-1 format shown in Figure 11.15.

11.4.1.5 SMPTE D-6

The D-6 format provides a data rate capability of up to 1.2 Gb/s, which is suitable for component HDTV recording at the highest resolution. It is based on 3/4-inch tape and the D-2 cassette and tape deck. A maximum playing time of one hour is provided. To reach the six-times higher data rate compared with that of D-2, eight recording channels are used. Since the scanner uses 180 deg wrap requiring two record heads per channel, and there are separate record and replay heads for the eight channels plus two flying erase heads, there are a total of 34 heads on the D-6 scanner.

The eight recording channels use azimuth recording and are recorded in a group of side-by-side tracks called a cluster. There are two clusters, corresponding to the two sets of heads required by the 180 deg wrap scanner. To facilitate editing of data on a cluster basis, there is a guard band between clusters and the flying erase heads are wide enough to erase all the tracks in a cluster at once. Editing of video and audio is possible on a field basis for interlaced scanning or a frame basis for progressively scanned video.

Signal processing is similar in concept to Figure 11.15. The video data distribution algorithm distributes on a complete pixel basis; luminance pixels go to even-numbered tracks and chrominance pixels go to odd-numbered tracks of the 8-track clusters. The track sequence for distribution varies from one cycle to the next to break any patterns that might appear when there are track errors. Reed-Solomon outer and inner coding are used, and the channel coding is an 8-12 group code. This code reduces the DC component and increases the minimum wavelength that has to be recorded.

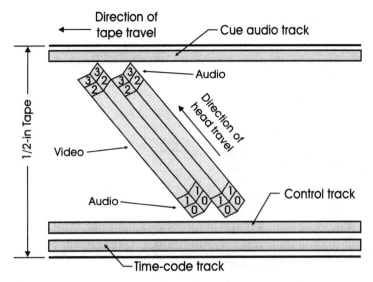

Figure 11.18 *D-3 records and parameters.*

Parameter	Value
Video format	Composite
Tape width	1/2 in
Cassette	D-3 standard
Tape speed	3.3 in/s
Tape usage	1.65 in²/s
Channels for video	2
Record heads/channel	2
Total heads on scanner drum	10
Number of audio channels	4
Video track width	0.8 mils
Azimuth recording	Yes
Drum diameter	3.0 in
Drum rotation speed	89.9 rps
Video channel coding	EFM
Video writing speed	847 in/s
Vide sample rate	4$f$sc
Total video data rate	115/142 Mb/s (NTSC/PAL)
Area density	69.7/86.1 Mb/in²
SMPTE standards	
Tape records	264M (525) 265M (625)
Cassette dimensions	263M

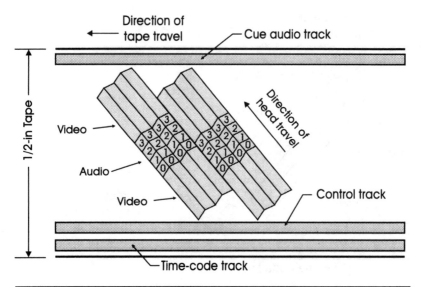

Parameter	Value
Video format	Component 4:2:2
Tape width	1/2 in
Cassette	D-3 standard
Tape speed	6.6 in/s
Tape usage	3.3 in²/s
Channels for video	2
Record heads/channel	2
Total heads on scanner drum	10
Number of audio channels	4
Video track width	0.8 mils
Azimuth recording	Yes
Drum diameter	3.0 in
Drum rotation speed	89.9 rps
Video channel coding	EFM
Video writing speed	847 in/s
Video sample rate—Y	13.5 MHz @10 bps
	18.0 MHz @ 8 bps
Video sample rate—chroma	6.75 MHz/9 MHz
Total video data rate	270 Mb/s
Area density	82 Mb/in²
SMPTE standards	279M

Figure 11.19 *D-5 records and parameters.*

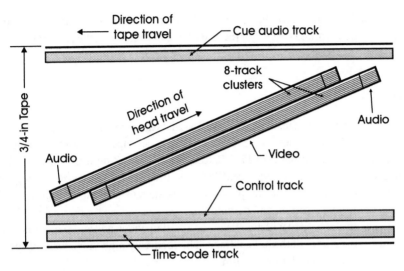

Parameter	Value
Video format	HDTV component
Tape width	3/4 in.
Cassette	D-1 standard (improved tape)
Tape speed	20.7 in/s
Tape usage	15.5 in²/s
Channels for video	8
Record heads/channel	2
Total heads on scanner drum	34
Number of audio channels	10
Video track width	0.8 mils
Azimuth recording	Yes
Drum diameter	3.8 in
Drum rotation speed	150 rps
Video channel coding	8,12
Video writing speed	1,773 in/s
Vide sample rate—Y	74.25 MHz (typical)
Video sample rate—chroma	38.12 MHz (typical)
Total video data rate	1.2 Gb/s (maximum)
Area density	77.4 Mb/in²
SMPTE standards	
Tape records	277M
Signal content of all records	278M

Figure 11.20 *D-6 records and parameters.*

Audio is recorded at both ends of the helical tracks; up to 10 channels of audio are available. Audio blocks are recorded twice—at the end of one cluster and at the start of the next cluster.

11.4.2 Betacam SX

Following on the popular Betacam analog professional camcorder line, Sony has developed a digital product family—Betacam SX, which is a ½-inch tape system for camcorder and studio use. The digital format uses ITU-R Rec. BT-601 4:2:2 digitization with 10:1 compression. The compression algorithm is MPEG-2 with a profile that has been designed specifically for professional use. The compressed video data rate is 18 Mb/s. Figure 11.21 shows the Betacam SX tape format and parameters.

The helical tracks are recorded with two heads and contain video and audio records. The audio records are at the center of the helical track. The relatively high video writing speed gives a minimum wavelength of about 35 μin.

Replay of the helical tracks uses four heads in a unique configuration that eliminates the need for a dynamic tracking servo. There are two heads at each azimuth setting, which are spaced one track apart on the drum. Their outputs are processed together so that between the two heads, all the content of a track is read, even when the track is not exactly straight on the tape. This also provides an additional important feature, which is that tracks can be played at faster-than- normal speed. Of course, the output data rate increases, but this is a useful feature for transmitting video and audio captured in the field back to a studio location. In news-gathering, getting the story to air quickly is a significant advantage.

11.4.3 DVC Home Recorders

As the cost of digital components has dropped, the time has come for a digital home video recorder. Many in the industry recognized this and began development and standardization—the result is the *Digital Video Cassette* (DVC) system. Both consumer and professional versions of this format have been developed.

DVC is based on ¼-inch tape in a small cassette that offers up to four hours recording time in DVC and two hours in DVCPro. A small-diameter, two-heads-per-channel scanner is used to record the single video channel. Tape record patterns and parameters for DVC are shown in Figure 11.22.

The basic sampling rates for luminance and chrominance are in accordance with ITU-R Rec. BT.601, 4:2:2 format; however, the recording format further subsamples the color-difference signals so that 525-line systems are recorded as 4:1:1, and 625-line systems are recorded as 4:2:0. The video data are then DCT-compressed to reduce the data rate by approximately 10:1. Two record channels with two heads per channel handle a data rate on tape of approximately 12 Mb/s.

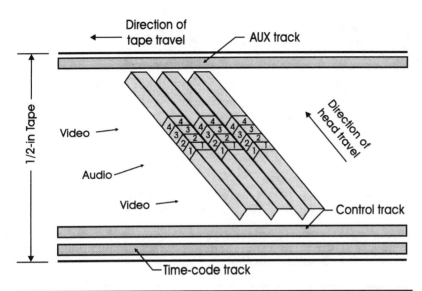

Parameter	Value
Video format	Component 4:2:2 compressed 10:1
Tape width	1/2 in
Cassette	Betacam SX standard
Tape speed	2.34 in/s
Tape usage	1.17 in²/s
Recording time	60 min (S-cassette), 180 min (L)
Channels for video	1
Record heads/channel	2
Total heads on scanner drum	8
Number of audio channels	4
Video track width	0.8 mils
Azimuth recording	Yes
Drum diameter	2.93 in
Drum rotation speed	74.925 rps
Video writing speed	689 in/s
Vide sample rate—Y	13.5 MHz
Video sample rate—chroma	6.75 MHz
Audio sampling rate	48 kHz
Audio bits/sample	16
Total video and audio data rate	21 Mb/s
Area density	18 Mb/in²

Figure 11.21 *Betacam SX records and parameters.*

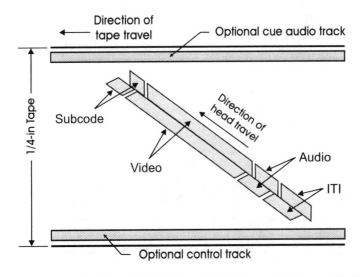

Parameter	Value
Video format	Component, compressed
Tape width	1/4 in
Cassette	DVC standard, small or large
Tape speed	0.75 in/s
Tape usage	0.187 in²/s
Playing time	2 hr, 4 hr
Channels for video	1
Record heads/channel	2
Total heads on scanner drum	4
Number of audio channels	2 (in helical tracks)
Audio sampling rate	48 kHz
Audio bits/sample	16
Helical track width	0.4 mils
Azimuth recording	Yes
Drum diameter	0.855 in
Drum rotation speed	150 rps
Helical writing speed	201 in/s
Video sample rate—Y	13.5 MHz
Video sample rate—C_R, C_B	6.75 MHz
Video decimation	4:1:1 (525), 4:2:0 (625)
Video compression	DCT plus RLC
Total video data rate after compression	12 Mb/s
Area density	64 Mb/in²

Figure 11.22 *DVC records and parameters.*

Each helical track contains four blocks of data: video, audio, subcode, and an insert-and-track information (ITI) code. The four blocks are separated by guard bands, and the scanner has flying erase heads so the blocks are separately editable. The subcode block has time code and other information that helps identify the tracks at high tape speeds in shuttle mode. The tape format provides for two optional longitudinal tracks, one at each edge of the tape, but the system can operate without either.

11.4.4 DVCPRO Professional Recorders

DVCPRO is a professional recording system based on DVC concepts. It is available in camcorder format and also in studio systems for editing. Video recording is 4:1:1 component at 13.5-MHz sampling with intraframe video compression. Two digital audio channels are provided with 48-kHz sampling at 16-bps. The DVCPRO record pattern and parameters are shown in Figure 11.23. The scanner diameter and rotational speed are the same as that of DVC, but the tracks are made wider, with a higher tape speed, and better tape is used to record a higher bit rate of 25 Mb/s.

To provide editing of audio or video, the helical tracks are divided into four sectors with guard bands between them as shown in the figure. The first sector of each track is the ITI sector, which contains codes that are used for tracking control and timing during insert editing. The second sector is the audio data with its sync and ID codes, and Reed-Solomon coded and shuffled audio data. The third sector contains the video data, with sync codes and Reed-Solomon coding. The final sector of each helical track is the subcode sector, which contains time-code information in a format that can be read reliably at varying tape speeds. This replaces the longitudinal track that is usually provided for time code in other professional recorders.

DVCPRO is one of the few professional recorders that use video compression. Because compression introduces some picture degradation, many in the video industry believe that it does not belong in professional equipment. However, the benefits are great in terms of data reduction and the performance degradation of the DVCPRO approach is minimal. DVCPRO compression is DCT based and is intraframe only so that editing is possible on any frame number. The compression performance provides 500-TVL resolution video with SNR greater than 54 dB. The audio performance provides a dynamic range greater than 85 dB and bandwidth from 20 Hz to 20 kHz.

11.5 OPTICAL RECORDING SYSTEMS

The high-density capability of optical recording along with the possibility of extremely-low-cost replication of recordings for mass distribution has facilitated several very successful mass-market products. These are based on the Compact Disc, which was originally developed for distribution of prerecorded audio to the home. Now, a successor to the

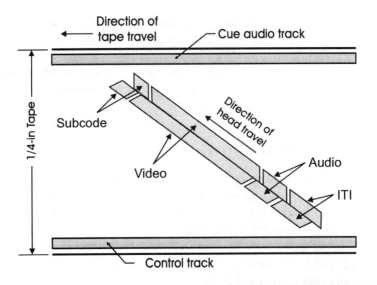

Parameter	Value
Video format	4:1:1 component, compressed
Tape width	1/4 in
Tape thickness, type	0.35 mils, metal-particle
Cassettes	DVC standard (L), DVCPRO (M)
Tape speed	1.33 in/s
Tape usage	0.33 in²/s
Maximum recording time	63 min (M), 123 min (L)
Channels for video	1
Record heads/channel	2
Total heads on scanner drum	6
Number of audio channels	2
Video track width	0.71 mils
Azimuth recording	Yes
Drum diameter	0.855 in
Drum rotation speed	150 rps
Helical channel coding	NRZI
Video writing speed	201 in/s
Video sample rate—Y	13.5 MHz
Video sample rate—chroma	3.375 MHz
Total video data rate (raw)	162 Mb/s
Total video data rate (compressed)	32.4 Mb/s
Area density	97.2 Mb/in²

Figure 11.23 *DVCPRO records and parameters.*

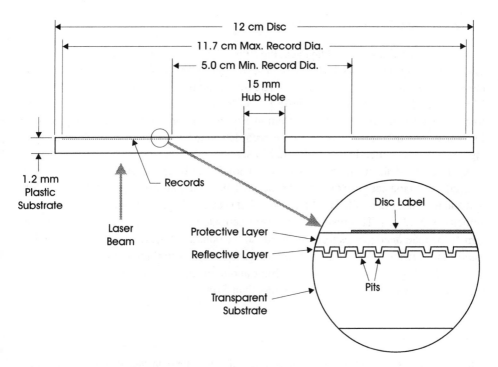

Figure 11.24 Construction details of the Compact Disc.

Compact Disc is becoming available with up to 25 times the data capacity on a single medium. These are discussed in this section.

11.5.1 Compact Disc

The Compact Disc (CD) standards are based on a 12-cm diameter (approximately 4¾ inches) plastic substrate. This design is shown in Figure 11.24. The record pattern is pressed on one side of the plastic substrate and then is covered with a reflective layer and a protective layer that becomes the label side of the disc. Reading is from the other side—through the plastic substrate. As a result, the pits in the original pressing appear as valleys to the reading laser beam. However, the recorded surface is very well protected from physical damage and the surface of the substrate is well out of focus because it is 1.2 mm away from the records. Thus, dirt or scratches on the disc surface will have a minimal effect on playback. The CD system is designed to use a laser light wavelength of 780 nm (10-9 m), and the performance parameters are closely tied to this wavelength.

11.5.1.1 Audio CD

As it is used for digital audio playback, the audio CD has a playing time of up to 74 min. The audio is digitized at 44.1 kHz at 16 bps, straight PCM without any compression, and there are two channels for stereo. This equates to a data rate of 1.41 Mb/s or 172 kB/s so, for 74 min of audio, the data capacity is 750 MB. Encoding for the audio CD uses a 588-bit frame structure that includes Reed-Solomon error protection, interleaving, and provision for synchronization and subcodes. This is recorded on the disc with EFM modulation, giving a resultant channel data rate of 4.32 Mb/s.

In its original form, the audio CD was available only as a replicated disc that was pressed from a master in an expensive process. This is the *CD-digital audio* (CD-DA) format and its standard is called the "Red Book." It uses CLV operation with a constant track velocity of 51.2 in/s. This results in the disc rotational speed varying between 500 to 200 rpm as the read head moves from the inside to the outside of the recorded area of the disc (recordings always begin at the inside.) There is a single spiral track that can be divided into multiple logical "tracks" to hold multiple audio selections. CD audio players are mass-produced and are available at retail for less than $100.

11.5.1.2 CD-ROM

The potential of CD technology for distribution of computer data was obvious, and another standard was developed for that service. Because better error protection (less than 10–13) is required for computer data than for audio, additional overhead was needed so the data capacity is a little less—680 MB, but still prodigious for such a small package. This standard is called the "Yellow Book" and the product is generally referred to as the CD-ROM (CD read-only memory.) The CD-DA's 588-bit block format is modified to provide two modes of operation for the CD-ROM—Mode 1 provides the extended error protection mentioned above, and Mode 2 provides the same error protection and data capacity as the CD-DA. Most computer applications use Mode 1.

Figure 11.25 shows the CD-ROM block structures for Mode 1 and Mode 2. Each CD-ROM block consists of 2,352 bytes, which fits into the data capacity of 98 of the CD-DA blocks (each 588-bit CD-DA block carries six 32-bit stereo audio samples or 24 bytes; 24×98 equals 2,352 bytes.) Thus, the CD-ROM block structure sits on top of the CD-DA blocks, and the error protection of both levels is active. Both modes provide a 12-byte synchronization code plus a 4-byte header, which contains a mode specifier and a 3-byte block address code. Mode 1 devotes 288 bytes of the remaining space to error protection coding, leaving 2,048 bytes of data per block. Since a CD-ROM can store up to 330,000 blocks, Mode 1 has a data capacity of 675,840,000 bytes. Mode 2 eliminates the extra error coding, giving 2,336 bytes per block, or 770,880,000 bytes per disc.

Because it was advantageous to share the drive design with mass-produced home CD-DA players, the CD-ROM standard adopted CLV operation, the same spiral track, and the same track speed as the audio system. CLV is not the most desirable for computers, which

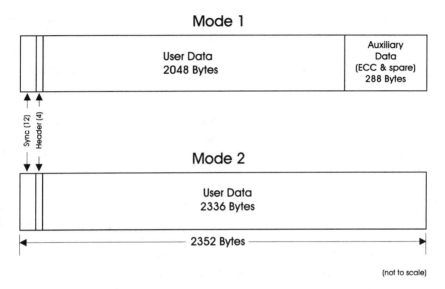

Figure 11.25 *Data block structures of CD-ROM modes 1 and 2.*

demand fast random access to the data, but it is what existed in an instant source of low-cost drives. Because of the use of CLV, CD-ROM access time must take into account the time to set the correct disc speed and tracking servo limitations. CD-ROM access times are 10 to 20 times longer than that of computer hard disks.

The Yellow Book only defines the medium and the format of the tracks on the disc; it does not describe the data content of those tracks. To be useful in computers, a further standard must define a data interface and a file system so data can be random accessed by a computer. The principal standard for CD-ROM file systems is ISO-9660, which provides the usual directory-subdirectory structure for organizing and retrieving files from a storage medium. ISO-9660 is understandable to most PCs that have suitable driver software.

As a market developed for CD-ROM drives, it became practical for manufacturers to make some changes to the drives to obtain better performance. The most important change was to increase the disc rotational speed and, therefore, the data rate and access time. This has generally been done in multiples of the base CD rate (150 kB/s), such as 2× (300 kB/s), 4× (600 kB/s), 6× (900 kB/s), and so on. It is a kind of horsepower race. In spite of these special features, CD-ROM drives are almost as inexpensive as audio players and also retain the feature of being able to play CD-DA discs!

11.5.1.3 Recordable CD

Although the CD-ROM has been extremely successful with computers, it is obvious to any computer user that it would be even more valuable if one could record on it in his or her computer. Recordable CD drives have been available for a number of years but they were too expensive for most PC users. Recently, however, prices have dropped to the $500 range, and the usage of CD recorders is growing rapidly. The system is called CD-R and uses blank discs containing an organic dye layer whose reflectivity is changed when "burned" by a laser light source in the recorder. To provide tracking and focus servo during recording, CD-R blank discs have a track structure in the form of physical grooves pressed into the recording surface. The grooves also have a built-in modulation that is used by the recording servos. A recorded CD-R disc is playable in most CD-ROM drives or CD audio players. Blank CD-R discs cost about $10, which is a very low price for 680 MB of removable storage. CD-R discs are recordable only once, however, so they become a permanent record, but that is very suitable for archiving.

Making a CD-R recording requires a PC with a lot of fast hard drive storage plus the special software to run the CD-R drive. The software allows a user to specify what files to take from the hard drives for the CD, and it can run a prerecord test to determine that a proper recording can be made. This is necessary because the recording process must run continuously once it begins and, if some data cannot be accessed quickly enough when needed, the recording will be ruined.

CD-R recorders typically run at 2× or 4× speeds, so significant time is required for a recording. If multiple copies are required, this time becomes an expense. However, the convenience of CD-R and its modest cost are very practical for one-off or small-quantity replication of all types of CDs.

11.5.1.4 Other Versions of the CD

It is possible to combine CD-DA audio and CD-ROM data on the same disc—this is called a *mixed mode* disc. The first track must always be a CD-ROM track, but other tracks on the disc can be CD-DA format. Such a disc cannot be played in a CD audio player because it will always start at the first track and find data that it cannot understand, but a CD-ROM drive in a computer will be able to read the first track and learn that there is digital audio in addition to computer data on the disc. The mixed mode disc is valuable when a computer application requires high-quality audio to be played while other activities may be absorbing the computer itself. This is because the CD drive plays the audio without involving the computer once it has been started. While audio is playing, the computer can do anything it wants except access the CD that is playing.

Other variations on the CD-ROM include CD-I (CD-Interactive–Green Book), CD-V (CD-Video), and CD-ROM XA (CD-ROM Extended Architecture). These provide enhanced capabilities in the data format to support audio or video along with other forms of computer data. None of them has become as widespread as the general-purpose CD-ROM, and most audio and video CD-ROM applications use the generic format.

11.5.2 DVD

The original CD-ROM data rate of 150 kB/s became a target for video compression developers to produce good-quality video that could be played from a standard CD-ROM. This could be a vehicle for distribution of video as part of computer games or other applications and could potentially replace videotape as the medium for distribution of motion pictures. An early digital video system was the Intel *DVI Technology*, which provided hardware and software that made possible the playback of full-motion, full-screen video on any PC. It became available in 1988 and has been widely used in interactive kiosks and computer-based training applications, but it has never caught on with the general market.

The approach for CD video that has been most successful in the general markets is software-only playback video. This can run on any PC with a fast processor and delivers low-quality video, typically in a window of quarter-screen or smaller size. Systems are Intel's *Indeo*, SuperMac's *Cinepak*, Apple *QuickTime*, and others. These systems run with a 1× CD-ROM, but they would run better with 2× or 4×. They are widely used in CD-ROM games and encyclopedias but are not suited for general distribution of movies because of their short playing time (74 min at 1×; less at higher speeds), and their poor picture quality. Late-model PCs often contain hardware accelerator that speeds up processing of software-only video and allows full-screen operation.

Recognizing that the original CD specifications date back to 1982 and were very conservative even at that time, developers and manufacturers have known for some time that there was an opportunity for a new optical-disc system that could have vastly better performance. Many developments have been done, and the industry has now reached a new standard, called *Digital Video Disc* (DVD) or *Digital Versatile Disc*.

The DVD system uses the same 12-cm diameter substrate, but with shorter wavelength lasers and advanced tracking methods, the density can be increased from 680 MB per surface to 4.7 GB per surface—a 7× increase! However, that is not all, because DVD provides two layers per side of the substrate and both sides can be used. The layers are accessed by refocusing the laser, and the sides are accessed by having two read heads in the drive. This gives 8.5 GB per side with two layers (the density per layer is slightly reduced to allow for potential interference between layers) or a total of 17 GB with both sides of the disc used.

The DVD plan provides specifications for a general-purpose DVD-ROM, a video version for DVD-V, an audio version for DVD-A and DVD-R and DVD-E. Not all these are complete at the time of this writing. DVD video will use MPEG-2 video at data rates in the range of 5 Mb/s, which provides video quality that is better than conventional broadcast television. The audio system is AC-3 5.1 channel audio, the same as specified by the ATSC ATV standard (see Section 9.4.5).

11.6 CONCLUSION

Digital video recording is a dynamic new field that is rapidly developing products that will eventually replace all analog recording products in applications ranging from the home to the highest professional levels. The promise of digital recorders that can perform repeated generations of recording without significant signal degradation has been realized, at least in the products that do not employ video compression. This is important to all recording applications that involve editing.

REFERENCES

1   Mee, C.D., and Daniel, E. D., *Magnetic Recording, Volume I: Technology*, McGraw-Hill, New York, 1987.

2   Watkinson, J., *The Art of Digital Video, 2nd Ed.*, Focal Press, Oxford, U.K., 1994.

Chapter 12

Postproduction Systems

12.1 INTRODUCTION

Motion picture creation inherently involves recording—the movie camera is a recorder and the film is the medium. The concept of separately shooting the scenes of a movie (*production*)* and putting them together after the film is developed (*postproduction*) was a necessity. That concept became highly developed for pictures and sound in the movies long before video (television) came on the scene. But early video could not be used that way because there were no video recorders. Thus, video became known as a live production medium and complete programs were produced and assembled on the fly in real time, as they were being broadcast. It was not until the development of video recording that "film-style" program creation could be performed in video.

The advantages of film-style program creation compared with live production are significant:

- The program can include scenes shot at different locations and different times. Scenes can even be taken from previously created programs.

- The program can be divided into scenes that can be shot at the convenience of the production staff, without regard for timing, effects, or sequence except within one scene. All scenes that involve a particular set or location can be shot in the same session, saving time and expense.

- Scenes can be shot over and over again until everyone is satisfied. In the case of film, the actual result cannot be seen until the film is developed, which is the reason that film productions have their takes developed quickly so the result can be approved

---

* The word "production" is often used to refer to the complete process of creating a program. In this book, the word "creation" is used for that and "production" refers only to the initial acquisition of program material.

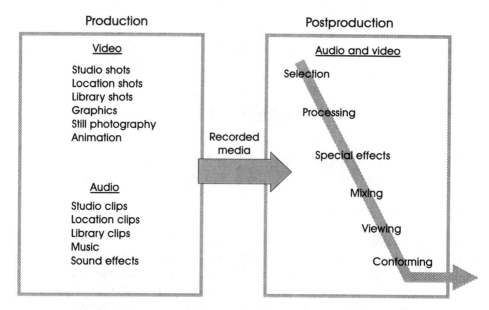

Figure 12.1 *Diagram of the production-postproduction process.*

before the scene is torn down. In video, this is not a problem because the result can be viewed immediately by replaying the recording.

- In postproduction, great care can be taken in the assembly of the scenes to achieve the exact sequence, effects, and timing required by the program. There is no time constraint on this process except that introduced by the cost of running the postproduction facility. If necessary, material can be sent out to specialty houses for special effects or processing. It is not necessary to have every conceivable capability in house.

- Audio and video can be separately handled in production and assembled in postproduction. This allows the production of each to be optimized without concern for the other and avoids tying up expensive video facilities while audio is being edited.

Although programs can still be created live and recorded all at once, the above advantages have such significance to the quality and cost of programs that nearly all program creation today is done this way.

12.2 THE PRODUCTION-POSTPRODUCTION STYLE

The flexibility of program creation afforded by the production-postproduction method can be seen in Figure 12.1. The production side of the figure shows the diversity of materials that can be acquired for use in a program. In postproduction, these materials are precisely selected, processed for quality control, effects added, and assembled or *mixed* into the program sequence. Postproduction is iterative—the assembly may be done in stages, which are then assembled into larger units, and finally all units are assembled into the program.

Audio postproduction usually is carried out separately from video, even when audio and video are shot together. This simplifies the tasks for each and allows dedicated facilities to be built and operated by experts in each medium. Program audio and video come together at the end of postproduction. However, postproduction facilities are designed for audio and video to be *viewed* together at any point so that decisions involving both can be made whenever needed.

12.3 TIME CODES

The coordination of separate audio and video is just one example why precise timing is required in the production-postproduction style of program creation. It is necessary that all materials coming into postproduction have means in them for precisely defining time locations. This is usually done in terms of video frames by adding a *time code* to every frame. Although audio does not inherently have frames like video, it is convenient to mark audio with virtual frames so that its timing can be handled the same as video.

Time codes take the form of sequential numbers given to sequential frames. It is usual to do this in terms of hours:minutes:seconds:frame numbering, so every frame includes a complete time location without reference to any other frame or for the need to count numbers from a base frame. There are several standards for doing this, but the most common one is the SMPTE time code, defined in SMPTE Standard 12M. That is an 80-bit-per-frame code (see Figure 12.2). At 30 frames per second, this is a data rate of 2,400 bps, which can be handled in almost any medium. The 80 bits provides 26 bits for the time value, 6 bit-flags to define the mode of operation, 16 bits for data synchronization, and 32 bits that can be defined by the user.

The time code should be created when the material is shot during production. On tape, it is usually recorded on a separate track from the video or audio—this is called *linear time code* (LTC). However, time code can also be merged into the bit stream of a digital recording medium or included in the VBI of an analog recorder—this is called *vertical interval time code* (VITC). These merged approaches have the disadvantage that it may be difficult to read the time code at the fast or slow play speeds that are often used in editing. Another form of time code is *burned-in* code, where the time code is placed right in the video picture. This can only be done on a copy of the video, of course, but it has the advantage that it can be viewed on recorders that do not have time-code-reading capability.

During production, it is useful to have readouts of time code available so the production people can make notes about shots or other production incidents in terms of the time code. One way to get convenient readouts is to base the time code on local clock time; then, every watch or clock is a time-code readout. Notes made this way will facilitate later searching of the recordings for specific points of interest.

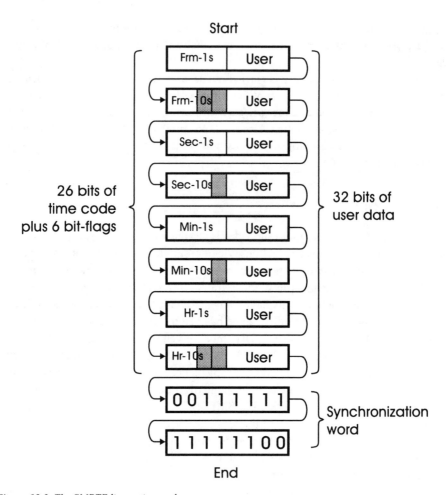

Figure 12.2 *The SMPTE linear time code.*

It is also possible to add time code to a recording that did not have it originally, by playing the material, detecting frames, and adding the time code in the proper places. Of course, when this is done, the time values have no meaning in terms of the production times, but they are still able to support precise editing.

12.4 EDITING

Postproduction is often equated to editing alone, but there is much more to it than that. However, editing is the most important and basic task in postproduction and it deserves discussion.

Editing is the process of joining selected segments from the production recordings into the exact sequence of the final program. The word "joining" might imply only butting the segments together (called *cut* editing) but, most of the time, joining employs *effects*, which are dynamic transitions, such as wipes, dissolves, fades, zooms, pans, rotations, and the like. Editing systems are often judged by the repertoire of effects they support.

Editing requires a recorded medium for both input and output. The medium can be videotape (analog or digital) or it can be computer mass storage (digital). Editing can be separated into a *decision-making* stage and a *conforming* stage. In terms of capabilities, an editing system must allow the editing operator to:

- Review recorded materials for the purpose of selecting exact segments to be used, defined as *edit points*. This is the start of decision-making and requires the ability to search through the recorded material at high speed, stop in the vicinity of the proposed edit point, and step frame-by-frame through that area to select an exact frame for the edit. If time-code numbers were noted in production, the system should be able to quickly seek to any exact time-code number. Editing systems should be able to act on any frame location and display an edit point exactly every time it is called up. The edit point at the start of a segment is called an *in-point*, and the end point is called an *out-point*.

- Record time code numbers for the edit points in an *edit decision list* (EDL). A computer is used for this purpose; it may be a dedicated computer built into an editing controller or workstation, or it may be a general-purpose PC running editing software. SMPTE standard 258M describes a format for EDLs that can be interchanged between editing systems.

- Choose an effect to be used for each edit; include that information in the EDL. Effects often have many parameters, such as durations, sizes, colors, and so forth. These must also be contained in the EDL. Effects also involve processing of more than one signal at a time. For example, a dissolve fades one signal out while fading another signal in. This means that the edit points must provide for the appropriate overlap of both signals during the effect.

Figure 12.3 is an example of an EDL for some simple edits. It is based roughly on the 258M format. Individual edits are identified by their edit number; multisource edits have more than one line in the EDL to define both sources. The mode field is coded A for audio-only, V for video-only, B for both. The effect column defines the type of effect and its parameters; C is for cut, D is for dissolve, W is for wipe (there are many other codes.) The source time code columns specify the start and end time codes in the source reel and the the the sync fields specify the start and end time codes in the target recording. The color bars and the black signals are still pictures, which is indicated by the (0) after their entry time codes. The dissolve in edit 03 has a duration of 5 sec (150 frames), and the wipe in edit 04 is wipe pattern 23 (a rectangle opening from the top of the picture) with a duration of 8 sec (240 frames).

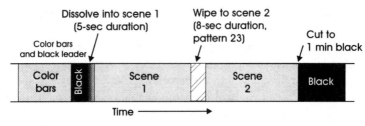

Edit Decision List

Edit No.	I.D.	Mode	Effect	Source Entry	Source Exit	Sync Entry	Sync Exit
01	CBARS	B	C	00:00:00(0)	00:00:00	00:00:00	02:00:00
02	BLACK	V	C	00:00:00(0)	00:00:00	02:00:00	02:15:00
03	BLACK	V	D 150	00:00:00(0)	00:00:00	02:15:00	03:00:00
03	SCENE1	V	D 150	05:13:22	05:58:22	02:15:00	03:00:00
04	SCENE1	V	W23 240	05:58:23	08:28:23	03:00:01	05:30:00
04	SCENE2	V	W23 240	01:30:00	04:00:00	03:00:01	05:30:00
05	BLACK	V	C	00:00:00	01:00:00	05:30:01	06:30:00

Figure 12.3 *Example of an edit decision list.*

Continuing the edit procedure:

- Preview individual or multiple edits made according to the EDL, including effects. The editor will make preliminary choices of edit points and effects and then he or she must view the edit to see if it produces the desired result. Often, this will mean viewing a series of edits with both audio and video to establish the tone of the entire scene. This should be able to be done quickly and precisely repeated as many times as needed. The edit decision-making process is very intense and stressful and should be conducted in its own room, away from external disturbances or interruptions. Usually the production staff will participate fully in editing along with the edit operator. Thus, viewing capabilities must provide for a number of viewers, and editing rooms often have an area dedicated specifically to viewing, but still in close personal communication with the edit operator.

- Make changes to the EDL and repeat preview until everyone is satisfied. The computer managing the EDL must have capabilities to make any types of changes precisely and quickly. It must also be able to save previous versions so changes can be undone, if necessary. When the EDL is complete, the decision-making stage is ended.

- Produce a final continuous recording containing an exact reproduction of the audio and video edits called for by the EDL. This process, often called *conforming*, can theoretically be done in a completely automatic mode once the EDL is in hand. It may be done by the same equipment used for decision-making, or it may be done on separate equipment that receives the finished EDL and automatically cranks out the final recording. The output of conforming is an *edited master* recording.

Depending on the degree of flexibility and the picture and sound quality required, editing rooms (called *editing suites*) can cost anywhere from a few thousand dollars to a million dollars. Because the decision-making process is the most time-consuming part of editing, many postproduction operations have simplified facilities available for use in preliminary decision-making by production people to use before they go into a full-scale editing room. Another approach is to copy the production material to a home recorder format that can be used for decision making. In that case, burned-in time code is used on the copies. These tape copies can be used with a low-cost home VCR to develop preliminary edit points or even a complete EDL. Using a copy of the original tapes to develop an EDL is called *offline* editing.

12.4.1 Videotape Editing

Electronic editing was developed first as a videotape feature and all the capabilities listed above are available in videotape editing. They are also available with most audio tape systems. However, there are important limitations in speed and accuracy caused by the need to search through tape for the edit points and the need to mechanically position the tape for editing. The latter limitation can be overcome at a price, but the speed limitation is fundamental and a lot of time is wasted in videotape editing waiting for tape to be searched or rewound. Because of the mechanical considerations, tape systems normally require a *preroll* period of a few seconds before every preview. This is needed to get the tape decks into synchronism so that the frame numbers are exact. Note that the mechanical limitations of videotape editing are the same whether the system is analog or digital. Because of the need to shuttle through a one-dimensional tape to find any location, videotape editing is called *linear* editing.

12.4.1.1 Videotape Editing Modes

There are two modes of videotape editing: *assemble* and *insert* (see Figure 12.4). In assemble editing, new recordings are placed at the end of previous recordings—a tape is built up by recording its scenes in their final sequence. To have a smooth edit without any disturbance on playback, the new recording must be properly synchronized with the previous one at the in-point. This is done by prerolling ahead of the in-point and playing the previous recording up to the edit point to achieve synchronization and then switching to record operation without disturbing the recorder timings. Once recording has started, the recorder

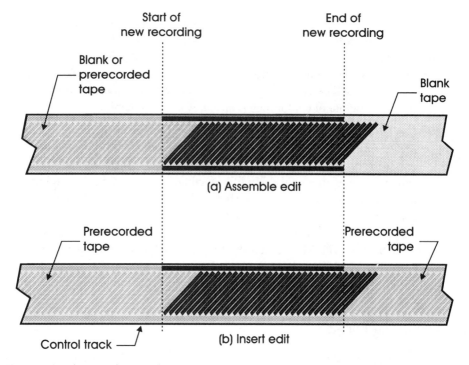

Figure 12.4 *Videotape editing modes.*

can continue with its own timing, since it is overwriting whatever was on the tape (there may be nothing there). A complete recording is made, including the control track and time-code track. As the name suggests, assemble editing is suitable for assembling a new tape, but cannot be used for changing an already-recorded tape. That is because assemble editing makes no attempt to synchronize with what is already on the tape at the out-point and a disturbance may occur there. Assemble editing is often used in shooting scenes for postproduction.

Insert editing requires that the entire tape to be edited have a continuous recording already in place. This is often done by recording black picture with silent audio on the entire tape. Having that, it is possible to make insert recordings at any place on the tape and in any sequence. The tape recorder synchronizes during an insert by using the control track of the tape, which is not rerecorded. At the end of the segment, video and/or recording is simply switched off, leaving the rest of the tape intact. Edited tapes are often assembled using insert, rather than assemble, editing because it allows edits to be repeated to make corrections. This method is the best way for live assembly of a sequence, if no postproduction is planned.

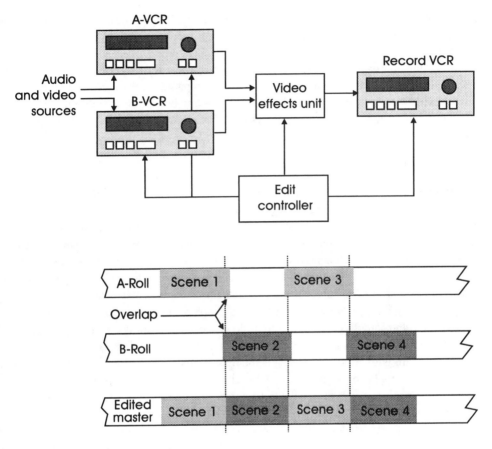

Figure 12.5 *A-B roll videotape editing.*

Note that insert and assemble editing are capable only of cut edits. No effects are possible. (Some consumer camcorders attempt dissolves or wipe transitions in assemble mode, but the quality achievable is not sufficient for professional use.)

12.4.1.2 A-B Roll Videotape Editing

When effects are planned in videotape editing, the A-B roll editing process is required. In this technique, shown in Figure 12.5, two tape players are used as the input to an effects unit. The output of the effects unit is viewed for previewing or it is recorded to make an edited master tape. The concept of A-B roll is to make two intermediate videotapes that contain the segments to be used in their proper time positions but alternately on the A or B tapes. If effects require overlap of the A and B signals, they are arranged that way on the A and B tapes. To preview, both tape recorders are started in synchronism and the effects controller is programmed from the EDL to make the transitions as desired. The output of the effects unit is viewed. Of course, this takes two tape recorders, and if more than two signals are to be combined in an effect, another recorder is required for each additional signal. However, the approach is very flexible, and this is the best way to do videotape editing. The disadvantage is that the A and B rolls have to be prepared ahead of time and need to be reedited whenever a change of timing is made. The A and B rolls are an additional generation of recording and, at least in analog systems, that causes some signal degradation.

12.4.2 Nonlinear Editing

An attractive possibility for editing is to place all the production material onto computer hard disks and perform editing by using the random-access capability of the hard disks to access the material for preview or conforming. With the hard disk's random access that can seek to specific frames and retrieve them essentially instantaneously, there is no need for A-B roll nor any waiting for tapes to rewind. Because of the random access, the editing system does not have to run tape linearly, so it is called a *nonlinear* editor. Until very recently, video editing was possible only with large computer systems and, at equivalent quality levels, it was considerably more expensive than videotape editing. Now, however, as the cost of computers and hard disk storage has come down, computer editing is a practical alternative to videotape and is rapidly being adopted at all levels of sophistication.

The problem with computer editing is the massive data requirements of digital audio and video, but small computers are rapidly reaching a capability that can deal with this. Of course, video compression makes the task even easier, and many nonlinear systems employ it. However, many professionals still are not happy about using *any* compression, so the highest performance computer editors generally avoid compression.

In theory, the computer can also do the digital signal processing needed for video effects, but real-time video processing is still out of reach for present computer speeds, so hardware effects units are generally used with computer editors. This is packaged as one or more add-in expansion boards to go into the computer. A block diagram for a typical nonlinear editing system is shown in Figure 12.6.

The architecture is a conventional PC bus structure, which supports control and display for the editing system. A central mass storage unit holds programs, EDLs, and A/V archives. However, the video processing is in hardware, with a compression unit, an effects unit, and a mixing unit. These are interconnected by a dedicated high-speed bus that is separate from the PC bus. This bus is capable of multiple simultaneous interconnections at the video data rate and provides mass storage and I/O for video and audio, which is the storage actually used during editing. In a low-end system, all the special hardware and the A/V bus would be built onto an add-in card, whereas in a more powerful system, it would be packaged on several add-in cards. In the latter case, the A/V bus connection would be made "over-the-top," with connections on the opposite edge of the boards from the PC bus connectors.

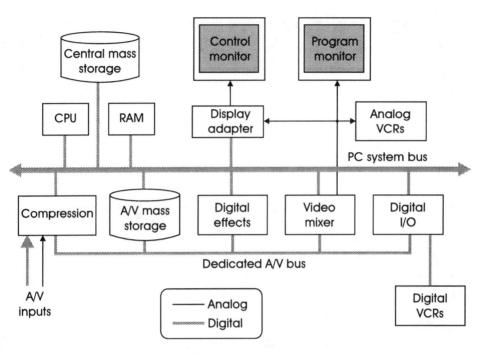

Figure 12.6 *Block diagram of a PC-based nonlinear editing system.*

Both analog and digital inputs are accommodated, with analog inputs being compressed according to the system's compression standard. The compressed input signals would then be stored on the A/V hard drives. This would take place before any editing was begun. Many systems use Motion-JPEG compression or varieties of MPEG compression that only use intraframe compression. In editing, the use of motion compensation would interfere with the ability to edit at every frame number, so interframe compression cannot be used.

When playing video, data are directed through the effects unit and/or the video mixer under software control. The video mixer contains a decompression unit with digital and analog outputs that support display or recording of the output signal. The figure shows two monitors—a "control" monitor and a "program" monitor. Usually, the control monitor shows several windows of video along with a representation of the EDL as a timeline or a table. Buttons on the control display respond to user touch or mouse actions for control of the process. It is possible to do all the editing using only the control monitor and viewing the video in the small windows of this display, but many editors wish to see full-screen video, which the program monitor provides.

Figure 12.7 shows a typical control monitor display. It should be realized that the configuration of this display is determined in software and could be anything. However, this example shows the basic requirements. The operation sequence for video is as follows:

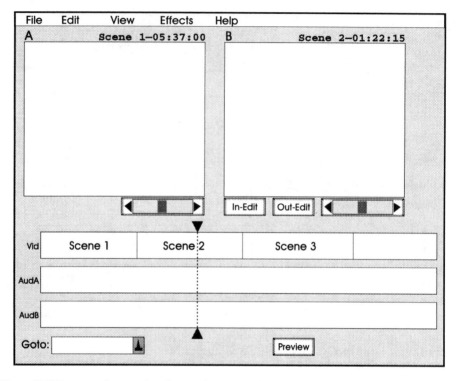

Figure 12.7 Drawing of a typical nonlinear editing control screen.

Edit decision-making begins by selecting a shot from the shot list. This would probably be done by a selection from the menu bar. The first frame of that shot is shown in video window B, with its time-code number below. If the operator has made time-code notes during shooting, the number of the proposed first frame can be typed into the Goto window, and the system instantaneously displays that frame. At any time, the operator can use the shuttle and jog controls to change the frame that is displayed. Once the proper frame is viewed, its time code is saved in the EDL by pressing the In-Edit button. The operator can then either shuttle and jog to the out-point or type its frame number into the Goto window. The same procedure is used to fine tune the out-point and that value is saved by using the Out-Edit button. A bar appears on the timeline display to indicate the duration of the first shot.

The operator then selects the video for the next shot to be used. At this point, the A-window displays the last frame of the first shot. The operator then repeats the procedure above to select the in- and out-points of the second shot and save them in the EDL. When this is complete, another bar appears in the timeline to represent the second shot. If there is room on the display, the names of the shots are displayed in the bars.

The preceding actions have set up the first two shots for a cut edit between them. This can be previewed by pressing the Preview button. The first shot instantaneously begins playing in the B-window and cuts to the second shot at the exact frame number that had been specified. If a program monitor is connected to the system, it also displays the preview. An alternative to a separate program monitor is to have an option for the control monitor to switch to full-screen video during a preview.

A cursor appears on the timeline display to indicate the point that is currently being displayed in the B-window. The operator can move this cursor with the mouse; the B-window instantaneously follows along. If the operator moves the cursor to the cut point between the two shots, a transition effect can be selected. This is done by calling up a separate transitions menu, choosing a transition, and specifying its parameters in yet another menu. That transition is then attached to that cut point, and the system automatically calculates and revises the EDL's in- and out-points to provide any necessary overlap of the signals.

Preview is now run to view the transition; again, the viewing is available instantaneously with no waiting. If the transition or its timing needs some fine-tuning, the previous steps are performed again to make adjustments.

Editing is continued by repeating the above steps for the other shots in the program and previewing as much of the program as needed to adjust each effect. When this is complete, the entire program can be previewed and displayed to other people who may have to approve the result. At any time, the editor can go in and adjust any timing or parameter until the complete program is approved.

The previous description was for video only. If audio is being edited at the same time, it will have its own timelines on the display, and the editing procedure is the same as described for video. On preview, both audio and video are played.

Note that adding audio editing to this scenario adds significant complexity because the audio is generally not cut at the same time as the corresponding video. If speech is involved, audio cuts must be at pauses; whereas video cuts are at the point where the visual change looks the best.

Nonlinear editors are available both as complete packaged systems or as boards and software to be put into a standard PC. Although the latter approach may be less expensive, the requirements of nonlinear editing make severe demands on a standard PC and, for most users who do not have a lot of technical expertise available, it probably makes sense to pay for a packaged system and get total responsibility from a single vendor.

12.5 VIDEO EFFECTS

The basic processes of video effects were described in Chapter 8. Effects can be classified in terms of the way they affect the signals involved. Many effects are performed on a single signal as, for example, zooming or panning. However, effects are also used for transition between two signals, such as dissolving or wiping, and, finally, effects can be used to simultaneously combine two or more signals on the screen, such as showing head shots of speakers from different locations in separate screen windows to conduct a teleconference. Thus, effects processors may process one, two, or more signals to a single output.

A further classification is based on whether the effect is static or dynamic. Static effects transform the picture in a stationary way that does not change with time; an example is a fixed rotation of the picture. Dynamic effects change their processing with time; transition effects are inherently dynamic—the effect must change with time to get from one picture to the other. However, a dynamic transition, such as a dissolve, may stop in the middle of its process and become stationary; for example, this might be done to combine shots of the same performer taken from different angles. The dynamic dissolve gives a smooth transition into the static effect and can be used again to get out of the effect. Figure 12.8 shows a number of effects classified this way.

The most convenient way to handle multisignal (more than two) effects is to have an effects processor that has enough inputs for all the signals at the same time. However, multisignal effects can also be built up using only a two-input processor by performing the effect on two signals, recording the result, and then passing the recorded effect through the effects unit again to add a third signal, and so forth. This method has a lot of capability but is inflexible in that making changes may require repeating the entire buildup process.

12.6 GRAPHICS

An important capability in postproduction is the insertion of titles or text overlays, which are examples of *graphics*. Anything that can be drawn with a computer graphics program can be overlaid, keyed, or dissolved into a video signal. If this insertion is done through an effects unit, the possibilities are endless. In the early days, graphics units were called "character generators" because text was all that they did, but today they are called "paint boxes" or simply "graphics" processors, and they are capable of all kinds of graphics effects, including text, drawings, cursors, maps, and animation. One of the best examples of graphics capability is seen on the weather segments of most major-market TV stations—a special animation processor receives current input from weather satellites and displays it in a three-dimensional animation that can be viewed from any angle, distance, or elevation. This is often combined with graphics drawn locally and chroma-keyed behind a live picture of the weathercaster who is presenting the report.

A graphics processor can be treated as another signal source in a postproduction system, in which case, its output should be a standard digital video signal that is passed through an effects processor to combine it with other signals. An alternative approach is that a graphics processor contains its own keying unit and other signals pass through the graphics unit to have graphics added. This latter approach is less expensive because it does not require an extra effects channel for graphics insertion but is also less flexible. It also means that the controls for setting up graphics insertion are different from the other effects controls in the system, which complicates the system control.

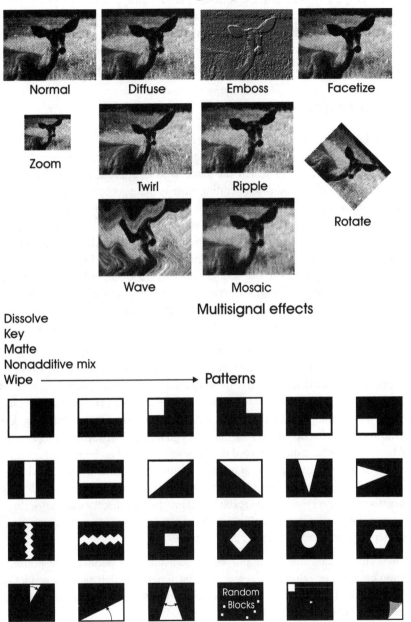

Figure 12.8 Video effects.

Because graphics often require time-consuming preparation, graphics processors should have separate workstations where material can be prepared by skilled operators or even artists and the results stored for easy callup when required during postproduction or programming. In the editing suite, convenient controls are provided for selecting and displaying preprogrammed graphics materials created at the workstation.

12.7 AUDIO POSTPRODUCTION

As explained in Section 12.1, audio is usually processed separately from video in postproduction. As shown in Figure 12.7, audio can be edited in a video nonlinear editor by handling it as separate tracks to which the same editing approach is used as the video. However, operation in an audio-only editing suite is done somewhat differently.

Audio is often captured for a program in a number of separately recorded tracks that must be combined (mixed) to create the final audio tracks. This style of audio editing calls for collecting or building a number of program-length tracks, which are combined in a final mix operation to produce the program audio tracks. This is shown in Figure 12.9. The editing system stores everything on hard disk just as with video but, rather than cutting scenes together to produce the final program, separate element tracks are built, which are assembled in the final mix. Typical audio elements are dialog, ambiance, sound effects, and music. The production and postproduction of the elements are described below:

- Dialog is the sound of the actor's voices. It is almost always captured during production at the same time as the video, but usually on separate audio tape. However, this original dialog is often not used in the final audio because the conditions for capturing audio are not optimal on the set or location where the video is shot and the voices may have a lot of other interfering sounds with them. A replacement dialog track will be made in postproduction by having the actors go into an *automatic dialog replacement* (ADR) studio where they rerecord their lines under ideal audio recording conditions. This is done by providing the actor with his or her original track played into headphones while the actor repeats the words exactly into the studio microphone. It is not as difficult as it seems, and the result is a clean dialog track for each actor that can be processed and used in the final mix with the ability to adjust level, reverb, and stereo pan separately for each voice in the program.

- Audio signals can often be improved by adjustment of frequency response, levels, stereo balance, or other parameters. Special functions such as noise reduction may also be needed. All these processes are called *sweetening* in the audio postproduction field. Their use is quite an art.

- Ambiance is the background sound for the scene, such as forest sounds, crowd noise, and the like. This also may be recorded during video shooting, but is often recorded separately and maybe not even at the same location. Having the ambiance on a

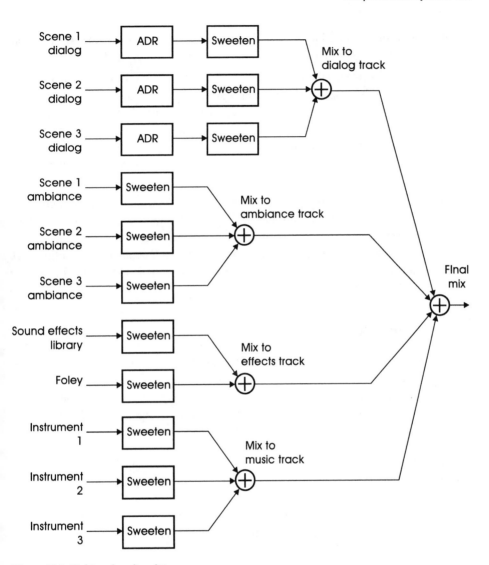

Figure 12.9 *Multitrack audio editing.*

separate track at the final mix allows the amount of ambient sound to be adjusted dynamically and appropriately spread out in the stereo field.

- Sound effects are the unique sounds that accompany action or activity. They include such things as footsteps, doors opening and closing, breaking glass, thunder, and so on. The sound effect track is built from sound effect libraries or by recording sounds that match the video action in a special venue known as a *Foley studio*. Here, there are various devices that a skilled operator uses to record appropriate sounds as he or she watches a copy of the edited video being played on a screen. Again, the effects levels, reverb, and stereo pan are adjusted in the final mix.

- Music can be produced live or computer-generated. In live-music production, it is often desirable to have separate microphones and record a separate track for each instrument so the level and stereo pan of each instrument can be fine-tuned in postproduction. Thus, there need be no concern for level balancing during the production. Because a multiinstrument music track can have many individual instrument tracks in it, the music is often mixed by itself to produce a single set of music-element tracks to go into the final mix.

The final mix involves playing all the element tracks and adjusting their contributions to each of the output tracks (stereo, surround sound, etc.). The mix may vary during the program and the system should be capable of controlling it dynamically from computer. Thus, the mix can be run repeatedly until exactly the desired result is obtained. The final mix room is usually also capable of displaying the video track along with the audio for viewing of the complete program.

12.8 POSTPRODUCTION SYSTEMS

Facilities for the various steps and processes of postproduction described above must be included in a complete postproduction setup. At the very low end, a single PC-based facility containing audio and video peripherals can be used to do all the tasks in sequence using a collection of specialty software for each part of the process. Some nonlinear editing systems provide all this in one hardware-software package. Hardware for such a system was described in Section 4.5.8.

At the other end of the scale in a large postproduction house, separate facilities are provided for each step of the process and all jobs pass through the types of facilities that they need. Central operations provide video and audio storage (servers), time codes, synchronization, and signal routing. In this kind of operation, the emphasis is on providing high capability in each area and managing the operation for maximum use of all areas as multiple projects are completed.

12.9 CONCLUSION

Production-postproduction is the preferred style of electronic program creation. The advent of digital video and audio has brought this approach to maturity and has made it possible at all levels of system sophistication from the single user-producer to the largest postproduction operations.

Chapter 13

Digital Multimedia

13.1 INTRODUCTION

The dictionary defines the word "medium" as

> an intervening thing through which a force acts or an effect is produced; any means, agency, or instrumentality; specif., a means of communication.[*]

Communication is so pervasive in modern life that we often do not think of the medium behind it, whether it is a book (print medium), television (video and audio medium), telephone (audio medium), or even face-to-face interaction (conversation medium). Often, several of these media are used at once. Applying the prefix "multi" to the word "media" is redundant since that word is already plural. In spite of that, the word "multimedia" is widely used. Unfortunately for good understanding, it is *over*used and overhyped. Therefore, it is necessary to carefully define it for this chapter.

Multimedia is

> the use of multiple formats of electronic presentation with user interaction for the purpose of conveying information, educating, or entertaining.

The two key phrases are "user interaction" and "formats of electronic presentation," both must exist for true multimedia. User interaction, called *interactivity,* is explored in the next section but the means of electronic presentation is discussed here. An example of multimedia is an electronic encyclopedia distributed on a CD-ROM. In addition to the usual text of an encyclopedia, it has images, drawings, audio, and video presentation.

Presentation is the display of information in a form that a viewer can understand; it implies a *means* of presentation and a *format* of presentation. The physical device or system whereby the information is presented is the means—such things as the telephone, a book, a

---

[*]   Webster's New World Dictionary, 1988.

Table 13.1

Means versus Format

Means	Format
Telephone	Speech (audio)
Book	Text, graphics, images
Television	Video and audio
Computer display	Text, graphics, images, video
Loudspeaker	Audio

computer display, or a loudspeaker. The format of presentation is the way the information is structured so that it can be understood. (See Table 13.1).

Thus, the "media" in multimedia are really presentation formats; the ones of interest are text, audio, video, graphics, images, and animation, which are discussed in Section 13.4. Multimedia makes use of these formats as necessary to convey information, teach, or entertain.

13.2 INTERACTIVITY

In television, the only control a viewer has over what is seen and heard is the changing of channels. The program content is whatever is being broadcast at the moment and requires only one-way communication—from the TV station to the viewer. Driving an automobile is a different situation. The driver commands the automobile via the steering wheel, pedals, and other controls and the automobile responds with its motion—it is an *interactive* environment. In this case, there must be two-way communication between the user and the machine: one way for the user to send his or her commands and the other way for the machine to respond.

An interactive environment is a feedback loop as shown in Figure 13.1, which diagrams the interactivity of a PC. The loop always contains three ingredients: two-way communication between machine and user, a user interface, and computing capability.

13.2.1 Two-Way Communication

User control during interactive presentation requires two-way communication: one channel to present the information to the user and a second channel to transmit the user's commands or choices back to the source of the information. Ordinarily, in interactive electronic systems, the second channel is low-bandwidth because the commands are generally simple and do not need to be sent very often. For example, a form of interactive television can be achieved by using a telephone for the control channel. The wide-bandwidth television channel sends the video and audio material, which is presented to the user by a

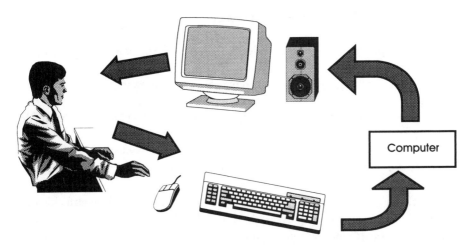

Figure 13.1 *The feedback loop of interactivity. From Inglis, A. F., and Luther, A. C.,* Video Engineering, *Second Edition,* McGraw-Hill, New York, 1996, reproduced with permission of The McGraw-Hill Companies.

video display and speakers, and the telephone line sends the user's commands back to the source so he or she can control what is being sent.

13.2.2 User Interfaces

All interactive devices, whether a kitchen spigot, an automobile, or a PC, must have a *user interface*. This is the means whereby the user commands the device or system and it must be carefully defined so that all users will know how to operate the system. The user interface of a spigot is so simple (two handles or a lever) that it is almost obvious how to use it but the interface of an automobile, while still rather simple, requires considerable skill and is usually learned through a training program of some sort. Since driving an automobile is a very important task and can be dangerous if it is done improperly, the operation of the user interface (steering wheel and pedals) is standardized and is the same in all cars.

Another standardized consumer product is the telephone; the telephone dial is known to everyone and is generally learned as a young child. However, on the so-called "feature" phones that have additional controls for such things as dialing memories, call holding, call answering, and so forth, the interface to the enhanced features is not standardized. Further, the features are less frequently used compared with the dial and consumers find that it is difficult to remember how to operate them when needed.

The user interfaces of consumer electronic products such as television receivers or VCRs are not well standardized and quickly become confusing to the consumer. Most consumers learn little more than how to change channels and adjust the volume. To exercise all the features of these products requires more learning and consumers often will not make the effort, so the features go unused. An important consideration in user interface design is achieving an appropriate match between the learning effort required, the importance of the feature, and its frequency of use. If these things are not in balance, the user will not take the trouble to learn the interface and the product falls into disuse or, worse yet, it is used incorrectly.

The complex editing systems described in Chapter 12 are examples of systems where the user interface is extremely complex to the point that a major training process is needed to learn them. This requires the concept of the *skilled operator*, a person who has made the effort to learn the system with the intention of making a career out of it. Few systems justify that, but editing is one case that does. It is now technically possible to bring editing capabilities to the casual user but the very significant learning curve of editing must be overcome before it will be a success.

An electronic system's user interface communicates with its user through a video monitor, other kinds of electronic displays, and sounds. The user returns his or her commands by means of a keyboard, mouse, touch screen, or a special control panel. The displays or sound must indicate when user interaction is possible or required. The user must know how to interpret these indications and also what he or she must do in response to them. This is where learning and standardization come in. Several devices are employed to help the user know what to do.

The most important of these is the *metaphor*—the system makes itself look or sound like something that is already familiar to the user. For example, a system that plays prerecorded linear programming can have the same kind of controls used on an audio tape deck or a VCR. The controls Play, Stop, Fast Forward, and Rewind are generally understood and can be modeled on a video screen as a group of four buttons with the usual arrow symbols or words on them. Another metaphor that is well understood is the book—an electronic encyclopedia can have a table of contents, an index, chapters, pages, and so forth. Most users will know what to do when they see these familiar objects.

The PC industry has developed its own set of metaphorical objects that are based on using the video screen with a cursor and a mouse or other pointing device that moves the cursor on the screen. These objects include radio buttons, check boxes, scroll bars, and selection lists. Schoolchildren are now exposed to these devices and their use—a new generation is growing up that is just as comfortable with mouse and keyboard as older generations are with books and pencils. Unfortunately, the PC metaphors do not go far enough—the devices are relatively standard but how they are used and what they mean are not very well standardized. Those problems can be solved by the use of text prompts and help screens but this is beginning to look like learning and the less sophisticated users will become leery if it appears too complex.

Schoolchildren learn that computers usually do not break when you mess with them, so they simply begin "mousing around" and try all the controls on the screen to see what they do. Designers should expect that and make sure that it is true their system will not break when this random behavior occurs. Better yet, they should help the user to learn when he or she clicks all around the screen. An example of that is used in some systems where, if you hold the cursor stationary over a control, a little prompt box appears next to the control to tell you what that control does. A similar feature is called *contextual help*—if a user press a special key (usually F1), a help window pops up and tells the user about the object that the cursor is on or it tells the user how to complete the most recent actions he or she has been doing. All of these devices become possible with a programmable computing device in the system and the best user interfaces employ the computer's power to help the user.

13.2.3 Computing Capability

PCs are clearly computing devices, but computers can also be *embedded* in devices or systems that are not considered to be computers. When this is considered, computers are everywhere. They are in automobiles (usually several of them), microwave ovens, VCRs, washers and dryers, telephone answering machines, and the like. In fact, if any significant amount of logical processing is required for the operation of a device, the best design solution today is probably an embedded computer. That is because such devices can be had as inexpensive single chips. Further, their programmability gives a tremendous amount of design flexibility. Many more complex processes can be performed than would be practical with dedicated logic. With an embedded computer, a more complex process simply means that program memory gets a little larger and processing time is extended a little. The impact on system cost is minimal. When the design is finished, the program is usually stored permanently in ROM on the computer chip and the resulting system is very robust and reliable.

When the interactive system can justify a full-scale PC, even more advantages accrue. All of the features of PC operating systems are available for support of mass storage, graphical user interfaces, communication, and data processing. Inexpensive PC parts can be used to build the system, standard software is available, software tools are available for designing custom software, and system expansion can utilize standard PC approaches. Of course, this all comes at a price—standard PCs begin in the hundreds of dollars whereas an embedded single-chip computer costs as little as a few dollars. You get what you pay for.

13.3 USES OF MULTIMEDIA

When someone goes to a library these days, he or she finds that there is a lot more than books and papers there—audio- and videotapes and various objects of art share space with the traditional printed and written matter. However, one has to search for the different types of information in different places because one needs different viewing equipment and viewing methods. A digital multimedia system takes care of that because all information is viewed on the same screen or heard from the same speakers and all information types can be searched in a single index. The library contents are fully integrated into a single environment.

Thus, one obvious use of digital multimedia is to perform a library function, and there are many products such as encyclopedias that fully use these capabilities to offer their

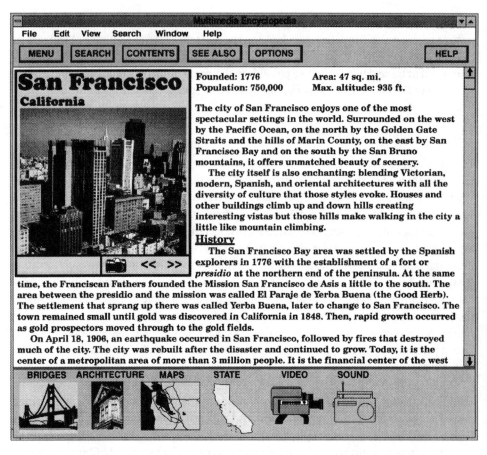

Figure 13.2 *A hypothetical screen from an interactive encyclopedia. From Inglis, A. F., and Luther, A. C.,* Video Engineering, Second Edition, *McGraw-Hill, New York, 1996, reproduced with permission of The McGraw-Hill Companies.*

information more richly. A hypothetical encyclopedia screen is shown in Figure 13.2. The basic story is told in text, but additional windows provide for a selection of images, sounds, or videos. Further controls allow quickly moving to related subjects or maps. At the top of the screen there is a menu bar for accessing other parts of the application and a row of buttons provides access to the index and searching tools.

The scope of multimedia is limited by the capacity of the storage medium—a CD-ROM fills up very quickly with multimedia library information. The DVD increases the possibilities for such products, but developers quickly learn how to fill them, too.

An interactive library is an exciting teaching medium, and there are many applications of multimedia in education and training. The dream of computer-based training (CBT) can well be fulfilled with a multimedia system.

The field of entertainment cannot be overlooked either; video games, humor, and interactive movies are other possibilities. All of these applications and more are being explored, developed, and marketed in the present explosion of CD-ROM products for PCs.

13.4 THE MEDIA OF MULTIMEDIA

The media types are familiar and there is little need to describe them further here. Instead, this section describes how the media types are used in interactive applications.

13.4.1 Text

Few multimedia applications can survive without text. About the only way would be to replace all text with audio, which is good in some situations but cannot support all uses for text. Audio also requires hundreds of times more data than text for the same message and that can quickly add up. Text has another advantage, which is that it is completely searchable, quickly and effectively. In fact, the best way to search other media types such as audio or video is to create text-based indices for them that include descriptions, key words, and locations for all the important points. Then, the tools for text searching can be used to search the other data types. Because of its information efficiency and searchability, nearly all large databases are mostly text, and it is not something to be avoided.

13.4.2 Audio

Audio is text converted to speech and much more. Music and sound effects are other important uses for audio and for which there is no substitute. It is not practical to search audio for its content so, if the content is available as text, that should be retained to support searching. For that reason, some applications use a speech synthesizer to create audio from text—the text is searchable and, once an item of interest is found, the speech synthesizer can read it to the user. Speech synthesizers work, but they have an unnatural sound that cannot convey all the expression of a good speaking voice, so there is a limit to their use.

Music can also be synthesized, and most PCs have a music synthesizer chip in their sound hardware. That technology has been highly developed by the musical instrument industry, and this work is spilling over into computers.

Audio has the advantage that the user does not have to be looking at the screen to get the message. Audio prompts can be received while the entire screen is being used for another purpose. Of course, with motion video, audio is essential for realism or to contribute to the feeling of a rich environment created by the presentation. Another use for audio is to present material that only exists as audio, such as a musical program.

13.4.3 Video

The success of television around the world demonstrates the potential of motion video to entertain, disseminate information, or to educate. That power comes at a price in a digital system in the form of prodigious data rates. Data compression can reduce the rates by 100:1 or more, but even then, video requires megabytes per minute of play. Since few systems have unlimited storage or transmission rates, video is used only where its presentation power is essential to the application.

Because of compression, there is a standards problem with video—the target system must have the hardware and software to run the compression algorithm used by the video. The software can be handled by supplying it along with the video, but the hardware must exist in the target system. Applications that use video must specify the hardware that they require. Fortunately, PCs are coming out with ever-more-powerful hardware, and eventually will reach the point where most hardware is fast enough to run any of the algorithms in software. Then, video is just a software problem.

13.4.4 Images

An image is a video still picture. However, images do not have to be refreshed many times per second as are video frames, so they can be handled differently. More time can be taken in loading and decompressing images since only one frame at a time is being handled. Thus, one can display higher quality images than would be practical with video. At the same time, spending a little more time per image means that lower data rates can be used than with video. Because of these considerations, if still images can tell the story effectively, they are a better choice than video.

13.4.5 Graphics

Graphics are to images as synthesized speech is to digitized speech—they are computer-generated. There are the same advantages and disadvantages—graphics usually take less data but they may not be as realistic. The latter is also an advantage because a graphics picture exists as a set of computer commands that are rendered at the time the picture is displayed. Thus, a graphics picture can be shown in different magnification or from different points of view. This offers greater flexibility. Very realistic graphics pictures are possible, as evidenced by some of the computer animation now being used in motion pictures. However, such realism requires massive amounts of computer power and long rendering times, which is not practical for many applications.

Another advantage that comes from graphics is they can be very precise, showing exact dimensions and relationships. Of course, a photograph is also precise in its own way, but that is only from the viewpoint of the taking camera. Once the shutter has clicked, no other view is available.

13.4.6 Animation

Continuing on the comparison of the last section, animation is computer-generated video. In animation, graphic objects are given specifications for how they move from frame to frame and the computer generates a motion video sequence of frames. This can be very effective and saves data just like graphics does; it also has the disadvantage of not necessarily being realistic. Animation also has the same disadvantage as motion video in that there are many animation algorithms and all systems may not support every one. However, most animation does not depend on special hardware beyond a graphics accelerator, so the problem can be handled by supplying appropriate software to run the animation on a "standard" system.

Animation is difficult to create. Although there are powerful programs available for animation creation, it is a complex task and the programs have significant learning curves. Also, as with movie animation, there is a substantial degree of art required by the process. Almost anyone can learn how to use a video camera and shoot passable video, but a lot of both learned and innate skill is needed to do animation. This is its biggest problem and makes good animation expensive.

13.5 THE WORLD WIDE WEB

The worldwide Internet (see Section 7.5.2) has been available for many years but it was in a form that required special equipment, software, and a text-based interface that took lots of computer skill to access. In spite of that, there are millions of Internet users in academia, industry, and governments around the world. Now, the potential user community is greatly expanding with the development of the *World Wide Web* (the Web), which is a protocol that can bring the Internet to anyone who has a PC or one of the so-called Internet computers (see Section 13.6.5).

13.5.1 Client-Server Architecture

The Internet consists of interconnected networks all over the world. Individual computers that offer information to the Internet are called *servers*, and computers that receive information from the servers are called *clients*. Special software is required to run a server and a full-time connection to the Internet is also necessary if the information on the server is to be available at all times. Client computers also run special software called a *browser* (see Section 13.5.5). They receive information by "logging-on" to a server.

13.5.2 URLs

Three key concepts are at the heart of the Web: the *Universal Resource Locator* (URL) addressing scheme, *hypertext*, and the *hypertext markup language* (HTML). With a URL, a

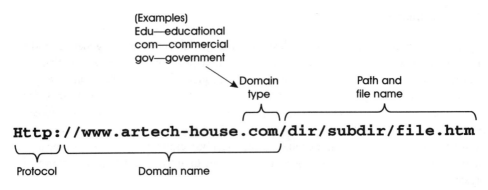

Figure 13.3 *The Web's URL addressing scheme.*

specific item on a server anywhere in the world can be addressed with a simple, easy-to-remember and -understand text string (see Figure 13.3). The Internet IP internally uses a numerical addressing system, but special servers called *nameservers* on the Internet perform the conversion from the URL to the IP address. By supplying a URL to a nameserver, one can quickly connect to any server on the Internet. The protocol on the Internet for this type of operation is http, which is an abbreviation for *hypertext transfer protocol.*

13.5.3 Hypertext

The second key to the Web is a system for embedding URLs anywhere in a document in a way that special software on a client computer will recognize. Thus, a document can contain embedded cross-references to other documents and the user can jump to them by simply invoking the indicated URL. Since this is most often done with text documents (although it is not limited to that), the system is called hypertext. Figure 13.4 shows an example of hypertext. It is used to traverse a chain of menus in the example and then to go to a more detailed page of text. On the Web, one can easily move through a complex list of cross-references by invoking the embedded hypertext links. In the vernacular, this is called *surfing* the Web.

13.5.4 HTML

The Web and hypertext work because of a special language called the *hypertext markup language* (HTML), which is a text language that provides a syntax for text documents, text formatting, and the embedded URLs needed for hypertext. In addition, other embedded commands in HTML documents allow for graphics, images, audio, video, and animation to be included in Web documents. HTML is managed informally by the *World Wide Web Consortium* (W3C), which has its own Web site at http://www.w3.org. The list of HTML enhancements is growing every day.

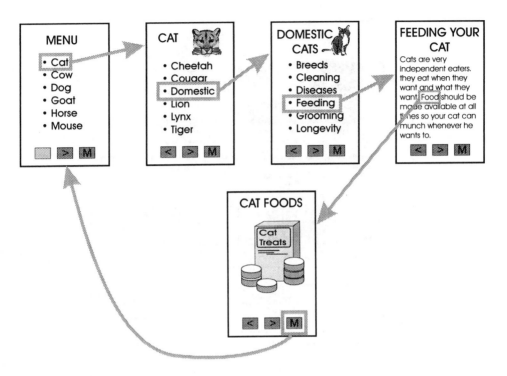

Figure 13.4 An example of hypertext.

A Web HTML document is called a *page*, and Web subjects are made up of multiple pages that are accessed by hypertext. Pages are usually separate HTML documents, but they are coupled together by their hypertext links [1]. As far as the servers and the Internet are concerned, HTML files are just text documents, but at the client machine they become true multimedia objects by means of a *browser* program.

13.5.5 Browsers

HTML files consist of text code that is interpreted to correctly display the contents; this is the purpose of a browser program. Figure 13.5 shows an example of an HTML page that displays an image, text in several sizes and formats, hypertext (the underlined text), and graphics (lines). In the HTML code, the tags are the items contained within the < and > characters. For example, the code <table> signifies the start of a table structure that contains an image (indicated by the img tag) and a <h1> heading side-by-side. The code </h1> marks the end of the heading and the </table> tag is the end of the table. Many other features are available in HTML and the list is continually being extended, not only by the W3C, but by browser manufacturers who are developing their own enhancements with the desire of having them standardized in future versions of HTML.

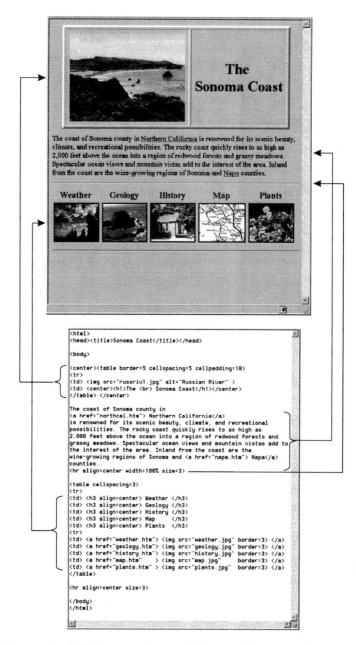

Figure 13.5 An example of HTML source code is at the bottom and the page displayed by a browser is shown at the bottom.

Since HTML is interpreted in a browser, it can run on any platform for which a browser is available. Nothing in HTML itself restricts its use to any system. This makes HTML *platform independent*.

13.5.6 Java

For all its attractions, HTML still only produces static pages. The addition of dynamic features to Web pages is an important enhancement to facilitate all the possibilities of interactive systems. Several languages have been developed to provide dynamic features by creating programs that run on a server and constantly send dynamic updates to clients. This works but is undesirable because it requires continuous communication with the client, thus tying up a communication channel, and also using up resources on the server. Now, languages have been developed that allow the server to download small programs to the client where they run top further involvement with the server. The most significant of these so far is the *Java* language developed by Sun Microsystems.

Java is a text-based language that runs by being interpreted in the browser program. It provides most all programming constructs and allows dynamic objects such as animations and any of the many other devices used in interactivity. Java is rapidly becoming a standard and is being incorporated into most new versions of browsers. Development tools for creating Java programs are also available.

13.6 MULTIMEDIA PLATFORMS

A *platform* is the hardware and software environment for running programs. Whether it is a computer or not is immaterial, but a platform must contain a microprocessor and an operating system with an API. A platform is capable of multimedia presentation within its capabilities of sound, display, and controls. Specific platform types are discussed in this section.

13.6.1 Personal Computers

PCs inherently include the capabilities for multimedia operation. They can run browsers or other types of multimedia programs (see Section 13.7). They are the most flexible approach to multimedia but are also the most expensive. PCs are available in nearly all offices and in a large percentage of homes, so multimedia capabilities exist in all these places without any additional hardware.

13.6.2 Television Receivers

The television receiver is available in nearly all homes and is a possible candidate for multimedia presentation because it has a video display and an audio system. However, most TVs do not have a microprocessor and thus lack one of the basic ingredients of a multimedia system. This is overcome by the use of a set-top box (see Section 13.6.2.1). A more fundamental problem with using a TV for multimedia is that TVs are designed for viewing ratios above 4:1 so their display resolution is low and, computer-generated objects look especially poor on a TV screen when viewed at the closer distances suitable for one-to-one interactivity. For example, TV resolution limits text to about 40 characters per line. Within these limitations, however, TV receivers can be and are used for multimedia.

13.6.2.1 Set-Top Boxes

The set-top box is a standalone (self-powered) unit that connects to video and audio inputs on a TV receiver and contains a microprocessor and the other hardware such as a CD-ROM drive or communications link needed for multimedia. The name comes because they are usually configured to sit on top of a TV cabinet. This concept is widely used to adapt TV receivers to cable distribution or to provide video game capability. A number of designs of multimedia set-top boxes have been produced, and a few are on the market. So far, none has shown much success, which is probably because there is not a universal standard for such a device and consumers are leery of investing in a proprietary system that may or may not continue to be available.

Much attention is being given to the Internet computer as a set-top box (see Section 13.6.5) because such a device will be less expensive if it is designed to use a TV for video and audio presentation.

13.6.3 Kiosks

Many special-purpose systems are in use for information dissemination in public places. These are called *kiosks* and usually contain a standard PC along with video and audio capability mounted in a freestanding cabinet that brings the video screen to about an average person's shoulder level. The user interface is usually a touch-screen monitor because that has proven to be easily learned by the public and it is nearly indestructible. Keyboards and mice do not meet either of those requirements.

Since most kiosks are intended for casual use by the general public, the user interface must be designed so practically no learning is required. The consumer wants to use the kiosk to get information quickly and then go on about his or her business. Somewhat more sophisticated kiosks are used in museums for presenting information. In that case, they are often used by children and the requirement for indestructibility is paramount.

13.6.4 Game Machines

Video game machines are designed to use the display and sound of a TV but are usually packaged differently because the game box should be with the players in front of the TV and connected by a single cable. Most games support more than one player, and a separate control unit is provided for each player. The heart of a game box is a special-purpose and usually proprietary microprocessor. Software is provided to the box either as a ROM cartridge or as a CD-ROM. Game machines have grown steadily more powerful over the years, but there is no standardization among manufacturers, and competition is on the basis of price and performance achievable through unique design. Some game machine manufacturers are coming out with Web-surfing add-ons.

13.6.5 The Internet Computer

One concept of the future of personal computing is that everyone will be connected to the Internet and will receive all programs from there and will store all data there. This mode of operation allows a PC to be simplified because it does not need mass storage. However, all the other PC components are still needed, so the degree of simplification is small. Of course, cost can be further reduced by making the product use a TV for its display and sound system but that has the problems of interlaced scanning and low resolution, which are major disadvantages for serious computing. The Internet computer also changes the model of software distribution because software now comes over the Net and it is impossible for users to own their software as they do now because they cannot store it locally. All software would be rented.

This concept seems to be motivated more by political or financial considerations on the part of manufacturers and software distributors than by the demands of users. The data demand that it would place on the Internet would be fantastic, especially considering that the Net is already reeling under the data demands of the Web. In this writer's opinion, the Internet computer is unlikely to become widespread. But as products are being developed, we will just have to see what happens.

13.7 AUTHORING

The development of a multimedia application is a nontrivial artistic *and* technical task. This is called *authoring* and includes audio and video production, graphic art, writing and scripting, programming, and distribution. Because of the sophistication of this and the desire of many people of limited skill to perform authoring, there are over 100 software products available for authoring. These products range from very simple ones that allow a completely unskilled consumer to build an application to extremely sophisticated products that are intended to be used by teams of experts to produce large and dynamic applications.

Table 13.2

Multimedia Capacity of One CD-ROM Disc, When Entire Disc is One Type

Data Type	Description	Number of Units
Text	Uncompressed	200,000 pages
Text	Compressed	400,000 pages
Images	640×480 JPEG, medium quality	20,000 images
Graphics	Line drawings	40,000 drawings
Audio	8-bit × 8kHz uncompressed	24 hours
Audio	16-bit × 22 kHz stereo uncompressed	2 hours
Audio	AC-3 compressed	3.9 hours
Video	320×240 MPEG-1	1.2 hours
Animation	320×240	4–8 hours

13.7.1 Languages

The heart of an authoring system is a *language* that is used to describe the application, its content, and its operation. One example of a language is HTML, which was described above, but there are many others. A language may be either compiled to produce an executable application or it may be interpreted by the target system at run time. The HTML used on the Web is an example of an interpreted language.

Programming languages such as C or Basic are quite arcane and require considerable learning to use. Some easier-to-use authoring languages have been developed but, if they are to have any power, the concepts of programming cannot be avoided. Therefore, many authoring systems provide a graphical interface where the user (author) can work with icons and flow charts or other representations to make the authoring process more intuitive. The authoring program then writes its multimedia scripts in whatever language it uses internally. Some of these products do not require an author to know anything about the underlying language. Others provide visibility of the language so a skilled author can work with features that may not be accessible through the graphical interface.

Because there are so many different authoring systems, selection of one is a difficult task. In selecting an authoring product, the author must consider what the target platforms will be and choose from systems that can support them. Then the author's own capability and degree of commitment for learning must be assessed. Finally, one must think through the types of features needed for the intended application. Books are available on the subject, but a potential author still needs to try out systems to find one with which he or she will be comfortable [2].

13.7.2 Authoring Systems

Authoring takes a lot more than software. A powerful PC or workstation is required with large mass storage, audio and video capture hardware, and software for authoring and manipulation and management of content. Because many different skills come into play for authoring, projects of any size involve a number of people of different disciplines. Usually, a network of computers is then required along with software capable of being used in a multiuser environment.

13.8 MULTIMEDIA DISTRIBUTION

A significant aspect of multimedia is the choice of how the program and content will reach the end user. All the available media for mass storage and transmission are candidates for this. This section discusses some of the considerations.

13.8.1 Recorded Media

The CD-ROM is the prime multimedia medium today because of its capacity, robustness, and low cost. It is available on nearly all PCs sold in the last three years and high-performance CD-ROM drives are now hitting the under-$100 price level. 680 MB of data represents a lot of content, as shown in Table 13.2. The table shows clearly that the data price tag for digitized audio or video is high compared with that of other types. Of course, most applications require a mix of data types.

The new DVD provides the capacity for much larger multimedia applications on a single disc, and this should keep the industry growing for some time.

Some applications require regular updating of the content of the application. This is particularly true for information kiosks. Of course, updating can be done by replacing a CD-ROM, but that is expensive if, for example, daily updating is required. The best approach is to use a transmission link to update information on a hard disk in the kiosk. Thus, the updating process is just a telephone call.

The data capacity of videotape is massive, but the difficulties of linear access make it quite unsuitable for interactivity.

13.8.2 Broadcasting

Many new services based on terrestrial or satellite broadcasting have been proposed. Broadcasting is a low-cost high data rate one-way capability that is appropriate when those characteristics are needed. It also requires an allocation of spectrum space, which is an extremely difficult hurdle if it does not already exist. Some services can be developed by utilizing unused capacity in existing broadcast services, such as the VBI of an analog TV channel. This avoids any new allocations but requires close coordination with the TV service and probably a change of those standards, which is also a difficult political process.

Since we are discussing interactivity in this chapter, a broadcast service must use some other type of medium for its return channel. Usually the telephone is chosen because it exists almost everywhere.

13.8.3 Wired Distribution

The primary wired high-bandwidth service in widespread use is cable TV. A lot of attention focuses on figuring out how to convert cable TV systems to digital distribution and how to make them multimedia-capable. Of course, multimedia requires two-way communication and, although the original concept of cable TV included a two-way capability, most systems have never implemented the return channels. It is a very expensive proposition to implement it now, especially when the magnitude of the market for interactivity is still uncertain.

The World Wide Web on the Internet is already a multimedia service but, for most people, is a very slow one because telephone modem communication must be used. One solution to that is to use the high bandwidth of a cable TV system to distribute the Internet to homes. Some cable systems are experimenting with this by offering "cable modems" to users and devoting a few channels to digital transmission. However, if this became widespread, there would still be a bandwidth problem because each Web user on the cable would require separate connection whenever he or she received data and the system would quickly load up. It also requires implementation of some form of return communication, either using the cable or the telephone.

Computer networks are another medium of communications that can be considered for multimedia wherever they exist. However, most network protocols now in use do not provide the real-time delivery required by digital audio and video. Approaches are being developed.

As the Internet gains more users, it is experiencing bottlenecks and overloads because of too much traffic on the backbone communications links. The slow connections through the telephone system are also a problem. Although these problems are being addressed, providing more bandwidth in the backbone and in connections to subscribers is going to increase costs, and it is not clear how much increase can be absorbed before the growth rate slows down. The concept of a high-speed Information Superhighway that is available to everyone is not yet a reality.

13.9 CONCLUSION

Digital multimedia has become pervasive in PCs as computers become more powerful and as the CD-ROM market expands. This has amply demonstrated the power of the technology to inform, educate, and entertain. However, multimedia has not yet penetrated the home market except as video games. Much industry activity is devoted to finding the product or products that will bring digital multimedia into the home.

REFERENCES

1. Graham, I. S., *HTML Sourcebook*, John Wiley & Sons, New York, 1996.
2. Luther, A. C. *Authoring Interactive Multimedia*, AP Professional, Boston, 1995.

Chapter 14

A Digital World

14.1 INTRODUCTION

It should be clear from the preceding chapters that digital audio and video have already affected many industries. But it is still the beginning. The objective of this chapter is to explore the future directions of digital audio and video. Since the future is not fact until it happens, such a discussion as this must be based on opinion—this writer's. Because of that, I will speak in the first person to help you remember that this is my opinion.

I will begin by discussing some of the trends that are visible in the many fields impinging on digital audio and video. Many of these have already been noted in previous chapters, but I will summarize them all here anyway. Then I will discuss some related subjects, such as standards and interindustry conflicts, and along the way you will see glimpses of the blue skies of the future. This chapter will show you that there are a lot of issues. But I do not have all the answers—no one does.

14.1.1 Industries and Markets

Digital audio and video are causing an unprecedented converging of industries and markets. Television, PCs, and telecommunications for the first time are all eyeing the same market—home and business information systems. The dream of a digital *Information Superhighway* that provides high-speed data communications to homes and businesses just like the telephone does for voice has been highly touted as the wave of the future. Everyone who has anything to do with video, digital technology, or communications wants a piece of this action.

At the same time, the existing markets for these industries are embracing digital technology to enhance their current services or to plan new services. It is an exciting time.

14.2 TRENDS

Although digital audio and video are still very new, there are already numerous factors influencing their development. The ones that are discussed here are shown in Figure 14.1. I am sure there are others.

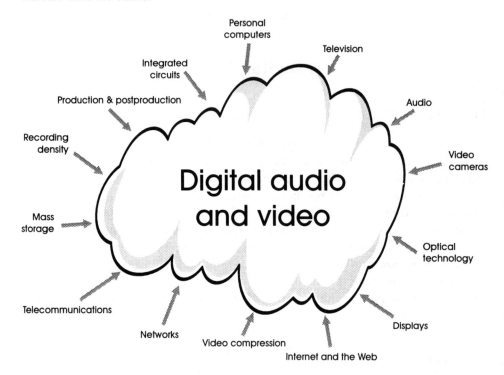

Figure 14.1 *Factors influencing the future of digital audio and video.*

14.2.1 Integrated Circuits

The enabling technology for digital audio and video is integrated circuits. Until the IC appeared, digital circuits were expensive, power hungry, and unreliable. It was difficult to imagine that large digital systems would ever be practical, or for them ever to become consumer products. But that has happened—today's home CD player contains a million or more transistors, it is hand-held and can run from batteries, it is completely reliable for years at a time, and it sells for $100 or less. Similarly, a PC, which can easily have a hundred million transistors, is reliable and inexpensive, considering its capabilities.

Since the IC was invented in 1965, the number of devices that can be integrated on a single chip has grown by more than six orders of magnitude and current chips can contain millions of devices. This has allowed entire systems to be constructed on one chip! It also has steadily increased the complexity of signal processing that is practical to use in low-priced products. This growth of IC capability was predicted early in *Moore's Law* (see Figure 1.1). It is expected that this exponential growth will continue unabated for many more years. Thus, we have to think about IC chips that have tens or hundreds of millions of devices or more on them. I will call these *mega-ICs*. What will we be able to do with such vast processing capability?

However, a specific IC design has to be produced in million quantities to reach the costs predicted by Moore's Law. That is because there is a large upfront investment in manufacturing facilities and design cost, which actually gets larger as ICs become more complex with more devices on a chip. Although it is possible to design custom or "application-specific" ICs, they become expensive when there is not enough production quantity to amortize the initial investment. A significant problem with larger and larger ICs is finding architectures that are general enough that million-quantity production will be possible. Products such as memory ICs or microprocessors fit this model, but not many others do.

It may be difficult to find very many 100-million-device IC designs that will be able to be sold by the millions. In this regard, the microprocessor is unique because the same device can fit many different applications through its software, which, of course, is not part of the IC itself. I think this means that there will be even more microprocessor applications because that may be the only way to bring the power of mega-ICs to problems that do not require million-quantity production. New microprocessor concepts will be developed to further facilitate this explosion of powerful embedded microprocessors.

14.2.2 Recording Density

Magnetic and optical recording systems have shown a progression in recording area density that is similar to Moore's Law but with a smaller exponent (see Figure 11.5 and Section 11.2.2). This progress has led to smaller, less expensive, and higher performing recorders. It also has made practical the digital video tape recorder and the digital video disc system. This trend is expected to continue for some time yet and will have a great impact on all types of digital recording.

Digital camcorders and VCRs are now available in all markets from the home market to the most demanding professional and broadcast markets. Although the home digital products are currently expensive, prices will come down as manufacturing investments are made and production quantities increase. However, the growth of digital recording in the home has to face the situation created by the VHS analog format, which currently dominates in the home. These VCRs are used primarily to play prerecorded material—movies, mostly. The replacement for that use is expected to be the DVD system; if that succeeds, there will be attrition in the market for VHS as it is being replaced by DVD. But the large inplace investment in prerecorded VHS tapes will make this a slow process. This scenario does not leave any market for the home digital VCR.

The impetus for the growth of home digital recording is the camcorder application and the possibility that higher resolution television comes into use. This will create an incentive to replace analog camcorders with digital to obtain higher performance in home recordings, because the performance gap between ATV and VHS will now be apparent to consumers.

In professional and broadcast recording, digital technology is already well on the way to complete acceptance. Within five years, I think all professional and broadcast recording will be digital.

14.2.3 Mass Storage

The mass storage requirements of digital audio and video are expressed in terms of data rate, data capacity, real-time performance, and random access. The latter characteristic is only available in disk-format storage and the recent thrust of the mass storage market has been to get all the other performance parameters of hard disk storage up to the requirements of digital video. This can already be done when video compression is used, and hard disk storage of up to 10 hr of compressed video is considered practical. In this case, the compression has to provide about 10:1 data reduction. However, some industry segments do not want to use *any* compression—for them, it takes 10× more hard disk storage, which is prohibitively expensive for all but the most cost-insensitive applications. But that will be overcome in the next few years, both by improved hard disks and by better compression that will have greater acceptance by the critical markets.

With economical hard disk storage, the video server concept (see Section 4.4.5) can come of age. Servers are already being used for online operation in broadcast and postproduction facilities. I think video servers will be practical for cable TV programming and for potential video-on-demand (VOD) services. However, I am not sure that the economics of VOD will provide a match to what viewers will be willing to pay for it.

14.2.4 Video Compression

Another technology that is at the heart of the digital video explosion is compression. One could not consider digital video in the consumer market without compression. The concepts of video compression date back to the 1980s and earlier but they could not be put to practical use until Moore's Law brought us to the level of processing required. Because of continued IC progress, video compression will continue to become more powerful and less expensive.

In the broadcast and production markets, video compression is viewed as a step backward. Digital technology began in those markets with the ITU-R BT.601 standard that provides an essentially transparent system for handling 525-line and 625-line video signals. After so many years of struggling with the built-in artifacts of analog NTSC and PAL composite systems, most industry people felt that digital video was the solution to a longstanding problem. No longer would one have to worry about accumulated degradation as signals passed through large systems or when multigeneration recording is required.

However, compressed digital video systems bring that problem back—every time that compression-decompression is done, there is some signal degradation because of the compromises that are made by the compression algorithm. Signal processing such as transitions and effects cannot be done with video in compressed format, so the conversion from to compressed to uncompressed and back cannot be avoided even in an all-digital system. It is the same analog problem all over again, which is causing many industry people to tell designers: "Don't use compression." I think this is a temporary situation because the continued performance and cost improvements that are built into the underlying technologies will soon allow broadcasters and producers to have the best of both possibilities—uncompressed digital video at a reasonable price and compressed digital video with minimal accumulated degradation at an even lower price.

Another compression issue has to do with standardization of algorithms and whether an algorithm is determined in hardware or software. From an idealized point of view, software algorithms are attractive because a software-based system can run many algorithms whereas a hardware system can only perform the algorithms it was designed for and there is no room for growth in the future.

With algorithms in software, there is more opportunity for innovation. This has been an important concept in the computer industry but there are a number of problems. First, a dedicated hardware processor can be many times faster than a software-based processor doing the same task with equivalent-sized ICs. Unfortunately, speed is an overruling issue with video because the processing must run in real time at the specified frame rate; there is no recovery from a processing slowdown except interruption of the video or audio. So a slower processor cannot perform as complex an operation during the time of each frame and the effectiveness of the compression must be compromised. It is fair to say that even with a hardware processor, the quality of compression is limited by the amount of processing available. At the present time, software-based compression systems are marginal. However, as CPU power increases, software-based compression will become steadily better, and I think it will be the best choice for all but the most demanding applications in a few years.

A second problem is the myth that software-based algorithms does not need standardization. A software-driven environment must specify a language and an API to work. This is a standard. For example, executable PC software is made up of CPU instructions—*standard* instructions—that is the language. However, one cannot write programs for a system without also knowing how the hardware in that system is accessed, which is the purpose of an API. The API specifies to the programmer how to do things such as reading and writing to the hard disk, reading what the user types at the keyboard, and so forth. The API is another standard. At this point, things would work if all systems had the same hardware but, of course, they do not. Further standardization is required to specify what hardware will be suitable for each piece of software. That is why there is a list of "recommended hardware" on software packages. This is most important for compression and decompression software, which is highly dependent on the power of the hardware it uses. Maybe the standardization of the algorithm itself could be avoided but the standardization of the *system* cannot be avoided.

A further problem occurs in software-based systems that allow the algorithm to vary between individual program segments—it becomes extremely difficult to edit or assemble programs from these segments. Transcoding has to be done so the output of editing holds to one algorithm or another but it cannot be more than one at a time. If wide distribution is going to occur and a suitable production-postproduction infrastructure is going to build up, algorithms need to be standardized.

14.2.5 Telecommunications

The worldwide telecommunications network grew up as an analog telephone service. However, it became one of the first applications of digital technology when it was realized that digital multiplexing was the most cost-effective way to build multichannel communication trunks between cities. Today, most of the telephone network is digital, except for the final connections to homes. High-speed digital circuits connect telephone central offices with each other and with the intercity trunks. However, most of this capacity is divided down into 64-kb/s digital voice circuits and used that way.

Although higher speed digital circuits are available from the phone companies, they are very expensive because pricing considers the tradeoff between using data capacity for many voice circuits or higher speed data. As long as there is voice traffic available to be carried, that is the more profitable way to use communication capacity. This must be overcome before a 1.5-Mb/s phone line into every home will be practical.

Many approaches are being offered by different members of the telephone community, but they are only confusing the market and do not yet have the price-performance that it is going to take to open the high-speed data market to the home or small businesses. In the meantime, others are offering different approaches for the high-speed line into every home (see below).

14.2.6 Networks

Computer networks are widespread in industry, government, and academia. They provide high-speed communication between computers at the same location and, with (expensive) leased-line connections, between computers at faroff locations. This technology offers data rates from 10 Mb/s to 100 Mb/s with wired connection, and much higher data rates with the emerging fiber-optic network technology. However, computer network technology has limitations regarding its use with digital audio and video.

Existing computer networks were not designed to provide real-time continuous delivery as is required with audio and video. Most other types of computer data can tolerate brief interruptions or delays, and network protocols make use of that tolerance. A standard computer network will not deliver continuous data at anywhere near its rated capacity unless that data are the only activity on the network. If a user wants to send a little data over the network while someone else is transmitting video, the network protocol will probably interrupt the video to service that other user. So, special network protocols are needed for digital audio and video. This is being worked on, but standards are not yet completed for an A/V-capable network. Network users are already trying to handle multimedia data, the demand is growing, and I believe that real-time computer networks will soon be developed.

14.2.7 Internet and the Web

The Internet is a network of networks, and the Web is the Internet's multimedia channel. All the comments above about computer networks apply to the Internet and the Web. In addition, there are bigger problems because the demand for data capacity is unbounded. Whereas a network in a corporate environment can be designed to serve a specific number of users or projected users doing specific things, no one knows how many users there will be on the Web or what they might start doing. So far, the approach has been to add capacity to the Internet as bottlenecks develop but it is very difficult to plan ahead. Thus, one could expect that there will always be bottlenecks coming and going as the Internet is molded to meet the demand.

Some people think further that this ad hoc growth may lead to a complete collapse of the Internet when demand passes the point of practical expansion. I do not know about that, but, as in many other cases where there is a recognized market demand for a service, the industry starts inventing and eventually fills the demand. That process is ongoing.

14.2.8 Displays

Video displays have been dominated by CRT technology for 50 years. Although alternative displays have appeared in certain niche markets, such as portable computers, the CRT is the display of choice for television receivers and PC monitors—the two largest existing markets for displays. However, as television grows to higher resolution, there will be demand for larger displays than the current 25 to 32-in diagonal sizes that represent the bulk of the market today. CRT technology rapidly runs out of steam when display size passes about 35 in because of size, power, and weight. The box becomes too large to get in the door of the typical home!

I should explain the reason why higher resolution TV requires larger displays. It has to do with the normal livingroom viewing environment where it is convenient for viewers to sit across the room from the TV display—an arrangement that makes most of the seating in the room usable for viewing. The typical viewing distance for TV today is about 9 ft, and the TV viewing ratio of 7:1 (see Section 2.2.1) is achieved with a picture height of 15.5 in, which is a picture diagonal of 26 in. If the resolution of that size of display is increased beyond present TV levels, viewers at the normal distance will not see it. Therefore, if higher-resolution displays come into the home, viewers must either sit closer (which I think they will not do) or displays must become larger. For example, a 1080-line HDTV display can support a 3.2:1 viewing ratio; at 9 ft distance, that means a picture height of 34 inches and a picture width (at 16:9 aspect ratio) of 60 inches. No direct-view CRT is ever going to do that!

However, large displays can be built with CRTs by projecting the output of small, bright display tubes. A 34×60 display is quite a reasonable size for projection, but the brightness and resolution performance of CRT projection displays is a difficult tradeoff, and they generally do not perform as well as direct-view displays. They also still require a large, deep box that is awkward to handle in the home. The digital micromirror device (DMD—see Section 10.3.4) addresses these limitations of CRT projection.

There is an opportunity for a large-screen display that is bright, high-resolution, low-power, small (which must mean thickness), and economical to produce. The two principal contenders at this time are plasma displays and DMDs. The former is a flat-panel direct-view technology, and the latter is a projection technology. Both are getting major development attention around the world. I am not expert enough in these technologies to make any prediction, but, from what I have seen, I would prefer the plasma display technology to have in my livingroom compared with any projection technology. But the conclusion will depend on which technology reaches the appropriate price-performance point at the time when the demand is there. (There is not yet any demand for HDTV.)

14.2.9 Optical Technology

Optical technology has found use in recording and transmission (fiber optics), and optical signal processing is being developed. The CD, CD-ROM, and DVD represent points on the curve of improvement of optical recording. This improvement will continue, and we can expect even higher density optical products in the future. Optically recorded products began as read-only and have progressed through write-once and write-many versions.

The write-once style, such as CD-R, has a market in archiving and small-quantity CD production, but the write-many optical systems will have a hard time competing with magnetic hard drives, and I do not think they will be a factor in the large markets. Write-once will be offered for the DVD for the same reasons that it is being used for CD, and I think that will be just as successful.

Fiber-optic transmission is widely used in telecommunications, and systems have been developed for cable TV and computer networks, but not much deployment has yet occurred. However, that will happen and the availability of fiber-optic gigabit networks and cable systems is not far off.

14.2.10 Broadcast Television

Broadcast television is the largest video market there is and it is all analog technology. Program production for television is rapidly moving to digital technology, but broadcasting is firmly based on the analog NTSC, PAL, and SECAM standards set in the 1950s and 1960s. The massive infrastructure of hundreds of millions of receivers and tens of thousands of broadcasting stations means that any transition to digital technology will be very slow. Such a transition will cost hundreds of billions of dollars, and there must be very important incentives to ever make it occur. However, there have been digital TV broadcasting developmental initiatives in most developed countries, and system choices may soon be made. The ATSC proposal in the United States is one of the leading systems. So what are the incentives to transition to digital broadcasting?

1. Digital broadcasting can provide substantially higher resolution in the same channel bandwidth now used for analog broadcasting. The ATSC proposal offers up to 1920×1080 resolution in a 6-MHz broadcast channel. Along with that, digital broadcasting can deliver multichannel audio at significantly higher fidelity than analog broadcasting.

2. Digital broadcasting can provide two, three, or more standard-definition TV programs in a single 6-MHz channel.

3. Digital broadcasting can occupy channel allocations that now have to be left unused because of interference problems with analog broadcasting. Using these extra channels for digital broadcasting will not interfere with existing analog channels.

4. Digital broadcast channels can carry new types of service along with television.

These incentives boil down to two things: many more TV channels can be available without any additional spectrum allocations, and the possibility exists for higher quality audio and video. But will broadcasters and the public make the hundred-billion-dollar investment necessary to put digital broadcasting in place? I think it does not make economic sense, but it may still happen over time if the right marketing approaches are taken. It is clear that television has a stronghold on the public, but it is not so clear how much they will pay to see more and better TV. That kind of a question was tested once before—with the introduction of color TV in the 1950s. It took ten years before any momentum developed, but then it did happen. This may be the same. But in the competitive 1990s and 2000s, will the industry stick it out until that happens? I do not know.

14.2.11 ATV and HDTV

More needs to be said about ATV and HDTV. These new systems are a direct outgrowth of digital audio and video and offer the possibility of departing from the concept of analog broadcasting where signals are produced completely in real time at the broadcast station or cable head end and receivers simply display them as they are received. However, a digital receiver does not have to do that—it can store signals, decompress them, transcode them, combine them, and perform many other processes before or while they are being displayed. From a standards point of view, a receiver can display signals in a completely different standard from the way they were transmitted. So, is that a good thing? If it is, what do you have to standardize?

It is too early to try to answer these questions because there is not yet much experience with ATV receivers outside of the research laboratory. The true cost impact of these receiver concepts is not yet determined.

14.2.12 Cable Television

The present concept of the television marketplace is that cable TV is just an alternative way of distributing television signals; it uses the same signal standards and the same receivers. Signals are RF-modulated on cable channels just the same way they are modulated on a broadcast channel. There can be some extra channels on cable because the cable can use frequency bands that are not available for broadcasting, and over time, all receivers have been made capable of receiving cable channels as well as broadcast channels. If digital ATV receivers are placed on the market, they will work on cable, too. From the point of view of a television receiver, cable is the same as broadcasting.

From the telecommunications point of view, however, cable is an existing wide-bandwidth connection into every home. Handled properly, it could be the Information Superhighway. This is an intriguing possibility and is being explored by both cable TV and telecommunications companies. The concept of a "cable modem" that connects the Internet to the home is being tested in some locations. I believe that cable TV systems will play an important role in the information superhighway, but I am not sure how we will move from here to there.

14.2.13 Personal Computers

Electronic computers have been digital since their beginnings. To a computer, digital video and audio are simply different data types, and computers are likely to try to handle them the same way they handle any other data. This causes problems, however, especially because of the real-time nature of audio and video. Computers, therefore, have made special cases of audio and video to provide for their real time requirements. This has not been easy and it is still somewhat in transition, meaning that there are many different approaches in use, and optimal solutions are not agreed upon.

The steady progression of Moore's Law makes computers more powerful every year, and much of this power is now being directed to the problems of audio and video. The objective of this is to reach the point where audio and video do not have to be special, and all data types can once again be handled the same way. Of course, that means using software instead of special hardware, and the industry will not be satisfied until that is possible. As I said above, the degree to which you can handle audio and video in software today depends on the picture and sound quality you need and, there is a performance point beyond which hardware is still required. That point is moving up every day, and I expect that sometime in the next five or ten years, everyone will be satisfied with an all-software approach. In the meantime, we are still in a transitional mode with multiple approaches being tried and no single standard has emerged.

14.2.14 Video Cameras

Over the past ten years, video cameras have made the transition from vacuum-tube imagers to CCD imagers. They are now making the transition to all-digital signal processing. Performance of the best digital cameras is spectacular and leaves little to be desired. However, as you move down the price scale, that is not the case and there is plenty of room for price-performance improvement. That is how Moore's Law applies to cameras. They will become lower in price and smaller and have more features at a given price.

The integration of cameras with recorders (camcorders) is also almost universal. Camcorders are available at all prices. At the high end, separate cameras and recorders are also available, and the "docking" configuration allows cameras and recorder types to be mixed in a single package.

14.2.15 Audio

Digital audio has been a mass market item in the CD audio system for more than ten years. This early system has had massive acceptance in the home and has also spawned the CD-ROM for computers. The audio CD is an extremely conservative design by today's standards—it employs straight PCM with no compression. There is a large opportunity for more audio storage at lower cost using the latest compression systems, such as AC-3 (see Section 9.4.5). AC-3, by the way is an example of a system that would not be practical without Moore's Law—it requires prodigious processing, but it now can be done on a single chip.

The increased data capacity of the DVD also stores a lot more audio than a CD. However, there may not be a large market for more prerecorded audio on a single disc. The real opportunity may be more in the idea of an audio server, where a single device stores all the consumer's CDs online. This would require a few hundred hours of audio to be stored in a recordable device with random-access playback. At AC-3 rates, 100 hr is 17.3 GB of data—that is only one four-layer DVD. However, a four-layer DVD is not recordable, so the answer (for now) would have to be a magnetic hard disk. A 17-GB hard disk is expensive today, but the price may become reasonable in the future. The concept could be explored today using a 3-GB hard drive—that would store about 17 hr of audio. Of course, audio servers also apply to postproduction use and are already being used there.

14.2.16 Production and Postproduction

Cameras, recording, and signal processing come together in production and postproduction. All of the digital advances in these components have contributed to a renaissance in program creation. Further, there are many more outlets for distributing programs today, and producers want to be able to address any of them. The trend is to produce in a high-definition format and then be able to transcode programs to other formats for distribution on broadcast, cable, CD-ROM, DVD, the Web, and so forth. There will be more distribution channels in the future and this type of multiformat program creation will grow.

Audio and video servers and nonlinear editing have taken over the postproduction market. The advantages are so great that analog systems are being phased out as fast as users can afford to replace the equipment. In only a few years, all postproduction will be digital.

14.3 STANDARDS

The products and markets that have been discussed in this chapter could not exist without standards. Standards let the purchasers of systems know that they are buying components that will interoperate with products from other manufacturers and that components will continue to be available over time. No mass market ever developed without standards. Most audio and video products require an infrastructure of content providers, hardware and software providers, training, and so forth. Standards are the way all these pieces can work together. This is extremely important, and developers of new technology have to consider right from the start how they will achieve the necessary standards.

In the digital world, standards do not have to be restrictive. If the product is software based, there will be much room for individual innovation through software. Even with hardware, the product can be made programmable to offer a range of options or features. A few more gates to provide programmability do not add much to the ICs already in the system.

14.4 COMPUTERS VERSUS TELEVISION

It should be apparent from some of the discussion in this chapter that the computer and television industries have some different views of how to handle audio and video and what standards and products should be like. This is not surprising when you consider the history of these two industries that have grown up in their own worlds until now.

Television is based very much on real-time delivery, no user interaction, and picture and sound quality tailored to a specific viewing environment and, until now, analog technology. In the case of computers, they have always been primarily digital, and delivery of information is seldom handled in real time because computers have been able to store their information locally until needed. User interaction is paramount in computers, and they provide elaborate user interfaces (sometimes too elaborate). Picture and sound quality in computers can be anything ranging from awkward simulated speech and postage-stamp video to better-than-HDTV video with high-fidelity audio. In addition, computers are controlled by software, so the same hardware can be configured to perform many different tasks—even things that the hardware designers never dreamed of.

One of the places where the computer and television views conflict is the matter of interlaced scanning. When TV was developed, interlaced scanning was the only way that the signals could be broadcast in a reasonable bandwidth. The factor of 2:1 that it offered was essential. The artifacts of interlacing such as interline flicker and gear-toothing were not visible at the picture sharpness and viewing distances normally used with TV. However, when computer displays are shown on TV screens, the flicker artifacts of interlacing becomes a serious problem. That is because computer-generated objects, such as text characters, contain a lot of information that appears isolated on one line. This inherently flickers at the frame rate, which is very visible. It is necessary to deliberately soften computer screens to make them usable on interlaced displays, and this is the reason why TV screens can only show about 40 characters per line of computer data.

Although the flickering of interlaced scanning can be removed by storing the incoming interlaced data in a screen memory and displaying that with progressive scanning at the field rate, it requires digital processing and increased scanning speeds so the price of a TV receiver is significantly increased. Some of the top-end receivers actually do this, but they are very few. However, all computer displays use progressive scanning, and the computer people are used to the way it looks. They are offended when they see an interlaced display. This has been a conflict in the ATV standardization because there, too, the highest resolution standards as developed by the TV industry call for interlacing. This has been compromised in the final standards by not specifying scanning standards at all. Although digital receivers could be built to be very flexible about scanning standards, that is expensive and it is expected that the industry will determine the preferred choices.

14.5 CONVERGENCE

Digital technology is providing both real and perceived opportunities in information distribution that are attracting the attention of the TV (consumer electronics), PC, and telecommunications industries. Some writers are expecting a battle for markets that will result in the demise of one or more of those industries. It does not have to be like that.

Of course, the largest opportunity is viewed to be the Information Superhighway—the high data rate digital channel into every home. All the industries are trying approaches that would "lock in" their share of this market and possibly knock out others' shares. This seems foolish to me. No one of the industries has all the technology marbles, and a system, if it ever develops and becomes cost- effective, requires ingredients from *all* industries.

The industries should work together toward this objective, and the way I think it should happen is by standardizing on a digital network for the home that will support digital audio and video as well as home control. Such a network will allow television receivers, computers, and telecommunications systems to share data throughout the home. Thus, audio and video could be presented on a television display in the livingroom, or it could be shown on computers in the home office, the kitchen, or the children's bedrooms. The distinction between TV and computer is based on whether the environment is the livingroom entertainment scenario or is it the one-on-one highly interactive computer situation. The extent to which these different environments actually shared data would be based on software—home owners buy the software that implements the features they want on their home network.

Telecommunications participates in this network by being a server on the network and handles incoming and outgoing data that then becomes available to all the TV or computing centers in the home. It is not necessary for telecommunications companies to begin making TVs or PCs to stake out their place in the home.

There are some initiatives in the industries to consider approaches like this, and I hope they will be pursued in a cooperative and compromising manner. Maybe this way, we may see the Information Superhighway develop and become connected into our homes in five or ten years.

14.6 CONCLUSION

Digital audio and video technology has come a long way to reach the present point. It can now demonstrate all of its opportunities. It is the task of industry, consumers, business, and governments to exploit those opportunities to bring us fully into the digital world.

Glossary

Italicized words in the glossary text refer to other glossary items.

3:2 pulldown A method for transferring 24 frames/second motion picture film to *NTSC* television, which displays one film frame for three TV *fields* and the next film frame for two TV fields.

4:1:1 component The option of the ITU-R Rec. BT.601 component digital TV standard that uses full-rate digitizing of the *luminance* component and quarter-rate digitizing of the *color-difference* components.

4:2:0 component A component digital TV standard that uses full-rate digitizing of the *luminance* component, half-rate digitizing of the *color-difference* components, and 2:1 line *decimation* of the color-difference components.

4:2:2 component The option of the ITU-R Rec. BT.601 component digital TV standard that uses full-rate digitizing of the *luminance* component and half-rate digitizing of the *color-difference* components.

A-B roll editing In videotape editing, a method that creates two intermediate recordings that are played in synchronism while assembling the final cut, which takes sequential or overlapped segments of the program from the two reels.

aberrations In optical imaging systems, the properties that cause distorted image reproduction.

AC-3 An audio compression system developed by Dolby Laboratories to provide up to 5.1 channels of surround sound. As used in the ATSC ATV system, it requires a data rate of 384 Kb/s.

access time In mass storage systems, the time from the issuance of a command to retrieve data until receipt of the first byte of data.

acoustics The science of sound waves.

active scan In a video system, the period of time during a line-scan cycle that picture information is actually displayed. The remainder of the scan cycle is the *blanking interval*.

acuity The ability of the human eye to distinguish fine detail.

adaptive differential PCM (ADPCM) A *differential PCM* scheme where the interpretation of the difference values is changed dynamically in some way according to the signal properties.

ADC See *analog-to-digital conversion.*

additive primaries In color image reproduction using colored lights, the three color lights that are mixed to produce a full-color image. The additive primary colors are usually red, blue, and green.

ADPCM See *adaptive differential PCM.*

ADR See *automatic dialog replacement.*

advanced TV (ATV) The proposed digital television system for the United States. It provides for broadcasting at a variety of resolutions from standard-definition up *to high-definition TV* using the existing 6 MHz television channel allocations. The proposal was developed by the *Grand Alliance* and is being completed by the *Advanced Television Systems Committee.*

Advanced TV Systems Committee (ATSC) An industry committee in the United States that is responsible for completing, testing, and promulgating the *advanced TV* standards.

aliasing In a *sampling* system, distortion caused by attempting to sample frequencies that are above the *Nyquist limit.*

alpha-wrap In a *helical-scan* videotape system, a design where the tape wraps completely around (360 deg) the scanner.

ALU See *arithmetic logic unit.*

ambiance In audio production and postproduction, the components of sound that result from the natural sounds of the environment, such as forest sounds, crowd noise, etc.

analog Any representation that characterizes a phenomenon by means of a continuous scale of values.

analog-to-digital conversion (ADC) The process of converting an analog signal to a digital representation. It includes the steps of *sampling* and *quantization.*

anechoic chamber A room for audio testing that has been designed to absorb all reflections of sound.

anti-aliasing A filter or process that reduces or eliminates *aliasing.* For example, an anti-aliasing filter having a frequency cutoff less than the *Nyquist limit* is used at the input when *sampling* an *analog* signal.

aperture (a) In a *scanning* system, the effective size of the scanning spot. See *aperture response*. (b) In a magnetic recorder, the effective size of the *head gap*. (c) In an optical imaging system, the opening in the lens that determines the diameter of the cone of light rays that can be passed by the lens.

aperture response The frequency response loss caused by scanning or sampling with a finite-sized *aperture*.

API See *application programming interface*.

application In a PC, a software package that performs a specific task.

application programming interface (API) In a PC, the part of the *operating system* software that defines how *application* programs communicate with the hardware resources of the system.

application-specific IC (ASIC) An IC that has been custom designed for a specific purpose.

area density factor In recording systems, the number of bits stored per unit area of the record medium.

arithmetic logic unit (ALU) In a *central processing unit*, the module that performs arithmetic and logic functions.

artifact Something unnatural. In audio and video systems, artifacts are distortions or effects that are not part of the originally recorded material.

ASIC See *application-specific IC*.

aspect ratio In a video system, the ratio of the width of the display screen to its height.

asynchronous transfer mode (ATM) A standard for a *packetized* transmission system. It provides data transmission of multiple signals over a single communication path.

ATM See *asynchronous transfer mode*.

ATSC See *Advanced Television Systems Committee*.

ATV See *advanced TV*.

audio Signals for the electronic reproduction of sound.

authoring In digital *multimedia*, the process of creating an *application*. It includes programming, production, postproduction, scripting, editing, etc.

automatic dialog replacement (ADR) A process in audio postproduction where the actors rerecord their dialog in a studio. The purpose is to improve the quality and avoid noise and interference that may have existed during the shooting.

azimuth In *magnetic recording*, the angle that the line of the *head gap* makes with the *track*.

ball chart A test chart to be placed in front of a camera for testing of *scan linearity*. The ball chart has an array of circles which, when reproduced by the camera, produces a signal that should align with an electronically created *grating pattern*.

BER See *bit error rate*.

binary A *digital* signal that has only two valid states: usually defined as 0 and 1, true or false, etc.

binaural The human hearing system using both ears.

biphase mark coding A transmission encoding scheme that transmits two channel transitions for a binary one and one transition for a zero. This eliminates the *DC component*.

bipolar A signal that has positive and negative values.

bit A *binary digit*.

bit error rate (BER) In digital transmission, the probability of occurrence of an error, expressed in exponential form. Thus, a BER of 10^{-9} means that the chance of an error is one in a billion (10^9).

bits per pixel In a digital video system, the number of bits used to represent one *pixel*.

bits per sample In a sampled system, the number of bits generated for each sample by the *quantization*.

blanking interval In a scanned video system, the period of time in a scan cycle during which no picture information is displayed.

Boolean algebra An algebraic notation developed by the English mathematician George Boole for describing and manipulating logic circuits.

burned-in time code A time code displayed in a window of the video itself. Thus, in still frame mode, each video frame displays its own time code.

burst errors In digital transmission, bit errors that occur together in a group.

bus In a computer, the group of circuits that connect all the units of the system. The units of the computer system communicate by time-sharing the bus.

camcorder A single unit that contains both a video camera and a video recorder.

capture In video and audio systems, the process of recording pictures and/or sound from live scenes.

cassette In a tape recorder, a housing containing two reels holding a length of permanently connected tape. An opening or door in the cassette allows the tape to be recorded or replayed by a suitable mechanism.

cathode-ray tube (CRT) A vacuum enclosure, usually glass, that has one or more electron guns at one end and a phosphor screen at the other end. High voltage is applied to accelerate electrons from the guns to hit the phosphor to emit light. By *scanning* the electron beam while modulating its intensity, an image can be displayed.

CAV See *constant angular velocity.*

CCD See *charge-coupled device.*

CD See *Compact Disc.*

CD-R The recordable version of the *Compact Disc.*

CD-ROM The computer-data version of the *Compact Disc.* It is a read-only medium.

central processing unit (CPU) In a computer, a programmable unit that performs processing in the system. In a PC, the CPU is a microprocessor IC.

character generator In a video system, a unit that produces computer-generated text and graphics for display along with other video signals.

charge-coupled device (CCD) In a video camera, a solid-state image sensor in the form of a two-dimensional array of cells on an integrated circuit. Light focused on the sensitive surface of the CCD is converted to a charge pattern in the cells, which can be read out as a video signal by applying appropriate scanning signals to the device.

chroma keying In a video system, a technique for combining two signals by, on a *pixel-by-pixel* basis, sensing a specific color in one signal to control the display of the other signal.

circle of confusion In an optical imaging system, the diameter of the bundle of light rays from a point source of light passing through the focused plane.

CISC See *complex instruction-set computer.*

client-server architecture In a computer network, some computers function as sources of information or processing (servers) and other computers function as displays or viewers (clients).

CLV See *constant linear velocity.*

code book In encoding and decoding for a digital transmission system, a table of data that is generated during encoding and is required during decoding to interpret the data being transmitted.

color correction In a video system, any process that modifies the color properties of hue, saturation, or brightness. See *masking.*

color-difference signals In a component video system, the two signals that convey color information but not brightness. Color-differences signals are produced by subtracting the *luminance* signal from the color primary signals, such as $R-Y$ or $B-Y$.

color table In a digital display, the pixel values are used as the index into a table of color values. The table can hold color values having more bits per pixel than the pixels themselves.

colorimetry The science of color measurement.

Compact Disc (CD) A record medium in the form of a 12-cm plastic disc that is read by an optical sensor. The first CD was developed in for distribution of prerecorded audio and was introduced to the home market in 1982. It employs *PCM* digital encoding of stereo audio with a recording capacity of up to 74 min. Subsequent developments have produced the *CD-ROM* for use with computer data, the *CD-R* recordable CD, and others. Note that the unusual spelling of "disc" when referring to the CD is part of the trade name.

companding The process of compressing the dynamic range of a signal before entering a process such as recording. After recording, the dynamic range is expanded back to the original values. This is most often used with audio.

comparator A circuit that changes the state of its digital output when it senses that the voltage of an analog input signal has crossed a predetermined "threshold" value.

compilation In computer software, a process that converts a program written in a *high-level language* into an executable module written in the instruction set of a specific *CPU*.

complements In color reproduction, the colors produced by mixing equal amounts of two primary colors.

complex instruction-set computer (CISC) A *central processing unit* architecture that employs a large instruction set. The CISC design concept provides many instruction types to facilitate efficient *compilation* of *high-level languages*. CISC computers are also characterized by varying execution times per instruction. An alternate architecture is the *reduced instruction-set computer*.

component video A color video system that handles three color components as separate signals. Component systems may employ *RGB*, *YUV*, or YC_RC_B components.

composite video A color video system that combines its color *components* into a single composite video signal. For example, *NTSC*, *PAL*, and *SECAM* are composite video systems. Composite systems require compromises to combine the signals; these may result in *artifacts* that are difficult or impossible to remove later.

compression In digital systems, any process that has the objective of reducing data without significant loss of information. Compression may be *lossless*, where absolutely no information is lost, or *lossy*, where some information is lost but in places where it may not be missed.

constant angular velocity (CAV) In a disk recording system, the disk rotational speed is held constant regardless of the position of the read/write *head*. This results in a varying *track* speed as the radial position of the head changes.

constant linear velocity (CLV) In a disk recording system, the disk rotational speed is changed as the **head** radial position is moved so as to maintain an essentially constant *track* speed under the read/write head.

constellation diagram In a digital transmission system, a display of all the possible states for the amplitude and phase of the channel signal, shown as points on a two-dimensional diagram.

contouring In color reproduction, an effect that appears in smoothly shaded areas when the reproduction employs too few colors. The shaded areas will jump abruptly from color to color, giving an effect similar to the contours on a geographical map.

contrast compression In a video system, a process that reduces the dynamic range of a video signal. This is usually done so that high-contrast scenes can be displayed on display devices that cannot reproduce the full original contrast range.

contrast ratio In a physical scene or a video display, the ratio of the intensity of the brightest point in the scene to the intensity of the darkest point in the scene.

CPU See *central processing unit.*

cross-interleaving In a digital system, the technique of using two nested *error protection* processes with *interleaving* done between them. This provides good error correction for both single-bit and *burst errors.*

CRT See *cathode-ray tube.*

DAC See *digital-to-analog converter.*

DAT See *Digital Audio Tape.*

data separation In a digital transmission or recording system, the process of separating binary information from the (analog) channel signal. See *eye pattern.*

dB See *decibel.*

DC component The long-term average value of a signal. See *modulation, run-length limiting.*

DCT See *discrete cosine transform.*

decibel (dB) The logarithm of the power ratio between two signals. For example: SNR (dB) = $20 \log(E_S/E_N)$.

decimation The process of periodically eliminating some data from a digital data stream. For example, in a sampled image, eliminating every other sample will reduce the data rate by 2:1. Of course, information may be lost. See *subsampling.*

density ratio In an *encoded* digital transmission system, the ratio between the minimal time between transitions of the channel signal and the minimal time between transitions of the incoming data stream before encoding. A higher density ratio indicates that more information is transmitted for a given channel bandwidth.

depth of field In an optical imaging system, the range of object distances within which the image appears to be in focus. See *circle of confusion*.

dichroic filter An optical filter that reflects one band of wavelengths but transmits all other wavelengths not reflected. A dichroic filter is often used in the light-splitting optics for a three-sensor video camera.

differential PCM (DPCM) A *PCM* system where the transmitted signal represents the differences between the incoming words or samples. See *predictive coding*.

digit One *symbol* of a *digital* value.

digital Representing by a fixed number of discrete points. For example, each *digit* of the common decimal system has only the values 0, 1, 2, 3, 4, 5, 6, 7, 8, and 9. Similarly, a *binary* digit (*bit*) has only the values 0 and 1.

Digital Audio Tape (DAT) A digital magnetic tape system that was originally developed for audio recording. It is also used for backup or archival recording in computers.

digital filter In a sampled digital system, a process that manipulates the sample values so as to modify the information content of the samples in the frequency domain. Typically, this is done by accumulating samples that have been delayed and weighted by different amounts. See *FIR*, *IIR*.

digital signal processor (DSP) A special-purpose microprocessor IC, usually of the *RISC* type, that is designed for digital signal processing tasks, such as *digital filtering*, *decimation*, etc.

Digital Versatile Disc (DVD) A new digital disc format for prerecorded audio, video, and *multimedia* use. It is the next generation of the *Compact Disc*. DVD-ROM and DVD-R versions are also planned.

Digital Video Cassette (DVC) A digital videotape system designed for consumer and semiprofessional use. It uses ¼-inch tape in a small cassette and employs video compression. *DVCPRO* is a professional version of the same system.

digital-to-analog conversion (DAC) The process of converting digital samples back to analog signals for processing or display.

digitize Another word for *analog-to-digital conversion*.

discrete cosine transform (DCT) In video *compression*, a form of *transform coding* that converts a two-dimensional array of pixels (usually 8×8) to a two-dimensional array of frequency coefficients. This transformation facilitates compression because many of the frequency coefficients have zero or small values and can be ignored.

disk drive A mechanism for recording or replaying *tracks* on a disk. It consists of a motor that rotates the disk and a *head* mounted on a mechanism that moves the head in a radial direction across the disk surface. Some disk drives have multiple disks and heads to increase storage capacity.

dither In a sampled and quantized system, a method for introducing randomness in the signal to minimize the effect of quantizing noise. Dither is often used in audio or video *analog-to-digital conversion*.

DPCM See *differential PCM*.

driver In computer software, a software module that interfaces between the operating system and a specific piece of hardware. The purpose of the driver is to add the capabilities of its hardware to the system's *application programming interface*.

DSP See *digital signal processor*.

DVC See *Digital Video Cassette*.

DVCPRO The professional version of the *Digital Video Cassette*.

DVD See *Digital Versatile Disc*.

EBU See *European Broadcasting Union*.

edit decision list (EDL) In audio or video editing, a list of commands and time code values that tells a suitable system how to perform the editing tasks necessary to assemble the program described by the EDL.

EDL See *edit decision list*.

EFM See *eight-to-fourteen modulation*.

EIA See *Electronic Industries Association*.

eight-to-fourteen modulation (EFM) In digital *encoding*, a specific version of a *group code* that takes 8-bit input bytes and encodes them as specific 14-bit words for transmission. Although six additional bits are transmitted for each 8-bit input byte, EFM can control the *DC component* and the *run-lengths* such that the channel data rate can actually be increased.

Electronic Industries Association (EIA) An association of electronics manufacturers in the United States.

emissive displays A display that produces its own light, such as a *cathode-ray tube* or a *plasma display panel*.

encoding In digital systems, the process of defining specific bit patterns for the incoming information.

entropy coding In digital transmission, *encoding* that exploits the statistical distribution of the data values. *Huffman coding* is one example of entropy coding.

envelope delay distortion In an analog signal system, distortion produced by a delay versus frequency characteristic that is not uniform.

Equally tempered scale In music, a scale of notes where the ratio of frequency of any note to its predecessor is a constant. For the most common scale, that ratio is $\sqrt[12]{2}$.

error concealment In a system that is capable of detecting errors but it cannot correct them, errors can be replaced by information derived from the signal so that the errors will be less visible.

error protection In digital systems, techniques for detecting and correcting for errors.

European Broadcasting Union (EBU) An organization of broadcasters in Europe.

eye pattern In a digital transmission system, an oscilloscopic display of the analog channel signal versus the recovered clock signal. This display shows the signal as fuzzy lines passing between the valid symbol levels of the signal. Open spaces in this pattern indicate where the amplitude and time sampling must occur to recover the data with the lowest *BER*.

f-number In an optical imaging system, the ratio of the lens *focal length* to the diameter of the lens *aperture*. Smaller f-numbers indicate greater light-gathering ability.

field In a video system employing interlaced scanning, one vertical scan period. During one field, one-half of the lines are scanned; the rest are scanned during a second field to make a complete *frame*. The two fields in a frame are named "odd" and "even" according to which line numbers they scan.

finite impulse response filter (FIR) A *digital filter* that synthesizes its output response by summing a finite number of delayed and weighted copies of the input signal. See *infinite impulse response filter*.

FIR See *finite impulse response filter*.

flash ADC An *analog-to-digital converter* that uses multiple *comparators* to simultaneously test all *quantizing* levels.

Fletcher-Munson curves A set of curves that show the typical frequency response of human hearing versus sound level.

flicker The psychophysical effect perceived by the eye when viewing an image that is periodically refreshed at too slow a rate.

flip-flop A digital circuit that has two possible steady states. It can be used to store a one-bit value.

floating point In digital number representation, a system of representing numbers as a mantissa and an exponent. Ordinarily, the bits defining one number are allocated to sign, mantissa, and exponent.

floppy disk In magnetic recording systems, a flexible plastic disk coated with a magnetic material. The disk is rotated in a *disk drive* for recording of concentric *tracks*.

flying-spot scanner A video scanning system for *capturing* from motion picture film that employs a *cathode-ray tube* light source whose *raster* is focused on the film. Light passing through the film is picked up by a photosensor device to create a video signal.

FM synthesis In music synthesis, a method that synthesizes by frequency modulating one or more carrier signals.

focal length In an optical imaging system, the distance between the lens and its focal plane when focusing on an infinitely distant light source.

Foley studio In audio *postproduction*, a facility for creating audio sound effects in synchronism with the action in an already-recorded video sequence.

foot-candle A unit of illumination equal to one *lumen* per square foot. See *lux*.

frame In a scanned video system, the period of time for a single scan of all the lines in the image. With *interlaced scanning*, a frame is two *fields*.

frame memory A memory that stores data representing one video *frame*.

frame synchronizer A *frame memory* that is written from an incoming signal and read at different timing so that the output signal is synchronized to a local video system.

full duplex A communication system that handles communication in both directions simultaneously.

gamma correction In a video system, manipulation of the gray scale characteristic to compensate for nonlinearities elsewhere in the system. The most common compensation is for a *cathode-ray tube* display. This requires a transfer characteristic having an exponent (gamma) of about 0.45.

gear-toothing In *interlaced scanning* systems, an artifact that occurs on vertical edges of moving objects because they are scanned at different times by each of the two interlaced *fields*. The effect is a horizontal splitting of alternate lines.

graceful degradation In an analog system, accumulated distortion causes the signal to be slowly degraded as it passes through more and more system components. The signal becomes progressively worse, but it does not fail completely.

Grand Alliance A consortium of organizations in the United States who developed the *advanced TV* standards now being completed by the *Advanced TV Systems Committee*.

graphics Computer-generated imagery, such as drawings or animation.

graphics primitives In computer *graphics*, one method of drawing is to build up images or drawings by using objects selected from a small number of primitive shapes. Typical primitives are lines, rectangles, ellipses, polygons, etc.

grating pattern An electronically generated test pattern used with a *ball chart* for measurement of scan linearity of video cameras.

gray scale In a video system, the brightness scale that is displayed. The term is often used to refer to the shape of the amplitude transfer characteristic even for signals that do not represent shades of gray.

group code In digital *error protection*, an *encoding* system that deals with groups or blocks of bits.

halation In an optical imaging system, stray light caused by internal reflections in the components of the systems. This is a common problem with lenses and *cathode-ray tubes*.

half-duplex A communications system that handles communication in only one direction at a time.

hard disk A rigid recording disk that operates with heads that do not contact the disk surface. Magnetic hard *disk drives* are widely used for computer *mass storage*.

harmonic distortion In an analog signal system, the distortion components that appear when the system is tested with a perfect sine wave input signal. In this situation, nonlinear distortion causes spurious frequency components to be created at the harmonics (multiples) of the sine wave frequency.

HDTV See *high-definition TV*.

head In recording systems, the device that interfaces with the record surface to create or read *tracks*.

head gap In a magnetic recording system, recording or replay occurs adjacent to a nonmagnetic gap in the magnetic circuit of the *head*. This is because the magnetic flux lines in the head tend to fringe out at the gap.

helical-scan In a magnetic tape recorder, a mechanism that has *heads* on a rotating wheel that the tape wraps around for recording or replay. Magnetic *tracks* produced by this mechanism are at an angle to the edge of the tape. See *alpha-wrap, omega-wrap*.

hexadecimal (hex) A system of notation for four-bit digital values. It uses the numbers 0–9 and the letters A–F to indicate the 16 possible values of a 4-bit number.

high-definition TV (HDTV) An *advanced TV* system that has significantly higher *resolution* than standard *NTSC, PAL*, or SECAM *television*. Resolutions up to 1920×1080 have been proposed. HDTV systems also typically have a higher *aspect ratio*, giving a wider picture. A common value is 16:9.

high-level language In computer software, a language that allows convenient programming. A high-level language program must be either *compiled* or *interpreted* before it can be run (executed).

horizontal resolution In a video system, the ability to reproduce fine detail in the horizontal direction, as caused by patterns of vertical lines. See *resolution, vertical resolution*.

HTML See *hypertext markup language*.

Huffman coding An *entropy coding* system that assigns bits according to the frequency of occurrence of values. For example, a high frequency-of-occurrence value is encoded with a small number of bits, whereas values that occur less often are encoded with words of more bits.

hypertext A system for display of text that allows specific blocks of text to be marked on-screen to indicate that they are buttons linking to more information. For example, button text may be underlined to show the user that placing the cursor over such text and clicking a button will move him or her to some new text that gives more or related information about the subject.

hypertext markup language (HTML) A language definition that adds tags delimited by special characters, such as '<' and '>.' Text within the tag delimiters provides formatting information for display or it indicates *hypertext* items and where to find the linked information. Additional tag types provide for most *multimedia* features.

hysteresis The property of magnetic materials to remember past conditions. Particularly valuable is the property to retain magnetization when the magnetizing force is removed. This is the basis for magnetic recording.

I/O See *input/output*.

IEC See *International Electrotechnical Commission*.

IIR See *infinite impulse response filter*.

illumination The aggregate of light from all the sources impinging on a scene. Measured in lux or *foot-candles*.

image enhancement In a video system, processes for modification of an image, such as sharpness, noise, *gray scale*, color, etc.

image stabilization In a video camera, a system for compensating the cameraman's unsteadiness in holding the camera so that the resulting video is more stable.

infinite impulse response filter (IIR) A *digital filter* that synthesizes its output response by summing an infinite number of copies of the input signal. This is normally accomplished by a recursive structure.

information superhighway The popular name given to the idea of a high data rate digital network that connects to every home and business.

input/output In a computer system, the hardware that connects to units external to the main chassis.

instruction set In a computer, the collection of commands that are used to directly program the *central processing unit*.

Integrated Services Digital Network (ISDN) A hardware and software protocol for a direct digital connection to the telephone system for a home or business. Data rates up to 128 Kb/s or more are available.

interframe compression Video compression that exploits the similarities between successive frames of a video sequence. One technique for doing this is *motion compensation*.

interactivity The ability of a system to be controlled by its user. An essential ingredient of *multimedia*.

interlaced scanning In a video system, the process of scanning half of the lines in each of two vertical scans (*fields*). This is accomplished by having an odd number of total lines and making the ratio of the horizontal scan frequency to the vertical-scan frequency equal to one-half the total line number. The result of this is that large areas of the picture appear to be refreshed at the field frequency, which reduces flickering of the picture.

interleaving In a digital transmission system, *burst errors* can be spread out by taking blocks of data at the input and temporarily storing them in a memory, which is read out in a different order. Usually this is done by viewing the memory as a two-dimensional array of data words that is read out in a direction orthogonal to the way it was written. After the transmission process, deinterleaving is done. Burst errors that occurred during transmission will now appear spread out over an entire block in the data.

International Electrotechnical Commission (IEC) An international standardizing organization.

International Standards Organization (ISO) An international standardizing organization.

International Telecommunications Union (ITU) An international standardizing organization.

Internet A public worldwide network of computer networks. Computers on the Internet can communicate with each other and exchange data. The *World Wide Web* is a multimedia part of the Internet that allows *hypertext* viewing of content located on computers anywhere in the world.

Internet Protocol (IP) Part of the protocols that make the *Internet* possible. IP and *TCP* are a *packetizing* system. IP handles the routing of packets through the network.

internetwork A network of networks.

interpolation In sampled digital systems, the process of creating samples between other samples. Because of the spectral content of a string of samples, interpolation of samples may require the use of digital filters to achieve the most accurate results.

interpreter In computer software, a program that reads commands written in a *high-level language* and converts them on the fly to instructions for immediate execution on a specific microprocessor. See *compiler*.

intraframe compression Video compression that compresses each frame separately without relying on information from other frames. This is necessary when editing may be desired at any frame location.

IP See *Internet Protocol*.

ISDN See *Integrated Services Digital Network*.

ISO See *International Standardizing Organization*.

ITU See *International Telecommunications Union*.

Java A high-level language developed for use on the *World Wide Web*. Java programs are downloaded to *client* computers on the Web where they are run by an *interpreter*. This allows dynamic or interactive features to be included on Web pages without requiring constant connection to the server system.

Joint Photographic Expert Group (JPEG) A subcommittee of the *ISO/IEC* that developed an image *compression* standard called JPEG. The standard provides a range of algorithms for compression of still images in both *lossless* and *lossy* modes.

JPEG See *Joint Photographic Expert Group*.

Kell factor In scanned video systems, a factor that relates the apparent *vertical resolution* (in *TV lines*) of a *raster* to the number of scanning lines in the raster. For CRT displays, it is generally taken as 0.7.

kiosk A freestanding cabinet containing an interactive *multimedia* system for public access of information.

LAN See *local area network*.

LCD See *liquid-crystal display*.

linear phase In an analog signal system, where the phase characteristic is a straight-line function of frequency. The slope of the phase curve is the delay of the system. If the phase curve is not linear, it means that delay is not constant with frequency and this causes *envelope delay distortion*.

linear time code (LTC) In a tape recording system, where a longitudinal (linear) *track* is provided on the tape for *time code*.

liquid-crystal display (LCD) A flat-panel display that uses the properties of liquid-crystal materials. Liquid crystals change the polarization of light that passes through them according to the intensity of an applied electric field. LCD panels are used in portable computers.

local area network (LAN) A network of computers connected by hard wiring, usually within the confines of a single building.

local bus In a computer system, a special *bus*, separate from the main system bus, that provides interconnection of high data rate peripherals such as *mass storage* and *video display adapters*.

lossless compression A data *compression* system that does not in any way change the information content of the data as a result of compression and decompression. Such a compressor can operate on any data without damaging it. However, the degree of compression is limited.

lossy compression A data *compression* system that may make changes to the information as a result of compression and decompression but it does that in a way that will have minimal effect on the use of the data. This type of compression requires that the compressor know the data format and its use, but knowing that, much more compression can often be achieved.

loudness In an audio system, the psychophysical response to sound intensity.

LTC See *linear time code*.

lumen A unit of light intensity.

luminance A video signal that represents the psychophysical attribute of brightness of an image. See *luminosity curve*.

luminosity curve A curve that shows the psychophysical brightness response of the human eye to spectral colors. It is often used to determine how to create a *luminance* signal from color signals.

lux A unit of illumination equal to one *lumen* per square meter. See *foot-candle*.

magnetic recording Recording that makes use of the magnetic *remanence* property of certain materials.

magneto-optical recording Recording that makes use of the Curie point property of magnetic materials. Replay of such recording is done by optical means using the Kerr effect.

masking In *RGB* component color systems, controlled *mixing* of the color channels to modify the colorimetry characteristic of the system.

Mass storage In a computer, hardware for large-capacity, nonvolatile storage of data. Typical mass-storage devices are *hard disks, floppy disks, CD-ROM*, magnetic tape, and so forth.

MIDI See *Musical Instrument Digital Interface*.

Miller code In digital transmission, a modified FM *encoding* scheme where a binary one is coded by a transition in either direction at the center of a bit interval, whereas there is no transition at that position for a zero. There is always a transition at the end of each bit interval. The *DC component* is small.

mixing In an audio or video system, combining signals by linear addition or logical processing.

modulation In a transmission system, the processing that makes the signal suitable to the characteristics of the transmission channel.

modulation transfer function (MTF) The response of an imaging system to sine wave patterns of different frequencies.

Moore's Law An empirical statement "the number of devices on an integrated circuit chip will double every two years." This was observed by Gordon Moore in 1965 and has proved to be true ever since.

motion compensation In video *compression*, a technique that examines sequential frames and determines the parts of the scene that have changed. Only the moving parts of the scene are transmitted to construct each frame from previous frames. This is *interframe* compression.

Moving Picture Expert Group (MPEG) A subcommittee of the *ISO/IEC* that developed the video *compression* standard that has their name: MPEG. This standard uses *discrete cosine transform* compression and *entropy coding* combined with *motion compensation*.

Motion-JPEG A motion video *compression* algorithm based on *JPEG* compression of individual frames. This is *intraframe* compression.

MPEG See *Moving Picture Expert Group*.

MTF See *modulation transfer function*.

mu-law (μ-law) A widely-used audio *companding* technique.

multiburst pattern A test pattern for measurement of high-frequency response in video channels.

multimedia The use of multiple formats of electronic presentation with *interactivity* for the purpose of conveying information, educating, or entertaining. Multimedia may include text, graphics, images, audio, video, and animation.

music synthesis Electronically generated music.

Musical Instrument Digital Interface (MIDI) A serial digital bus standard for connecting electronic musical instruments.

National Television Systems Committee (NTSC) The organization in the United States that developed that country's color TV standard (called NTSC color television) in 1953.

neutral-density In optical imaging systems, a filter that attenuates all colors equally. Such a filter appears gray.

nonemissive displays Displays that operate by controlling the reflectance or transmission of light from a separate source.

nonlinear editing Audio or video editing that uses random-access storage (usually a hard disk) to assemble edits in real time.

nonreturn to zero (NRZ) A digital encoding technique that encodes a binary one as one amplitude level and a zero as a different level.

NRZ See *nonreturn to zero*.

NTSC See *National Television Systems Committee*.

Nyquist criterion In a sampled system, the *sampling* frequency must always be at least twice the highest signal frequency to be sampled. If this criterion is not met, the result is *aliasing*.

offset binary In binary encoding of bipolar signals, zero is given the value of one-half the maximum binary range. This has the problem that the offset values add up in addition. See *two's complement*.

omega-wrap In *helical-scan* tape recording, a design where the tape is wrapped only part of the way around the scanner.

Open Systems Interconnect (OSI) A set of digital transmission protocols defined by the *ISO* as standard IS 7498 (1984).

operating system In computer software, the software modules that control the overall system and provides the *application programming interface* and the *driver* interface.

optical recording Recording by modifying the optical properties of a material so that records can be read by reflection or transmission of a light beam.

orthogonal sampling In a two-dimensional sampling system, where the sample points in each line are aligned directly above and below the samples in other lines.

OSI See *Open Systems Interconnect*.

oversampling In a sampled digital system, where the sampling frequency significantly exceeds the *Nyquist criterion*.

overscanning In a television receiver, the technique of scanning the picture larger than the screen mask so that edges of the *raster* are never seen.

packetizing In digital transmission, the technique of breaking the incoming data into a series of blocks (packets). Packets may either be fixed in size or variable-size, and each packet is handled separately by the transmission system.

PAL See *Phase-Alternating Line*.

parallel In digital transmission or signal processing, where each bit of a data word is handled with a separate circuit.

parity In digital transmission, the technique of adding an extra (parity) bit to each word to make the bit values of the word plus the parity bit have an even sum (even parity) or an odd sum (odd parity). By testing the parity of each word after transmission, single-bit errors can be detected.

PCI See *Peripheral Connect Interface.*

PCM See *pulse-code modulation*

PDF See *probability density function.*

PDP See *plasma display panel.*

peripheral In a computer system, all units connected to the *bus* other than the *central processing unit* and system memory.

Peripheral Connect Interface (PCI) A high-speed *local bus* standard for personal computers.

persistence of vision The property of human vision that causes a rapidly flashing light to appear steadily illuminated. See *flicker.*

phase shift In an electrical signal path, the integral of the delay versus frequency characteristic. A system having uniform delay (which does not introduce delay distortion) has a *linear phase* characteristic.

Phase-Alternating Line (PAL) A *composite* analog color TV standard developed first in Europe and now used by many countries around the world. PAL is based on most of the concepts of *NTSC* but has some improvements. The name comes from the line-to-line alternation of the color subcarrier phase that causes some types of transmission distortion to cancel.

pipelining In a digital processing system, a technique for speeding up a process by breaking the process into steps that are performed by multiple processing units in series.

pitch In music, the analog of frequency.

pixel A point in an image. Each pixel has separately definable brightness and colors. An image is a two-dimensional array of pixels.

plasma display panel (PDP) A flat-panel *emissive display* that uses a UV glow discharge in an inert gas to excite phosphors.

platform In computers, a specific definition of a system including *central processing unit*, *peripherals*, and *operating system*. A platform contains all the ingredients necessary to run *application* programs designed for that platform.

platform-independent A hardware or software unit that can be used on many different *platforms.*

postproduction In audio and video program creation, the process of assembling materials from *production* into a complete program.

predictive coding In digital *encoding*, the technique of coding only the information necessary to make corrections to a prediction made at the decoder using the information that has already been received. For example, *DPCM*, which sends differences, is predictive encoding where the prediction simply assumes that the new value is the same as the previous value.

preemphasis In transmission systems, the technique of enhancing parts of the frequency spectrum where it is known that signal amplitudes will always be lower than the channel could handle. The preemphasis is undone at the receiving end and results in a *signal-to-noise ratio* improvement.

primary colors In color reproduction, a set of colors (usually three) that are added to produce the reproduction of any color. See *additive primaries, subtractive primaries.*

probability density function (PDF) A curve of the probability of something happening versus an independent parameter. For example, a PDF that shows the probability of a particular voltage occurring in a video signal versus the voltage.

product code In digital *error protection*, the technique of viewing a block of data as a two-dimensional array and performing error coding for each row and each column.

production In audio and video program creation, the process of *capturing* all material to a storage medium.

progressive scanning In a scanned video system, where all the lines of the *raster* are scanned in every vertical scan. See *interlaced scanning.*

psychoacoustics The science of perception of sound.

pulse-and-bar pattern A video test pattern that tests the analog transient response of a system. The pattern consists of a narrow *sine-squared* pulse followed by a wide pulse on a group of lines so as to make a vertical line and a rectangle on the screen.

pulse-code modulation (PCM) In digital transmission, *encoding* of audio or video sample values using *pure binary* or *two's complement* .

pure binary *Encoding* numerical values by assigning the bits of a word to successively higher powers of two. Thus, an 8-bit word can represent values from 0 to 255.

quantization The process of converting a continuous-function *analog* value to the nearest one of a set of *digital* values.

qunicunx sampling In a two-dimensional sampling system, where the sample points in each line are located horizontally halfway between the samples in adjacent lines.

raster In a scanned video system, the pattern of lines produced by the *scanning* motion over the scanned area.

reduced-instruction-set computer (RISC) A computer that has a simplified *instruction set* intended to speed execution of instructions. See *complex instruction-set computer*.

Reed-Solomon code In digital *error protection*, a set of algorithms for generating error protection codes for specific-size blocks of data to give a specified degree of error correction.

registers In a *central processing unit*, internal memory areas that are directly accessible through the CPU *instruction set*.

remanence In a magnetic material, the property of the material to remember some magnetization after the magnetizing force has been removed. See *hysteresis*.

render In computer graphics, the process of creating a picture from the computer graphics commands stored for the picture.

requantizing In a sampled digital system, if the number of bits per sample must be reduced, requantizing is done to make sure that as much information as possible is kept in the remaining bits.

resolution In a video system, the ability to reproduce fine detail. In digital systems, resolution is often specified by giving the number of *pixels* in horizontal and vertical directions on the screen. In TV systems, resolution is specified by "television lines per picture height" (TVL), which is a count of the maximum number of black and white lines that can be reproduced in a distance equal to the picture height.

reverberation Multiple sound reflections in an enclosed room. This causes a sound to decay slowly after the sound source has stopped.

RGB Acronym for red, green, and blue—the three *additive primary* colors. It refers to *component* color video systems that use the primary colors directly.

RISC See *reduced instruction-set computer*.

RLE See *run-length encoding*.

RLL See *run-length limiting*.

routing switcher In a large video system, a switching system that allows all signal sources and all recorders to be connected to any of a group of control rooms.

run-length encoding (RLE) In digital transmission, an *encoding* scheme that codes repeated values in the data stream as a count number and a value.

run-length limiting (RLL) In digital transmission, any *encoding* that controls the maximum number of repeated ones or zeros that may occur in the data stream. This is important is making the data stream *self-clocking* and in controlling its *DC component*.

safe title area In television, the area of the *raster* that is guaranteed to be visible on the screen of *overscanned* receivers.

sampling The process of making a series of values equally spaced in time out of a continuously varying analog signal. Each sample is the instantaneous value of the analog signal at the time of sampling (see *sampling width*).

sampling frequency The frequency of *sampling* an analog signal. The rate of occurrence of samples.

sampling width Recognizing that *sampling* is not truly instantaneous, the sampling width is the time over which the sampler averages the analog signal to produce the sample value.

saturation In a magnetic material, the property that limits the maximum magnetizing flux that can be produced in the material with an arbitrarily large magnetizing force.

scan linearity In a scanned video system, the extent to which the scanning velocities (line or vertical) are constant.

scanning In an image reproduction system, the process of sweeping a pattern over the image to sequentially determine values at each point of the image. Most scanning uses a rectangular pattern of lines called a *raster*.

SECAM See *Sequential Couleur Avec Mémoire*.

self-clocking In a digital transmission system, the ability of the modulated signal to support extraction of a data clock directly from the signal.

separation loss In magnetic recording, the signal loss caused by physical separation between the *head gap* and the magnetic tape or disk.

Sequential Coleur Avec Mémoire (SECAM) The *composite* color television system developed in France and used there and in the countries of the former Soviet Union. SECAM uses a baseband luminance signal and two frequency-modulated subcarriers that carry the *color-difference signals*.

serial In digital transmission or processing, the handling of the data bits in sequence in a single path.

set-top box A unit designed to be connected to the audio and video channels of a television receiver in order to access the display capability of the receiver for a purpose other than broadcast TV reception. Set-top boxes are used for cable TV, pay-per-view, video games, and the new Internet viewers.

shift register A digital component that has a string of interconnected memory circuits (usually *flip-flops*) that are controlled so that data bits entering at one end of the string pass step by step through the circuits until they come out the other end of the string. A clock signal controls the shifting from stage to stage.

signal-to-noise ratio (SNR) In a signal system, the ratio of the desired signal to spurious noise produced in the system. In audio systems, SNR is the ratio of rms signal to rms noise, usually expressed in *dB*. In video systems, SNR is the ratio of peak-to-peak video (black-to-white) to rms noise, also expressed in dB.

sine-squared pulse A pulse shape often used in analog video transient response testing because it has a frequency spectrum that is not infinite and thus, it can be perfectly reproduced by a good system.

SMPTE See *Society of Motion Picture and Television Engineers*.

SNR See *signal-to-noise ratio*.

Society of Motion Picture and Television Engineers (SMPTE) An organization of engineers that develops standards in the fields of audio, video, recording, and motion pictures.

soft decision decoder In certain types of encoding, not all possible *symbol* values are used and not all possible sequences of symbols are valid. One encoding technique like this is *trellis coding*. In decoding such a signal, a soft decision decoder will examine symbol sequences that may contain some errors and decide what is the most likely correct sequence to apply.

software In a computer, the sequences of commands that tell the computer to perform specific tasks.

spatial offset In three-sensor *charge-coupled device* color cameras, horizontal resolution can be improved by offsetting the pixels of the three sensors with respect to one another. This can be interpreted in the signal processing to double the number of effective luminance pixels in the horizontal direction.

state machine A digital circuit that sequences through a set of predetermined conditions or states to perform a process.

stereo In audio reproduction, the use of two channels (left and right) for *binaural* reproduction of sound.

subsampling In a sampled system, the use of a divided-down sampling rate for one part of the system compared with another. For example, in a *component video* system of the 4:2:2 type, the *color-difference* components are sampled at one-half the sampling rate of the *luminance*.

subtractive primaries The primary colors used in color printing: magenta, cyan, and yellow. They are called "subtractive" because they cause certain colors to be subtracted from the light reflected from white paper. See *additive primaries*.

suppressed-carrier modulation A *bipolar* amplitude-modulated system where the zero-signal condition is zero carrier. The carrier phase shifts 180 deg between positive and negative modulating signals.

surround sound A sound reproduction system that uses speakers in front of and behind the listener to provide a more natural sound environment.

symbol In a transmission system, the basic unit of data carried at one moment of time by the channel signal. Symbols may carry one or more bits.

sync generator A circuit that generates horizontal and vertical timing signals to control the scanning of multiple video devices so they will be synchronous.

system bus In a computer, the main *bus* that connects all units and *peripherals* of the system.

tape deck The main mechanism of a tape recorder that handles unrolling the tape from the supply reel, passing it over the *heads* or *helical-scanner*, and rolling it up on a takeup reel. Other tape deck functions can include *cassette* loading and tape rewinding.

TCP/IP See *transmission control protocol*.

telecine The name given to a video camera designed for video reproduction from motion picture film.

tempo In music, the beat rate, which determines the speed of playing notes.

threshold In a *comparator*, the predetermined input level at which the comparator will change its output state.

timbre In music, the dynamic harmonic and amplitude properties of a note.

time-base instability In a signal system, the degree of instability of the frequency of a fixed-frequency signal that has been passed through the system. Time-base instability in the system causes frequency modulation of the fixed frequency.

time code A digital code that identifies video *frames* or their audio equivalents according to a standard sequence of hours, minutes, seconds, and frames.

track In magnetic or optical recording, the pattern recorded on tape or disk by the passage of the recording device.

transducer A device that converts information from one form to another. For example, a microphone is a transducer that converts sound waves to electrical signals. Similarly, a CCD is a transducer that converts an optical image to a video signal.

transfer smear In a CCD camera, an artifact of vertical smearing on highlights in the scene. It is caused by spurious charge that is collected during the vertical blanking interval in some types of CCD.

transform coding In compression systems, the processing of blocks of data from one form to another to expose signal aspects that then may be compressed. For example, the *discrete cosine transform* is used in video compression to transform a block of pixels to the frequency domain where the higher frequency components can be treated differently to achieve compression. An inverse transform is used to restore transformed data to its original form.

Transmission Control Protocol (TCP) Part of the TCP/IP that makes the *Internet* possible. TCP and *IP* are a *packetizing* system. TCP is the first layer of protocol.

transparent In a signal processing system, the capability to process signals without any distortion being visible to the end users.

trellis coding An *encoding* scheme for multilevel *symbols* that combines with *soft decision decoding* to provide better data transmission through a channel.

trichromatic theory The theory of color reproduction by mixing three primary colors.

truth table A diagram that shows the result of all possible combinations of input to a digital logic circuit.

two's complement An *encoding* scheme for bipolar numbers that eliminates the problem with addition in *offset binary* encoding.

universal resource locator (URL) The addressing system used on the *World Wide Web*.

URL See *universal resource locator*.

user interface The way a user interacts with an interactive system. It includes the hardware and software for the two-way communication between user and system required for interactivity.

VCO See *voltage-controlled oscillator*.

vectorscope An oscilloscopic display of the chrominance components of a *composite video* system. It is a polar-coordinate display that shows color subcarrier amplitudes and phases.

vertical interval time code (VITC) A *time code* that is transmitted during the vertical interval of a television signal.

vertical resolution In a video system, the ability to reproduce fine detail in the vertical direction, as caused by patterns of horizontal lines. See *resolution, horizontal resolution*.

vestigial sideband modulation A modulated-carrier system where part of one sideband is suppressed. It is used for analog television broadcasting and also for digital ATV broadcasting.

vibrato In music, a small frequency modulation of the *pitch*.

video display adapter In a PC, a hardware module that interfaces between the system *bus* and a video display monitor.

video effects In a video program, the various processes that are used to produce transitions between scenes or shots or to create dynamic combinations of multiple signals. Typical examples are dissolves, wipes, quad splits, zooms, pans, and so forth.

video RAM (VRAM) A special form of random-access memory that has two separate ports. One port is the conventional random-access interface to a computer bus, and the other is an onchip *shift register* that is loaded from a block of the RAM in one cycle and can then be separately clocked to shift out its contents at the same time the other port of the memory is doing other things. VRAM provides a speedup of operation in a *video display adapter.*

video server A *mass storage* unit capable of storing a large amount of digital video and outputting one or more real-time video streams under random-access control.

videoconferencing The use of video and audio communication to carry out conferences among people at different locations. Each person can see and hear all the other people, regardless of their actual physical locations.

viewing ratio In viewing a video display, the ratio of the viewing distance to the picture height.

VITC See *vertical interval time code.*

Viterbi detector A form of *soft decision decoder.*

voltage controlled oscillator (VCO) An electronic oscillator generating a signal whose frequency is controllable by a voltage.

VRAM See *video RAM.*

W3C See *World Wide Web Consortium.*

WAN See *wide area network.*

wavelength For periodic signals transmitted through a medium, the wavelength is the speed of propagation through the medium divided by the frequency of the signal.

wavetable synthesis In music synthesis, a method where natural sounds are captured and played back with pitch control to synthesize notes at any frequency. It often produces more realistic sounds than other methods of music synthesis.

weighting filter In signal systems, a filter that modifies the frequency characteristic to simulate the way that a person would perceive the signal. It is often used for *SNR* measurement.

white balancing In a video camera, the process of adjusting the signals in the three component channels so the system will reproduce white in the scene as white perceived by the viewer at a display.

wide area network A computer network that covers long distances, ordinarily requiring some type of telecommunications links.

World Wide Web (the Web) The protocol on the Internet for multimedia. The Web is based on the *hypertext markup language* and allows users to jump among information sources located anywhere on the worldwide Internet.

World Wide Web Consortium (W3C) An informal organization that manages the standards on the Web.

wow and flutter   In audio systems, the manifestation of *time base instability*.

YC$_R$C$_B$ The name often given to a component video system that uses luminance and the two color-difference signals, *R–Y* and *B–Y*.

YUV   The name given to a component video system that uses luminance and the two color-difference signals *U* and *V*, defined in the *PAL* standard.

Bibliography

GENERAL DIGITAL TECHNOLOGY

Dorf, R. C., *Electrical Engineering Handbook*, CRC Press, Boca Raton, 1993.

Negroponte, N., *Being Digital*, Knopf, New York, 1995.

Rzeszewski, T. S. (Ed.), *Digital Video: Concepts and Applications Across Industries*, IEEE Press, New York, 1995.

Watkinson, J., *The Art of Digital Video, Second Edition*, Focal Press, London, 1994.

TELEVISION

Baron, S. N. (ed.), *Implementing HDTV:Television and Film Applications*, SMPTE, White Plains, NY, 1996.

Benson, K. B., and Whitaker, J., *Television Engineering Handbook*, McGraw-Hill, New York, 1992.

Inglis, A. F., and Luther, A. C., *Video Engineering, Second Edition*, McGraw-Hill, New York, 1996.

Society of Motion Picture and Television Engineers, all publications: http://www.smpte.org.

Institute of Electrical and Electronics Engineers, *IEEE Transactions on Broadcasting*, IEEE Operations Center, 445 Hoes Lane, P. O. Box 1331, Piscataway, NJ 08855-1331. http://www.ieee.org.

AUDIO

Benson, K. B., *Audio Engineering Handbook*, McGraw-Hill, New York, 1988.

Pohlmann, K. C., *Principles of Digital Audio,* 3rd ed., McGraw-Hill, New York, 1995.

Keyboard Magazine, published monthly by Miller-Freeman, Inc. 600 Harrison St., San Francisco, CA 94107. http://www.keyboardmag.com.

VIDEO CAMERAS AND PRODUCTION

Anderson, G., *Video Editing & Postproduction: A Professional Guide,* 3rd ed., Focal Press, Boston, 1993.

AV Video magazine, published monthly by Montage Publishing, Inc., 701 Westchester Ave., White Plains, NY 10604.

Hamalainen, J., et al., "Facts and Fiction: Some Aspects Regarding the Design of Digital Television Cameras Using CCD Image Sensors," *International Journal of Imaging Systems and Technology,* vol. 5, pp. 314–322, 1994.

Millimeter magazine, published monthly by Intertec Publishing Corporation, 5 Penn Plaza, 13th Floor, New York, NY, 10001.

TV Technology Magazine, published biweekly by IMAS Publishing, P. O. Box 1214, Falls Church, VA 22041.

Videography magazine, published monthly by Miller-Freeman PSN, Inc., 460 Park Avenue South, New York, NY 10016.

Videomaker magazine, published monthly by Videomaker, Inc. P. O. Box 4591, Chico, CA 95927.

Zettl, H., *Sight Sound Motion: Applied Media Aesthetics*, 2nd ed., Wadsworth, Belmont CA, 1990.

VIDEO RECORDING

Kubota, Y., et al., "A System for Consumer-Use Digital VCR," *IEEE Transactions on Consumer Electronics*, vol. 42, no. 3, pp. 274–278, Aug. 1996.

Mee, C. D., and Daniel, E. D., *Magnetic Recording Volume I: Technology*, McGraw-Hill, New York, 1987.

Watkinson, J., *The Art of Digital Video,* 2nd ed., Focal Press, London, 1994.

MULTIMEDIA

Graham, I. S., *HTML Sourcebook,* 2nd ed., Wiley, New York, 1996.

Keyes, J. (ed.), *The McGraw-Hill Multimedia Handbook*, McGraw-Hill, New York, 1994.

Koegel Buford, gentlemen. F. (ed.), *Multimedia Systems*, ACM Press, New York, 1994.

Luther, A. C., *Authoring Interactive Multimedia*, AP Professional, Boston, 1994.

Luther, A. C., *Using Digital Video*, AP Professional, Boston, 1995.

Ritchey, T., *Java!*, New Riders, Indianapolis, 1995.

Stout, R., *The World Wide Web: Complete Reference*, Osborne McGraw-Hill, Berkeley, 1996.

STANDARDS

Advanced Television Systems Committee (ATSC), http://www.atsc.org.

Institute of Electrical and Electronics Engineers (IEEE), http://www.ieee.org.

International Standards Organization (ISO), http://www.iso.ch.

International Telecommunications Union (ITU), http://www.itu.ch.

Society of Motion Picture and Television Engineers (SMPTE), http://www.smpte.org.

COMPUTERS

Byte magazine, published monthly by the McGraw-Hill Companies, Inc., P. O. Box 552, Hightstown, NJ 08520.

Computer magazine, published monthly by the IEEE Computer Society Publications Office, 10662 Los Vaqueros Circle, P. O. Box 3014, Los Alamitos, CA 90720-1314.

Hennessy, J. L., and Patterson, D. A., *Computer Architecture: A Quantitative Approach,* 2nd ed., Morgan Kaufman, San Francisco, 1996.

IEEE Computer Society, http://www.computer.org.

DATA COMPRESSION

Huffman, D., "A Method for the Construction of Minimum Redundancy Codes," Proc. IRE, pp. 1,098–1,101, Sept. 1952.

Jayant, N. S., and Noll, P., *Digital Coding of Waveforms*, Prentice-Hall, Englewood Cliffs, 1984.

Kespret, I., *ZIP Bible*, Abacus, Grand Rapids, 1996.

Nelson, M., and Gailly, J., M&T Books, New York, 1996.

Ozer, J., *Video Compression for Multimedia*, AP Professional, Boston, 1995.

Riley, M. J., and Richardson, I. E. G., *Digital Video Communications*, Artech House, Boston, 1997.

Schaphorst, R., *Videoconferencing and Videotelephony: Technology and Standards*, Artech House, Boston, 1996.

DATA TRANSMISSION

Agnew, P. W., and Kellerman, A. S., *Distributed Multimedia: Technologies, Applications, and Opportunities in the Digital Information Industry*, ACM Press, New York, 1996.

Gibson, J. D. (ed.), *The Communications Handbook*, CRC Press, Boca Raton, FL, 1997.

Inglis, A. F., *Satellite Technology: An Introduction*, Focal Press, Boston, 1994.

Keiser, *Broadband Coding, Modulation, and Transmission Engineering*, Prentice-Hall, Englewood Cliffs, 1989.

Kessler, G. C., and Southwick, P., *ISDN: Concepts, Facilities, and Services,* 3rd ed., McGraw-Hill, New York, 1996.

Lu, G., *Communication and Computing for Distributed Multimedia Systems*, Artech House, Boston, 1996.

Minoli, D., and Keinath, R., *Distributed Multimedia Through Broadband Communications Services*, Artech House, Boston, 1994.

Ohta, N., *Packet Video: Modeling and Signal Processing*, Artech House, Boston, 1994.

Index

The Artech House Audiovisual Library